The Great Prophecies Concerning the Gentiles, the Jews, and the Church of God

G H Pember

Copyright © BiblioLife, LLC

This book represents a historical reproduction of a work originally published before 1923 that is part of a unique project which provides opportunities for readers, educators and researchers by bringing hard-to-find original publications back into print at reasonable prices. Because this and other works are culturally important, we have made them available as part of our commitment to protecting, preserving and promoting the world's literature. These books are in the "public domain" and were digitized and made available in cooperation with libraries, archives, and open source initiatives around the world dedicated to this important mission.

We believe that when we undertake the difficult task of re-creating these works as attractive, readable and affordable books, we further the goal of sharing these works with a global audience, and preserving a vanishing wealth of human knowledge.

Many historical books were originally published in small fonts, which can make them very difficult to read. Accordingly, in order to improve the reading experience of these books, we have created "enlarged print" versions of our books. Because of font size variation in the original books, some of these may not technically qualify as "large print" books, as that term is generally defined; however, we believe these versions provide an overall improved reading experience for many.

THE GREAT PROPHECIES

CONCERNING

THE GENTILES, THE JEWS, AND THE CHURCH OF GOD.

BY

G. H. PEMBER, M.A.,

AUTHOR OF
"EARTH'S EARLIEST AGES," ETC.

THIRD EDITION, REVISED AND ENLARGED.
WITH A COLOURED CHART.

London:
HODDER AND STOUGHTON,
27, PATERNOSTER ROW.

MDCCCLXXXVII.
[*All rights reserved.*]

Printed by Hazell, Watson, & Viney, Ld., London and Aylesbury.

PREFACE.

THE Supreme God has deigned to give revelations whereby He seeks to communicate His purposes to men, and thus, by a gentle process, to bend their minds to His mighty and irresistible will. Nevertheless, myriads of professing Christians are content to reach the end of life in total ignorance of these gracious disclosures, while accredited ministers of Christ are too frequently unable to expound them.

But, since God has thought fit to set them before us, are we not deliberately charging Him with folly while we neglect them? And is not the significance of our conduct much the same if we persist in perverting them from their proper meaning and use—as, for instance, those do who can find little in the Apocalypse save events that had become history before it was written, and doctrines that are fully taught in other parts of Scripture; although the Lord Himself declares that the object of the Book is "to show unto His servants the things that must shortly come to pass"?[1]

[1] Rev. i. 1. With the future, then, dating from the time when it was written, and with that future alone, the book is concerned. And we do not violate this rule, as we have been accused of doing, when we interpret the Travailing Woman, in the twelfth chapter, of the Church in affliction. For although her sorrows had commenced many years before John saw the vision, yet they were still going on at the time, and were destined to continue for some eighteen hundred years afterwards.

And again, may we not attribute much of the apathy of Christendom, the Laodicean spirit with which we are surrounded, and the worldliness of popular Christianity, to the fact that believers will not give themselves to those studies and contemplations which God has provided for them.

A passage in the Epistle to the Hebrews seems to force such a conclusion upon us. The inspired writer complains of the difficulty of communicating what he wishes to say concerning Melchizedec, because those to whom he is writing are dull of hearing and unskilful in the Word of Righteousness; and their condition draws from him a severe rebuke, followed by the exhortation;—

"Wherefore, leaving the word of the beginning of Christ, let us press on unto perfection; not laying again a foundation of repentance from dead works, and of faith toward God, of baptisms of instruction, and of laying on of hands, and of resurrection of dead persons, and of eternal judgment."[1]

We may observe that this list of foundations includes nearly all the doctrines ordinarily heard from our pulpits. And yet the Apostle compares those who are incessantly occupied with them to one who wastes labour and time by repeatedly laying down and taking up again the foundation of a building, when he ought to be raising the superstructure. He, therefore, solemnly urges the Hebrews to pass on from first principles to perfection, and presses his exhortation with the words—

"For it is impossible in the case of those who were once enlightened, and tasted of the heavenly gift, and were made partakers of the Holy Ghost, and tasted the

[1] Heb. vi. 1

good word of God and the powers of the World to Come, if they shall fall away, to renew them again unto repentance ; seeing they crucify to themselves the Son of God afresh, and put Him to an open shame." [1]

Now, without entering into the full meaning of these words of terror, we must admit that the context leaves us in no doubt as to the manner of persons who are in danger of the lapse contemplated and the appalling judgment which must inevitably follow it. They are those who refuse to look beyond the first principles of Christ ; those who will not study, meditate upon, and suffer the Holy Spirit to mould their minds by, the revelations which God has provided for that purpose, and with which He has bidden us to fill our heart and satisfy our intellect ; those who vainly strive to excuse their indolence, and want of appetite for heavenly things, by affirming that the simple Gospel is enough for them—as if the effect of tasting the good things of God were to make us desire no more of them, although His banquet is spread, and He ceases not to say ;—" Eat, O friends ; drink, yea, drink abundantly, O beloved."

Thus, throughout the whole Christian dispensation, spiritual apathy and the peril of apostasy have ever been threatening those who neglect to become acquainted, as accurately as they may, with the Divine utterances, whereby alone we are enabled to estimate earthly things aright, and are moved to look for the blessed hope and glorious appearing of the great God and our Saviour Jesus Christ.

What, then, shall we say of ourselves upon whom the end of the age has come, who seem to be living

[1] Heb. vi. 4-6.

in times when the predictions of old are on the point of fulfilment! How far more cogent is the word of exhortation to us, who can even see the Day approaching!

Isaac Taylor thought that God would ultimately divide between those who support and those who oppose the truth by means of the Book of the Revelation. And undoubtedly his general idea is correct; for a far higher and absolutely unimpeachable authority has said of the Old Testament Apocalypse;—

"The words are closed up and sealed until the time of the end. Many shall be purified, and made white, and tried; but the wicked shall do wickedly. And none of the wicked shall understand; but the wise shall understand." [1]

Such, then, will be the distinctive mark of God's elect in the world's last hour of trial; and to the wise of that generation, whether it be our own or another, the word of prophecy will seem no matter for slight or neglect, but a revelation of transcendent importance.

Nor can we tell what mighty issues may be depending upon its reception even in the case of those who will not live to see it become history. The great Creator acts upon us during the present life in ways that we know not, and with results which will not fully appear until this mortal shall have put on immortality. And surely a patient and prayerful study of revelations which set forth His purposes must produce a frame of mind favourable to sanctification and spiritual growth, and likely to affect our eternal condition in no insignificant degree. God's prescribed means of education must be the best, and even those who think that they

[1] Dan. xii. 9-10.

have done greater things by labours of a different kind may find their hopes crushed by the stern rebuke ;— " Behold, to obey is better than sacrifice, and to hearken than the fat of rams ! "

But the cause which most powerfully moves men to neglect God's revelations of the future is the repugnance of the human mind to anything which is contrary, either to its experience, or to the aspirations of its fallen nature. There was a wondrous depth of truth in our Lord's rebuke when He said ;—" O fools, and slow of heart to believe all that the prophets have spoken ! "[1]—not slow of heart to know, or to understand, but to believe. It was an instinctive aversion to the course of God's will which led the very disciples to misunderstand the predictions of the first advent ; a similar feeling will cause many Christians to be taken by surprise at the second.

Such an aversion is, however, rarely acknowledged ; it is usual to assign its results to unreal causes, of which the most frequently urged is the great diversity of expositions. But this perplexity is indefinitely increased by the careless recognition as an interpreter of almost any one who presents himself. In such circumstances what wonder that we hear of strange and wild interpretations! But if the Church would awake from her indifference, and be at the pains to apply proper tests, the mischief would be speedily checked and restricted. And two obvious tests are these.

No one may claim to be more than a tentative expounder of prophecy, unless he can formulate a complete and consistent scheme.[2]

[1] Luke xxiv. 25.
[2] With permission to manipulate selected passages at will, it

And no system can be the true one, unless *all* the main prophecies of the Bible will fall easily and naturally into place in it.

We are well aware that many object to the very mention of a system of prophecy : but surely it does not require much reflection to discover that such a sentiment is simply irrational. If the prophecies are all utterances of one and the selfsame Spirit, they must be capable of reduction to an orderly scheme, and certainly cannot be comprehended in any other way. And unless we find out what this scheme is, woe to us ; for if, as nearly all Christians seem to agree, we are now on the borders of the last times, the knowledge of it will soon become the distinguishing mark of those whom God has chosen. For, at the time of the end, "none of the wicked shall understand, but the wise shall understand."

The scheme, which commends itself to our mind, is set before the reader in the present volume, and is constructed with careful reference to certain clues, which we believe to have been given for the purpose, and which are explained in the last six chapters of the Prolegomena.

The most important of them are a recognition of the three distinct classes into which mankind are divided, a knowledge of the three prophetic periods, and an acquaintance with the simple principle upon which God computes the chronology of Jewish history. A clear apprehension of these points will, we believe, remove

would, of course, be possible to apply prophecy to any given event or events—just as almost every conceivable doctrine has been already taught from the Bible by a skilful, but frequently unscrupulous, use of isolated texts.

all difficulty and uncertainty in regard to general and systematic interpretation.

But when we enter into details, it is no longer possible to speak with the same confidence; for there are, doubtless, some predictions which will not be perfectly understood until their fulfilment is actually impending. None the less, however, must we study and firmly grasp them with our minds: and if we do so, that which is lacking to us will be revealed in the hour of need; and at the crisis perplexing to others, or, perhaps, altogether unperceived by them, we shall have full understanding of what is about to happen, and of what we ought to do.

The early disciples were probably unable to explain the Lord's command, that they should flee to the mountains as soon as they saw Jerusalem compassed with armies. How, they may have thought, can we flee in such circumstances? Surely the very sign which He has promised will render obedience impossible.

But in due time all became clear to them; and their hearts must, indeed, have overflowed with gratitude when they perceived that the Lord's gracious arrangements had given, not merely the signal, but also the opportunity, for their flight, and had at the same time removed out of the way their bigoted countrymen who would have hindered it.[1]

"They shall not be ashamed that wait for me."[2]

In preparing this work for a second edition we have

---

[1] For an account of this deeply interesting event, see the note on p. 241.
[2] Isa. xlix. 23.

subjected it to careful revision and correction; much explanatory matter and several new chapters have been added; and it is hoped that the book may now prove useful as a systematic manual for students of prophecy. It does not, however, include the whole of the subject, but only such portions of it as seem most nearly to concern those who are waiting for the summons of their Lord. The detailed events of the Last Week, the descent of Christ upon the Mount of Olives, the Millennial Age, the Final Judgment, and the Eternal State, are reserved for future treatment.

A few replies to adverse criticisms have been embodied in the text; but we may at once mention three points in regard to which we do not recognise the need of a defence.

The fact that an event is, so far as we can see, improbable, is no reason whatever for refusing it a place in God's revelation of the future.

We have been repeatedly asked what ground we have for inserting events between the sixty-ninth and the seventieth of Daniel's weeks. Simply that in so doing we follow the prophecy, which makes the cutting off of Messiah take place after the close of the sixty-ninth week, and then interposes the events in question before it proceeds to the seventieth. It is for those who violate this order to defend their position.

Lastly, we are accused of Pessimism, and have no wish to deny the charge, but confess to have learnt that distrust in the power of fallen man to recover himself, which is inculcated in the Scriptures from Genesis to Revelation. But our Pessimism, derived from such a source, is not hopeless; though there be little help in ourselves, we look for the coming of One

Who is mighty to save. Be the sky never so dark, we know that the Sun is still shining in His strength behind it, and presently, when the tempestuous clouds of the Great Tribulation shall part asunder, His light and warmth will be revealed to the rejoicing earth.

The coloured chart prefixed to the present edition will, we trust, facilitate the reader's acquaintance with the scheme.

CONTENTS.

PROLEGOMENA.

		PAGE
I.	INTRODUCTION. SCHEME OF INTERPRETATION	3
II.	THE SIGNS OF THE TIMES	18
III.	THE SEVEN DISPENSATIONS	27
IV.	THE THREE LINES OF PROPHECY	36
V.	THE THREE PROPHETIC PERIODS	42
VI.	MYSTIC CHRONOLOGY	45
VII.	SUPERNATURAL JUDGMENTS	48

PART I.—THE GENTILES.

I.	THE PROPHECY OF BALAAM	53
II.	THE KINGDOM OF THE TEN TRIBES	58
III.	THE DREAM OF NEBUCHADNEZZAR	60
IV.	THE VISION OF THE FOUR WILD BEASTS	75
V.	THE VISION OF THE RAM AND THE HE-GOAT	91
VI.	THE GREAT RED DRAGON	106
VII.	THE WILD BEAST FROM THE SEA	114
VIII.	THE WILD BEAST FROM THE EARTH	126
IX.	MYSTERY, BABYLON THE GREAT	132
X.	THE SEVEN KINGS AND THE EIGHTH	139

CONTENTS.

	PAGE
XI. THE OVERTHROW OF ECCLESIASTICISM BY SECULARISM	150
XII. THE NAPOLEONIC THEORY	153
XIII. THE REBUILDING OF GREAT BABYLON	169

PART II.—THE JEWS.

I. THE PURPOSE OF GOD CONCERNING ISRAEL	185
II. THE PERPLEXITY OF DANIEL	188
III. THE PROPHECY OF THE SEVENTY WEEKS	190
IV. THE INTERVAL FORETOLD BY ZECHARIAH	208
V. THE INTERVAL RECOGNIZED BY MATTHEW	210
VI. THE INTERVAL IN OTHER VISIONS OF DANIEL	216
VII. THE SCHEME OF THE SEVENTY WEEKS IS THE KEY TO ALL PROPHECY	219
NOTE ON THE BRETHREN OF THE LORD	226
VIII. THE RETURN OF THE JEWS TO PALESTINE	236
IX. THE SERMON ON THE MOUNT OF OLIVES	238
X. THE TWENTY-FOURTH CHAPTER OF MATTHEW	242
XI. THE PRESENT CONDITION OF THE JEWISH NATION AND LAND	261

PART III.—THE CHURCH OF GOD

I. THE MYSTERY HIDDEN FROM THE AGES	283
II. THE SEVEN PARABLES	291
III. THE PARABLE OF THE SOWER	295
IV. THE PARABLE OF THE TARES	300
V. THE PARABLE OF THE MUSTARD TREE	306
VI. THE PARABLE OF THE LEAVEN	311

		PAGE
VII.	THE PARABLE OF THE TREASURE IN THE FIELD	319
VIII.	THE PARABLE OF THE PEARL OF GREAT PRICE	321
IX.	THE PARABLE OF THE NET CAST INTO THE SEA	324
X.	SUMMARY OF THE SEVEN PARABLES	325
XI.	THE PLAN OF THE APOCALYPSE	327
XII.	THE EPISTLES TO THE SEVEN CHURCHES	336
XIII.	EPHESUS	339
XIV.	SMYRNA	347
XV.	PERGAMOS	352
XVI.	THYATIRA	365
XVII.	SARDIS	376
XVIII.	PHILADELPHIA	385
XIX.	LAODICEA	403
XX.	THE PRESENCE AND THE APPEARING	417
XXI.	THE FIRST RAPTURE, AS REVEALED TO THE THESSALONIANS	425
XXII.	THE MYSTERY FINISHED	433
XXIII.	CONCLUSION	453

PROLEGOMENA.

PROLEGOMENA.

I.

INTRODUCTION. SCHEME OF INTERPRETATION.

THE Son of God has already visited our earth once since it became the abode of sin and death. For many centuries prophets had announced His coming, and foretold the things which should befall Him; nevertheless, when He actually appeared at the predicted time, and began to fulfil before the eyes of men all that had been spoken of Him, they failed to recognize the great Deliverer. Even the chosen people, to whom the Divine revelations had been specially entrusted, misunderstood and rejected Him. But they were shortly overtaken by the gravest consequences. Not many years had elapsed before the flames of Jerusalem were casting their glare upon the agonized faces of her leading citizens as they hung upon crosses ranged around the walls. And the remainder of the unhappy people either fell by the edge of the sword, or were led into captivity among all nations. Such were the fearful results of neglecting or perverting the prophecies given by God for the guidance of those who loved Him, and to serve as lamps in the dark places through which they had to pass.

The unspeakable importance of understanding what has been revealed concerning our own age and its close is thus sufficiently evident; and it is hoped that this volume may prove helpful to some who are desirous of acquiring the necessary information. With such an object in view, we have examined only those prophecies which would enable us to construct the scheme of God's dealings with our race, so far as it has pleased Him to disclose them. For if we can but discern the grand outline, all details will easily fall into place.

These pages are, however, put forth without any feeling of dogmatic certainty: the writer is well aware of the feebleness of the human mind in its attempts to cope with so vast a subject, and of the proneness of the human will to see only that side of a matter which is favourable to its own foregone conclusions. Nevertheless, he judges that the Scriptures, being a revelation to men, *can*, therefore, be comprehended by them, if they ask the Spirit's aid. And, so far as he is conscious, the system here propounded was not first constructed and then justified, but has been gradually evolved by a close study of the Divine oracles.

With the different modes of interpretation the reader is, probably, more or less acquainted, and they have been so often discussed that but little need be said about them.

Some years ago the great conflict was between Millenarians and Post-Millenarians—those who were expecting the return of the Lord to introduce the Millennium, and those who thought that the thousand

INTRODUCTION. SCHEME OF INTERPRETATION.

years of peace and blessing would be brought in by the efforts of the Church, and would, therefore, precede the coming of the King.

But among serious students of prophecy this distinction is no longer recognised. It is now generally admitted that the consistent testimony of Scripture represents the world as growing worse and worse, until the Lord appears to destroy the corrupters and take the Kingdom. Attempts have indeed been made to refer the predictions of human failure and depravity to the revolt which follows the Millennium : but these predictions are often found to contain direct evidence connecting them with the close of the present age. And, even if nothing more could be adduced, the parable of the Tares alone would be sufficient to refute such a theory, since it admits of no interval of universal blessing between the sowing and the harvest, but represents the tares as continually growing flourishing and ripening, until the angel-reapers gather them for the fire.

Again ; many passages, which for centuries were quoted without challenge in support of the Post-Millenarian theory, have, after more careful investigation, been appropriated by those who maintain the opposite view. We may instance the parables of the Mustard Tree and the Leaven, both of which may be demonstrated, in the light of their context and of other Scriptures, to indicate the spread, not of truth, but of corruption.

Lastly ; several isolated texts, which those who were hoping to convert the world had been wont to regard as conclusive, have been found, upon examination of their settings, to refer to times subsequent to the second advent. Such is the well-known prediction of Isaiah, that "the earth shall be full of the knowledge of the Lord, as the waters cover the sea":[1] for a glance at its context reveals the significant fact that it is preceded by a description of the fall of Antichrist[2] and the reign of the Lord Jesus,[3] and is also closely connected with the restoration of the Kingdom to Israel.[4]

So much, then, for the Millenarian controversy. But there are also three well-defined and fundamentally antagonistic schemes of interpretation which claim a brief notice, and which are known as the Praeterist, the Historical,[5] and the Futurist.

The Praeterist view was first put forth as a complete scheme by the Jesuit Alcasar in his work entitled "Vestigatio Arcani Sensus in Apocalypsi," which was published in 1614. It was thus unknown in the early times of the Church, and has found but little favour save with Roman Catholics and with expositors of a rationalising tendency.[6] It limits the scope of the Apocalypse to the events of the seer's life and some other things which he might well have guessed, and affirms that the whole prophecy was fulfilled in the destruction of Jerusalem by Titus and the subsequent

[1] Isa. xi. 9.
[2] Isa. x. 20-34.
[3] Isa. xi. 1-10.
[4] Isa. xi. 11-16.
[5] Sometimes called the Continuist, and, still more frequently, the Protestant interpretation.
[6] With Rationalists, because it helps them to eliminate the supernatural from prophecy. Roman Catholics formerly used it as a shield by which to turn off the darts of their Protestant assailants from Papal to Pagan Rome. But the Protestants urged that, if the fall of Babylon be interpreted of Pagan Rome, then Rev. xviii. 2 must be a description of the same city under Papal rule. The logic of the retort was inexorable, and the Praeterist system ceased to be popular with Romanists.

fall of the persecuting Roman Empire, that is, in the successive overthrows of Judaism and Paganism.

The Historical view, also unknown to the early Church, seems to have first appeared, about the middle of the twelfth century, in the teachings of the heretical Cathari. By the beginning of the thirteenth century it was systematised by the Abbot Joachim, whose mantle descended upon our own countryman Walter Brute. Subsequently it was adopted and applied to the Pope by the precursors and leaders of the Reformation and by the Protestant Churches, and may be said to have reached its zenith in Mr. Elliott's "Horæ Apocalypticæ." It is frequently called the Protestant interpretation, because it regards Popery as exhausting all that has been predicted of Antichristian powers, and can find nothing but it either in the Harlot or the two Beasts. And herein the system betrays its weakness : it is the exposition of men who gazed at a contemporaneous power of evil until they could conceive no other, and who have, consequently, forced the Scriptures into accord with their own contracted minds.

As we might expect in such a case, its interpretations are vague and unsatisfactory : they are altogether lacking in that exact and literal precision which characterised the fulfilment of prophecies connected with the first advent—a fulfilment which is our only reliable guide if we would know how to deal with predictions relating to subsequent times.

Very conspicuous among the failures of this School are its wholly inadequate attempts to explain the Sixth Seal and the Two Witnesses. These have, however, been noticed so often that we may pass from them to some other points which more nearly affect our present purpose.

As we remarked above, those who support the Protestant interpretation believe Romanism to be the great evil power in which all the prophecies respecting Antichrist will find their fulfilment; and, consequently, they hold that it will continue until it is destroyed by the Lord at His appearing.

If, however, we turn to the latest prediction on this subject, the seventeenth chapter of the Apocalypse, a difficulty seems to lie in the way. The vision set before us is that of a wild Beast, which may be readily identified with the Fourth of Daniel's vision, and, therefore, represents the secular power of Rome. But the Beast wears no crowns, as he does in the thirteenth chapter, for a very obvious reason: he is ridden and directed by a Woman who is universally admitted to be the Church of Rome. We are thus able to recognize a picture of the times during which the Roman Empire has been in abeyance, and an ecclesiastical sovereignty has more or less taken its place.

But what is the end of the vision? The Woman is hurled from her seat, and destroyed with hatred and violence, not by the Lord, but by the Ten Kings, who can be identified with the toes of Nebuchadnezzar's image. And after her destruction, these kings transfer the sovereignty, which she had claimed, to the Beast, or secular power.

If, then, the usual, and undoubtedly correct,[1] Pro-

[1] Correct, that is, so far as it goes: for the symbol of the Woman comprehends much more than the Church of Rome, nothing less, indeed, than the entire Babylonian system, which has overspread the world, and of which Romanism is but a local and comparatively recent development. See Part I., chap. ix.

INTRODUCTION. SCHEME OF INTERPRETATION.

testant interpretation of the Harlot is to stand, we have a clear intimation that Popery will be exterminated *by human agents*, and will be succeeded by a secular and altogether antagonistic power. And the latter is that which Christ will consume at His appearing; for then the Beast—and not the Woman—will be slain, and his body destroyed and given to the burning flame.[1]

Thus the fact that the Woman and the Beast are distinct and finally antagonistic powers seems to break up the frame-work of the so-called Protestant interpretation. And we have but to look around us if we would see the marshalling of the forces to which Ecclesiasticism must shortly succumb.[2]

Again; according to the Historical view, the Ten Kings appeared some thirteen centuries ago. But surely such a conclusion overlooks the fact that Nebuchadnezzar's vision exhibits the whole course of Gentile secular dominion until the Lord's appearing; that, according to inspired interpretation, the image is gradually and regularly formed from the head to the feet, as each new empire arises or changes its shape; and that the toes are the parts last added, after which there is nothing more to come but the instantaneous descent of the stone.

Moreover, the kings represented by the toes could not have appeared until the Eastern and Western Empires, prefigured by the legs, had finished their course. Yet Elliott reckons up the Ten Kingdoms "at the epoch of A.D. 532";[3] whereas the Eastern empire cannot, at least, be said to have fallen until the capture of Constantinople by the Turks, in A.D. 1453! And even

[1] Daniel vii. 11. [2] See Part I., chap xi.
[3] Hor. Apoc., vol. iii., p. 140.

then, Russia claimed to be continuing its dominion, and, on that ground, styled her emperor the Czar, or Cæsar, and adopted as her standard the two-headed eagle, which was the symbol of the divided Empire. As to the Western division, if the reader will consult our chapter on the Napoleonic theory he will see that it continued to represent the very Empire founded by Augustus until it succumbed to the forces excited by the French Revolution of 1789. The latter epoch probably marked the transference of power to the feet;[1] while the toes are still undeveloped.

And yet again ; Historicists forget that, since five of the toes are on the right foot and the same number on the left, consistency requires that we seek five of the Ten Kings in the Western and five in the Eastern division of the Roman Empire.

But want of space forbids us to continue these remarks: we will mention only one other error of the Historical School, that which regards the Euphrates as representing the Turkish Empire. There appears to be no foundation whatever for this idea, as, indeed, many who accept it seem to feel: for it is frequently introduced with the vague remark that such is the generally admitted interpretation. Some, however, cite the fact that the river is in the Turkish Empire, which is not conclusive ; others affirm that the Turks began their migrations from the Euphrates, which is scarcely true, since we can trace them back some hundreds of miles into the interior of Asia.[2]

Such, then, is the Historical system, to which, per-

And also, as we hope presently to show, the fall of the Sixth Head of the Beast and the rise of the Seventh.

[2] See Part I., chaps. ii. and xi. Scripture appears to intimate that the Turkish Empire, as it was before the revolt of the Greeks,

haps, the most serious general objection is that it eliminates the supernatural from the judgments of God, and so contradicts the word of the Almighty Himself.[1] And we cannot better conclude our observations upon it than by quoting the subjoined graphic sketch of its rise and future disappearance.

" A thousand years passed away, and still the Master came not. To fill up the interval, some sought present accomplishments of prophecies till then understood to belong only to the end. In this way was produced the Historical School of interpreters, which has since flourished uninterruptedly, and bids fair to flourish, till the first sound of Apocalyptic judgment shall dispel the dream, and Prophecy, too long degraded and trifled with, shall appeal from the visionaries of the closet to the consent of a terror-stricken world."[2]

The third or Futurist system, which is adopted in the present volume, dates in modern times only from the beginning of this century. It is, however, a revival of the earliest of all interpretations which, together with much other long-lost truth, is in these last times restored to the Church, that she may be cleansed from her corruptions, and in purity of doctrine and holiness of life go out to meet her Lord.

But since the distinctive characteristic of the Futurist School has been often misrepresented, a few words of explanation will be necessary. And in the first place, its very name is a misnomer: for it by no means relegates all prophecies to the future, and ignores

must ultimately be divided into four kingdoms, with one of which Antichrist will be connected. See Part I., chap. v.

[1] Exod xxxiv. 10. See Prol., chap. vii.
[2] Maitland's "Apostolic School of Prophetic Interpretation," p. 4.

neither Romanism nor the trials and troubles of the true Church during the present age. But it is so termed because it groups most of the prophecies around the two advents, and so refers the greater part of the Apocalypse[1] to the last of Daniel's Seventy Weeks, which is yet in the future. The reasons for this method of interpretation will appear in the following pages, and the reader will perceive that the charges usually brought against the Futurist School do not apply to the scheme here laid before him.

For it does not omit the Papacy, but finds it strongly marked in prophecy, and described in such a manner as to expose its real nature. It sets forth Romanism as having been hitherto the master-piece of Satan, and the great enemy of the true Church; but it further teaches, in accordance with Scripture, that mystery Babylon will fall by the hands of men, and be succeeded, for a brief space, by a secular power even more wicked and terrible.

It cannot be said to ignore the Church, for it discovers two charts—drawn by the Lord Himself—of all that should befall her, from the beginning to the end of her career.

It is not a mere human speculation, but a scheme believed to be unfolded by God in the cardinal revelation which gave skill and understanding to Daniel, and enabled him to comprehend his visions. And, consequently, it will be found to agree with and explain every Scripture upon which it bears, and especially the Sermon on the Mount of Olives and the Apocalypse. Indeed this is the strongest point of Futurism: it is the only system which is based solely upon the great

[1] Rev. iv.-xix.

interpreting message vouchsafed to Daniel, and the Lord's own division of the Apocalypse into "the things which thou sawest, and the things which are, and the things which shall come to pass after these." And, accordingly, it is found to be a return to the interpretation preached by the apostles among the earliest converts, and a return in clearer light: for the Christians of old could only contemplate the mighty events of the end from an unknown distance; while we, owing to the subsequent fulfilment of prophecy, and its gradually unfolded interpretation, are enabled to discover that the age is almost exhausted, and its closing scenes on the point of commencing.

But objectors also urge that the Futurist system crowds too many great events into the short space of three years and a half, whereas the doings ascribed to the personal Antichrist would be more likely to be performed in the course of twelve hundred and sixty years by a series of Antichrists; and, further, that it is in the highest degree improbable that God would have given prophecies so important merely to warn Christians of the nineteenth century against a single foe.

To this we reply, generally, that it is dangerous to argue respecting the probability or improbability of God's dealings with men. His ways frequently differ altogether from our expectations, nor can we know anything concerning them except it be revealed. And, in regard to particulars, there is no warrant for the supposition that, when days are mentioned in prophecy, years are intended: nor is there any hint in the New Testament of a continuous line of Antichrists, the great rebel being always treated as a single individual.

As to the shortness of the time, the space of three years and a half has already been rendered memorable as the time of Christ's ministry: it shall be so once again as that of the Antichrist's tyranny. Logical consistency requires this: for in Scripture "the Christ"—ὁ Χριστός—is opposed to "the Antichrist"—ὁ Ἀντίχριστος. Lawlessness, also, shall finally culminate, as righteousness has done, in a single person, and be exhibited unveiled to the world for the same period.

Nor is the description of what shall happen within so contracted a time useless to the Christians of eighteen centuries: for since our first father *did* taste of the fatal tree, it has now become necessary for us also to acquire so much knowledge of the consequences of the fall as will give us a humbling sense of the sin in which we have become involved. We must, therefore, study the predicted doings of Antichrist and his worshippers, that we may understand something of the depths of Satan, may be warned to resist the beginnings of evil, and may be filled with gratitude as, with startled gaze, we behold the horrible and loathsome disease from which we have been saved only by the sacrifice of the beloved Son.

Plainly does Paul intimate the lesson set before us, when he says;—"For the mystery of lawlessness *doth already work:* only there is One That restraineth now, until He be taken out of the way. And then shall the Lawless One be unveiled, whom the Lord Jesus shall slay with the breath of His mouth, and bring to nought by the manifestation of His presence."[1]

Men are ever ready to break out into the appalling wickedness of the end: we live over a mine which

[1] 2 Thess. ii. 7, 8.

might be sprung at any moment; but hitherto there has been a restraining power. The Spirit, Who descended at Pentecost, is still with the Church, and so mightily convinces even *the world* of sin, of righteousness, and of judgment, that men dare not do their worst. Nevertheless, defiant rebellion is in their hearts; and, as soon as the Spirit leaves the earth with those believers who are to be gathered to their Lord, then the Powers of Darkness and their earthly subjects will manifest their real character.

Accordingly, that character is revealed to us beforehand, that we may know the true nature of the lawlessness around us, disguised though it be by plausible excuses and specious philosophies; and that we may avoid the guilt which Christians too often incur through such manifestations of it as disobedience to parents, disrespect to elders, indifference to the relations of life, proneness to speak evil of dignities and to despise lordship, and all similar strivings to be first where God has called us to be last, to take the higher room when He has bidden us to the lower. "Thou shalt do no murder," was the commandment of old; and the Lord tells us that it meant, "Thou shalt not be angry without a cause." And, just in the same way, the lawlessness of Antichrist is set before us that we may beware of everything which could possibly lead in the direction of his bad eminence.

We cannot, therefore, admit that a Futurist interpretation is useless to all except those who live in the actual times of fulfilment; for God undoubtedly instructs and disciplines the minds of believers by visions and revelations of the things which must shortly come to pass as the natural consequence of sin.

In regard to our scheme of interpretation, it has been, so far as we are aware, entirely deduced from the Scriptures; and its conclusions are as follows.

We gather that there are three peoples upon earth in connection with whom God has revealed His purposes —the Gentiles, the Jews, and the Church.

The predictions respecting the first of these three are very simple. Beginning with the kingdom of Nebuchadnezzar, four successive empires were to run their course, the last of them continuing until the appearing of Christ. But the third should fall apart into four dominions, after existing for a short time as one. And the course of the fourth should be even more varied, including three phases of sovereignty: it should rule over the earth first as one undivided power, then as two more or less connected empires, lastly as ten kingdoms confederated under a great and blasphemous president who should be destroyed by the Lord Himself. But, between its second and third phases, this fourth empire should be for a while deprived of its sovereignty, and be dominated by an ecclesiastical hierarchy. Thus the times of the Gentiles should flow on without interruption until the return of Christ.

The Jewish prophecies are a little more intricate, and Daniel was unable to comprehend the purposes of God concerning Judah and Jerusalem until he had received a special revelation to give him skill and understanding. This revelation disclosed that God was about to take four hundred and ninety years out of the times of the Gentiles for the special discipline, under covenant, of the Jews; that these years would commence from the issuing of an edict to rebuild the destroyed city and walls of Jerusalem; that after four

INTRODUCTION. SCHEME OF INTERPRETATION. 17

hundred and eighty-three of them had passed by, Messiah would be cut off, and, in consequence of His rejection, the covenant would be broken, and a long and unknown interval elapse, during which the Jews would be scattered and disowned of God ; that at the close of the interval they would again be found in their own land, and that the last prince of the Fourth Empire would make a covenant with the majority of them for seven years ; that God would at the same time resume His dealings with them, and so complete, in the time of Antichrist's covenant, that which still remained of the four hundred and ninety years ; and that, after they had experienced a fearful discipline during the final three years and a half, the Deliverer should come to Zion, and give to the remnant of Israel " the greatness of the Kingdom under the whole heaven."

In regard to the third people, the Church of God, we find that they began to be gathered out of all nations shortly after the Jewish covenant had been suspended, and that their age was to occupy the interval which followed. They were to undergo a variety of trials and struggles, concerning which they were instructed and warned in two prophecies uttered by the Lord Himself. They would feel their love growing cold as time went on ; they would have to pass through the fires of persecution ; they would be allured from the path of humility by a vision of earthly greatness ; their faith would be stealthily corrupted and changed, until they would become mingled with idolaters unawares, and be fast caught in the net of the Mother of Abominations. After a weary season they would break through her meshes, only to find another temptation spread before them ; they would be surrounded by a drowsy and indifferent orthodoxy, which would ultimately develop into Deism, Pantheism, and Atheism, or into a self-satisfied religionism. Yet among the faithful there would, in the latter days of the dispensation, be a revival of love which would urge some to wash their stained robes, to keep the word of Christ, and to confess His name. And so the interval would come to its close. The Lord Jesus would descend into the air : those of the Church who had died would hear His voice and come forth from their graves, while the living who had been able to endure, in spite of temptation, would be at the same moment changed, and caught up together with them into His Presence. There they would remain during the last seven years of the Jewish covenant, before the close of which they would be joined by some of their fellows whose unready condition caused them to be left behind for a season. And then the whole multitude, arrayed in white, would appear with their King in glory, and, after the destruction of His enemies, rule as His subordinates over the redeemed earth.

Such is an outline of the prophetic scheme which the writer believes to be God's revelation : whether he is able to substantiate his opinion, or not, the reader must judge.

II.

THE SIGNS OF THE TIMES.

WHEN the blue-grey clouds begin to gather in the sky and move towards each other, though we may as yet have perceived neither flash nor sound, we know that a storm is impending, and that the quiet hills and valleys will soon be startled by the forked lightnings and heavily pealing thunder.

"Ye hypocrites," said our Lord to the Pharisees, "ye can discern the face of the sky and of the earth ; but how is it that ye do not discern this time ?"

He spoke thus of His first coming, the signs of which are not nearly so fully depicted in Scripture as those of His second.

What, then, will He say to us if we fail to discover the secret of God in the things which are taking place around us, when we have so wonderful a commentary whereby to explain them ? Even the statesmen philosophers and thinkers of this world are expecting great changes in its social and political condition. Surely, then, it becomes us to search and see whether the ceaseless preparations which are everywhere apparent, the tendency of opinions in matters civil and religious, and the generally unsettled and frequently lawless state of Christendom, do not show that the last times of our age have come ; that the world will shortly be confronted by her despised but rightful and all-powerful King ; and, therefore, that His Church—the living and the dead alike—no longer *may* but *must* speedily be summoned to meet Him in the air.

Were we floating on a broad river which at no great distance was hurling itself in mighty cataract to a lower level, what should we infer when we found that we were being borne along more swiftly by the quickening stream, when we perceived an ever increasing agitation in the waters around us, and began to hear mingling with their tumult the sound of a deeper roaring ? Should we not at once understand that we were already within the rapids caused by the terrific fall?

And have we not exactly described the present condition of the stream of time? For both the prophets and the Lord Himself foretold a mighty catastrophe which will usher in a new age; a season of perplexity and trouble immediately preceding the times of refreshing from the presence of the Lord; a general disruption and disintegration of society, amid wars tumults and the most appalling calamities, to be followed by the glorious reign of the Prince of Peace. And are not signs of our approach to these predicted days of terror continually multiplying around us? Do not events, which were wont to float by in slow procession, now chase each other before our bewildered eyes with such rapidity that they pass away in months, or it may be even in weeks, instead of years? Have not the currents of public opinion ceased to originate merely in the schemes of a few princes and statesmen, and is not every country torn by antagonistic factions which drag the State, now in this direction, now in that?[1] Nay, are there not also multitudes of private individuals, who have each his own nostrum for divers ills, ever agitating the surface of society by thrusting themselves into notice?

Doubtless one chief cause of all this confusion has been that very thing which the world regards as a

[1] In a speech delivered at Aylesbury, September 20th, 1876, the late Lord Beaconsfield thus alluded to another formidable element of distraction;—"In the attempt to conduct the government of this world, there are new elements to be considered with which our predecessors had not to deal. We have not to deal only with emperors, princes, and ministers, but there are the secret societies —an element which we must take into consideration—which at the last moment may baffle all our arrangements, which have their agents everywhere, which have reckless agents, which countenance assassination, and which, if necessary, could produce a massacre."

cure for every evil—the spread of knowledge. For many of those who acquire a little learning—and the majority of mankind can do no more—are not slow to give proof that in very deed "shallow draughts intoxicate the brain"; and are wont, by a confident and persistent setting forth of their opinions, to lead astray those whose ignorance exceeds their own, and in this manner to confound the counsels of wiser and more experienced guides.

Education of a certain kind has indeed become general; but, alas! not with the expected result, since morals seem at the same time to be degenerating in inverse ratio. For how common is the lack of truthfulness, and that not merely in commercial life, but in all ranks of society! And this evil does not only exist, but is recognized as at least a venial fault, if not an absolute necessity. The law, "Swear to thine own hurt and change not," has no popularity in the present age, and he who breaks it will find many advocates and defenders.

Meanwhile, the growing impatience and irritability of men, arising from the indulgence of generations, the abuse of stimulants and narcotics, and the painful pressure and excitement of modern life, are beginning to manifest themselves in deeds of recklessness and violence, such as may be found in the records of any newspaper; while lawlessness and crime of every description are increasing, and—which is still worse—often assume shapes difficult to detect or punish.

And over all this sin and misery the giant forms of still more terrible woes are projecting their advancing shadows. Europe is armed to an extent hitherto unknown, and has been converted into a vast camp through the jealousy of the great Powers, which are simply waiting for an opportunity of carrying out their aggressive schemes. The most cruel and bloody war of our days has lately terminated in a peace which can be no more than a lull in the storm ; for the dreaded Eastern problem is still unsolved. Few are those who expect more than a brief respite before the air is again tormented with the rush of shot and shell, and polluted with the smoke of burning villages and homesteads. And even during the short armed truce in Europe, wars have been raging in parts of Asia, Africa, and America.

Yet again, the rapid spread of Socialistic principles among all the nations of Christendom, and the numerous secret leagues organized for their propagation, are giving statesmen grave cause to apprehend a revolutionary outburst which may shatter the whole framework of society.

And lastly ; breaches have been made in the barriers set by God to separate the dwellers upon earth from the spirit-world, so that an avowed intercourse is now established between men and demons.

Nor are physical commotions wanting to heighten the excitement. The last few years have been unusually prolific in violent storms and inundations destructive to life and property. Earthquakes have become alarmingly frequent, and seem by their ubiquity to betoken a widespread disturbance in the bowels of the earth which may culminate in some appalling catastrophe. And although the greater number of shocks are at present comparatively slight, yet there have been not a few grave disasters—such as those at Casamicciola, Chio, Ischia, and Java, the last of which has been characterised by competent authorities as the most stupendous convulsion on record. Famines, too, have occurred in divers places—in different parts of India, in Persia, in China, in Morocco, and in several other countries; while various kinds of sickness and disease seem to be more than usually prevalent.

Now all these things, and many others which might be mentioned, do indeed forebode disasters and widespread distress, but not necessarily the last tribulation, the final throes of the world. For earth has had her times of convulsion, suffering, and change, in former days. God's sore plagues, war, famine, pestilence, and the beasts of the earth, have often desolated her lands in past years, and yet the end has not followed. Nay, were we to feel the solid ground trembling beneath us, and behold the mountains lifted up and cast into the sea, even such a sight would not in itself prove that the great Day of the Lord had come.

Men have often forgotten this, and, when appealing to Scripture, have too frequently drawn their inferences from an exaggeration of one or more detached texts, instead of carefully considering *all* that the prophets have spoken. Hence there have been many false alarms and panics.

A remarkable instance occurred at the close of the sixth century. At that time men had become so accustomed to the domination of Rome that they believed her power could only perish with the world itself. And so, when they saw her apparently in the pangs of dissolution, with her lands wasted by war, famine, and disease, to such a degree that many once populous places had become pestilential through neglect;[1] when they beheld her supplies cut off, and not a few of her buildings destroyed by storms and inundations, they imagined that the world also had run its course, and that the last dread judgment was near at hand.

Gregory the Great was strongly imbued with this idea, and, in a letter to King Ethelbert, he thus expresses it;—"We know from the word of Almighty God that the end of the present world is now at hand, and that the reign of the saints, which can never be terminated, is about to commence. And now that the end of the world is approaching, many things will take place which have not happened before. For there will be atmospheric changes, terrors from heaven, deranged seasons, wars, famines, pestilences, and earthquakes in divers places."[2]

And since there was an Antichrist required for the last days, Gregory was sure he had detected him in the Patriarch of Constantinople, John the Faster, who had just irritated the See of Rome by proclaiming himself Universal Bishop.

Again, in the tenth century, there was a still more general panic. It was imagined that Satan had been bound from the time of our Lord's first appearing, and that, since the thousand years were almost accomplished, he was about to be loosed as a preparation for the last judgment. As the supposed time of this

---

[1] See Gregory's sermon on the plague, and Gibbon, chaps. xliii. and xlv. From a passage of Procopius (Anecdot. cap. xviii.), quoted by the latter, it appears to have been calculated, in regard to the times of Justinian, that no fewer than 100,000,000 of human beings " had been exterminated under the reign of the imperial demon."

[2] Bede, " Eccles. Hist.," i. 32.

event drew nearer the terror of men became piteous. Some handed over their property to the monkish foundations, and set out on a pilgrimage to Palestine, whither they expected Christ to descend. Many actually bound themselves by solemn oaths to be serfs to churches or monasteries, in the hope that, if they were found acting as servants to the servants of Christ, they would be more gently dealt with at the judgment. Buildings were allowed to fall into decay, since it was supposed that there would be but little further use for them. And if there happened to be an eclipse of the sun or moon, affrighted crowds would fly to the caverns of the rocks, or to any other places which they thought might shelter them from the glory of the dreaded appearing.[1]

But the year One Thousand passed by; nothing happened, and presently the excitement subsided.

Now these alarms, and many others, sprang from crude and baseless arguments which do not for a moment endure the test of intelligent investigation. And their result was something worse than the mere delusion of those who were affected by them: for they caused a general discredit of, and distaste for, the prophetic scriptures; since men are ever ready to cast upon the word of God the blame of that failure which is solely due to their foolish and short-sighted interpretation.

Certainly, then, our duty is to take heed that we be not carried away by such vain excitements, of which there are too many in our days; but we must

[1] See Mosheim, "Eccles. Hist." Cent. X., part ii. chap. iii.; and Robertson's "History of the Christian Church," book iv. chap. v.

be still more careful to avoid the opposite extreme. It is better to be troubled by many false alarms than to be once taken by surprise. The inhabitants of earth must awake some morning to find that the Day of the Lord is present; and as a snare will it come upon all those who have not understood the warnings of revelation. We should, therefore, pray for wisdom that we may understand, and for the power of the Spirit that we may watch. Nor could words be stronger than our Lord's injunction upon this point. "Take ye heed," He said, "watch and pray: for ye know not when the time is. For the Son of man is as a man taking a far journey, who left his house, and gave authority to his servants, and to every man his work, and commanded the porter to watch. Watch ye, therefore, for ye know not when the Master of the House cometh, at even, or at midnight, or at the cockcrowing, or in the morning; lest, coming suddenly, He find you sleeping. And what I say unto you, I say unto all, Watch!"

To stimulate obedience to our Lord's command, by tracing out the main streams of prophecy, and endeavouring to ascertain our own position in regard to them, is the object of this book. And if we discover that the revealed counsels of God place before us the translation of the Church as the next event to be expected; and, still further, that the present bent of human opinion, and the general condition and tendency of the world, are already in the direction of those apostasies, convulsions, revolutions, and judgments, which will affect men after the withdrawal of the Church; then we shall indeed have reason to believe that our age has entered upon its last days, and that those who would be Christ's at His coming have urgent need to keep their garments, lest He be suddenly revealed, and they be found naked, so that all men see their shame.

III.

THE SEVEN DISPENSATIONS.

WHY man, immediately after his introduction into the world, should have been exposed to temptation and sin with all its attendant miseries, we cannot explain. We are altogether unable to decide whether he is now passing through a fiery trial which is intended to humble him and eradicate the rebellious feelings conceived in former ages,[1] while the blood of the Lord Jesus atones for them; or whether some other and, perhaps, widely different cause has shaped the wise and merciful counsels of the Most High in regard to our race. Nor can anything be more foolish than the attempt to penetrate a mystery so utterly beyond our ken—a mystery which, in spite of all our efforts, must remain hidden until, in some

[1] We do not mention this to express belief in a previous existence of man, but only in the possibility of it. Should it prove to be an actual fact, the foundation of nearly all the hard speeches which ungodly sinners have spoken against God would be swept away in a moment. Should it not, God has some far better solution of difficulties, which He may hereafter show to those who love Him. It has been supposed that the description of man's creation precludes the question of his pre-existence, because God is said to have breathed into his nostrils the breath of life. But this expression is not materially different from that which is found in the prophecy to the dry bones, " Behold, I will cause breath to enter into you, and ye shall live." And again, " Come from the four winds, O breath, and breathe upon these slain, that they may live" (Ezek. xxxvii. 5, 9). Since, then, the words of this passage are confessedly used of resurrection, it

future age, it shall please the Almighty to draw back the curtain with His own hand, and so to reveal, to those who could trust Him amid the darkness of this life, the depths and faultless wisdom of His unwearying love.

Yet, although we may not search into the deep things of God, we cannot but be struck with one feature of His dealings with mankind. For while the government of this world has undergone several changes, which we, following the example of Paul, term dispensations; still, these dispensations, vary as they may in laws and conditions, are ever constant to one main object. They all combine to prove that in no conceivable circumstances are men able to preserve their integrity and save themselves from corruption; that their sole hope lies in a direct interposition of the Eternal, and so miraculous an infusion of His Holy Spirit that an entire change is wrought in their nature. And this fact certainly points to some deep-seated alienation from and tendency to rebellion against God, which must be eradicated before peace and harmony can be restored to the human race.

would seem that the verse in Genesis does not decide against the possibility of pre-existence, but must be regarded as neutral. Yet let us not dwell upon this impenetrable mystery; for, while a passing glance *may*, perhaps, help a weak faith, any attempt to speculate upon it *must* be fraught with the gravest danger, since there is no revelation. "The secret things belong unto the Lord our God; but those things which are revealed belong unto us, and to our children for ever." Oh that there were a deeper reverence among us for the hidden things of the Almighty, which are withheld for our discipline, and that we might be taught to say with David;—"Lord, my heart is not haughty, nor mine eyes lofty; neither do I exercise myself in great matters, or in things too high for me." And let us ever remember the words of a greater than David;—"Except ye be converted, and become as little children, ye shall not enter into the Kingdom of the heavens."

Whatever he be, or whatever the mystery which enwraps him, it is at least clear that man has failed to comprehend the lesson of absolute dependence which creation should have been sufficient to teach, and can now learn it only through a redemption more wonderful than creation itself.

In the first dispensation, Adam and Eve were created in a state of innocence and entire freedom from pain toil or anxiety, and were placed in a garden of delight. As a test of that spirit of obedience to the Creator which is both reasonable and necessary, but one small thing was required of them— they were merely commanded to abstain from the fruit of a single tree in the garden. Easy, nay, imperceptible, as this yoke must have been—for surely nothing but the distempered fancies of pride and self-will could have made them feel it at all— they, nevertheless, broke it from off their necks. And so they were expelled from the Paradise of joy, after having shown that man cannot retain his innocency when he has it: no, not even if he be aided by the most favouring circumstances.

A different age succeeded. Adam and his descendants were now tested to see whether, after the painful experience of the fall, they could recover themselves by their own innate goodness and without law or government. But, instead of improvement, they grew worse and worse, until earth was so filled with corruption and violence that God was compelled to sweep every living creature out of it. And thus it appeared that man, if freed from restraint and left to himself, will not merely fail to effect his salvation, but also rush headlong to destruction.

When the flood had passed away, Noah came forth from the ark, and a third dispensation commenced. God now invested man with the sword of the magistrate, directing that violence should thenceforth be checked by the execution of the murderer, and thus placed His fallen creatures under the discipline of visible and earthly government. But political union so intoxicated them with its new power that they deliberately rebelled against Him, and were only hindered from a daring act of defiance by the confusion of tongues. And while their government served to unite them against their Creator, it at the same time utterly failed to restrain their moral corruption. This we may learn from the miserable history of the cities of the plain, whose catastrophe seems to have closed the third or Noachian period.

From the beginning of the fourth dispensation, which may be termed the Pilgrim Age, God gave up the world as a whole, and chose out for Himself a single family, purposing first to regenerate the people who should spring from it, and ultimately, through them, to restore and bless all nations. Abraham and his descendants by Jacob were, consequently, separated from the remainder of mankind, that they might be brought into communion with Jehovah. They were caused to wander about as strangers and pilgrims, having no dwelling-place of their own ; and when at last they seemed to have settled in Egypt, they were suddenly made to feel the hostility of the land in which they lived by finding themselves reduced to a cruel and hopeless bondage. Yet even this severe discipline of separation and affliction, though it was closed by a wondrous display of God's faithfulness and power, failed to subdue their rebellious self-will, as we may see by their conduct after deliverance. Nor did the treatment which they had received from the world change their inclination towards it. For when, on their journey to Canaan, they began to be dissatisfied with God, they longed for the flesh-pots, the fish, the cucumbers, the melons, the leeks, the onions, and the garlic, of Egypt, and turned back in their hearts to the land which had so ruthlessly oppressed them.

The time at last arrived for the establishment of the chosen nation as a Kingdom upon earth, and the introduction of the fifth age. Accordingly, the Israelites, awe-struck by the marvels of their deliverance from Egypt, were led through the Wilderness of Sin— being meanwhile sustained by bread which fell from heaven, and water which streamed from the smitten rock—until they halted in full view of the steep and rugged heights of Sinai. There, amid the most awful manifestations of the presence of Jehovah, the laws of the Kingdom were delivered to them, and were afterwards written, in order that they and their children might thenceforth know those things by which, if they did them, they should live. But from the very first they grievously failed to obey; and, in consequence, delayed their entrance into the promised land for forty years. And when God did at last establish them in Palestine, they quickly showed themselves to be the same stiff-necked and wayward people. Neither their marvellous training, nor the possession of the written law of God, availed to effect a radical change in them. they grew weary of Jehovah as their sole Ruler, and demanded an earthly monarch. This request was granted ; but, after three successive reigns, dissensions arose which caused the separation of the people into two distinct and, for the most part, hostile states. These kingdoms, in spite of the warnings of the prophets and the oft-repeated chastisements of God, proved so incorrigibly prone to sorcery and idolatry that at length the Almighty permitted the destruction of Israel, and some time afterwards suffered Judah also to be carried away captive.

After seventy years the exiles of the latter kingdom were allowed to return to Jerusalem, and to rebuild the Temple and the ruined walls. Their affliction had cured them of open idolatry, and they practised it no more. They did not, however, on that account, draw nearer to God, but merely substituted for their former sin a hypocritical formality or a sceptical indifference.

And thus they became so entirely carnal that, when God, in the fulness of time, sent His only begotten Son into the world, instead of hailing Him as the long-desired Messiah, they rejected and crucified Him. In anger God suspended His covenant, refused at that time to restore the Kingdom to Israel, again gave up the city and sanctuary to destruction, and scattered the Jews among all nations for a second and far longer and more severe captivity.

Then followed the parenthetical dispensation of grace, during which the Israelite is cast aside for a season, but not forgotten in the counsels of God. For one object of the present age appears to be the removal of the obstacle to Israelitish obedience. It was the rebellious Prince of this World, assisted by his angels and the spirits of the air, who continually enticed the children of Abraham either to idolatry or hypocrisy. Accordingly, preparations are now being made for the expulsion of these hostile powers—" the High Ones that are on high "—and the substitution of a new spiritual government, that of the Lord Jesus and His Church. To this end the apostles were commanded to declare the significance of the death of Christ upon the cross. He had offered Himself as a sacrifice for the sins of the whole world, and from that time all who loved and were willing to follow Him should be considered to have died in Him, and so to have paid in full the penalty of their sins. Nay, further, God would regard them as clothed with the perfect righteousness of their Saviour ; and, after a short season of trial for their sanctification, they should, at the close of the age, be caught up, whether dead or alive, to meet their Lord in the air, and with Him become the spiritual rulers of the world in place of Satan and his angels. And, in the ages to come, the Creator would show forth the exceeding riches of His grace in His kindness toward them through Christ Jesus.[1]

Surely such an exhibition of love on the part of the Most High God, coupled with such glorious offers to His fallen and undeserving creatures, should have constrained every inhabitant of earth to join in one mighty ascription of praise to Him That sitteth on the Throne and to the Lamb ! But no ; men have received the announcement with stolid apathy, or have even been roused by it to feelings of bitter hatred and opposition. Only a few, whose hearts the Lord has opened, have heard, believed, and rejoiced. These are, for the most part, found among the poor and despised of men ; but they are known to the great King, and He will shortly confess their names before His Father and the angels.

[1] Eph. ii. 7.

The rest of the world will grow worse and worse, until this sixth age also ends in complete failure, proving that not even the revelation of the love of God in Christ Jesus can soften the rebellious heart of man.

Then will follow the last seven years of the fifth dispensation.[1] The majority of the Jewish people, which would not receive Christ, will accept a covenant with Antichrist, and the Lord will close the dread times of tribulation by appearing, with His redeemed Church, in glory to take the Kingdom.

During the Millennial Age, the seventh and last trial of the human race, Christ will reign in the heavenly places, the region now in the possession of the fallen angels, and will make His people Israel the Kings of the Earth upon the earth. Then will the promises to Abraham and the glorious predictions of the Old Testament prophets be at length fulfilled. The Tempter and his hosts of wickedness will be cast into the abyss, and their evil influences will no longer impregnate the air with incitements to sin; the curse will be removed from the earth, and the visible glory of the Lord will be present at the Temple in Jerusalem; while the carcases of the rebels slain in the valley of Jehoshaphat will be ever exposed to view.[2]

But not even this age of marvels, blessings, and warnings, with its total immunity from spiritual temptation, will bring about the recovery of fallen man. The Israelitish people will indeed be perfect, yet only through the power of the Spirit of God, Who, in accordance with the promised new covenant, will then have written His law upon their hearts.[3] But other nations,

---

[1] The reader will find a proof of this assertion in Part II.
[2] Isa. lxvi. 24.   [3] Jer xxxii. 40.

though awed into acquiescence, will yield but a feigned submission;[1] and when at last the Tempter is let loose, as a final test of obedience, they will gladly listen to his suggestions, and gather themselves together in open rebellion against God. The forbearance of the Almighty will then, however, have become exhausted. Fire will be hurled from heaven to destroy the rebel host ; and, after the general judgment, the eternal state will follow, that age of unsullied glory when righteousness will not merely reign, as in the Millennium, but will dwell in the renewed heavens and earth.

Thus, by seven distinct and altogether diverse tests, it will have been proved that no possible circumstances can give man the power of recovering himself from sin ;[2] that he must either cry out for the help of the Lord, or perish from His presence for ever.

[1] Twice in the Psalms—lxvi. 3, and lxxxi. 15—the Hebrew כָּחַשׁ is used to describe the attitude of the Gentiles towards Christ during the Millennium : and yet again it appears in Psalm xviii. 44, where the ultimate application, at least, seems to be the same. Now, when followed by a dative case, as in each of these passages, the word signifies "to lie to" a person, and then "to cringe," "fawn upon" through fear, or, as the margin of the Authorised Version has it, "to yield feigned obedience to."

If, then, such a word can be used of the general condition of the world at a time when men will not merely be freed from temptation by evil spirits, but will also be awed by the visible presence of the Lord, it is evident that their outward submission, however complete, will be rather the result of fear than of love. Consequently, at the close of the age, as soon as Satan is loosed from his prison, and is again able to stir up and direct human wickedness, the last great rebellion ensues.

[2] Not, of course, that God needs any proof, for He knows all that is in the heart of man : but it appears to be necessary to His purposes that man himself should be convinced. And this is no easy matter, as every experienced Christian is too well aware. It is one thing to subscribe to an historical belief in the depravity of the human race, and quite another to be humbly conscious of the appalling fact in our own person. All the trials of believers

IV.

THE THREE LINES OF PROPHECY.

BEFORE we can attempt to interpret the prophecies of Scripture, it is necessary to ascertain to whom they severally belong: for God is now dealing with three distinct classes of men upon earth, and with each of them on lines peculiar to itself.

Until the close of the third age He seems to have given all His revelations, and to have issued every command, to the whole human race without distinction. But by the covenant with Abraham He called out one tribe from among the families of the world to be peculiarly His own. And some two thousand years later He proclaimed the formation of another elect body, and men of every kindred and tongue and people and nation were invited to join the Church of Christ, and so to become separate from Israelites as well as Gentiles.

Thus the population of the earth is at present divided into three great orders, each of which will be found to have its own laws, covenant, sovereignty, and prophecies.

I. To the Gentiles, or world at large, belong those primal laws which were given from the creation of Adam to the call of Abraham.

Their covenant is the Noachian, which God made between Himself "and all flesh that is upon the earth,"[1]

---

are needed to bring them to a realisation of their true condition; and yet how often, when the burden which has bowed them down to the dust is removed, do they rise from their lowliness and join the company of the confident, until another affliction repeats the lesson they have so quickly forgotten.

[1] Gen. ix. 17.

THE THREE LINES OF PROPHECY.

and the conditions of which are still in force in the case of those who are neither Israelites nor members of the Church. Indeed God's great controversy with the Gentiles, after the translation of waiting believers and before the Kingdom is restored to Israel, has special reference to breaches of this covenant, as we may fairly infer from the appearance of its tokens about the judgment throne, which is encircled with a rainbow and attended by the Cherubim.[1]

Their sovereignty is earthly: it has failed once already, and they are now nearing the end of their second trial. In the times of the early Babylonian monarchy they were permitted to exercise dominion, and the result was a general revolt against God. Yet again, because of Israel's idolatry, the supremacy reverted to them in the person of Nebuchadnezzar, and has ever since remained in their hands.

Their prophecies—apart from those primeval utterances which belong to all mankind—are very easily distinguished, since they are written, not in the usual Hebrew of the Old Testament, but in Chaldee, the language of the first great Gentile world-power. Six chapters of Daniel are thus marked off for the nations,[2] and in the book of Jeremiah there is a still more significant instance. God sends a short message through the prophet to the Gentiles, and this message, though occupying but a single verse, is, nevertheless, expressed in Chaldee.[3]

II. Passing on to the second division, we know that

---

[1] Rev. iv. 3. 6-8. For an exposition of the Cherubim and their connection with the Noachian covenant, see the author's "Earth's Earliest Ages," chap. viii.
[2] Chapp. ii.—vii.
[3] Jer x. 11.

the hope of Israel lies in the covenant with Abraham, and that their law was given through Moses.

Once already the Kingdom has been within their grasp, but they proved unworthy to possess it, and were, therefore, cast out for discipline. At the close of the times of the Gentiles the sovereignty will be restored to them, but not until they have become regenerate through the Spirit of God, so that there will be no fear of a second failure.

All the Old Testament prophecies are theirs, save the few mentioned above as belonging to the Gentiles;[1] while, in the New, predictions which concern them may be readily distinguished, either by the context, or by some indication which connects their fulfilment with the Jewish economy and excludes it from our own.

III. For the Church, whose calling is heavenly, laws have been laid down by the Lord Himself and by those apostles who received from Him the power to bind and to loose. Her covenant is that of grace, the glorious Gospel of the blessed God. The Kingdom, which in her case is heavenly, has never yet been delivered to her; but the time will presently come for the Saints of the High Places to take it, and then her reign will be with Christ. Her prophecies are all contained in the New Testament.

Such, then, are the three great divisions of our race, to one of which every human being belongs. And it

---

[1] The Church, as we shall presently show, was a mystery hidden from the ages until it was made known by the Lord and His Apostles. There are, therefore, no direct prophecies of the heavenly election in the Old Testament, but only a few allusions which could not have been understood without further revelation, and will always be found to have reference to the connection between Israel and the Church.

must be remembered that all unfaithful Jews and merely nominal Christians are included in the first class, the only difference between these and absolute Pagans being that an awful responsibility rests upon the former from which the latter are free. Consequently, two-thirds of the Jews will perish in the great tribulation ;[1] and when the Lord appears to plead with all flesh by fire and by His sword, the rebellious peoples of Christendom will be destroyed :[2] but He will send messengers of peace to the nations that have not heard His fame nor seen His glory.[3]

There are many allusions in the Bible to the threefold division of mankind, and it will be well, before we dismiss the subject, to call attention to some of them.

First, then, a notable instance occurs in the fiftieth Psalm, the commencing verses of which run as follows.

1. " The God of gods, Jehovah, hath spoken,
    And called the earth from the rising of the sun unto the going down thereof.
2. Out of Zion, the perfection of beauty, God hath shined.
3. Our God will come, and will not keep silence :
    A fire will devour before Him,
    And it will be very tempestuous round about Him.
4. He shall call to the heavens above,
    And to the earth, that He may judge His people.
5. Gather My saints together unto Me,
    Those that have made a covenant with Me by sacrifice !
6. And the heavens shall declare His righteousness,
    For God Himself is Judge. (Selah.) "

The general meaning of these verses is sufficiently evident, they set before us a grand description of the coming of the Lord. His summons to the heaven

[1] Zech. xiii. 8.   [2] Matt. xiii. 40-42.
[3] Isa. lxvi. 15-19.

above and to the earth beneath seems to refer, as the context indicates, to the gathering to Him of New Testament saints, whether they chance to be then waiting in the Paradise of God, or are still alive upon earth. These have made with Him a covenant founded upon sacrifice : that is, they have confessed their need of atonement, and have accepted Christ as the propitiation for their sins. And they are assembled from earth and sky in order that God may judge His people, that is, Israel : for as soon as the Church is removed from earth, Israel will again become His people.

The Church, then, is summoned to meet the Lord in the air, and the heavens declare the justice of God in so exalting her : for Christ who knew no sin has been made sin for her, and now she must needs be manifested as the righteousness of God in Him. The destiny of the first of the three classes is made clear and the solemn pause indicated by the word *Selah* shows that the subject is about to change.

The remainder of the Psalm may be divided, at the close of the fifteenth verse, into two sections.

Of these, the first contains a tender appeal to the sons of Jacob, exhorting them to trust no longer in mere outward and formal sacrifices, but to bring spiritual offerings to their God. And it ends with the gracious promise that, if they hearken to His voice, they shall call upon Him in the day of trouble, that is, in the great tribulation, and He will deliver them, and they shall glorify Him.

But the sixteenth verse begins a very different strain, an address to " the wicked," those who, whatever they may deem themselves, can in God's judgment

THE THREE LINES OF PROPHECY.

be ranked neither with Jews nor Christians, and are, consequently, in danger of the impending wrath. Their hypocrisy is denounced in scathing terms: they are disobedient ones who know the Lord's will and do it not; nay, who even dare to preach it to others, though they are themselves workers of iniquity. Such conduct God abhors, and in special detestation does He hold the deceit by which they rid themselves of His fear, that is, by representing His attributes according to their own depraved conceptions, and not according to His revelation. Therefore, utter destruction is before them, unless they quickly repent, and bring forth fruits meet for repentance by giving glory to God.

Again, the three classes are set before us just as clearly in the seventh chapter of Daniel, where we find mention of the Four Beasts, or Gentile World-powers; of the Saints of the High Places, or the Church, so called because they are destined to reign in the High or Heavenly Places with Christ; and, lastly, of the People of the Saints of the High Places, that is, of the Israelites, who will be in intimate connection with the Church during the Millennial period.

Yet another instance occurs in Paul's First Epistle to the Corinthians, where, according to our Authorised Version, we read;—"Give none offence, neither to the Jews, nor to the Gentiles, nor to the Church of God."[1] Thus translated the passage needs no comment: but upon referring to the original, we find that Paul wrote "Greeks," and not "Gentiles." This fact does not, however, appear to affect the sense: for in warning

[1] 1 Cor. x. 32

the Corinthians not to put a stumbling-block before individuals belonging to any of the great divisions of the world, the apostle terms the second class "Greeks" merely because the Gentiles in contact with the Corinthians were mainly of that nationality. Moreover, the term Greeks was then applied to all civilized nations in opposition to the rest of mankind who were characterised as Barbarians.

Other passages might be cited, but these will suffice to show how distinctly the Scriptures recognise that threefold division of the human race upon which the interpretation of the present book is founded.

V.

THE THREE PROPHETIC PERIODS.

THERE is yet another fact, the knowledge of which is indispensable to those who would comprehend Divine revelations of the future. Prophetic time, from the commencement of the Seventy Weeks to the Second Advent, is divided into three grand periods, which are plainly marked out in the book of Daniel, and as plainly recognised in the Apocalypse. The evidences to this fact will be given in their proper place: for the present we shall merely make a statement of it, in order that the principles which guide our interpretation may be at once laid before the reader.

In glancing through the book of Daniel we observe that the prophet could not understand his earlier visions in the seventh and eighth chapters;[1] that in the ninth chapter an angel is sent, in answer to his

[1] Dan. vii. 28; viii. 27.

earnest prayer, to give him "skill and understanding";[1] and that, after receiving this communication, he readily comprehended the final vision,[2] which is narrated in the tenth and following chapters. It is clear, then, that the four verses[3] which contain the angel's words are the key to the whole book.

Now the purport of these verses is, that God had divided what was then future time into three periods.

I. The first, a definite time of four hundred and eighty-three years, beginning with the issue of a mandate for the rebuilding of the city and walls of Jerusalem, and ending with the presentation of Messiah as her King to the daughter of Zion, four days before His death.

II. The second, an indefinite period, beginning immediately upon the close of the first, and ending with the resurrection of the dead in Christ and their translation, together with all waiting believers who are then upon earth, to meet the Lord in the air. This is the present age, the time of the Church, during which all Jewish prophecies are suspended.

III. The third, a brief period of but seven years, beginning on the day when Antichrist shall make a seven years' covenant with the majority of the Jewish nation, and ending with the glorious appearing of the Lord Jesus to set up His Kingdom. This is a time of judgment, God's strange and short work, during which He will resume His dealings with the Jews by casting them into the refining furnace, carry on His controversy with the Gentiles, and permit the fulfilment of the prophecies concerning Antichrist and the Great Tribulation.

Dan. ix. 22. [2] Dan. x. 1. [3] Dan. ix. 24-27.

Now with these three distinctly marked times before us, let us remind ourselves of two facts.

First : the Scriptures cannot be broken or disagree. We may, therefore, justly expect to find in the Apocalypse a recognition of the periods disclosed to Daniel.

And, secondly, John wrote many years after Christ's entry into Jerusalem. Therefore, the first of Daniel's periods had then passed away, and the apostle was living in the second or Church period.

Turning now to the Apocalypse, we shall find that its contents are given to us by the Lord Himself in the nineteenth verse of the first chapter, where He says ;—" Write, therefore, the things which thou sawest, and the things which are, and the things which shall be after these things."

We have, then, the following harmony with the scheme of the Seventy Weeks.

I. Daniel's first period had passed by.

II. What John had already seen is written in the first chapter, which describes his vision of the sanctuary arranged for the present dispensation. Then, occupying the second and third chapters, come "the things that are," or prophecies of the age in which John was living, which is still going on, and which answers to Daniel's second and indefinite period.

III. Lastly ; stretching from the fourth to the nineteenth chapter, come "the things that shall be after these things," that is, in Daniel's third period, the seven years of judgment.

A careful application of this Divinely revealed scheme will dispel confusion, and enable us to range the predictions of the two great prophets, as well as those of all others, in their proper order.

VI.

MYSTIC CHRONOLOGY.

WE must not close our introductory remarks without mention of the mystical chronology which inspired writers sometimes use in dealing with the times of Israel, and which is based upon a very simple principle.

Israel once brought out of Egypt should have been the people of God for ever without any intermission. But they provoked Him by their idolatries, so that He repeatedly "sold them" into the hands of their enemies. And whenever He did so, the theocracy was suspended, and the time of their servitude was not reckoned in the mystic chronology.

We shall meet with a remarkable illustration of this fact when we examine the prophecy of the Seventy Weeks. There the whole time from the Lord's rejection as King by the daughter of Zion to the still future day on which Antichrist will make his covenant with the Jews, is omitted from the calculation, because it is the *Lo-ammi*-period, during which no Israelites of any tribe can be nationally recognised as the people of God. But of this we shall have to speak presently.

There is, however, another instructive instance which we shall not need to mention again, and will, therefore, endeavour to set forth now.

In the Book of Kings, we are told that Solomon began to build the Temple in the fourth year of his reign, and "in the four hundred and eightieth year after the children of Israel were come out of Egypt."[1]

But if we turn to the thirteenth chapter of "Acts"

[1] 1 Kings vi. i.

we shall meet with a very different computation. For there Paul speaks of the Israelites as having passed forty years in the wilderness,[1] four hundred and fifty under the judges,[2] and forty under Saul.[3] If to these five hundred and thirty years we add the forty during which David was king,[4] and the three of Solomon's reign which had gone by before he commenced his great work, we see that Paul reckons five hundred and seventy-three years between the Exodus and the building of the Temple.

Here, then, is an apparent discrepancy of no small magnitude. For the same period contains

According to Paul	573	years
And according to the Book of Kings	480	,,
So that the difference is	93	,,

Now some chronologists defend Paul's calculation, some that of the Book of Kings: but, for aught they say, the result is in either case equally disastrous, since one of the two inspired writers is always shown to be wrong.

If, however, we apply the principle stated above, the discrepancy vanishes, and it appears that neither the author of the Book of Kings nor Paul is mistaken; but that the former is reckoning by the mystical and the latter by the ordinary chronology. Nor is there any difficulty in demonstrating the fact.

During the period in question the only instances of God's formal, though temporary, rejection of His people occur in the Book of Judges. And turning to that

---

[1] Acts xiii. 18.
[2] Acts xiii. 20.
[3] Acts xiii. 21.
[4] 1 Kings ii. 11.

book we find that He sold them to Chushan-rishathaim, king of Mesopotamia, for eight years; to Eglon, king of Moab, for eighteen; to Jabin, king of Canaan, for twenty; to the Midianites for seven; and to the Philistines for forty.

There is also mention of an oppression by the Ammonites lasting eighteen years; but this was contemporaneous with that of the Philistines,[1] and may, therefore, be omitted from our calculation.

The times, then, during which their enemies ruled over the Israelites, and the theocracy was, consequently, suspended, were as follows.

Chushan-rishathaim					8	years.
Eglon					18	,,
Jabin					20	,,
The Midianites					7	,,
The Philistines					40	,,
					93	,,

Thus the sum of the times of servitude is ninety-three years, which, as we have just seen, is the exact difference between the lengths assigned to the period from the Exodus to the Temple in the "Acts" and the Book of Kings.

This instance unquestionably demonstrates the principle of the mystic chronology as applied to the history of Israel. And, among other lessons, it warns us to beware of finding mistakes in the Scriptures. If a discrepancy so utterly hopeless, to all appearance, as that which we have been considering is made to vanish in a moment by the discovery and application of one

[1] See Judges x. 7, where the double oppression is mentioned, and the historian immediately proceeds to describe that of the Ammonites, returning to the Philistines in chap. xiii.

of the Divine laws, should we not unhesitatingly attribute other difficulties which we may encounter to our own ignorance of the clue rather than to error in the revelation of God?

VII.

Supernatural Judgments.

The last general principle of interpretation to which we would invite the reader's attention is the necessity of recognising a supernatural power in the closing events of the age.

The Praeterist, of course, openly denies this: the Historicist is virtually on the same side, since he explains the seals trumpets and vials by ordinary occurrences, and thereby suggests, whether intentionally or not, that whatever still remains to be fulfilled will also pass into history in a natural course of things. But such a suggestion can be received only by those who are willing to ignore the words of the Almighty Himself.

When the Israelites had committed their great sin, and had broken the second commandment a few days after the terrors amid which it had been given, Moses interceded for them, and offered his own soul for their sake. But God refused the proffered substitution with the significant words;—"Whosoever sinneth against Me, him will I blot out of My book."[1] For Moses was himself a guilty man: there was but One Who, being sinless, could be made sin for others, and, having no transgressions of His own, could bear those of His fellows.

[1] Exod. xxxii. 33.

SUPERNATURAL JUDGMENTS.

At length, however, the Lord revealed Himself as the Saviour of apostate Israel; and, in answer to the earnest entreaties of Moses that He would still take them for His inheritance, He replied as follows;—

"Behold, I make a covenant: before all thy people I will do marvels, such as have not been done in all the earth, nor in any nation: and all the people among which thou art shall see the work of the Lord: for it is a terrible thing that I will do with thee."[1]

Now these words were uttered shortly after the destruction of Egypt by the ten plagues, after the dividing of the Red Sea, and at a time when the awful appearing of the Divine majesty upon Mount Sinai was still fresh in the minds of the people. Events, therefore, more marvellous and more terrible than these ancient wonders must take place at the close of the times of the Gentiles, before Israel can again dwell securely in the Holy Land, and be manifested as the inheritance of God.

If we bear this in mind, we shall be led to understand in a literal sense many predictions which we may hitherto have regarded as symbolic, and shall not fail to notice the similarity of the more universal Apocalyptic plagues to those which fell upon the land of Egypt.

So, too, the appearing upon Mount Sinai will be repeated, with terrors indescribably more appalling, when the trump of God shall cause the whole earth to tremble, and "the Lord Jesus shall be revealed from heaven, with His mighty angels, in flaming fire taking vengeance on them that know not God, and that obey not the gospel of our Lord Jesus Christ."[2]

[1] Exod. xxxiv. 10.   [2] 2 Thess. i. 7, 8

To this Paul refers when, quoting from Haggai, he says ;—"Whose voice then shook the earth : but now He hath promised saying, Yet once more I shake not the earth only, but also heaven."[1]

It will not, therefore, be long before God begins to answer the scoffings of Positivists, Evolutionists, Theosophists, and every other kind of unbelievers, in a manner which they little expect.

It will not be long before a Power—far mightier than the supernatural energies which are now troubling the world—will be manifested in the disorganisation of the laws of nature, vainly supposed to be unalterable, and in the infliction of plagues which will cry with ever increasing voice ;—

"Fear God, and give glory to Him ; for the hour of His judgment is come : and worship Him That made heaven and earth and the sea and the fountains of waters."[2]

The second Psalm seems to be on the point of receiving its ultimate fulfilment. The rebellion against the Lord and against His Anointed is gathering strength, and louder and louder every day waxes the defiant cry ;—"Let us break their bands asunder, and cast away their cords from us !"

Meanwhile the Lord still sits in heaven, veiled with thick clouds, and silent as though He heard not the boastings of the sons of men : but presently He will speak to them in His wrath, and trouble them in His sore displeasure. The anger of the Son will at length flash forth as the lightning, and blessed, indeed, will they be who have put their trust in Him.

[1] Heb. xii. 26.   [2] Rev. xiv. 7.

PART I.

THE GENTILES.

I.

The Prophecy of Balaam.

THE sons of Abraham are the destined "Kings of the Earth upon the earth." They may, therefore, with reason have supposed that, from the day of their settlement in Canaan, supreme power would be at once and for ever withdrawn from all other nations. And doubtless this would have been the case, had their own hearts been wholly surrendered to their God. But they were stiff-necked and rebellious; and, consequently, while they were yet in the wilderness, Moses was instructed to foretell the woes and captivities which would befall them in later days.

And again, towards the close of their wanderings, God plainly declared, by the mouth of Balaam, that their enemies would have power to trouble them, and drive them from their land; that a time of Gentile sovereignty must intervene before the fulfilment of the promises to Abraham; but that his seed should at length be delivered by the advent of a mighty and all-victorious King. This utterance is so grand and impressive—bringing into sight, as it does, the dim and threatening form of Gentile power, though it was separated from the prophet's standpoint by the vast stretch of eight centuries—that we subjoin an amended translation of the greater part of it. After declaring that his words had reference to "the end of the days,"[1] or the time when God's purposes in regard to Israel would begin to find their fulfilment, Balaam proceeds as follows ;—

" I see Him—but not now ;
I behold Him—but not nigh.
A Star goes forth from Jacob,
And a Sceptre arises out of Israel,
And smites the corners of Moab,
And destroys all the children of tumult.
And Edom becomes a possession,
And Seir becomes a possession, His enemies ;
And Israel acquires strength.
And a Ruler arises from Jacob,
And destroys what is left out of cities.[2]
And he saw Amalek, and took up his parable, and said ;—
Beginning of the nations was Amalek :
But his end is destruction.
And he saw the Kenite, and took up his parable, and said ;—
Durable is thy dwelling,
And upon the rock is thy nest laid.
For should Kain[3] be destroyed,
Until Asshur[4] shall carry thee away captive ?

[1] בְּאַחֲרִית הַיָּמִים. An important prophetic phrase. See Gen. ᵈlix. 1 ; Isa. ii. 2 ; Dan. x. 14 ; Mic. iv. 1. "This expression enotes, not only here but in every other place of its occurrence, the time when the promises and hopes of salvation given to any age should all be fulfilled. As Hävernick has aptly observed, it always points to the horizon of a prophetic announcement. For any particular age ' the end of the days ' commences when such anticipations of salvation as are not yet fulfilled, but occupy the forefront of hope, patient waiting, and longing desire, first begin to pass by fulfilment into the sphere of reality."—KURTZ.

[2] "מָעִיר is employed in a collective and general sense, as in Psa. lxxii. 16. Out of every city in which there is a remnant of Edom, it shall be destroyed."—KEIL.

[3] Kain, the name of the tribe-father, is used poetically for the tribe which he founded.

[4] Asshur was originally the name of Assyria ; but it was afterwards applied to the great Asiatic Empire in its later stages under

THE PROPHECY OF BALAAM.

And he took up his parable, and said;—
  Woe! who shall live when God does this?
  And ships come from the side of Cyprus,
  And press Asshur, and press Eber;
  And he[1] also goes to destruction."

Thus the prophecy opens with a grand vision of the second appearing of Christ as King of kings and Lord of lords.[2] Until this great event the enemies of Israel should remain; but then they should be either exterminated or reduced to submission.

Amalek, however, which had been the first to attack the chosen people—for such is the evident meaning of the expression, "first of the nations"—should be destroyed long before.[3]

Babylon and Persia. In 2 Kings xxiii. 29, Nabopolassar is called "the king of Asshur": in the apocryphal Book of Judith a similar title is given to Nebuchadnezzar, and his general Holofernes is described as "the chief captain of the army of Asshur." Again, in Ezra vi. 22, Darius Hystaspes is styled "the king of Asshur."

[1] Obviously the ultimate reference is to the last head of Western power, that is, to Antichrist.

[2] It is impossible to apply the opening paragraph to the first advent, as many have endeavoured to do. None of the details are concerned with the humiliation or sufferings of Christ, but only with the glory which is yet to follow. The power of Moab was not shattered at the first advent; and in place of Edom becoming a possession of Israel, it was just at that crisis that the Edomite family of the Herods became rulers in Judea. Nor did they disappear until the Jewish state was destroyed by the Romans: indeed Herod Agrippa II. fought on the victorious side in the final struggle. It is unnecessary to add that Israel acquired no strength in that time of trouble, nor did any Ruler arise out of Jacob to save the miserable people from destruction, and from the exile which is not yet ended.

[3] For an account of the unprovoked assault of the Amalekites, see Exod. xvii. 8-16. God manifested His hot displeasure by at once declaring, "I will utterly put out the remembrance of Amalek from under heaven." The cause of the severity is thus explained by Ebn Ezra;—"He had provoked the wrath of the Lord; for whilst the princes of Edom, the Moabites, and the Philistines, were overwhelmed with fear on account of the signs which the

On the other hand, the friendly Kenite should endure until Israel itself should be carried away captive by Asshur, an Eastern foe.

Nor would this captivity be the last of the troubles; for mightier nations would come from the other side of Cyprus, that is, from the West, and oppress both Asshur and Eber, or the Asiatics on both sides of the Euphrates. Yet these also should be destroyed when the Sceptre of Israel should smite the corners of Moab.

Thus, although at this early date—about B.C. 1452—not one of the destined world-powers was as yet in existence, so that it could be distinctly named, Balaam, nevertheless, foretold that the sovereignty would be delivered, first into the hands of Eastern, and then into those of Western Gentiles. And many centuries later it was further revealed, through Daniel and Zechariah, that this temporary dominion would

Lord had done in Egypt and at the Red Sea, this Amalek came, notwithstanding, to combat against Israel, and had no fear of God."

A direct command was afterwards given to the Israelites to execute the sentence of Jehovah as soon as they had established themselves in the land of Canaan (Deut. xxv. 19), and in the reign of Saul it was obeyed (1 Sam. xv.), but only in part. The Amalekites who were spared became troublesome to David, and were repeatedly chastised by him (1 Sam. xxvii. 8; xxx; 2 Sam. viii. 12). In the reign of Hezekiah, five hundred Simeonites went to Mount Seir, and smote a remnant of Amalekites who were dwelling there (1 Chron. iv. 42, 43).

In the book of Esther, Haman is called "the Agagite": the Jews affirm that he was a descendant of Agag, and in that way account for his hatred of their nation. If this statement be true, there is something very instructive in the rise of this scion of the accursed race after so many centuries, and in the fact that he all but effected the destruction of the people who had disobediently suffered his ancestors to live. And it may be that in the death of Haman and his family the doom of Amalek was accomplished.

be sustained by four successive empires, of which the first and second were Asiatic, the third and fourth European. Such is the most ancient prediction of the times of the Gentiles, containing, as is usual with the earlier prophecies, the germ of all that should follow, and delivered, most appropriately, before a Gentile king by a prophet who was himself without the pale of the chosen people.

Before we proceed, a modern theory, which confuses the house of Israel with some of the nations of the Fourth Empire,[1] will oblige us to say a few words concerning that portion of it which revolted from Rehoboam.

[1] The Anglo-Ephraim theory would render the great prophecies of Daniel unintelligible. These are times of Gentile domination, and, as the Lord tells us, they will continue until their close is announced by signs in the sun, moon, and stars. Since, therefore, such signs have not as yet appeared, none of the Ten Tribes could at present be holding so commanding a position in the world as that of England ; nor indeed—if our exposition on pp. 58 and 59 be correct—could they even be living on this side of the Euphrates. The mistake of Anglo-Ephraimites, like that of Post-millenarians, is that they adduce Millennial prophecies, and apply them to this age. Many of their assertions will not bear the test of Scripture: for instance, the idea that royalty must always remain with Israel is a direct contradiction of Hosea's words ;—" For the children of Israel shall abide many days without a king, and without a prince, and without a sacrifice, and without an image, and without an ephod, and without teraphim " (iii. 4). But, worst of all, they confuse the heavenly calling with the earthly, and in place of that tribulation which the Lord warned us to expect in the world until He calls us out of it, point us to earthly glory. They are not content to say with Paul, " For our citizenship is in heaven, whence also we look for the Lord Jesus " ; but tell us that we have a nation and a land here, and are not, therefore, strangers and pilgrims upon earth. Yet the New Testament never offers Israelitish promises to Christians, but, on the contrary, informs Jews by birth that, if they would be followers of Christ, they must give up their Jewish privileges, for that in Him there is neither Jew nor Greek.

II.

THE KINGDOM OF THE TEN TRIBES.

THE sad story of the Israelites is well known. From the earliest days of their settlement in Canaan they altogether failed in fulfilling God's purpose that they should be a separate and holy people, and after a while the nation was divided into two kingdoms. That of the Ten Tribes quickly began to worship "other gods and molten images," so that the Lord pronounced sentence upon them before the death of their first king. It was uttered by the mouth of the prophet Ahijah in these terrible words ;—"For the Lord shall smite Israel as a reed is shaken in the water, and He shall root up Israel out of this good land which He gave to their fathers, and shall scatter them *beyond the river*"—that is, the Euphrates—/ "because they have made their groves, provoking the Lord to anger."[1] This was the decree; but the mercy of God delayed its execution for more than two hundred years, at the end of which time Shalmaneser transported the captive Israelites to localities in Assyria and Media, on the other side of the Euphrates.

There is great significance in the place of exile. When God called Abraham from Ur of the Chaldees, He bade him leave the idolatrous country of his kindred, and cross the Euphrates into a land which He would show him. Abraham did so, and was forthwith termed a Hebrew—that is, "one who has crossed over"—by which name his descendants were from that time known to foreigners.

[1] 1 Kings xiv. 15.

But because the Ten Tribes rent themselves from the house of David, and lapsed into Demonism and Idolatry; therefore God would allow them to be Hebrews no longer, but sent them back again to the place from whence He had taken them. And there, beyond the river, they have remained, and apparently must still remain—whether in Affghanistan, China, or elsewhere—until the times of the Gentiles are ended. Then, at the bidding of the Lord, they will return towards their own land, and as they approach the barrier-river, He will dry it up before them, as He did the Jordan, and reveal His chosen people as "the Kings from the East."[1] Thenceforth both they and

[1] Rev. xvi. 12. Since they will have to cross the Euphrates, they must necessarily come from the East—$ἀπὸ\ ἀνατολῆς\ ἡλίου$: and after they have effected a junction with their brethren, the Jews, from the West, "the Kingdom and Dominion, and the greatness of the Kingdom under the whole heaven," will be given to them. The drying up of the Euphrates to make a way for the return of Ephraim is twice mentioned in the Old Testament, and is coupled in both places with a similar miracle in regard to the Egyptian Sea, by which a passage is opened for other Israelites, probably Jews, who come through Egypt. In Isaiah xi. 15, 16, we read;—"And the Lord shall utterly destroy the tongue of the Egyptian Sea; and with His mighty wind shall He shake His hand over the river, and He shall smite into the seven streams, and make men go over dryshod. And there shall be a highway for the remnant of His people which shall be left from Assyria, like as it was to Israel in the day that he came up out of the land of Egypt." Now the river in this passage must be the Euphrates, because the way made through it will be a highway from Assyria to Palestine; and the drying up must be literal, because we are told that it shall be like the drying up of the Red Sea and the Jordan when Israel went out of Egypt in the days of old. The remnant from Assyria are, of course, the Ten Tribes, who were led into captivity by the Assyrians; and if the reader will glance at the fourteenth verse, he will find a sufficient explanation of the Apocalyptic title, "Kings from the East." For all the nations must yield to their sway: "they will fly upon the shoulder of the Philistines towards the West; together they will spoil the sons of the East: they will seize upon Edom and Moab; and the

their brethren will dwell within the river, and their boundaries will extend, according to the promise given to Abraham, "from the river of Egypt unto the great river, the river Euphrates."[1]

III.

THE DREAM OF NEBUCHADNEZZAR.

IN the manner just related the Ten Tribes disappeared from the prophetic scene, and will enter it no more until the glorious times of the Lord's return. But the case of those which remained faithful to the house of David is very different. For a hundred and fifty years after the desolation of Israel, God still continued to plead with Judah. But neither warnings, chastisements, nor deliverances, availed to produce anything more than a temporary repentance; so that at length the patience of God began to be exhausted.

In the fourth year of the reign of Jehoiakim, Nebuchadnezzar appeared for the first time in the streets of Jerusalem, the city which he was destined so soon to destroy. It was a critical period of the world's history: for the recent battle of Carchemish had laid Egypt low and exalted Babylon to be mistress of the nations. Pharaoh-Necho had come up as the Nile-flood, his waters had rolled along like its streams: he had said, "I will go up, and will cover the earth; I will destroy

---

children of Ammon will obey them." A similar prediction may be found in Zechariah x. 6-11, where the drying up of the sea of Egypt and the river of Assyria is again mentioned. And the sixth and seventh verses seem to indicate that Judah is concerned with the Egyptian Sea, and Ephraim with the river Euphrates.

[1] Gen. xv. 18.

the city and the inhabitants thereof."[1] But the boasting was vain : the crown of the world had been given to Babylon, and soon the cry went forth, "Pharaoh, king of Egypt, is lost : he has suffered the appointed time to pass by."[2]

Immediately after the victory Nebuchadnezzar pushed on to Jerusalem to chastise the Jews for their rebellious alliance with Egypt. Their resistance was speedily overpowered : the city was taken, and king Jehoiakim loaded with fetters to be carried as a prisoner to Babylon. But just at this time some unknown cause so changed the feelings of Nebuchadnezzar towards his captive that he released him, and set him again upon the throne to rule, as a tributary, over his shattered and miserable kingdom.

The proud conqueror would not, however, return from Jerusalem empty-handed. He plundered the Temple of a portion of its vessels, and also gave directions to Ashpenaz, the prince of his eunuchs, to select, from those of royal or noble birth, the most comely and intellectual of the Hebrew youths, and to convey them to Babylon, that they might there be instructed in the language and wisdom of the Chaldeans. And so the young captives, among whom were Daniel, Hananiah, Mishael, and Azariah, were brought to the great metropolis of the world, and placed under a course of training which was to fit them for the king's service.

Shortly after their appointed time of instruction had come to its end, Nebuchadnezzar had a strange dream. He had been victorious over all his enemies ; his power was now unrivalled ; there was none to dispute it. Nor was there any city which could be compared for

[1] Jer. xlvi. 8. [2] Jer. xlvi. 17.

glory and strength to "great Babylon." One day, however, the king became thoughtful, and, remembering how quickly the glories of other monarchs had passed away, wondered what would be the end of his own magnificence, and who would arise after him. While he was thus striving to peer into the dark future, he fell into a slumber; but was even then unable to dismiss the troubled thoughts, which seemed to move like black and agitated clouds before his eyes. Presently a faint light began to steal upon the gloomy vision, and gradually to assume a dim and glimmering form of colossal proportions. Imperceptibly it became more lustrous and more clearly defined, until at length the clouds had passed away, and lo! the king was gazing upon a majestic statue, whose brightness was excellent, and the form thereof terrible.

It was an image of metal, but not of one metal only; for at the first glance Nebuchadnezzar perceived that it was shedding four diverse gleams. The head was of fine gold; the breast and the arms were of silver; the belly and the thigh-part of brass; the legs of iron, and the feet part of iron and part of clay.

With awe the king beheld the dreadful apparition: and then, casting his eyes upward, he saw, towering far above the lofty statue, a rock whose top reached to the clouds. While he continued to watch, a stone was detached without hands from its summit, and hurled down with mighty force upon the image. With a crash it struck the feet, and in a moment clay, iron, brass, silver, and gold, were broken in pieces together, and became like the chaff of the summer threshing-floor, so that the wind carried them away.

Nebuchadnezzar was astonished; so quickly had the

form of majesty disappeared, and yielded its place to the destroying stone. As he still looked on, he saw the stone beginning to grow larger, to spread forth its sides and raise higher its top, until at length it had become a vast mountain and filled the whole earth.[1]

Then the king awoke in trouble and perplexity. He had indeed seen a marvellous and never-to-be-forgotten vision; but who should unfold to him its dark enigma? He instinctively recoiled from the thought of consulting his soothsayers and sorcerers. Hitherto they had satisfied him; but during that night the messengers of the living God had been with him, and he could no longer regard the magicians of Babylon with confidence.

There were, however, none others to whom he could go; and so at last he summoned his wise men, determining at the same time to put them to a severe test. Accordingly, he bade them first relate to him the dream as a guarantee of their power, and then declare the interpretation. If they complied with his request, they should receive splendid gifts: but if they did not, the ministers of death should punish their deception. In vain the miserable Chaldeans pleaded that, if he would only show them the dream, they would tell him the interpretation. Nebuchadnezzar was inexorable, and curtly replied, "The word has gone from me"; that is, I have made the decree, and will not relent.[2]

[1] It is very important to notice that the stone does not begin to increase until *after the total disappearance of the image*. This fact emphasises the absurdity of attempting to interpret the descent of the stone as a prediction of the first advent.

[2] Such is undoubtedly the sense of the original. The ninth verse proves that Nebuchadnezzar could not have forgotten his dream. Moreover, if he had really done so, it is too probable that the Chaldeans would have attempted some deceit.

And so the slaughter of the wise men of Babylon had actually commenced, when Daniel went to Arioch, the captain of the guard, and boldly told him that, if a little time were granted, he would do what the king required. The offer having been accepted, Daniel returned to his home, where, in answer to the earnest prayer of himself and his companions, the matter was revealed to him in a vision of the night. Then, after uttering a glorious ascription of praise to the God of Israel, he hastened into the royal presence, and having first described the vision with minute accuracy to the awe-struck king, proceeded to unfold its interpretation.

The Most High God had deigned to gratify Nebuchadnezzar's wish, to draw back the curtain of futurity, and to reveal to him the things which were coming to pass. Israel had been rebellious; therefore the sovereignty of the world should now be delivered to the Gentiles, in order that they might, if they could, prove themselves more obedient and worthy to hold it. And the image, whose brightness was excellent and the form thereof terrible, was a representation of Gentile power from the time of Nebuchadnezzar, its first head, till the reign of that Lawless One whom the Lord shall consume when He appears to take the Kingdom.

Daniel, therefore, announced to Nebuchadnezzar that the world-power, previously reserved for Israel, was now given to him; and that he was, consequently, a king of kings over all the children of men. Hitherto each of the kingdoms of earth had been as a wild beast held in by a leash; till Israel was rejected none of them might obtain the supremacy. But now all restraint was removed from the royal lion of Babylon

THE DREAM OF NEBUCHADNEZZAR.

and he was permitted to ravin at his will. Nebuchadnezzar was the head of gold. And after him should arise three other kingdoms in succession, the last of which should pass through certain stages of development. Thus the outline of Balaam was to some extent filled in, and it was discovered that the Eastern and Western dominion of which he spoke would include the rise and fall of four empires.

In regard to the names of these powers we have no perplexity; for Scripture reveals them all, becoming in this as in every other case, if we only know how to use it, its own interpreter.

The first kingdom, Babylon, is indicated by Daniel while interpreting the vision to the Chaldean monarch—"Thou art this head of gold."[1]

The second he points out, in his account of Belshazzar's feast, by the emphatic words, "In that night was Belshazzar the king of the Chaldeans slain, and Darius the Median took the kingdom."[2]

The third empire may be discovered in the eighth chapter. For after the ram has been overcome by the he-goat, Gabriel explains that the vision represents the Medo-Persian kingdom and its destroyer, the Grecian.[3] The same succession appears also in the tenth chapter, in the words, "Now will I return to fight with the Prince of Persia: and when I am gone forth, lo! the Prince of Grecia shall come."[4]

To find the fourth power, we must turn to the ninth chapter. There it was predicted that Messiah should be cut off, and that, afterwards, Jerusalem and the Temple should be destroyed by the people of a great

[1] Dan. ii. 38.
[2] Dan. v. 30, 31.
[3] Dan. viii. 20, 21.
[4] Dan. x. 20.

Prince destined to meet his end in the last indignation, that is, by the people of the fourth World-power.[1] (And we know that the destroyers of Jerusalem, about forty years after our Lord's death, were the Romans.) Also in the Gospel of Luke we read of a decree of the Roman Emperor that all the world should be taxed.[2] Augustus is thus recognised in the Word of God as the head of the fourth World-power, since the dominion of Greece had then passed away.

(The four great empires are, therefore, Babylon, Medo-Persia, Greece, and Rome.) And if we turn to secular history, this succession is most plainly corroborated.

There is doubtless a significant appropriateness in the parts of the human body apportioned to each kingdom.

The head seems to point to the unity and compactness of the Chaldean empire, as being maintained by one dominating people under the absolute control of one sovereign. And since the head is the natural director and governor of all the members, it may also here stand for the Babylonian autocracy because such a form of government most nearly resembles that of God, and is the only one which can ever be perfect.

The breast and arms, a twofold part, are assigned to the Medo-Persian empire—the right arm and breast signifying the Persians, the stronger of the two nations; the left indicating the Medes.

The belly with the thighs, or rather, with the thigh-part, a combination of two portions of the body associated respectively with sluggishness and vigour, aptly represents the kingdom of Alexander, in which the

[1] Daniel ix. 26. See amended translation in Part II.
[2] Luke ii. 1.

ever active Greek ruled over the placid Asiatic, but could not imbue him with his own qualities.

The word which in our version is rendered "thighs" has the possessive suffix of a singular noun, and is only made to appear plural by the pointing of the Rabbis.[1] Of the six parts of the image which are mentioned, the one in question and the head, which is indisputably singular, have the same suffix; while the Chaldean expressions for the breast, arms, belly, and legs, are all plural, and are uniformly furnished with the plural suffix. There can thus be little doubt that ירכתה is singular, and means "the thigh-part," that is, the lateral part of the lower belly from which the thighs issue.

Lastly, the legs point to the great division of Rome into the Eastern and Western Empires, and the toes to the final division into ten kingdoms. At the same time the legs and feet were appropriate members to symbolize that power of which we are told, in the seventh chapter, that it should tread down and break in pieces the whole earth.[2]

We may remark that although the two great nationalities of the fourth kingdom were united for a while, they did not amalgamate. From the first Rome was made up of two distinct parts,[3] the Greeks were never completely merged in the Empire, but retained their

---

[1] Possibly the Rabbis may have followed the Septuagint, which has οἱ μηροί.

[2] Dan. vii. 23.

[3] "The edict by which Caracalla extended to all natives of the Roman world the rights of Roman citizenship, though prompted by no motives of kindness, proved in the end a boon. Annihilating legal distinctions, it completed the work which trade and literature and toleration to all beliefs but one were already performing, and left, so far as we can tell, only two nations still

THE GENTILES.

individuality, until at length the artificial bond of union was severed.

By the different metals of the image a gradual deterioration of government appears to be indicated.

Nebuchadnezzar received his power directly from God; and the prophet, after declaring how absolute it was, exclaimed, "Thou art this head of gold." On another occasion also, Daniel said of the same king;— "All people, nations, and languages, trembled and feared before him: whom he would he slew; and whom he would he kept alive; and whom he would he set up; and whom he would he put down."[1]

The second kingdom is said to be inferior to the first, and its metal is silver. For the Medo-Persian empire was not an autocracy, but a monarchy dependent upon the support of an hereditary aristocracy. The king could by no means do what he willed; and this we may see in the case of Darius, who earnestly desired to save Daniel from the lions' den, but was unable to resist the pressure of the presidents and princes. Similarly Ahasuerus could not rescind his order for the slaughter of the Jews, but could only issue a counter-decree permitting them to stand for their lives and slay those who would assault them.

The metal of the third empire is brass; and the government of Alexander was a monarchy supported by a military aristocracy of a far coarser grain than the hereditary nobles of Persia.

---

cherishing a national feeling. The Jew was kept apart by his religion, the Greek boasted his original intellectual superiority." Bryce's "Holy Roman Empire."

Of course the image which Nebuchadnezzar saw did not include the Jews: it was a portrayal of Gentile power exclusively.

[1] Dan. v. 19.

THE DREAM OF NEBUCHADNEZZAR.

The iron power of the Cæsars showed a still further depreciation. For they were nominally elected by the people ; they were merely called First Magistrates of the State, or Generals ; and for a long time they wore no diadem, but only the laurel crown of a successful commander. They had also a Senate which was supposed to counsel and control them. Yet, underneath this vail of popular authority, they usually wielded an absolute power. The people were neither allowed to legislate for them, nor to interfere with them. If a senator attempted to be independent, he was quickly put out of the way, and had cause to congratulate himself should the penalty be nothing worse than banishment to a desert island.

Thus the Empire remained metallic : it was coherent and strong as iron. But, as time went on, those northern hordes, which had long been the foes of Rome, began to assert their superiority, and gradually drew nearer and nearer to the imperial city. Many a time they retired, as if in fear lest some supernatural power should burst upon and destroy them if they essayed to offer violence to Rome ; but at length the spell was broken, and the world began to look upon the great city as the Philistines did upon Samson when, shorn of his locks, he had become weak as other men.

The citizens must have felt this bitterly at the second approach of Alaric, king of the Visigoths. For the embassy, which they sent to terrify the barbarian by threatening to oppose to him a numerous and well-disciplined army, could only evoke the insolent rejoinder, " The thicker the hay, the easier it is mowed." Finding him indifferent to their menaces, the ambassadors changed their tone, and requested to know upon what terms he would consent to withdraw. His conditions were so grasping that they exclaimed in despair ;—" If such, O king, are your demands, what do you intend to leave us ? " " Your lives," was the brief reply. Alaric was, however, bribed to retire for a while ; but he soon returned, and the fatal day arrived on which Rome herself experienced those horrors which she had for centuries inflicted upon other cities. A long period of more or less anarchy succeeded, and the modern kingdoms of Europe were gradually evolved, but under the presidency of an ecclesiastical hierarchy which for some centuries occupied the place of the emperor.

It was by the irruption of these northern barbarians, and the spirit which they brought with them, that the clay began to be mingled with the iron in what we call constitutionalism, the nature of which is to be ever inclining more and more to pure democracy. But it is impossible that governments so modelled should long cohere. Men cannot be ruled, and at the same time be themselves the rulers. Such an arrangement may indeed be, in certain circumstances, the best palliative during the present age ; just as poisons are often medicinally useful to diseased bodies. But it can be nothing more than a palliative : there will be no settled rest for the fevered inhabitants of earth until they be placed under the sway of an Autocrat of never-failing wisdom, absolute righteousness, and perfect love.

And this is the solution of mundane difficulties which God proposes.

This is the hope which rose in glorious vision before the eyes of David at the close of his chequered life, and called forth the last words of the sweet Psalmist of Israel—

"A Ruler over men, just;
A Ruler in the fear of God!
And He is as the light of the morning when the sun riseth,
As a morning without clouds!
From the sunshine after rain verdure springeth out of the earth!"[1]

The Ten Kingdoms are not yet clearly manifested, but are doubtless, amid the many changes of these restless times, now in process of formation. The portion of the prophecy which has been already fulfilled assures us that in this case also the figure will be strictly carried out; so that, just as five of the toes of the image were on the right foot and five on the left, in like manner five of the kingdoms will spring from the Western, and five from the Eastern division of the old Roman Empire. Of the latter, four, as we shall presently show, will be the resuscitated kingdoms of Alexander's generals, covering the area at present occupied by Greece, by the Turkish empire in Europe, Asia, and Africa, and by the independent states between it and Russia. The fifth *may* be Persia, which, it would seem, must be included in the last great empire;[2] though, of course, not neces-

[1] 2 Sam. xxiii. 3, 4. The translation is literal, and the order of the Hebrew words is carefully preserved. But only one acquainted with the East can rightly appreciate the beauty of the metaphor in the last sentence—one who has seen the marvellous change which passes over the face of the earth, burnt and whitened by a long drought, when at last a copious rain is succeeded by the clear shining of the morning sun, and the tiny green blades begin to appear in their countless millions. Such is the figure set before us of the effect physical and moral which will be produced by the rising of the Sun of Righteousness with healing in His wings. Let not men call those pessimists who, however great their distrust of human powers, are looking for such a consummation; who dare to believe that in a few short years sin may be suddenly suppressed, the miseries of life turned into gladness, and the whole creation made to rejoice, by the coming of the King.

[2] Persia has never yet submitted to Roman sway, but even after

sarily as one of the Ten Kingdoms, but probably as a mere dependency.[1]

For since the image is standing complete in all its parts when the stone strikes it, and since all the parts are destroyed at the same moment, it seems to follow that the Ten Kingdoms will either comprise or dominate all that has ever pertained to the Babylonian, Persian, Grecian, or old Roman empires.

And, moreover, since the Fourth Empire in its final phase will include the feet and toes of the image which have never yet belonged either to its own dominion or to any of the other empires, it is manifest that it will exceed, not merely its own ancient limits, but also those of the three previous kingdoms. For at the addition of each of the other limbs there has always been an increase of territory to the prophetic earth; nor is there any reason to suppose that a rule which has invariably held good will fail in the single remaining case to which it can apply in the future.

It would seem, then, that those who take pains to trace out the bounds of the ancient Roman Empire, under the impression that it will, in its revival, be confined within the same exact limits, are mistaken. And something yet stronger might be said of the interpreters who persist in affirming that England must be separated from Ireland, and lose India and other dependencies,

these paration of East and West remained the determined foe of the Byzantine empire, until the Saracen made his fell swoop upon both of the exhausted combatants.

[1] Although there can be but ten *sovereign* kingdoms, yet it must be remembered that no limit is set to their dependencies, which may include the whole of the known world. Indeed, something like this seems to be implied in the Apocalyptic account of Antichrist: for it is said that "there was given to him authority over every tribe and people and tongue and nation" (Rev. xiii. 7).

because these countries were not formerly under the sway of Rome. For their mistake becomes a practical mischief, helping, in its degree, to bring about the calamity which they predict. If the imperial spirit of England declines, and she becomes weak and mean in her counsels, she may very probably lose both Ireland and India, and with them all the prosperity which her vast empire has sustained for her—nay, the very security of her existence. And were so dire an event to befall her, we could not but recognize it as a just judgment of God upon a nation which, though most highly favoured by Him, has continually abused its privileges. But it would be no fulfilment of prophecy, though its causes might afford a striking illustration of the proverb—" Whom God will destroy, He first deprives of sense."

To the delay in the development of the Ten Kingdoms we may find many parallels if we study the past translations of God's purposes into history. This vision, like some others, may seem to tarry, yet it is for an appointed time ; at the end it shall speak, and not lie. But that the Roman Empire would disappear for a while as a secular power, and afterwards recover its sovereignty in the last days, is plainly intimated in the seventeenth chapter of the Apocalypse. There the Beast, which represents it, is seen discrowned, and ridden by a Woman under whose sway it has fallen. This Woman, as we hope presently to show, is the ecclesiastical power which lifted itself up to the throne of the Empire, and has for centuries hindered the rise of the Ten Kingdoms. But they must shortly appear, and then their kings will hate the whore, and make her desolate and naked, and eat her flesh, and burn her with fire.[1]

[1] Rev. xvii. 16.

This they will do because God will put it in their hearts to fulfil His will by destroying the false Church, and reviving the fallen Empire under the presidency of the last and greatest of the Cæsars. And when all these things have been accomplished, the time for the descent of the stone will be at hand.

But here a remarkable instance of God's justice presents itself: for destruction will not come upon the world-empire until the masses of the people are themselves responsible for their condition. Gentile dominion passes gradually from the head to the feet, from the organ which ought to direct to the members which are only formed to carry the body whither the head guides it. While it remains with the autocrat, there is some excuse for those who are under his rule ; and the same remark applies, though in a less degree, to every form of government short of the absolute sovereignty of the people. Therefore the stone has not yet fallen upon the image. But as soon as the power is really vested in the people, then the multitudes of mankind will themselves become responsible to their Creator for the ungodliness and rebellion of the world. And so judgment will be no longer deferred, and the stone will descend to strike the image upon the *feet*,[1] that is, to destroy the body politic out of which the ten democratic kings arise, and of which they form a part.

This awful event will take place, with the swiftness of lightning,[2] when the Lord Jesus is revealed in flaming

[1] Dan. ii. 34.

[2] It is strange that the rapid descent of the stone, and the instantaneous pulverization of the image, could ever have been interpreted of a gradual conversion of the world from the time of the first advent. For—to pass by the hopeless incongruity of the metaphor—if such were the meaning to be conveyed, how could

fire, as is described in the nineteenth chapter of the Apocalypse. The World-power of Christendom will be destroyed in a moment. And when the Messiah shall, like David, have gained the victory over all His enemies, He will become the great Antitype of Solomon; and His Kingdom of peace, beginning from Jerusalem, will spread over the whole earth.[1]

Such, then, was the dream and its interpretation. The vision was granted to Nebuchadnezzar; but he could not understand it until Daniel came forward as the interpreter. For although earthly power had now been transferred to the Gentile, the mind of God still remained with the Jew. He had not yet poured out His Spirit upon all flesh, nor did He do so until Israel had rejected the Messiah.

IV.

THE VISION OF THE FOUR WILD BEASTS.

ONLY a short time after his memorable dream, the rebellion of Jerusalem obliged Nebuchadnezzar to march

the stone strike the image upon its feet when as yet there were neither feet nor legs? The division of Rome into the Eastern and Western Empires—to say nothing of the formation of the Ten Kingdoms—did not take place till centuries after the first advent.

[1] This will take place rapidly, no doubt, but not instantaneously. Irresistible though it be, it is no more than a stone which descends, and, consequently, the immediate effect of its descent is locally restricted. But after the destruction of the image, it *becomes* a great mountain and fills the whole earth.

From other Scriptures we gather that the agency by which Christ will then spread His Kingdom will be similar to that which He now uses, while the circumstances will be altogether changed.

The word will go forth no longer in weakness, but in manifested power; its ministry—as we learn from Isa. lxvi. 19—will be committed to the children of Abraham; and the opposition of the spiritual powers of wickedness will have been removed.

against that city. His invasion was irresistible; and having deposed and—as the prophecies of Jeremiah seem to imply—slain Jehoiakim, he placed the youthful Jehoiachin upon the throne, and departed to press the siege of Tyre. But a fatal impulse moved the dominating party in Jerusalem to resume their intrigues with Egypt, and caused the prompt return of Nebuchadnezzar, whose determination so terrified the Jews that Jehoiachin, his mother Nehushta, and all the royal princes and officers, went out and surrendered themselves to be carried as captives to Babylon. With an unwonted clemency, which can only be ascribed to the impressions wrought on him by the revelations of Daniel, the wrathful autocrat still refrained from destroying the city. His forbearance resulted, however, in nothing more than a short respite: for Zedekiah, who had sworn to rule as his vassal, was soon discovered, like his predecessors, to be "sending his ambassadors into Egypt, that they might give him horses and much people."[1] Then the Chaldean king gave vent to his just anger; and, after a little delay, Jerusalem was levelled to the ground, and the Temple, in which the bigoted but ungodly Jews had placed their trust, was consumed with fire.

Yet God would not altogether give up Israel: sinful as the inhabitants of Judah had been, they were still His people, and His prophets continued among them.

Stationed with the miserable remnant in Palestine was Jeremiah, who, while he sternly rebuked their sins, nevertheless foretold that earth would soon be moved at the ruin of great Babylon, but that fallen Israel should rise again. And if any of his countrymen were

[1] Ezek. xvii. 15.

THE VISION OF THE FOUR WILD BEASTS.

humbled in spirit before Jehovah, he could comfort them with the sweet assurance ;—" For I know the thoughts that I think toward you, saith the Lord, thoughts of peace and not of evil, to give you an expected end."[1]

And even when the Jews, rebellious as ever, determined against the will of God to flee to Egypt for refuge, Jeremiah still remained among them, and prophesied to those who dwelt at Migdol and Tahpanes and Noph and in the country of Pathros.

Nor were the captives by the river of Chebar forgotten. With them was the prophet Ezekiel, who saw indeed mournful visions of the departure of the glory from the Temple, and of the punishment of Jerusalem ; but who also declared that the Spirit of the Lord should yet pass over the dry bones of Israel, and cause the people to arise from their graves, an exceeding great army ; and that the Messiah should, in happy times, build a structure far surpassing the Temple of Solomon, to which the glory of the Lord should return, and abide in it for ever.

Such, then, was the distribution of prophets among the Jews, who in all their afflictions did not cease to be the people of Jehovah, until they had filled up the measure of their iniquities by contemning His Son.

And since the sovereignty was now, according to the purpose of God, delivered to Nebuchadnezzar, and the Gentiles were being put to the test, a prophet was stationed at Babylon also, to reveal the Divine will, and to direct or warn as occasion might require. And so the new era commenced.

It is, of course, with the revelations of the prophet

[1] Jer. xxix. 11

appointed to minister to the Gentiles that we are at present concerned. We have already considered his interpretation of Nebuchadnezzar's vision, of the great image which represented Gentile dominion, noble and terrible as it would appear to the eyes of men. We saw that by it four great empires were disclosed as destined to run their course before the times of the Gentiles should be ended, and the Lord return to restore the Kingdom to Israel. That the fourth empire would be first divided into two, and then, after it had become more or less democratic, into ten kingdoms, which would nevertheless be in some way united under one head. That the parts of the body were significant of the unity, or the composite character, of the empires symbolized by them. That the arrangement of the metals intimated a continual degeneracy in the form of government. That judgment will not come until power has descended to the feet, or to the lowest order of the people. And, lastly, that the fourth empire will, in its final phase, include, together with new accessions, all the territory previously possessed by the others.

Such is the first great prophecy which relates exclusively to the Gentile powers. Most significantly it is not written in Hebrew, but in Chaldean, the world-language of that time. This is also the case with the five following chapters of Daniel, the last of which contains a second vision of the Gentile empires; while the intermediate four, though strictly historical, seem to be at the same time prophetic, since they are illustrative of the spirit which animates the World-powers, and also foreshadow scenes which will take place on a far grander scale in the closing years of the age.

In the third chapter, the golden image which Nebuchadnezzar set up in the plain of Dura was apparently suggested by his dream. Some have found difficulty in admitting this, because no exact copy of the vision-statue was attempted. But since the king knew that the head of gold represented himself, it was surely natural that he should use that metal alone to form the symbol of his own power. Homage to the statue may *possibly* have been intended to mean nothing more than submission to the king by a recognition of his gods as superior to those of vanquished nations. But far more probably it was a worship of himself—such as that which Darius received in the second empire, which was offered to Alexander as he entered Babylon, and which the Roman emperors were ever striving to exact from the Christians of the early Church. And in this case how completely does the scene in the plain of Dura foreshadow that which shall be hereafter! (For the last king of the Gentiles, like the first, will also set up his image for worship ; and the false prophet who stands before him will cause all those who refuse him Divine honour to be put to death.)

Again ; the contents of the fourth chapter—Nebuchadnezzar's second dream, its interpretation, and the sequel—are clearly a type of the whole course of God's dealings with the Gentiles. This is much more plainly brought out in the seventh chapter, in which we find that the World-powers are regarded by God as wild beasts ; while, in contrast to them, the Lord Jesus takes the government upon His shoulders as a Son of man—that is, of man as God originally made him, before he fell into the bestial condition. And what hope there is for the human race in the restoration of Nebuchadnezzar to his sovereignty and glory, and in the noble confession by which he shows that his chastisement has been made a means of healing to him!

The types in the fifth and sixth chapters are striking and obvious. In the seventh we come to a vision which affords us another glimpse of the Gentile empires, but this time from an altogether different point of view. For the seer is no longer the head of the World-power gazing upon Gentile dominion displayed before his eyes in the noble appearance and fair proportions of a majestic human form, but the prophet of God, who is made to see things as they really are. Hence we have now no mere disclosure of the number of the coming empires, and of their gradual descent from absolute monarchy to democracy, but an insight into their real character as it appears, not to men, but to God.

It was in the first year of Belshazzar's vice-royalty at Babylon—when the armies of Cyrus were advancing, and perhaps the defeat of the Babylonians had already forced their king Nabonadius to take refuge in Borsippa—that Daniel, who was doubtless pondering the impending changes, received a further revelation.

He thought he was standing on the shore of the great sea, and lo! from the four corners of heaven, violent blasts were hurling themselves upon its restless waters, and lashing the whole surface of the deep into a tumult of dark foam. The prophet gazed with awe upon the troubled scene, and, while he was looking, a huge monster gradually lifted itself up from the boisterous waves, a creature in shape like to a

THE VISION OF THE FOUR WILD BEASTS.

lion, but with eagle's wings. Suddenly its great pinions were torn away, and it was raised up so as to stand upon its hind legs in the posture of a man, beast though it still was; and a man's heart was given to it. Then a second creature, like to a ponderous bear, came forth from the waters; it raised its right side, and was holding three ribs between its teeth. And the prophet heard a voice crying to it;—"Arise, devour much flesh." Anon a third beast appeared, resembling a spotted leopard; but upon its back were four wings, not like those of an eagle, but of a more ordinary bird. It had also four heads, and dominion was given unto it. Lastly, there arose a fourth monster, diverse from all the others, with a form unlike that of any earthly creature, having iron teeth and claws of brass, with which it devoured, brake in pieces, and stamped the residue under foot. Upon its head were ten horns, and while it was passing before Daniel, another small horn sprouted, uprooting, as it gradually increased, three of the ten. And the prophet perceived that in this horn were eyes like the eyes of a man, and a mouth speaking great things.

Turning his face toward heaven, Daniel saw that judgment thrones were being set[1] in the empyreal height, the same probably as those described by John in the fourth chapter of the Apocalypse—that is to say, the Throne of God and those of the twenty-four elders. Then, in indescribable majesty, the Ancient of days appeared surrounded by innumerable angels, the books were opened, and Daniel saw in vision the great Assize

[1] Such is the sense of the original: the rendering of the Authorized Version, "till the thrones were cast down," is incorrect.

which shall hereafter be held over the as yet unconscious world. By its sentence the career of the fourth monster was suddenly arrested; because of the blasphemies of the horn the beast was slain, and his body given to the burning flames. His fate thus differed from that of the other beasts; for though successively deprived of their dominion, their lives had, nevertheless, been spared.

Then, in place of the beasts, Daniel saw One like to a son of man brought before the Ancient of days; and to Him was given all power, so that His dominion should, unlike those which had preceded it, be everlasting, and His Kingdom one which should never be destroyed.

Such, then, was the vision, a partial interpretation of which was given by an angel who stood near. But by comparing the previous revelation the prophet might have perceived that the four beasts represented the same four empires which had been displayed to Nebuchadnezzar in the parts and metals of the image; and that the vision foreshadowed the course and end of those Gentile powers to which God had delegated the sovereignty of earth, during the chastisement of His people Israel.

Daniel thought that he was standing on the shore of "the great sea," an expression which in the Old Testament always signifies the Mediterranean.[1] This indicated the locality of the world-powers; they must all border upon the Mediterranean before they could have anything to do with the vision.[2]

[1] Num. xxxiv. 6; Josh. i. 4; ix. 1; xv. 12.
[2] It is worthy of notice that each empire in succession acquired a greater extent of Mediterranean coast-land, until at last the whole of "the great sea" became a Roman lake.

THE VISION OF THE FOUR WILD BEASTS.

In the dark and troubled sea we have a symbol of the confused anarchy of the nations, the tumults of the peoples, out of which empires are wont to rise; just as did that of Napoleon from the French revolution and Reign of Terror.

But unless they had been provoked, the waves would never have lashed themselves into the fury of a storm. They were impelled by external forces, the blasts which were breaking upon them. And these blasts represented the evil powers of the air, the angels and demons of darkness, which by their ceaseless assaults keep men in a perpetual state of unrest, excite their passions, and drive them on to every kind of wickedness.

The fact that there were four winds, corresponding to the four quarters of heaven, pointed to the universality of the influence, and showed that people of all regions of the earth would be affected by it, and moved hither and thither in violent commotion.

The first beast which arose from the seething foam was in form like a lion, but had also the wings of an eagle. Such figures—of a colossal size, and probably reminiscences of the Cherubim—were well known in Nineveh and Babylon, and many of them have been disinterred by Sir Henry Layard, and are now in the British Museum. The apparition would, therefore, suggest to Daniel the Babylonian Empire; and he would recognize the combination of the lion, the king of beasts, with the eagle, the chief of birds, as a symbol similar in meaning to the golden head of the image. And the kingdom of the Chaldeans had indeed ruled royally like the lion, and winged its conquering flight over the world like the eagle. For nothing was more characteristic of Nabopolassar and Nebuchadnezzar than the energy and rapidity of their irresistible movements.

But while Daniel was gazing upon the beast, its wings were suddenly plucked off; so that it could no more fly victoriously over the earth, or hover as a ruler above it. Then it was lifted up, and made to walk as a man upon two feet instead of four, while at the same time a man's heart [1] was given to it. It was still a beast, but it assumed the attitude, and was endowed with the intellect, of a man. It no longer trusted to the savage strength of its claws and teeth, which had failed it, but had recourse to human artifice and skill. By this means it was yet able to compass its ends in spite of the loss of its brute force. For although a man, if he be opposed to wild beasts with no other defence than his natural limbs, will have little chance in the struggle, yet let him only plan and make his weapons, and he will quickly destroy the most terrible monsters.

The wings of the lion were old and heavy when Cyrus marched against its Lydian ally: there was then no Nebuchadnezzar to hasten to the scene of action, and vigorously arrest the progress of the conquering Persian. So dilatory had the Chaldeans become, that their confederates, the Lydians and Egyptians, were defeated, Sardis was captured, and Crœsus made a prisoner, before their army had even started from Babylon. When they heard of these disasters, they no longer dared to think of advancing out of their own country, but began to construct huge

[1] We must remember that the Hebrews regarded the heart as the seat of the intellect as well as of the emotions.

defensive works. The fierce brave spirit of that bitter nation, the Chaldeans, had been taken from it: it could no more go forth conquering and to conquer. Fifteen years after the capture of Sardis, Cyrus invaded Babylonia, swept everything before him, and at last took the great city itself. Then the wings of the Chaldean beast were plucked off for ever: he was deprived of all his brute strength, and was no longer the acknowledged head of the beasts and birds of the earth.

He was not, however, destroyed, but assumed the attitude and received the heart of a man. This description appears to glance at the subsequent history of the Chaldean caste. While its members wielded the still vigorous power of Babylon, they were enabled to rule the world by force; but when they were driven out of the city by Cyrus and the almost monotheistic Persians, they retired to Pergamos, and there sought by machination and craft to compass that which they could no longer obtain by force. Of their success, and by what means they recovered the sovereignty of the world, first through the Empire and then through the Church of Rome, we shall have to speak presently; and shall then be able to explain the manner in which the existence of the first beast is prolonged to the times of the end, and discern a reason for the breaking out of its spirit in the fourth, as well as for the transference of the name of Babylon to Rome.

The second empire is likened to a bear, the strongest beast after the lion, distinguished for its voracity, and called by Aristotle " an omnivorous animal." It has none of the agility and majesty of the lion, but is awkward in its movements, and effects its purpose with comparative slowness, by brute force and sheer strength. As it appeared upon the scene of Daniel's vision, it raised up itself on one side in readiness to attack, it held three ribs in its mouth, and the command was given to it;—" Arise, devour much flesh."

Now all these points find a ready interpretation in the characteristics and history of the second empire. It was ponderous in its movements: it did not gain its victories by bravery or skill, but overwhelmed its enemies by hurling vast masses of troops upon them, armies the greatest that have ever been collected. For instance, when Darius Hystaspes invaded Scythia, he took with him 700,000 men, and, in addition, a naval force of 600 ships manned by 120,000 sailors and marines. Xerxes' expedition against Greece was undertaken with 2,500,000 fighting men gathered from fifty-six nations. Adding the camp-followers, the whole body made up some 5,000,000 souls, a vast multitude, which, as Justin remarks, were able to drink up rivers on their march, but could not exhaust the royal treasury. Artaxerxes Longimanus used 600,000 men to subdue the one province of Egypt, and raised 1,200,000 to crush the rebellion of his brother Cyrus. Even in the last throes of the empire, Darius Codomannus opposed nearly 600,000 troops to Alexander at the battle of Issus. And after his defeat he made another supreme effort, and appeared in the plain of Gaugamela with a well-equipped army of 1,000,000 infantry, 40,000 cavalry, and 200 scythed chariots.

In the movements of such enormous bodies of men much flesh was indeed devoured, and that not merely

THE VISION OF THE FOUR WILD BEASTS.

by the sword, but by famines in the countries requisitioned for the vast armies, and also by a reckless waste of life in the armies themselves.

The side of the bear which was raised up to attack seems to signify Persia, in which lay the chief strength of the twofold empire. It will thus correspond to the right breast and arm of the image; and also to the horn of the ram which came up last, but was higher than the other.[1]

The three ribs are the three kingdoms of Lydia Babylon and Egypt, which formed a league to check the Medo-Persian power, but were all destroyed by it.

The third beast, which represents the Grecian empire of Alexander, was like a leopard. This is the most agile and graceful of creatures; but its speed is here still further assisted by wings. Slight in its frame, but strong, swift, and fierce, its characteristics render it a fitting symbol of the rapid conquests of Alexander, who, followed by small but well-equipped and splendidly brave armies, moved with the greatest celerity and skill, and in about ten years overthrew the unwieldy forces of Persia, and subdued the whole civilized world.

The four heads and four wings must be interpreted of different things, and not taken together; for otherwise there would have been but two heads to correspond to the four wings.

Probably the wings denote spreading and extension of dominion to the four quarters of the earth. But they are only the wings of a fowl, and not those of an eagle; the progress would not be so royally victorious as that of the Chaldean power.

The four heads, on the other hand, are the four king-

[1] Dan. viii. 3.

doms into which the empire of Alexander was divided by his generals, namely, Thrace and Bithynia, Macedonia and Greece, Syria Babylon and the East, and Egypt. In these kingdoms the empire of Alexander was continued until, in B.C. 31, Egypt, the last survivor of them, was destroyed by the Romans.

The fourth beast, diverse from all its predecessors, was indescribably dreadful and terrible, and exceedingly strong. And certainly the career of the Roman Empire has already, even in the past, been more bloody than those of all the others, while its crimes include the murder of the Son of God Himself. Daniel beholds it as it arose and destroyed the Grecian empire; but nothing is revealed to him of its after career until the yet future time of the Ten Kingdoms. To Nebuchadnezzar, the Gentile, its intermediate division into two Empires, the Eastern and Western, is foretold: but that event took place in the period during which Hebrew prophecy is in abeyance;[1] therefore it was not disclosed to Daniel. He sees only the beast and its ten horns—the Empire in its first phase till the destruction of Jerusalem by Titus, and its final condition, in the last seven years of God's dealings with Israel, when the ten horns, corresponding to the ten toes of the image, will be developed. He is instructed that the ten horns are ten kings, and that another shall arise among them, diverse from all the rest, who shall subdue three of the ten, and gain the ascendency over them all. That this king will be distinguished by intelligence and great intellectual power is indicated by the eyes of the horn; while the mouth speaking

[1] The reader will find this explained by the comments on the Prophecy of the Seventy Weeks in Part II.

great things shows that he will be boastful and blasphemous. He is the last monarch of the Gentiles, who will with stupendous magnificence bring up the rear of that long procession which was headed by Nebuchadnezzar the Chaldean nearly two thousand five hundred years ago.

The brief account of this potentate here given to Daniel exactly corresponds with the descriptions in the thirteenth and seventeenth chapters of the Apocalypse. He will speak great words against the Most High, wear out the Saints of the High Places,[1] and think to change times and laws. And his power will be limited only by his will for a time, times, and the dividing, or half,

[1] It is interesting to distinguish the meanings of three expressions in the seventh chapter of Daniel.

In verses 18, 22, 25, and 27, the Authorised Version translates, "Saints of the Most High," whereas it should read, "Saints of the High Places." Daniel could not of course understand who these would be—for the mystery of the Church was not then revealed—but we can easily recognise those who will live and reign with the Lord in the heavenly regions, taking the place of "the host of the High Ones that are on high." In ver. 25, the reference is specially to that portion of them which will be upon earth during the great tribulation, but will suffer martyrdom rather than worship the Beast or his image.

In ver. 27, there is also mention of another class, "the people of the Saints of the High Places;" that is, the people which stand in close relation to these saints, namely, the Israelites. To the latter "the kingdom and the dominion and the greatness of the kingdom *under* the whole heaven shall be given." That is, they shall become "the Kings of the Earth upon the earth," in the stead of the destroyed Gentile powers (Isa. xxiv. 21).

In ver. 21, the simple expression, "the saints," seems to embrace all the people of God who are upon earth at the time, the believers who pass through the tribulation, and the pious Jews. In ver. 22, it includes still more, nothing less, indeed, than the completed Church and the whole Israelitish people; for the reference is to the Millennial age, and "the Kingdom" comprehends both the heavenly and the earthly portions of Christ's government.

of a time—that is, probably, for three years and a half, or, as it is elsewhere called, for forty and two months.[1] At the end of that time God will sit in judgment, the dominion will be given to the Lord Jesus, and He will go forth to consume the Lawless One with the breath of His mouth. "Because of the voice of the great words which the horn spake, I beheld even till the Beast was slain, and his body destroyed, and given to the burning flame."

Since the Beast, which represents the body politic, is slain because of the blasphemous words of the horn, it is evident that Antichrist will be in perfect sympathy with the ungodly inhabitants of earth. There is here no illustration of the famous line of Horace,

"Quidquid delirant reges plectuntur Achivi."[2]

Unlike the kings of former times, this monarch will be an exact exponent of the will of the people; therefore, they will justly share his punishment. Their community of feeling is strikingly set forth in the seventeenth chapter of the Apocalypse, where the eighth king, who corresponds to the little horn, is said to be the Beast himself.[3]

The previous empires were not destroyed when their power was taken away; for Babylon prolonged its life in the manner described above, while Persia and Greece remain as insignificant kingdoms to this day. But with the fourth empire all must meet their doom; for, in the vision of the image, the stone which strikes it upon the feet breaks the whole into pieces, so that gold, silver, brass, iron, and clay, are mingled together in one indistinguishable ruin.

[1] Rev. xiii. 5.   [2] Hor., Epist. i., 2, 14   [3] Rev. xvii. 11.

We must not forget the peculiar significance of the vision of the four beasts to Daniel and the Jews, for they learnt from it how long Jerusalem must be trodden down of the Gentiles. Four World-empires were to run their course, and then the times of the Gentiles would be ended, and the Lord would descend and restore the Kingdom to Israel.

This foreordained purpose was also disclosed to Zechariah, when he heard the angel of the Lord crying;—" O Lord of hosts, how long wilt Thou not have mercy on Jerusalem, and on the cities of Judah, against which Thou hast had indignation these threescore and ten years?" For the Lord spoke comfortably both to the angel and to the prophet, while to the latter He showed *four* horns and four smiths. Zechariah asked for an explanation, and the reply was;—" These are the horns which have scattered Judah, so that no man did lift up his head: but these are come to fray them, to cast out the horns of the Gentiles, which lifted up their horn over the land of Judah to scatter it."[1]

V.

THE VISION OF THE RAM AND THE HE-GOAT.

THE eighth chapter of Daniel reveals the connection which will be found to exist between the third empire and Antichrist—a connection which may, perhaps, serve to identify him when he appears, and which at the same time hints that his rule will be characterized by the intellectual brilliancy and defective morality of Greece, as well as by the iron force of Rome.

[1] Zech. i. 12-21.

It was some two years after the grand vision of the four beasts, when another wonderful sight was presented to the eyes of Daniel. The time was critical, and the prophet may have felt the need of further guidance and prayed for it; for the siege of Babylon was being pressed, and her end was so near that in the new revelation it is tacitly assumed, and the predictions begin with the power which overthrew her.

Daniel's past experiences, and his close walk with God, had probably quickened his spiritual perceptions; and, accordingly, the Divine communications could now reach him without needing the medium of a dream. While awake, and fully conscious, he seems to have been caught up—like Ezekiel—by the Spirit of God, and conveyed out of beleaguered Babylon to the far distant city of Susa, that he might there behold in vision the fall of the Persian empire, of which it was a capital, and be instructed in regard to the third empire and the arch-enemy who should arise from one of its four kingdoms in the latter days.

He soon found himself standing on the banks of the Ulai, and, lifting up his eyes, saw a ram with two horns, one of which was higher than the other; but the higher had come up last. This ram was pushing Westward and Northward and Southward, so that none were able to stand before him: consequently, he did according to his will and became great. But while the prophet was considering the sight, a he-goat suddenly appeared, coming from the West with such speed that he seemed not to touch the ground, and having one great horn between his eyes. In the fury of his power he made for the ram, smote him, shattered his horns, cast him down, and trampled

THE VISION OF THE RAM AND THE HE-GOAT.

upon his prostrate body: nor could the ram either resist him, or find a deliverer. Then the he-goat waxed powerful; but in the midst of his strength the great horn was broken off, and in its place four others came up towards the four winds of heaven.

Out of one of these sprang a little horn, which became exceedingly great towards the South, and toward the East, and towards the glory—that is, the land of Israel. Nay, it even grew up to the host of heaven, and cast down some of the host and of the stars to the ground, and trampled upon them: it magnified itself against the Prince of the host, and took away the daily sacrifice, and destroyed the sanctuary.

Then Daniel saw two angels in conversation, and, endeavouring to hear what they were saying, seems to have failed to understand the first speaker, but caught the meaning of the other, who inquired;—" How long shall be the vision concerning the daily sacrifice, and the transgression of desolation, to give both the sanctuary and the host to be trodden under foot?" And the first replied;—" Unto two thousand and three hundred days: then shall the sanctuary be cleansed." These words were unintelligible to Daniel, and caused him the greatest anxiety; but, while pondering them, he was suddenly startled by the consciousness of an apparition facing him in the distance, a supernatural presence in human form. And then he heard a voice of command—proceeding, apparently, from one who was hovering above the waters of the Ulai—which said;—" Gabriel, make this man to understand the vision."

Instantly the heavenly being began to move toward him, and Daniel, though he was the greatly beloved, experienced the indescribable horror which seizes upon every sinful man when he is brought face to face with perfect holiness. He fell to the ground, just catching, before he fainted, a single sentence from the lips of his celestial instructor;—" Understand, O son of man : for the vision has reference to the time of the end."

Here, then, is the first clue to the interpretation. The vision is no prophecy of Antiochus Epiphanes : the little horn is another and far more terrible persecutor who shall arise in the last days.

While Gabriel was speaking, Daniel had fallen into a swoon : but the angel restored him by a touch, set him on his feet, and then continued ;—" Behold, I will make thee know what shall be in the last end of the indignation : for it relates to the appointed time of the end."

Here is another solemn warning against misapprehension. The first part of the vision, which was soon to be fulfilled, is merely used to introduce, connect, and render intelligible, what follows ; while its main burden is a prediction of the closing days of that indignation which Moses threatened to disobedient Israel, and under which the Twelve Tribes are now suffering, and will suffer until the times of the Gentiles be ended.

Gabriel then explains that the ram signifies the king of Media and Persia, and the hairy goat the king of Greece. In the former vision these two powers were represented by a bear and a leopard ; but the symbols are here changed, perhaps for the sake of more certain identification. In the earlier vision the representative beasts seem to have been selected for the purpose of delineating the characteristics of the kingdoms for which they stood: here there is also a reference to heraldic devices.

Most of the great Asiatic powers were founded by mountaineers or nomads, the Persian among them: and this probably explains the fact that its recognized emblem, or one of them, was a ram. In Taylor's "Calmet" there is an engraving of a Persian coin displaying a ram's head on the obverse, and a ram recumbent on the reverse. The same symbol is found among the sculptures of Persepolis, which was the capital of Persia proper from the time of Darius Hystaspes until its wanton destruction by Alexander. And it seems to have been long retained: for Ammianus Marcellinus, in describing the march of Sapor, tells us that the Persian king rode in front of his army wearing "a golden figure of a ram's head set with gems, instead of a diadem."[1] We may add that, in the Zendavesta, Ized Behram, the guardian spirit of Persia, appears "like a ram with clean feet and sharp-pointed horns."

The ram corresponds to the bear in that it also is a heavy and strong animal. Its two horns, the one higher than the other, indicate the twofold character of the empire, as well as the superiority of the Persians to the Medians.[2] The same facts are marked by the right and left arms of the image; and in the vision of the four beasts by the attitude of the bear, who raises himself up so as to strike with the side on which he is strongest.

Amm. Marc., xix. 1.
The higher horn is said to have come up last, because the Median dynasty was earlier than the Persian.

The pushing of the ram in three directions seems, like the three ribs in the bear's mouth, to indicate the conquest of the kingdoms of the league, Lydia Babylon and Egypt, of which the first two were subjugated by Cyrus, the last by his son Cambyses.

And finally, the overthrow of all other beasts, and the note that none could deliver them from the power of the ram, answer to the command given to the bear ; —" Arise, devour much flesh."

Thus far, then, for the ram. The goat, on the other hand, owing to its connection with the famous legend of Caranus,[1] was the national emblem of Macedonia, and is found on the coins of that country, the ancient capital of which was called Ægæ, or the Goat-city, and the people Ægeadæ; while the adjacent waters received the name of the Ægean, or Goat-sea. Hence the son of Alexander by Roxana was called Ægus, or "son of a goat," and some of his successors are represented on their coins with goat's horns. And in his life of Pyrrhus, Plutarch describes the enthusiasm with which that

[1] One of the Heraclidæ, and the founder of Macedonia. His story is thus related by Justin ;—" But Caranus also, who was followed by a large number of Greeks, when he had been bidden by the answer of an oracle to look for settlements in Macedonia, came to Emathia, and seized the city of Edessa. He took it by surprise, a dense rain and mist having prevented the inhabitants from descrying his approach ; while he contrived to find his way to the place by following a flock of goats which were flying from the storm. After the capture he called to mind an oracle by which he had been bidden to seek for a kingdom under the guidance of goats, and was, consequently, induced to make the city his capital. And from that time he was scrupulously particular to have the goats in front of his standards whenever he marched out with the army, in order that he might retain, for all his undertakings, those guides which had put him in the way of gaining his kingdom. To commemorate their service, he changed the name of the city of Edessa, and called it Ægæ, and his people the Ægeadæ " (Just. Hist. vii. 1).

monarch was recognised by the Macedonians when he had put on his helmet adorned with a lofty plume and a crest of goat's horns.[1]

In the ram and the he-goat there is the same contrast of dull strength and nimble energy as in the bear and the leopard; and the he-goat comes from the West— that is, from Greece, which is to the West of Persia.

He had a notable horn between his eyes, a symbol of pre-eminent strength directed by intelligence; and this, as the angel explains, represents the first king of the Grecian World-power, Alexander the Great, whose marvellous energy was guided by an equally marvellous intellect.

The fury and violence of the goat well depict the vigour of Alexander's attack, which carried everything before it, and of which a wonderful example was given in the very first encounter, the fiery assault on the Persian positions at the Granicus. All conditions of peace were refused, and Alexander openly declared to the ambassadors of Darius that he would pursue their master to the death, not as an honourable enemy, but as an assassin and poisoner. The decisive battle of Arbela followed; after which Alexander, at the instigation of an Athenian courtesan, wantonly destroyed Persepolis, the ruins of which prove it to have been one of the grandest cities the world has ever seen. Then, taking with him a compact army, he made a forced march of three hundred miles in eleven days in hot pursuit of Darius.

But while the goat was at the height of his strength,

---

[1] It is possibly in allusion to such a crest that Alexander is called Dhu'lkarnein, or the Two-horned, in the Koran (chap. xviii., "The Cave").

the notable horn was suddenly broken off: and so, in the midst of his glory, with plans inconceivably vast in his mind, Alexander "succumbed to marsh fever and intemperance" at Babylon, in the thirty-third year of his life. The great centre of power was broken; but the intelligence and energy of the Greeks remained, and soon four horns sprang up in the place of the one: the World-empire fell apart into four dominions extending toward the four winds of heaven. For after the battle of Ipsus, four of the generals of Alexander divided his territories among themselves in the following manner.

Ptolemy took possession of Egypt, Cyrene, Cœlo-Syria, and some of the northern parts of Asia Minor.

Cassander of Macedon and Greece.

Lysimachus of Thrace, Western Bithynia, Lesser Phrygia, Mysia, and Lydia, with the Meander for a boundary.

Seleucus of the remainder of Asia Minor and the East.

Just after the appearance of the four horns, Daniel saw a little horn issuing from one of them, and becoming exceedingly great. Had the vision been transmitted to us without interpretation, we must have supposed this last to indicate some monarch, or state, arising from one of the four kingdoms not long after their establishment. But the interpreting angel explains that the power represented by it will not appear until "the latter time of their kingdom, when the transgressors are come to the full." Hence we perceive that at this point the vision passes on to "the time of the end," with which, as we have previously seen, it is mainly concerned.[1] Now the four kingdoms were all merged in the Roman

[1] See p. 94.

Empire before the birth of Christ—the last survivor being Egypt, which continued until the defeat of Mark Antony and Cleopatra by Augustus, B.C. 31.[1] They will, however, be resuscitated; for "the latter time of their kingdom" must be synchronous with "the time of the end" and "the last end of the indignation." Otherwise, no part of the vision would refer to that crisis, and the solemn declarations of Gabriel would be without meaning. And so we understand that the period of the little horn will not arrive until the closing days of the dispensation in which Daniel lived—that is, until the seven years which yet remain to it, after our parenthetical age has run its course.[2]

But in the previous vision there also arises, from among the ten horns of the fourth beast, a little horn, which has been usually distinguished from that which we are considering, on the ground that the former springs from the fourth beast, and the latter from the goat, which corresponds to the third.

This, however, when carefully examined, proves to be a very superficial reason. The moral features of the two powers are precisely the same. Both of them are violent and blasphemous oppressors of God's people: both dare to defy the Powers of heaven, the Most High and the Prince of princes. Both exist at the same time: for the horn of the seventh chapter continues until Christ comes to take the Kingdom; while that of the eighth prospers until the last end of the indignation, which is also closed by the appearing of the Lord.

[1] At this date, therefore, what we may call the former time of their kingdom came to its end.
[2] The reader will find this statement fully explained in Part II., chap. 3.

Both become exceedingly great upon the earth, and destroy terribly; and, finally, both are at last struck down by the direct interposition of God. Scarcely would there be room in the world for two such beings at the same time: the descriptions seem to be of one and the same person.

The apparent difficulty of the diverse origin may be easily explained. We have already seen, from the seventh chapter, that the Roman Empire when resuscitated will consist of ten kingdoms, locally governed each by its own king, but welded into one great dominion under Antichrist. And again, from the eighth chapter, we find that the four kingdoms of Alexander's successors will also be in existence during the Last Week. But these were merged in the Roman Empire before its disappearance; and even if they had not been, we are, nevertheless, taught by the vision of Nebuchadnezzar, as well as by the description of the Beast in the Apocalypse, that the fourth World-power, just before its fall, will comprise all the dominions of the three previous empires.

It follows, then, that if the kingdoms of Alexander's successors are to be in existence at the end, they must be among the number of the ten which will at that time make up the Roman Empire.[1] And so, while the seventh chapter tells us no more than that Antichrist may arise from any one of the ten kingdoms, the subsequent vision limits this statement, and declares that he will proceed from one of the four which were formed out of the territories of

[1] The phrase, "in the latter time of their kingdom," evidently indicates that they will not be found in the revived Empire as mere dependencies, but be reckoned among the ten sovereign states.

Alexander. To speak roughly, two of these four will fill the peninsula south of the Danube, Bulgaria Turkey and Greece, the third will probably be Asia Minor, and the fourth Egypt. Greece is already a separate kingdom, and there are not a few indications that the Turkish empire is about to break up into some such portions as the other three.

If, therefore, this interpretation be correct, Antichrist will spring from the dominions of the third empire, but will hold sway over the fourth, which will include all the others.

Now the third and fourth world-powers were diverse. The former was distinguished for its intellectual splendour, though at the same time it was utterly devoid of truth and morality.[1] It excelled in everything that could beautify and adorn outward life, and it has educated the world: its poets, philosophers, historians, orators, painters, and sculptors, have been models for

---

[1] As a specimen of Greek morality, we may cite the following account of the way in which the Athenian commander Paches gained possession of Notium. "But he invited Hippias, the officer in command of the Arcadians who were in the fortified quarter, to a conference, on the condition that, if he failed to propose anything acceptable to the other, he should restore him safe and sound to the fortress. Upon this understanding Hippias came out to him, whereupon he held him in custody, but did not put him into chains, and having suddenly assaulted the fortress takes it, since the garrison were not expecting an attack, and puts to death all who were in it, whether Arcadians or foreigners. Afterwards, in accordance with his promise, he brings Hippias to the fortress, and, as soon as the latter was fairly within it, seizes him and shoots him down" (Thucyd. iii. 34). This is the account of the philosophical historian Thucydides, who coolly relates it as an ordinary transaction against which no one would think of raising an objection. The reader will notice the diabolical scrupulosity of Paches, which made him avoid putting Hippias into fetters, lest his prisoner should be bruised, and it should thus become impossible to restore him safe and sound to the fortress.

all succeeding generations. Even the conquering Romans owned the power of Greece, acknowledging her superiority in the intellectual sphere; and Paul. in his Epistle to them, divides the whole Gentile world into Greeks and Barbarians.[1] For this division, which originally meant Greeks and foreigners, had, by reason of Greek influence upon the world, become not so much a designation of nationality as of degree of culture. And so the Romans themselves were reckoned as Greeks, because they had imported into their country, and become imbued with, the language and culture of Greece.

The characteristics of the fourth power, on the contrary, were its iron will, its maintenance of law, and the mighty strength with which it bent everything to its rule. Virgil has well delineated the features of either empire in a celebrated passage, which we may translate as follows;—

"Others will mould with softer touch the breathing brass—
I grant—the living face from the cold marble draw;
Will urge with rarer eloquence their client's plea;
Will trace with skilful rod the tangled ways of heaven,
And tell the rise and setting of each silver star.
But, Roman, thine it is to make the world obey!
These are thy noble arts: to fix the terms of peace,
To spare the vanquished suppliant, and fight down the proud."[2]

It would, then, seem that Antichrist will fascinate the world by an intellectual brilliancy like that of Greece, which he will use to direct the irresistible will of Rome. And so when the fourth beast appears in his last phase, he is no longer diverse from all the others, but is "like unto a leopard";[3] has assumed

[1] Rom. i. 14, 15.   [2] Virg. Æn. vi. 847-853.   [3] Rev. xiii. 2.

THE VISION OF THE RAM AND THE HE-GOAT. 103

much of the outward grace and beauty of Greece, while retaining the might and force of Rome. And in the chapter under our consideration the interpreting angel seems to point to the same thing. For the king is "fierce of countenance"; that is a characteristic of Rome, which, indeed, is elsewhere described in the very same words, as "a nation fierce of countenance."[1] But the next clause, "understanding dark sentences," presents the subtlety of the Greek mind.[2]

Possibly some of the considerations just advanced may explain the fact that Israel and Greece are brought into sharp collision, at the time of the end, in Zechariah's prophecy;—"When I shall have bent Judah for Me, filled the bow with Ephraim, and raised up thy sons, O Zion, against thy sons, O Greece."[3] And it is not unworthy of notice that, at the first advent, the three kingdoms of Greece Rome and Israel are found together in the inscription on the cross.[4]

When it is said of the fierce king that "his power shall be mighty, but not by his own power," we are reminded of those other words, "And the Dragon gave him his power, and his throne, and great authority."[5] Strengthened by such a helper, he will spread havoc in a wondrous manner, will by his cunning make the deceit which he devises successful, and will destroy many by professions of peace, or, as the words may mean, by unexpected and malignant attacks in times of security. It is especially mentioned that he will work the ruin of "strong ones and the people of the saints." The latter would seem to be the Jews, of

[1] Deut. xxviii. 50.
[2] Dan. viii. 23.
[3] Zech. ix. 13.
[4] Luke xxiii. 38.
[5] Rev. xiii. 2.

whom—if we render the twelfth verse more correctly—we have already been told that " a host shall be given up, together with the daily sacrifice, because of transgression." It is more difficult to find out who are indicated as the " strong ones," but probably they are that nation, or those nations, which, comprising many believers in Christ, will at first be moved to resist Antichrist with the sword, and will, consequently, have to pay the penalty with which those who do so are threatened.[1]

The king will further defy God by destroying the Temple, and will at last stand up against the Prince of princes Himself: but he will then be broken without hand, dashed to pieces by the stone cut without hands from the mountain.

The words of the angel in regard to the two thousand three hundred days are mysterious. The literal Hebrew expression is, not "days," but "evenings mornings," which proves that actual days of four-and-twenty hours are intended; just as when we hear of forty days and forty nights, or of three days and three nights. And we should note that seven full prophetic years would contain two thousand five hundred and twenty days; that is, that the time mentioned by the angel is two hundred and twenty days short of seven years.

Now it may be that the vision of the daily sacrifice and the transgression of desolation refers to the whole period of Antichrist's connection with Jerusalem. If so, he is to make a covenant with the majority of the Jewish nation for seven years, as we shall see in a later chapter, and after the first three years and a

[1] Rev. xiii. 9, 10.

THE VISION OF THE RAM AND THE HE-GOAT.

half will cause the sacrifice and oblation to cease. The remaining three years and a half will be the time of the great tribulation. But the Lord Jesus has promised that those days shall be shortened for the elect's sake.[1] Possibly, then, the angel's words are intended to give us the extent of this shortening; and if so, God will spare His people two hundred and twenty days from the last year.

We have thus examined some of the most remarkable prophecies of the Old Testament which relate to Gentile dominion. Before the later Scriptures were written three of the great World-powers had passed away, so that we no longer hear of Babylon Persia and Greece, but only of Rome. And even of Rome but little is said, until she is set before us embodied, as she will be, in her last king. At that time, as we shall presently see, many Jews will be dwelling in their own land, having been gathered thither to endure that purification by the Spirit of judgment and burning which shall prepare the meek among them for their glorified inheritance. And then, when God begins to remember Israel, His dealings will resume their direct reference to the government of earth; so that at this point prophecy again enters into details of earthly matters. But of what will happen to the kingdoms of this world during the dispensation of grace only the barest outline is revealed. For believers in Christ have a heavenly calling, and are commanded not to mind earthly things, but to be ever waiting for the coming of their Lord.

We will now briefly consider some New Testament predictions respecting the fourth empire.

[1] Matt. xxiv. 22.

VI.

The Great Red Dragon.

THE second of the wonderful signs which John describes in the twelfth chapter of the Apocalypse is a great red Dragon, having seven heads and ten horns, and seven crowns upon his heads.

Now the Dragon himself is afterwards declared to be "the old serpent, he that is called the Devil and Satan, the deceiver of the whole world."[1] But the ten horns indicate also the fourth beast of Daniel's vision, and later revelations make the seven heads equally characteristic of it. The symbol seems, therefore, to represent the spiritual Power of Wickedness who impresses his image upon, and works in the sphere of flesh, by means of the fourth World-kingdom; in other words, it sets before us Satan in active energy through the medium of the Roman Empire.

The meaning of the heads and horns, in their earthly development, will be discussed presently. We will only remark in anticipation that the former are seven *consecutive* rulers of the Latin realms,[2] special agents of Satan in his various attempts to corrupt or destroy the followers of Christ; and that they appear crowned because the vision includes the reigns of all the monarchs who are represented by them.

The ten horns, on the contrary, are *contemporaneous* kings,[3] the same as the toes of the image and the horns of Daniel's fourth beast; and their crownless condition intimates that those who are signified by them will not receive kingdoms while this scene of the

[1] Rev. xii. 9.   [2] Rev. xvii. 10.   [3] Rev. xvii. 12, 13.

vision is in process of fulfilment, but will begin their part in the great drama at some period subsequent to the removal of the Man-child.

Such, then, was the monster which appeared in heaven : nor was he standing in idle pose ; for his eyes were fixed, and his energies concentrated, upon a Woman who was writhing in travail before him, while he was waiting to devour her child as soon as it should be born.

Now in Scripture a Woman is the symbol of a system or Church ; [1] and the one before us seems to represent the perpetual system of God in the world, the corporate body of those who, in whatever dispensation they may live, are recognised as His servants, and employed by Him as instruments to work out His great will upon earth, and to bring salvation to individuals whom He has chosen. It is to this latter function that we must refer the appropriate figure of a mother.

In the previous dispensation such a symbol would not have comprehended all Israel, but only the really faithful, the Israelites indeed. At the close of their age, these were found to be exclusively "the poor of the flock," [2] who when they heard the voice of the great Shepherd, waited upon Him, and were gently led out of Judaism into the covenant of grace.

The description of the Woman seems to connect her with three dispensations. Her head was crowned with twelve stars, which, if we interpret them as in Joseph's dream, may signify the twelve sons of Jacob and refer

[1] Frequently also of a city; but such an explanation would be inappropriate to the present case, in which the Woman flies into the wilderness, and is pursued.
[2] Zech. xi. 11.

to the Patriarchal age. The moon is now beneath her feet: it was not, perhaps, always so. In the Mosaic dispensation she needed its reflected light at a time when no better was available, when she could seek the rays of her Lord's glory only as they glanced with diminished splendour from the Law. But now she is clothed with the sun, and appears, not on earth, but in heaven: for the Lord has revealed Himself to her, has become her glorious covering, and has raised her in Himself to the Heavenly Places.

As John gazed upon her, he saw that she was with child, and cried out travailing in birth and in pain to be delivered—a particular which enables us to discover the time of this scene accurately marked out for us both in the Old and in the New Testament.[1]

In the last chapter of Isaiah, there is also mention of a subsequent delivery of the same Woman in very different circumstances. For in speaking of the restoration of Israel at the second advent, the prophet exclaims;—" Before she travailed, she brought forth; before her pain came, she was delivered of a Manchild. Who hath heard such a thing? Who hath seen such things? Shall the earth be made to bring forth in one day? Or shall a nation be born at once? For as soon as Zion travailed she brought forth her children."[2]

Here, as in the passage before us, a Man-child is born; but there is no long period of travail as in the other case. Nor is this child caught up to God and to His throne: on the contrary, he is nursed and comforted in Jerusalem, and the glory of the Gentiles

[1] Micah v. 1, 3; John xvi. 19-22.
[2] Isa. lxvi. 7, 8.

comes to him and his mother like a flowing stream.[1] In other words, he represents the ruling body upon earth, not those who shall reign with Christ in heaven.

Of the birth with which we are now concerned Micah speaks when he foretells that his people will smite the Judge of Israel upon the cheek, and then adds ;—" Therefore will He give them up until the time that she which travaileth hath brought forth : then the remnant of His brethren[2] shall return together with the sons of Israel." [3]

Thus the travailing occupies the whole time of Israel's rejection, that is to say, the Church-period, or space between the two advents. Guided by Micah's prophecy we may regard it as commencing with the anguish of the disciples when the body of their murdered Lord was lying in the grave, and their despair could find vent only in the heart-broken lamentation, " We had hoped that it was He which should redeem Israel." And ever since, it has gone on in the trials afflictions and persecutions of the Lord's people, and will go on, until that night when of two sleeping in the same bed, the one shall be taken and the other left.

Precisely the same commencing and ending dates were also given by the Lord Himself, when, on the night before His death, He uttered the solemn words ;— " Do ye inquire among yourselves concerning this that I said, A little while and ye behold Me not, and again

[1] Isa. lxvi. 12, 13.
[2] That is, the brethren of he Lord according to the flesh, or the Jews.
[3] Micah v. 3.

a little while, and ye shall see Me? Verily, verily, I say unto you, that ye shall weep and lament, but the world shall rejoice: ye shall be sorrowful, but your sorrow shall be turned into joy. A woman when she is in travail hath sorrow, because her hour is come: but when she is delivered of the child, she remembereth no more the anguish, for joy that a man is born into the world. And ye, therefore, now have sorrow: but I will see you again, and your heart shall rejoice, and your joy no one taketh away from you."[1]

Thus, then, the period of travail and anguish is exactly co-extensive with the time of the Lord's absence from His Church.

The offspring of the Woman is a male child as opposed to a female: for he is to rule in strength. Indeed the only particular given to us for his identification is his destiny " to rule all the nations with a rod of iron."

Now, in the second Psalm, the nations and the uttermost parts of the earth are promised to the Lord Jesus, with the added words;—"Thou shalt break them with a rod of iron; Thou shalt dash them in pieces like a potter's vessel."[2]

And again, in the Apocalypse, when He comes forth to take possession of His inheritance, it is said;—"And out of His mouth goeth a sharp sword, that with it He should smite the nations; and He shall rule them with a rod of iron."[3]

Therefore the destiny of the Lord Jesus and that of the Man-child are the same.

But when the Lord appears, the unity of Himself and His Church will be made manifest: whatever He

[1] John. xvi. 19-22.   [2] Psalm ii. 9.   [3] Rev. xix. 15.

has, she will share with him. And that the prerogative of the Man-child is no exception to this law He Himself assures us when He says to the remnant in Thyatira;—"But that which ye have, hold fast till I come. And he that overcometh, and he that keepeth My works unto the end, to him will I give authority over the nations. And he shall rule them with a rod of iron, as the vessels of the potter are broken to shivers; as I also received of My Father."[1]

The prerogative was, then, originally given to Christ, and He has bestowed it upon all who overcome and keep His works to the end. And so the Man-child, as being heir to an inheritance common to the Lord and His people, seems to prefigure a mystic Christ of which the personal Christ is the Head, and the first-fruits of the Church the body; while the attitude of the Dragon points to the great object for which Satan uses the World-power, namely, to destroy the people of God.

We have said that the Man-child includes only the first-fruits of the Church: for a consecutive perusal of the twelfth and thirteenth chapters of the Apocalypse gives us the following order of events:—

I. The Man-child caught away to God and to His throne.

II. Satan cast out of heaven.

III. Antichrist evoked from the sea.

It is then evident that the believers represented by the Man-child will be caught away to God and to His Throne—that is, the Throne described as set for judgment in the fourth chapter—before the appearance of

[1] Rev. ii. 25-2

Antichrist, whose persecutions they will, therefore, escape.

Nevertheless, when the whole Church is assembled, we find that it consists not only of those who sit upon thrones, or the class of believers just mentioned, but also of others who have suffered death under the power of Antichrist; or, at least, have persisted in their refusal to worship him or receive his mark. These latter are the remnant of the Woman's seed whom the Dragon presently persecutes, those who will come out of the great tribulation, and who, whether alive or dead, will be caught up to their Lord at its close, just as the Man-child was before it began. But of this we shall say more in its proper place.

Thus the travailing of the Woman will go on until the number of the first fruits is accomplished. Then the Man-child will be completely born, and straightway the whole body of waiting believers will be caught up to God and to His Throne. And the Church having been thus broken up as an earthly institution, the Lord will begin to work the redemption of Israel, a sequence of events which is also signified in the passage just quoted from Micah, which declares that as soon as the travailing Woman shall have brought forth, the remnant of the Lord's brethren, that is, the Jews, will return together with the sons of Israel."[1] And again, it corresponds with Paul's statement;—"A hardening in part has befallen Israel, until the fulness of the Gentiles be come in; and so all Israel shall be saved."[2]

Thus the vision of the travailing Woman and the Dragon seems to exhibit the action of Satan in his

[1] Micah v. 3.   [2] Rom. xi. 25, 26.

THE GREAT RED DRAGON.

endeavours to destroy the Church by means of the Fourth Empire, and the manner in which the Lord Jesus will finally baffle him by summoning His saints to meet Him in the air.

Immediately after the rapture of the Man-child, Satan and his angels are driven out of the Kingdom of the Air —which, as the World-rulers of this Darkness, they are now occupying—and forced down to earth, there to be confined within narrow bounds, until the Lord shall cast them into a still lower and more contracted prison. There is great significance in the mention of the agent chosen to expel them: for it would seem that Michael is the angel who was appointed to lead the children of Israel into Canaan, and to be, under Christ, their spiritual prince, at least until the promises have been fulfilled.[1] His appearance, therefore, shows that the sons of Abraham are again coming into remembrance before God, and identifies the conflict with that to which the heavenly interpreter alludes when he tells Daniel, "And at that time shall Michael stand up, the great prince which standeth for the children of thy people, and there shall be a time of trouble, such as never was since there was a nation even to that same time: and at that time

[1] Exod. xxiii. 20-23; xxxii. 34; Num. xx. 16. That Michael was this angel-guide appears from passages in which he is described to Daniel as "your prince" (Dan. x. 21), and as "the great prince which standeth for the children of thy people" (Dan. xii. 1). We may also find a strong corroboration in Jude 9, where there is an allusion to the rescue of Moses' body from him that hath the power of death, in order that it might be preserved from corruption. For the archangel, who as the ruler of God's host confronts the Prince of Darkness, is Michael. Those who have attempted to identify Michael with Christ must have overlooked Dan. x. 13, where it is plainly stated that the archangel, mighty though he be, is not Lord of all, but only "one of the chief princes" (אַחַד הַשָּׂרִים הָרִאשֹׁנִים).

thy people shall be delivered, every one that shall be found written in the book."[1]

Thus will the air be cleared of those evil powers which are now defiling it, and Satan must thenceforth direct his earthly realms from their own level. At the same time the heaven will be prepared for Christ and His Church, and will resound with the loud cry of joy;— " Now is come the salvation, and the power, and the Kingdom of our God, and the authority of His Christ : for the accuser of our brethren is cast down, which accuseth them before our God day and night. And they overcame him because of the blood of the Lamb, and because of the word of their testimony ; and they loved not their life even unto death. Therefore rejoice, O heavens, and ye that are tabernacling in them." But the voice which speaks gladness to heaven has a very different message for the world beneath it ;—" Woe for the earth and for the sea ; because the devil has gone down unto you, having great wrath, knowing that he hath but a short time."

VII.

THE WILD BEAST FROM THE SEA.

WHEN the Dragon had been cast out of heaven, John saw him endeavouring to vent his disappointed fury upon the Woman ; but the two wings of the great eagle were given to her, and she was enabled to fly into the wilderness and avoid his persecutions.

At this point there seems to be need of careful attention ; for if the Dragon could assail the Woman *after*

[1] Dan. xii. 1.

he had been cast out of heaven, it is clear that she also must have in some way descended. And this is just what we should expect; for the rapture of the Man-child is the signal for a dispensational change. The Jew has again become the great centre of the Divine action, and the Church has ceased to be the system of God upon earth, though its numbers in heaven are not yet completed. Believers still remaining below must, therefore, be considered as stragglers, and recruits enlisted by them, who will presently join the main body above. Meanwhile, though they preach and teach with power, they will not be able to affect the world at large, but will merely influence individuals, by whose conversion the number of the heavenly elect will be accomplished.

The period may thus be regarded as one of transition—the old order having ceased as a recognised system, though many are still being brought to salvation by it; while the new is already in force, and the discipline of those who shall presently carry it out in power has commenced.

And so the Woman now represents faithful Israelites whom God will lead into the wilderness for refuge from the persecuting Dragon, just as once He led His people out of Egypt, and saved them from the hand of Pharaoh, bearing them upon eagle's wings.[1]

Upon the Egyptians the waters of the Red Sea returned, and they sank like lead into the deep: now the earth opens her mouth, and swallows up the pursuing hosts which the Dragon again sends in hot chase after the Israel of God.

With baffled rage he turns back to make war upon

[1] Exod. xix. 4.

the remnant of her seed, " which keep the commandments of God, and hold the testimony of Jesus "—a description intended, possibly, to include all the people of God who will at that time be exposed to his malice, whether they be pious Jews, or Christians who were not found worthy to escape the impending woes. In order to carry out his purpose, he stands upon the shore of the sea, and evokes from its raging waters a seven-headed and ten-horned monster, the symbol of the great Empire which at the time of the vision was ruling the earth, and will again be needed by the Powers of Darkness as the end approaches.

The Wild Beast thus called forth by the Dragon will, however, be found to differ from the fourth of Daniel's vision in that it has seven heads. For the revelation given to the Jewish prophet was confined to those particulars which affected his own nation; therefore the Beast which he saw was merely one-headed, as being the power which would destroy Jerusalem; but, nevertheless, ten-horned, because during the reign of the Ten Kings God will have resumed His covenant with Israel. Thus the career of the Roman Empire was exhibited to Daniel only at its points of contact with his city and people.

Again: the Beast which now emerges from the sea of human revolution and anarchy—far from being diverse from all the others, like the fourth of Daniel's vision—is described as displaying the graceful body of the Grecian leopard, the feet of the Persian bear, and the cruel mouth of the Chaldean lion. It seems, therefore, to represent that last and compound form of Roman power which shall include all the territories, the strength, and the characteristics, of the four empires, and which stands before us, in Nebuchadnezzar's dream

THE WILD BEAST FROM THE SEA.

erect and complete in all its parts up to the moment when the stone descends from above and grinds it to powder.

The seven heads are no longer sparkling with diadems, because the time of their dominion has passed away. But the horns are crowned; for the Harlot Babylon, of whom we shall hear presently, has been overthrown, and the Empire is now in the hands of the ten confederate kings, who give all their power to their great chief.

While, however, the Beast doubtless represents the Fourth World-power in the energy of its last phase, it has also a restricted meaning which is more especially set before us. In the seventeenth chapter we are told that, after the seven heads have fallen, one of them shall revive, and will then be the Beast himself.[1] Hence we may understand why, in the present passage, the description is, not that of a state, but of a man—the great Antichrist, who, as concentrating in his own person all the power and intelligence of the Roman Empire, and directing it according to his will, is here identified with it.

In regarding the Beast as the last emperor, we may consider the sea out of which he arises to indicate that which is below it, namely, the abyss, called in the Authorized Version sometimes "the deep," sometimes "the bottomless pit." Indeed, in another part of the Apocalypse[2] it is plainly stated that Antichrist will ascend from the abyss, or, in other words, that he will be a re-incarnated spirit from the dead.[3] How this

[1] Rev. xvii. 10, 11. Compare xiii. 3.
[2] Rev. xvii. 8.
[3] For further proofs see remarks upon Rev. xix. 20, p. 143.

may be, we learn from the account of the fifth trumpet,[1] at the sounding of which John saw a star which had some time previously fallen from heaven,[2] "and there was given to him the key of the pit of the abyss." Now there can be little difficulty in identifying the fallen star with Satan after his expulsion from the heavenly places by Michael. And, since the power has been granted to him, just as he opens the shaft of the abyss to let loose the infernal locusts upon the earth, so we may infer that he also unbars the gates of Death for the escape of Antichrist.

The description of the Beast shows how mighty will be the dominion and manifold the energies of the prince that shall come. He is like to a leopard; he will display the quick determination and marvellously rapid action of Alexander, and at the same time carry out his plans with such grace and plausibility as to secure the admiration of the world. His feet are as the feet of a bear with all their terrible strength and power of crushing; he will add the vast fleets and armies of the second World-power to the agility of the third, and will possess forces sufficiently large to overwhelm and destroy all his enemies. His mouth resembles the mouth of a lion, the terror of the forest: for his power will be as that of Nebuchadnezzar, of whom it was said, "And for the majesty that He gave him, all people, nations, and languages, trembled and feared before him."[3]

Just as the Lord was about to enter upon His

---

[1] Rev. ix. i.
[2] ἀστέρα ἐκ τοῦ οὐρανοῦ πεπτωκότα εἰς τὴν γῆν, "a star which had fallen out of heaven to the earth."
[3] Dan. v. 19.

public ministry, Satan stood in the way, and offered to surrender into His hands all the kingdoms of the world and the glory of them, if He would but do homage to the god of this age; but the Saviour repelled the blasphemous temptation. The proposal will, it seems, be repeated to Antichrist, and will not meet with a second rejection. Then Satan will fulfil his part of the covenant, and will give to the Beast his power, his throne, and great authority; so that the hearts of all men will turn to the latter, and he will receive a dominion, not seized by force, but assumed with an unimpeachable title based, probably, upon a plebiscite of all Christendom. And when, in addition to this, the new hero is invested with a halo of supernatural glory by the discovery that he is an illustrious leader of ancient times who has returned to his place after a long sojourn in the regions of the dead, then, indeed, the whole world will be moved to wonder after him.

It may, perhaps, be difficult to conceive how a spirit from the abyss could be thus recognised, after the lapse of so many centuries, as one who had already played a great part in the drama of men. Nevertheless, it is clear from the third verse of the thirteenth chapter that there will be a recognition sufficiently startling to draw the whole world in wonder after the Beast: how it will be brought about the day must declare. But so much progress has been made during the last few years in the demolition of the partition-wall between men and demons that it is impossible to say to what lengths the forbidden intercourse may not shortly be carried.

Some have supposed that the seventh king will be

slain; and that his body will then be restored to life, with the mark of the fatal wound upon it, by the entrance of another spirit. But such a solution of the difficulty does not seem to be in accord with what is revealed. The eighth king must be one of the first five resuscitated; since at the time of the vision in the seventeenth chapter he had already passed to the place of the dead after the completion of his first life,[1] and only five of the kings had then fallen.[2] It is in exact agreement with this that, in the earlier vision, John sees one of the heads of the Beast "as though it had been smitten—or, more literally, " slain "—unto death " at some previous time: for the participle ἐσφαγμένην is in the perfect tense.[3] And this is the head which subsequently revives.

Such, then, is the inconsistency of the human heart; men scoff at the resurrection of Christ, but will shortly be prostrating themselves before a lost spirit from the pit.

Nay, they will go still further, and worship also the Dragon—that is, the Devil—who will be openly acknowledged by the resurrected king as his Saviour. And, startling as such an idea would have been some years ago, the currents of thought are now so changed as to make it quite conceivable. For the terror once inspired by the mere name of the Prince of Darkness has been gradually dissipated by the denial of his very existence, by the theories which include him in a universal redemption, and by a general disposition to regard him—if there be such a being—as not altogether bad or irreclaimable; so that it will be easy for those who have gone thus far

[1] Rev. xvii. 8, 11. [2] Rev. xvii. 10. [3] Rev. xiii. 3.

to go farther, until at length they are willing, like the Yezidis, to worship him as the giver of all earthly good, in other words, of all that carnal men care to have. Such direct worship he has already received in former times even from great nations, and "the thing that hath been, it is that which shall be." Nor would a return to the practice indicate a more violent change in human opinion than others which have been characteristic of our age. Indeed, the way to it is even now being pointed out by the multiform revival among modern Spiritualists and Theosophists of the Gnostic doctrine, that the serpent is the true friend of man, as having guided him to that which is the source of all his power—to the tree of knowledge.[1]

As regards the Beast, a large portion of Christendom is already prepared to worship a man of transcendent ability and unbroken success. For, to pass by the adoration of saints in the Roman and Greek Churches, there is even now in existence a Positivist Calendar, in which each day is appointed for the "cultus" of some man remarkable in art, literature, philosophy, or in any other of those pursuits which are considered glorious among men. Meanwhile the general tendency of the world to hero-worship is daily increasing, and

[1] As an illustration of this reversal of doctrine, which is becoming popular, we quote an extract from the letter of the Paris correspondent of the *Record* (May 27th, 1881). He is speaking of an Anti-clerical Congress which had just been convoked by M. Schoelcher, an eminent senator, and of which he gives the following account. "This Congress showed its true spirit in electing as Vice-President Miss Maria Deraisme, a notorious atheistic lecturer. In a long speech she drew a parallel between Eve and Mary—Eve who freed mankind by the tree of science, while the education given by Mary to Jesus brought them again under bondage. One of the members of the assembly proposed that all children should be educated in the hatred of God.'

manifests itself, not only in verbal praise, but also in the frequent erection of statues, in the celebration of centenaries, and in many other modes. To how great a height, then, will this feeling be raised when it is called forth by one who will concentrate in himself the consummate warrior, statesman, legislator, king, and philosopher; who will dazzle the world by the inexhaustible brilliancy of his abilities, and still more by continual flashes of supernatural power;[1] so that, to the carnal eye, he will seem to be some great deity who has at last appeared among men, to heal their sorrows, and bring in that golden age for which they have long been sighing.

In their wonder we are told that they will say, "Who is like unto the Beast? who is able to make war with him?" In the last clause we may, perhaps, detect an allusion to the fulfilment of that which is represented in Daniel's vision by the uprooting of three horns before the little horn; and possibly also to the eleventh chapter of the Apocalypse, in which the Beast makes war upon the Two Witnesses, and by slaying them relieves the earth of their terrors and plagues.

The remainder of John's description contains a thrice-repeated phrase, "it was given unto him"; an expression which emphasizes the fact that what follows

---

[1] In 2 Thess. ii. 9, the English Version reads, "lying wonders," which conveys the impression that the wonders themselves will be mere delusive tricks, like that of the blood of St. Januarius; but this seems to be incorrect. The literal rendering of the Greek is, "with all power and signs and wonders of a lie;" that is, connected with or belonging to a lie, used for the purpose of authenticating it. The signs and wonders will be real enough in themselves, and will be effected by the exercise of Satanic power, as we are plainly told in the beginning of the verse; but they will be used to gain credence for the lie that Antichrist is God.

will be specially allowed by God as a means of forcing half-hearted believers to self-denial and decision, and of hardening the godless for their doom. And, first of all, we are particularly warned that the Beast is *permitted* to utter his blasphemies. For his words against the living God will be so stout and defiant, that those who hear them, and see no interference, might start back appalled, and be led to doubt the very existence of Jehovah, had they not been previously told that so it must be. They will be comforted also by knowing that a limit is set to the power of this terrible one ; during forty and two months he must practise and prosper,[1] and then he will fall to rise no more. This period seems to be "the hour of temptation, which shall come upon all the world to try them that dwell upon the earth,"[2] the great tribulation, and the latter half of Daniel's Seventieth Week.

The blasphemy of Antichrist will not, however, expend itself solely against God: he will also assail "them that are tabernacling in the heaven"[3]—for so the words should be rendered—that is, those believers who have been caught up from earth, and of whose departure and place of sojourn he will evidently be aware. But they will be removed far beyond his reach ; therefore he will turn fiercely upon the people of God who still remain in the world, and refuse to worship himself and the Dragon. Against them it is said that he will " make war," an expression which supposes an organized resistance on their part. But such a resistance will be useless, and could only be attempted in culpable ignorance of the Divine revelation ; for power will be given to the Beast over all kindreds, and tongues, and nations,

[1] Rev. xiii. 5.   [2] Rev. iii. 10.   [3] Rev. xiii. 6.

and he will be irresistible until he is confronted by the great King.

There are, however, not a few Christians who would soon drift into a policy of resisting evil by force of arms, because they are at all times disposed to neglect precepts and revelations which are not in accord with their own feelings. Such are those, who, forgetting their Lord's warning to beware of the leaven of Herod, and the fact that if their citizenship be in heaven they must be strangers and pilgrims here, plunge into the politics of this world with as much animation, and often with more manifest emotion, than they evince in striving for the Kingdom of the Heavens. They talk, too, of what they call liberty, little regarding the law of their King, which knows no liberty save that wherewith Christ has made us free; recognizes no citizenship but that which is in heaven; and, while bidding its hearers obey in earthly things the powers that be, teaches them such complete indifference to their worldly condition that it commands, "Wert thou called being a slave, let it not be a trouble to thee; but if thou art even able to become free, use it—that is, remain in slavery—rather."[1]

Christians who turn away from the spirit of such precepts are often enticed to mind earthly things when they should be watching for the King from heaven, and many of them are even now unconsciously aiding the

[1] 1 Cor. vii. 21. ."This rendering, which is that of Chrysostom, Theodoret, Theophylact, Œcumenius, Photius, Estius, Wolf, Bengel, Meyer, De Wette, and others, is required by the usage of the particle εἰ καὶ, by which the καί, 'also,' or 'even,' does not belong to the εἰ, as in καὶ εἰ, but is spread over the whole contents of the concessive clause. . . . It is also required by the context; for the burden of the whole passage is, Let each man remain in the state in which he was called."—*Alford*.

Roman apostasy to recover its power over England. Anon they will rue their own work; the Woman shall again direct the Beast, and become drunken with the blood of the saints. Then, as soon as the other great foe, popular infidelity, arises and assails the false Church, they will probably for a while sympathize with the new movement, hoping that it will tone down to their standard of right. When, however, the Lawless One tears away his veil, and the decree goes forth that all must worship him or die, these carnally-minded believers will receive a second sharp rebuke.

But yet another lesson will be needed; for as soon as Antichrist, upon their refusal to pay him adoration, prepares to move his hosts against them, they will altogether forget the example of the Captain of their salvation, Who would not suffer His servants to take up the sword in defence of His own body, and Who bade them remember that the disciple is not greater than his Master. Not knowing the Scriptures, they will say, God cannot permit so great wickedness! Who is this Philistine, that he should defy the armies of the living God? And so they will go forth to war: scenes of bloodshed and slaughter will follow, and as they perish in battle, or are captured and put to death, their eyes will at length be opened, and they will, perhaps, remember the words of the angel to Daniel;—"And some of them of understanding shall fall, to try them, and to purge, and to make them white."[1] But hard is the lot of those who will not be instructed by the word of Jehovah, and can be turned from earthly things only by a bitter discipline which must pursue them to the last hour of life.

[1] Dan. xi. 35.

With a warning to those believers who will be disposed to defend themselves by arms, John concludes his account of the first Beast. If any, he says, are for leading into captivity, into captivity they must go; if any wish to kill with the sword, with the sword they must be killed.[1] God will not bless their efforts; for, as the last sentence of the verse declares, this will be a time when the saints must have no weapons but patience and faith.

VIII.

THE WILD BEAST FROM THE EARTH.

WHILE John was still wondering at the monster from the sea, he saw a second Wild Beast ascending out of the earth. In this case also we may probably look for a double meaning, and again regard the symbol as representing a system as well as the man who organizes it. In the first application, "the earth" may signify a settled state of things brought about, perhaps, by the former Beast, who quells the tossing anarchy out of which he arises and consolidates society: it may point to some such condition of affairs as the first Napoleon had already effected in revolutionary France, when he essayed to move the Pope from Rome to Paris, and make him his subordinate and coadjutor.

In the second or personal application, since this being also is a spirit from Hades, we may take "the earth" in its literal sense, and compare the words of the witch of Endor in regard to Samuel's appearance; —"I saw a god ascending out of the earth;" "an old man cometh up." The same idea is also found in the

[1] Rev. xiii. 9, 10.

fourth verse of the twenty-ninth chapter of Isaiah, which should be rendered ;—"And thy voice shall come up like that of a demon from the ground, and thy speech shall mutter out of the dust." And in the tenth Psalm, the second Beast is described as "the man from out of the earth."

He is sometimes called "the False Prophet"; while the seven-headed monster is invariably termed "the Beast." He is said to have the horns of a lamb, but the voice of a dragon; there is in his outward appearance and profession a travesty of the meekness and gentleness of the Spirit of Christ; but, whenever the fulness of his heart finds vent through his mouth, he proves himself to be inspired by the great Dragon "which deceiveth the whole world." He is thus the chief of those of whom the Lord said, "Beware of false prophets, which come to you in sheep's clothing, but inwardly they are ravening wolves." While, then, the first Beast assumes the place of Christ and demands worship, the second stands before him as his prophet. There is no mention of priests; for the new deity knows nothing of substitution or vicarious sacrifice, and needs only a prophet to declare and execute his will.

This at once shows us that we have here no reference to Popery, at least in any form in which it has hitherto appeared.

Though the place of the False Prophet is subordinate, he, nevertheless, exercises all the authority of his chief, and uses it for the one purpose of compelling men to worship the Beast, on the ground that he has been slain, and has risen again from the dead. To this end he puts forth miraculous power, and, like Elijah, calls down fire from heaven in the sight of wondering multitudes. The effect of such a display will be very great, more especially in the case of Jews; and we must remember that it will be counteracted neither by a Satanic spirit of scepticism, nor by anything unpalatable in the doctrines which it supports. The False Prophet will follow up his advantage, and at once cause an image of the Beast to be made for adoration, into which, when it is completed, he will send a spirit to command from its mouth the slaughter of any who refuse to bend the knee. And that none may escape the ordeal, all grades of men, the small and the great, the poor and the rich, the bond and the free, will be compelled to imprint upon their foreheads or right hands a visible mark, consisting either of the name or the number of the Beast, and exhibited as an open profession of their devotion to him.

On the part of the Beast and False Prophet, none will be allowed to buy or sell without showing the mark; so that those who refuse to receive it will be reduced to starvation if they conceal themselves, or be put to death if they are discovered. But, in vindication of God, an angel will be sent to fly in mid-heaven with the awful proclamation;—" If any man worshippeth the Beast and his image, and receiveth a mark on his forehead, or upon his hand, he also shall drink of the wine of the wrath of God, which is prepared unmixed in the cup of His anger; and he shall be tormented with fire and brimstone in the presence of the holy angels, and in the presence of the Lamb: and the smoke of their torment goeth up for ever and ever; and they have no rest day and night, they that worship the Beast and his image, and whoso receiveth the mark of his name." To this dreadful threat succeeds an exhortation;—" Here is the patience of the saints, they that keep the commandments of God, and the faith of Jesus." They must prove themselves to be saints and obedient believers by firmly, but quietly, refusing to sanction in any way the rebellion against God and His Christ. If they yield, in the very least degree, to the terrible pressure which will be brought to bear upon them, they are lost; for this is the testing time, the great hour of temptation. No wonder that John immediately hears a voice from heaven, saying;—" Write, blessed are the dead which die in the Lord from henceforth."[1] For as soon as this Reign of Terror commences, from that very moment, the greatest favour which God can show will be to gather in quickly those whom He loves with the sickle of death.

In such fearful straits will those believers find themselves who are not ready at their Lord's first summons: so bitter will be the discipline from which

[1] It is the custom to quote these words as if they might be used indiscriminately of those who die in the Lord at all times; but the limitation, "from henceforth," should have checked this general application. That death is not always a blessing to the saved is evident from the fact that Paul declares it to have been inflicted as a punishment upon certain careless Corinthian Christians. "For this cause," he says, "many among you are weak and sickly, and not a few sleep" (1 Cor. xi. 30). It is possible for a believer to lose his reward by being cut off in the Lord's anger before his work is done, and the passage quoted above seems to show that this is a thing of not very infrequent occurrence. Just in the same way the wicked may by aggravated sin shorten their time of grace. "How oft is the candle of the wicked put out"—not suffered to burn out (Job. xxi. 17). "Bloody and deceitful men shall not live out half their days" (Psa. lv. 23).

they must learn to be thenceforth unhesitating in their obedience to the great King. But strength will be given to them, so that neither they, nor their converts, nor the God-fearing Jews, will yield to Antichrist; but will rather submit to be destroyed in a persecution more furious than any which has yet raged against the servants of God. One of many passages in which it is described is the tenth Psalm, the first verses of which, when more carefully translated than in our version, run as follows.

1. "Why, O Jehovah, standest Thou afar off?
   Why hidest Thou Thyself in times of trouble?
2. Through the pride of the wicked the afflicted is feverish with fear;
   They are taken in the plots which they (the wicked) have devised.
3. For the wicked boasteth of his soul's desire;
   And the spoiler he blesseth; he despiseth Jehovah.
4. The wicked, such is his haughtiness, (saith);—'He will not require.'
   'There is no God,' is the sum of his thoughts.
5. Strong are his ways at all times:
   Far above are Thy judgments, out of his sight.
   As for all his adversaries, he puffeth at them.
6. He saith in his heart, 'I shall not be moved;
   From one generation to another I am he who shall not be touched by evil.'
7. Of cursing is his mouth full, of deceit and oppression;
   Under his tongue is mischief and wickedness.
8. He sitteth in the ambush of the villages;
   In the secret places he slayeth the innocent;
   His eyes are privily fixed upon the helpless.
9. He lieth in wait in his secret places, like a lion in his lair;
   He lieth in wait to catch the afflicted;
   He catcheth the afflicted by drawing him into his net.
10. And crushed he (the afflicted) sinks down and falls,
    The helpless among his strong ones."

That this Psalm refers to the persecution shortly to be carried on by the second Beast seems to be intimated by its concluding verse, in which the oppressor is described as "the man from the earth." It opens with the cry of the persecuted, which ascends to God like that of the Lord Jesus in the extremity of His agony, "My God, my God, why hast Thou forsaken Me!" Then their terrible condition is graphically depicted. They are feverish with fear: life is not secure for a moment: at any time they may be discovered, dragged before the image of the Beast, and there forced either to worship or to die. From morning till night snares are incessantly being laid to entrap them into an avowal of their faith: nor do they dare to enter any of the markets or shops; for not even the smallest necessary can be bought unless the purchaser first uncover his forehead or hand, and show that he is stamped with the sign of the Beast.

The third verse intimates that all the desires of the False Prophet will be towards the Wicked One who is set over him: that he will bless him and give thanks to him, cruel spoiler though he be, while at the same time he will despise Jehovah.

Indeed, from the following clauses we may infer that his chief characteristic will be an utter ignoring of God, a development of the infidelity which is even now daily increasing in popularity. And whatever may be his professions of truth, he will be crafty and altogether unscrupulous.

The eighth verse returns to the energetic cruelty of his persecutions. Neither village nor secret place will be safe from his agents: with untiring activity they will search every remote corner, and hunt down all those who will not bow before the image, whether they be believers in Christ, or conscientious Jews.

But possibly the secret places may be establishments like the Inquisition, with its subterranean dungeons and hidden chambers of torture and death. And with this interpretation the next clause seems to agree, alluding, as it probably does, to some frightful system of espionage.

IX.

MYSTERY, BABYLON THE GREAT.

WE have now to consider a mysterious and deeply interesting subject, and in order to understand it must carefully examine the seventeenth chapter of the Apocalypse. In that famous passage we shall find a vision which closely affects ourselves : for, among other things, it foreshadows a mighty convulsion, the premonitory rumblings of which seem to be even now forcing themselves upon our ears, and threatening the present generation with the terrific violence of its shock. Of the particulars which are revealed, we wish, in the first place, to call attention to the following :—

That for a time the Roman Empire would cease to exist as a united and secular power ; but that, in the meanwhile, its parts would be held together and dominated by an ecclesiastical system which would rule from its ancient seat of government, the city of Rome.

That this system would grievously persecute and destroy the saints of God.

That, in the end, secular factions would gather strength, and, after a fearful struggle, overthrow the ecclesiastical power amid scenes of the greatest violence and cruelty.

And that, at the same time, the Roman Empire, arranged in Ten Kingdoms, would be openly re-united under a great emperor, a re-incarnated spirit, beneath whose sway it had already once bowed before the time of the vision.

In the beginning of the chapter, John is bidden to come into the wilderness that he may see the judgment of the great Whore, or Babylonian false Church, and to his amazement she appears mounted upon the Beast! We can easily enter into his feelings; for up to that time there had been only war between the Church and the world, and the Master had declared that so it should be until the end. Well, therefore, might he be bewildered when he saw her who pretended to be a Church, not merely suffering herself to be upheld by the Christ-hating World-power, but actually rejoicing to sit as a queen and direct its course, though it was still as ever in its fallen and bestial condition. The apostle was gazing upon the depths of Satan, learning something of those wondrous counterfeits and phantoms by means of which the god of this age deludes our feeble intellects and diseased spirits, and allures into the dismal swamp of Death all those who are willing to abandon the King's highway.

On looking at the Beast, John observed that neither its heads nor its horns were crowned: it was, therefore, exhibited to him at a time when its ruling powers would neither be any of the seven heads, nor the eighth emperor with his confederate kings, but the ecclesiastical system symbolized by the Woman. And it needs but little study of the Bible to teach us that the figure of a whore would scarcely be used of a system *avowedly* hostile to Christ; but rather of one which gives itself out to be the Church, though its doctrines and practices are altogether opposed to its claim, and it may not even care to disguise its hatred of true believers.

The name, Mystery, Babylon the Great, intimates that in some enigmatical sense the Woman is Babylon, although we are afterwards told in plain terms that she is Rome. But with our present knowledge the riddle is quickly solved, and we find that each of the two great cities was in its turn the seat of her power, so that she was identified with one of them in earlier times, and with the other in a later age. For we have here exhibited to us that great organization, that instrument of Satan for deceiving and enslaving the hearts of men, of which, in Old Testament days, it was said, "The nations have drunken of her wine; therefore the nations are mad":[1] while, in the New Testament, the same power is depicted as a Woman who is called "the Mother of the harlots and of the abominations of the earth."[2]

Of her long concealed history, which has been at last brought to the light by the discoveries at Nineveh and Babylon, our limits will permit no more than a slight sketch. It appears that a secret organization of unbelievers was formed soon after the death of Nimrod, at a time when open apostasy was dangerous, and that its members established their headquarters at Babylon. From that centre they laboured, with ceaseless activity, to confuse and destroy the knowledge of Jehovah in the world, and to bring men under the yoke of demon-

[1] Jer. li. 7.   [2] Rev. xvii. 5.

gods. They soon became a powerful and influential body, but found their original method of procedure so effective that, even when they had altogether forgotten the fear which suggested their precautions, and were, indeed, likely soon to be supreme in every land, they, nevertheless, did not change the character of their corporation, but continued to be a secret society. Those who wished to share their power and privileges could only do so by passing through the ordeal of initiation, which included a baptism, after which the initiate was termed twice-born, or regenerate (διφυής).

Their worship was originally offered to a Trinity consisting of father, mother, and son. But the first person was very commonly confused with the third, and at last almost entirely forgotten; so that the prominent deities were the mother and son. Of these, the former was by far the most popular, and has been known, according to time and place, as Queen of Heaven, Mother of the Gods, Mylitta, Astarte, Diana of Ephesus, Aphrodite, Venus, Isis, and the Blessed Virgin.[1]

The earthly head of the society was a priest-king, who thus usurped a dignity which God will permit to

[1] Mary is never called "the Virgin" in the Bible after the birth of her first-born Son, but always "the Lord's mother," or "His mother." How completely the identification of the Romish Virgin Mary with the Egyptian Isis has been demonstrated, may be seen by the following extracts from King's "Gnostics and their Remains" (pages 71, 72). "To this period belongs a beautiful sard in my collection, representing Serapis seated with his attributes, as Macrobius had seen him, whilst before him stands Isis, holding in one hand the sistrum, in the other a wheatsheaf, with the legend ἡ κυρία Ἴσις ἁγνή, 'Immaculate is our lady Isis,' the very terms applied afterwards to that personage who succeeded to her form, titles, symbols, rites, and ceremonies Thus her devotees caried into the new priesthood the former

no one until He come Whose right it is, and Who shall be a Priest upon His Throne.[1]

Babylon, as we have before said, was the ancient seat of this rebellious confederation, and from thence its influence was disseminated throughout the world. But, after the capture of the city of Nebuchadnezzar by the Medo-Persians, its leaders, driven from that stronghold, removed their headquarters to Pergamos, and remained there for some centuries.[3]

badges of their profession, the obligation to celibacy, the tonsure, and the surplice, omitting, unfortunately, the frequent ablutions prescribed by the ancient creed. The sacred image still moves in procession as when Juvenal laughed at it (vi. 530)—

'—— grege lnigero circumdatus et grege calvo.'
'Escorted by the tonsured surpliced train.'

Her proper title, Domina, the exact translation of the Sanscrit Isi, survives with slight change in the modern Madonna."

Mr. King goes on to explain that the lotus of Isis is re-named the lily for the later goddess: and that the tinkling sound of the sistrum is replaced by that of the bell, which latter instrument "came directly from the Buddhist religious usages, where it forms as essential an element as of yore in early Celtic Christianity, when the holy bell was the actual type of the Godhead to the new converts." In a note he adds that "the 'Black Virgins,' so highly reverenced in certain French cathedrals during the long night of the Middle Ages, proved, when at last examined critically, to be basalt figures of Isis."

[1] Zech. vi. 13.
[2] "Where Satan's throne is." Rev. ii. 13.
[3] Possibly the dispersion consequent upon the fall of Babylon may have given an impetus to the missionary efforts of the initiated, and caused the revival of their rites and doctrines in many parts of the world. In less than a century after the death of Belshazzar a new or rather a reformed faith was spreading in India, the Buddhist religion, which is but a slightly changed Babylonianism, and bears the strongest resemblance to Romanism. Indeed, Professor Max Müller has lately pointed out that Buddha himself is actually a saint in the Roman Catholic Calendar, under the name of St. Josaphat. For the story of Josaphat and Barlaam, which first appears in the works of John of Damascus, a theologian of the early part of the eighth century, and became extremely popular in the Middle Ages, has now been certainly

MYSTERY, BABYLON THE GREAT.

Meanwhile the fourth Gentile power was rapidly overshadowing the world, and, unlike the Persian kingdom of Cyrus, professed the faith of the Chaldeans. For the religion of Rome was instituted by the Etrurian, Numa Pompilius, its second king; and recent researches prove that the Etrurians were a colony, either from Babylonia itself, or from some

---

identified with that of Buddha. According to it, a devout monk named Barlaam received a Divine command, and, in obedience to it, travelled to India disguised as a merchant. There, having gained access to the young prince who afterwards became the founder of Buddhism, he unfolded his dogmas to him, and especially the blessings of a monastic life. (See Yule's " Marco Polo," vol. ii., pp. 304-309.)

But it must not be forgotten that Buddhism was merely a reformation by which the original faith, corrupted through the priestcraft of the Brahmans, was restored to something like the form in which the Aryan emigrants had brought it from Babylon after the confusion of tongues.

To pass to another quarter of the world, Prescott tells us that, when the Spaniards conquered Mexico, they were astonished to find stone crosses set up on the roads, and were easily able to convert the Mexicans to Popery, because the difference between it and the Aztec system was but slight. Mr. Pascoe, who has been long a missionary in the country, declares that the Mexican religion was purely Chaldean, and substantiates his assertion by the most startling particulars. He says;—" They had a regular priesthood, gorgeous temples, and convents: they had processions in which crosses, and even red crosses, were carried; and incense, flowers, and fruit-offerings, were employed in their worship. They confessed to their priests, and generally confessed only once, receiving a written absolution, which served for the remainder of their lives as an effectual safeguard against punishment, even for crimes committed after receiving the said absolution. They worshipped, and afterwards ate, a wafer-god, an idol made of flour and honey, which they called 'the god of penitence'; and they always ate him fasting. They also venerated the black calf, or bull, and adored a goddess-mother with an infant son in her arms. They sacrificed human victims to the god of hell, of whom they considered the cross to be a symbol, and to whom human victims were sacrificed by laying them on a great black stone and tearing out their hearts." (Speech at the Mildmay Conference, 1876.)

neighbouring country which had adopted the Chaldean creed. And so it happened that the authority of Pergamos was never disputed by the Pontiffs of the seven-hilled city; and at last Attalus the Third, at his decease, left his royal priesthood, his dominion, and his vast wealth, to the Roman people. Since, however, their government was a republic, they had no citizen who could undertake the kingly functions of Attalus, until Julius Cæsar, who had been previously elected Pontifex Maximus, became emperor also, and was thus enabled to succeed to all the dignity of the Babylonian Pontiff. Forthwith he declared himself to be a descendant of the goddess Venus: and from that time the Roman emperor was styled "divus," or "divine," and was adored as a god.

The vast World-power of Rome had thus been mounted by the Babylonian Woman before Christ appeared, and, at her instigation, the whole machinery of the Empire was set in motion to crush His Church, and persecution followed persecution in bloody succession. But it was only after the failure of these efforts that she exhibited herself as the Harlot by a false profession of allegiance to that Jesus Whom she had persecuted. By open violence she had effected nothing: she tried hypocrisy and corruption, and in an incredibly short space of time the Christian Church was completely Heathenized, and persuaded to receive all the old deities under the new name of Saints, together with the doctrines, ritual, and vestments of Paganism. And finally, in A.D. 366, by skilful manœuvring and not a little violence, Damasus, a leader of the conspirators, was pushed into the bishopric of Rome, and, having thus become the head of the Christian Church, was also elected Pontifex Maximus of the Heathen world. The Pagans could have no further scruple. They flocked into the Church in crowds; the amalgamation was soon completed, and its result was the Church of Rome, whose chief ruler, under the old title of Pontifex Maximus, which he retains to this day, soon towered above all secular monarchs, and claimed supremacy over Christendom.

Such, then, is the history of the Babylonian Society, which after swaying the first World-empire, and probably having much to do with the third, had, in the time of John, made itself mistress of the fourth; so that the Woman, by governing the world from the seven-hilled city, had become identified with Rome, and the angel was able to describe her as "the great city which reigneth over the kings of the earth."[1] But she was exhibited to the apostle as she would be at a later stage in her history, when, partially disguised beneath a robe stolen from the Church of Christ, she would have ceased to govern secretly through the medium of the secular powers, and would have openly placed herself above them, and be ruling with supreme authority. And, accordingly, in this vision, the Beast, which always stands for the secular power, appears crownless, wearing diadems neither upon his heads nor his horns, but ridden and directed by the Woman.

X.

THE SEVEN KINGS AND THE EIGHTH.

IN explaining the significance of the Beast to John, the angel told him that its seven heads had a double

[1] Rev. xvii. 18.

meaning, and were to be interpreted in one way in their reference to the Woman, and in another when they were taken in connection with itself. As regards the Woman, they denoted seven mountains on which she sat; and since it was usual in those days to speak of Rome as the City of the Seven Mountains,[1] or, Hills, the apostle would easily perceive what was intended, even before the angel added that the Woman was the imperial city which was then ruling the world.

But, when taken in their connection with the Beast, the seven heads have a very different meaning: for they are then said to signify seven kings, while the Beast himself represents an eighth. Of these eight monarchs, we are told that five had already fallen, that one was in existence when John wrote, and that a seventh was yet to come; and then an eighth, who would be one of the seven, and would be so identified with the World-power, so perfect an exponent of the popular will, that he is not called a head, but rather the very Beast himself.

The five kings are said to have fallen. From the use in the Apocalypse of the verb "to fall" we may,

---

[1] Although the city soon exceeded its ancient limits, yet the Romans never reckoned more than seven hills. Indeed, as Niebuhr remarks, "when Augustus divided the city into regions, though it was entirely for practical purposes, he determined their number by doubling that of the oldest divisions. Christian Rome, too, was very early divided into seven regions."

The custom was doubtless perpetuated by the Septimontium, or Festival of the Seven Mountains, held annually to commemorate their inclosure within the walls of Rome. Curiously enough Suetonius (Dom. iv.) mentions a celebration of this Festival by Domitian, the Emperor in whose reign the Apocalypse was written. About a century afterwards Tertullian (De Idol. x.) complains that Christian schoolmasters were in the habit of attending it, in order to obtain fresh pupils.

perhaps, infer that they died by violent, and not by natural, deaths.[1]

In the description of the thirteenth chapter, we are told that names of blasphemy were upon the seven heads of the Beast; in that of the seventeenth, that his whole body was full of them. This apparently indicates that each of the seven kings, as well as the eighth, who is the Beast, would set themselves forth as gods to the world. So far, therefore, we seem to have the following data for the identification of these kings.

I. They are all monarchs of the fourth, or Roman, World-power.

II. Five of them had already died by violent deaths, before John saw the vision.

III. A sixth was reigning at the time of the vision.

IV. The seventh and eighth were yet to come.

V. All were, or would be, worshipped as gods.

Now, so far as we can judge from their history, the five who had fallen were probably Julius Cæsar, Tiberius, Claudius, Caligula, and Nero.[2] The sixth was doubtless Domitian, during whose reign John appears to have received the revelation.[3] He was the

[1] Whether the sixth and seventh kings were to perish in like manner the prophecy does not determine.

[2] We have supposed the remaining Cæsars to be excluded from the prophecy for the following among other reasons. Augustus Vespasian and Titus, because their lives were terminated by ordinary disease: and Galba Otho and Vitellius, on account of their insignificance and the probability that no one of them became an acting Grand Master of the initiated.

[3] The almost universal testimony of antiquity is in favour of the Domitianic date of the Apocalypse : and against such an array it is impossible to give any weight to a statement of the notoriously inaccurate Epiphanius of Salamis, who flourished at the end of the fourth century. As a specimen of the evidence on the other side,

last of the twelve Cæsars, and directed the second persecution of the Church.

Between the sixth and the seventh it may be that a considerable space of time intervenes: there is possibly a hint of this in the words, "The other is not yet come; and when he cometh, he must continue a little

we may cite that of Irenæus, who had been taught by Polycarp, a disciple of the Apostle John, and who died at the close of the second, or beginning of the third, century. Speaking of the Apocalyptic vision, he says;—"For it was seen, not long ago, but almost in our own generation, in the last days of the reign of Domitian" (Advers. Haer. V. cap. xxx. 3). Such a witness is not likely to be mistaken, and he is corroborated by many others (*e.g.*, Eusebius, Tertullian, Victorinus, Jerome, Sulpicius Severus), and also by the fact that what we know of John's banishment is in perfect accord with the procedure of Domitian; whereas Nero's persecution does not seem to have extended beyond the immediate district of Rome, or ever to have expended itself in the punishment of exile.

As to the alleged historical arguments from internal evidence, which have been lately revived, such reasonings can only affect those who believe the book to have been prompted by, and solely concerned with, contemporaneous events. To one who regards the vision as a Divine prediction, there is nothing strange in the fact that Jerusalem and the Temple are represented as standing, though they had just been destroyed by Titus (Rev. xi. 1, 2); for the prophets contemplated their restoration. Nor do we find any difficulty in the mention of the Twelve Tribes as still existing (vii. 4-8); for the Bible elsewhere assures us that they will yet be gathered.

To explain why the Greek of the Apocalypse is less polished, and contains more Hebraisms than that of the Gospel and Epistles, which were written earlier, may be difficult; but such a difficulty cannot be allowed to overthrow direct evidence. Men do not necessarily continue to improve in a language which they have acquired; and since John wrote his last book in extreme old age, it may be that he was an illustration of that comparison which likens an old man's mind to a palimpsest; and that, becoming somewhat forgetful of the Greek which he had learnt, he occasionally recalled phrases and constructions of the speech of his youth. Or, possibly, the subject of the book, which is much more Jewish than his other works, had some influence upon the style.

while." Perhaps he is still in the future; but there are some reasons—which we will presently consider—for believing that he has already appeared in the person of the first Napoleon.

In regard to the eighth king, we seem able, by putting together the information of the thirteenth and seventeenth chapters, to deduce the following particulars. The seventeenth chapter describes him as one of the seven kings—that is, one of them resuscitated. And, this being the case, there is no mention of an eighth head, but only of an eighth king. In the thirteenth chapter also there is no notice of an eighth head; but John perceived that one of the seven had been slain unto death—that is, had been unmistakably slain—and while he was gazing upon it, the head revived, and thus plainly indicated the meaning of the statement in the later vision that the last king "is of the seven."

Thus the eighth king is one of the seven raised from the dead; and, accordingly, it is said that the Beast which represents him will ascend out of the abyss, or place of the dead.[1] By keeping this in mind we shall understand his ultimate fate, and also that of the False Prophet; for being both of them re-incarnated spirits, and having, therefore, already experienced the first death, they are not, when seized at the height of their rebellion, cast into the abyss, but hurled alive into the lake of fire and brimstone.[2] For it is ap-

[1] Rev. xvii. 8.
[2] Rev. xix. 20. Their immediate punishment is thus more severe than that of Satan himself. The latter, never having suffered the first death, must do so before he can be subjected to the second; and will, therefore, be confined in the abyss until the close of the Millennium, Rev. xx. 1-3. See also the exposition of Psa. lxxxii. in "Earth's Earliest Ages." Chap. III.

pointed unto men *once* to die, and afterwards comes the judgment.

Again ; John is told of the Beast which is the eighth king, that he " was, and is not, and is about to come up out of the abyss, and to go into perdition." Or, in other words, he had been upon earth before John saw the vision, was then in the place of the dead, and would in future time ascend therefrom, and head the great rebellion which would cause him to be consigned to everlasting perdition. Therefore this terrible being, who will a second time trouble the world, cannot be the sixth or seventh king, but must be one of those who had already fallen at the time of the vision ; that is, if the names just mentioned be correct, one of the five Cæsars, Julius, Tiberius, Claudius, Caligula, and Nero.

Further than this we can only proceed by conjecture; yet by conjecture so strongly supported that it is at least worth mention.

We have shown that the Beast is a symbol of double signification, which denotes the World-power as well as the eighth king. And, in considering the vision of the thirteenth chapter with a view to the former interpretation, we observe that he combines features taken from the other three monsters ; for he has the body of the leopard, the feet of the bear, and the mouth of the lion. The peculiarity seems, as we have already stated, to set forth the last form of the World-power, when it will represent the totality of the four empires, and include within itself all that has ever belonged to them together with accessions of its own.

In working out this interpretation the heads cannot of course be individual kings, but must stand for seven different forms of government, which is precisely the number indicated in the visions of Nebuchadnezzar and Daniel. They will be found to be as follows: the first is Babylon; the second Medo-Persia; the third Alexander's empire; the fourth the four kingdoms of his successors; the fifth the Roman Empire in its unity; the sixth the Eastern and Western Empires; the seventh the Ten Kingdoms.

Now, in analogy with the personal interpretation, we may suppose that one of those forms of government which have disappeared will be restored under Antichrist; and that one will doubtless be the Roman Empire in unity, or the fifth head, which will be revived when the Ten Kings surrender their power to the Beast, and so sink into the position of mere governors of provinces. Is it not possible that, in correspondence with this, the fifth king also will be the one who will ascend from the abyss? If so, provided the five kings be those whom we have just mentioned, Antichrist would be the re-incarnated spirit of the terrible Nero. Could there be found another instrument so fitted for Satan's purpose?

Should we admit this conclusion, we could certainly find startling corroborations of it in the history of Nero, as well as in the conceptions formed of him, and the rumours circulated, by his contemporaries and those who came after them, Pagans and Christians alike.

To begin with his acts, some of them were very suggestive foreshadowings of what Antichrist will hereafter do. For he was the first to wield the imperial power against the Christians, and the bitter cruelties of his persecution—among the victims of which was

Paul, the apostle of the Gentiles—were imitated too well by succeeding emperors. And again, it was Nero who sent out the expedition, under Vespasian and Titus, which ravaged Judea and ultimately destroyed Jerusalem and the Temple.

Not less remarkable were the ideas prevalent respecting him in the Heathen world: for it was believed that he would be deprived of his power, and afterwards restored to it; nay, according to some soothsayers, *Jerusalem* was to be the capital city of his second Empire. The following is a passage from his biography by Suetonius.

"It had been long ago foretold to Nero by the astrologers that his fate was to be sometime forsaken of all. Hence that very famous saying of his;—

'Any land maintains an artist.'

And for this reason he was wont with greater indulgence to cultivate the art of playing on the lyre, an art which was pleasing to him as the first man of the state, and would be indispensable when he became a private person. Certain astrologers, however, promised him the dominion of the East after he had been forsaken of all; some, particularly, the kingdom of Jerusalem; a greater number the restoration of all his former good fortune."[1]

Reports of these predictions spread far and wide, and abundant evidence may be found in the Classical writers of the deep and lasting impression produced by them. For instance, Suetonius, after mentioning the general joy at the death of Nero, adds;—

"And yet there were not wanting those who for a

[1] Sueton. Nero xl.

THE SEVEN KINGS AND THE EIGHTH. 147

long time used to deck his tomb with spring and summer flowers ; and sometimes they would put forth robed statues of him in the Rostrum, sometimes they would issue edicts, as though he were still living, and would shortly return to the great woe of his enemies.

"Moreover, Vologesus, king of the Parthians, when he sent ambassadors to the Senate to renew an alliance, urgently entreated this also, that the memory of Nero might be reverenced. Lastly, some twenty years afterwards, when I was a youth, a man of uncertain origin stood forth, and boasted that he was Nero. And so attractive was the name among the Parthians that he was strenuously assisted, and surrendered at last with reluctance."[1]

Three times, in the reigns of Galba, Titus, and Domitian, the Parthians were on the eve of fighting for impostors who took the name of Nero. There is something striking in this : for although it seems necessary to the fulfilment of Nebuchadnezzar's vision that Persia should ultimately belong to the Fourth Empire, yet the Parthians, who were then in possession of that kingdom, successfully resisted all the efforts of the Romans to subdue them, and maintained their independence. If, therefore, Nero is to be Antichrist, there seems to have been an almost prophetic instinct in the respect which these sturdy warriors paid to his name, and in their willingness to follow him, as though they recognized a destined chieftain.

Tacitus mentions the incident related by Suetonius,[2] and also the subsequent disturbance of Achaia and Asia through a false alarm that Nero was alive, and on

[1] Sueton. Nero, lvii.   [2] Tac. Hist. i. 2.

his way to the East.[1] Similar accounts may be found in Dion Cassius, Zonaras, and other writers; but we have said enough to indicate the strange ideas respecting this emperor which were floating about in the Heathen world.

And if, again, we turn to the Christian communities, we shall be no less startled at the rumours which everywhere meet us. For there was a common belief in the early Church that Paul, when speaking of the " Man of sin" and the Lawless One, pointed to Nero the reigning emperor, though he would not mention his name. Hence arose the opinion that Nero was the head of the Beast which had been fatally wounded; and that he would, therefore, be raised from the dead, and be the last great persecutor as he had been the first. Lactantius[2] and Augustine[3] both mention this idea as being prevalent in their respective times, but do not subscribe to it.

It is, however, adopted without hesitation in the earliest Apocalyptic commentary which has come down to us, that of Victorinus of Petau, who adds the following remark;—" For it is plain that, when the cavalry sent by the Senate was pursuing him, he himself cut his throat. Him, therefore, when raised up, God will send as a worthy king; but worthy in such a way as the Jews merited." Commodianus also, when treating of Antichrist, affirms that he will be Nero raised up from Hell, and in describing the last seven years of the age says;—" But Elias shall occupy half of

---

[1] Tac. Hist. ii. 8. The appearance of a third spurious Nero, in the reign of Titus, is mentioned by Zonaras (xi. 18).
[2] Lactant. De Mort. Persec., cap. ii.
[3] August. De Civit. Dei, xx. 19.

the time, and Nero shall occupy half. Then, the whore Babylon being reduced to ashes, its embers shall thence advance to Jerusalem; and the Latin conqueror shall say, 'I am Christ Whom ye always adore.'" Lastly, Sulpicius Severus mentions the opinion of many in his days that Nero is yet to come as Antichrist, and explains thus ;—" It is uncertain whether he destroyed himself. Whence it is believed that, although he may have pierced himself with a sword, yet he was saved by the cure of his wound in accordance with that which is written, 'And his deadly wound was healed.' At the close of the age he is to be sent again, that he may exercise the mystery of iniquity." Similar statements may be found in the Sibylline prophecies, and in many other ancient writings.

Such, then, are specimens of the ideas prevalent among Heathens and Christians respecting Nero, from his own times until the fifth century. That they are very remarkable and interesting, and seem to accord more or less with Scripture, must be admitted; that they may prove true in the main is by no means impossible; but further than this we cannot go.[1]

[1] Soon after the issue of our first edition Canon Farrar published his "Early Days of Christianity." We much regret the rationalizing theory which he has applied to the interpretation of the Apocalypse, but the following passage is curious and interesting.

"So died the last of the Cæsars . . . but . . . his history does not end with his grave. He was to live in the expectation alike of Jews and Christians. The fifth head of the wild beast of the Revelation was in some sort to re-appear as the eighth : the head with its diadem, and its names of blasphemy, had been wounded to death, but in the Apocalyptic sense the deadly wound was to be healed. The Roman world could not believe that the heir of the deified Julian race could be cut off thus suddenly and obscurely, and vanish like foam upon the water. The Christian felt sure that it required something more than an ordinary death-stroke to destroy the Antichrist, and to end the vitality of the wild beast

XI.

THE OVERTHROW OF ECCLESIASTICISM BY SECULARISM.

BEFORE the interpreting angel discloses the manner in which the alliance between the Woman and the Beast will end, he pauses for a moment to explain an obscurity in his description of the Woman. He has called her "the great Whore that sitteth upon many waters," and it is necessary to inform the apostle that these waters signify "peoples and multitudes and nations and tongues." Now we must remember that, since she herself is the mystic Babylon, the waters upon which she sits must be the mystic Euphrates: therefore this often cited river is no symbol of the Turkish empire, as so many have expounded, but represents the peoples over which the Babylonian system has dominated since its establishment at Rome: it does not signify Moslem power—which, with all its faults, has ever been the enemy of Babylonianism—but the kingdoms of Christendom, those countries which have bowed to the sway of the false Church, but will shortly welcome the rule of Antichrist and his Ten Kings.[1]

from the abyss, who had been the first to set himself in deadly antagonism against the Redeemer, and to wage war against the saints of God."

[1] We have already expressed an opinion that the drying up of the Euphrates in Rev. xvi. 12 is to be understood literally, and not figuratively as in xvii. 15. If this point be conceded, the river cannot in the former passage signify the Turkish empire. Nor, indeed, can it if we prefer a figurative interpretation; for in that case, since the drying up of the Euphrates is the consequence of the sixth vial, and the fall of Babylon follows the outpouring of the seventh, there is a manifest allusion to the capture of the great

After this preface—by which the angel probably intended to indicate with greater clearness the nations involved in the prophecy—the scene is changed, and we see before us the terrific struggle between Ecclesiasticism and Secularism for which all Europe is manifestly preparing, and in which one of the contending parties will be the Romish Church, and all who have imbibed her ecclesiastical principles, while on the other side will be ranged the daily increasing forces of Socialists, Communists, Nihilists, Positivists, Agnostics, and Freethinkers of all kinds. In every country of Christendom men are even now rapidly filing off to one or other of the two great camps, and the final struggle is not likely to be long delayed. But its issue has been already decided. Ecclesiasticism

city by Cyrus, which was a subject of prophecy. And it is well known that the Persian leader turned the stream of the Euphrates, and so dried it up, not absolutely, but only in regard to Babylon. He was thus enabled to march through the channel of the no longer opposing river, and gain access to the city. See Isa. xliv. 27—xlv. 3; Herod. i. 191; and Xenoph. Cyrop. vii. 5. Hence it would appear that the sixth and seventh vials are related to each other as cause and effect.

In applying this to the figurative interpretation, it will follow that the mystic Euphrates must be some active power which protects the mystic Babylon. And since, in Rev. xvii. 15, we are told that it represents peoples and multitudes and nations and tongues, these must be the peoples which support the system of Babylon, whatever that may be. If, then, we allow the system to be Romanism, the peoples must be the nations of Christendom.

As to the meaning of the drying up of the waters, since in the actual siege the volume of the river was not diminished, but only turned away from Babylon, so as no longer to protect it; similarly in the figurative application we must understand, not the ruin of the nations of Christendom, but only their alienation from Ecclesiasticism, which would render the destruction of the Woman by the Ten Kings an easy task. Such seems to be the fair method of interpretation for those who insist upon taking the passage figuratively.

will be destroyed with fearful bloodshed, and Satan's delegate will sit upon the throne of this world as king and god, and receive that adoring homage of its peoples and multitudes and nations and tongues which was formerly given to the Woman.

It may be that Rome's influence is already waning to its end; that the shocks which she has been continually sustaining since the commencement of the great French revolution have so shattered her that, when the Ten Kings appear, she will need but a final stroke. On the other hand, it is possible that the time of her power is not altogether exhausted. In some quarters she is showing signs of renewed strength, especially in England and Germany; and we may yet see a sudden, though very short-lived, reaction setting in throughout Europe. She may for a moment find herself again firmly seated upon the Beast, and, by taking advantage of her popularity to renew her old policy of persecution, become once more drunken with the blood of the saints. And it may be that her bloodthirstiness will cause that revulsion of feeling and intense hatred in which she will be consumed.

The fact that none but the Ten Kings are mentioned as the agents of her destruction, and that they will effect their purpose with extreme violence, would seem to imply that she will be in full vigour when they fall upon her. And it is in analogy with other dealings of God that the hardened criminal should meet his doom while red-handed with a last crime. So Jerusalem, which had already killed the prophets, and stoned them that were sent unto her, was permitted to persecute the Lord and His disciples also, that upon her might come all the righteous blood shed upon the earth, from the blood of righteous Abel unto the blood of Zacharias, the son of Barachias.[1]

Should this last view prove correct, there would yet be two great persecutions before the appearing of the Lord, one by the Harlot, and a second by the Beast. And who can look around on the corrupt and inert masses of professing Christians without admitting that they have in truth need of cleansing fires, if they are ever to join the purified and white-robed company which shall appear with the Lord in glory?

XII.

THE NAPOLEONIC THEORY.

FROM the time when Faber suggested it, there has been a gradually increasing opinion that Napoleon Buonaparte was the seventh king, and that the eighth will also emerge from his family. That there is some ground for this opinion cannot be denied: it is well, therefore, that those who would understand the signs of the times should keep watch in the direction indicated. But, since the evidence is not irresistible, to dogmatize is foolish, to point out any particular member of the Buonaparte family as Antichrist is far worse. For certainly it is unbecoming in Christians to slander any man, and much more so to accuse him of being the great enemy of God and His Christ, when there is no proof whatever of the assertion. And it would seem that Antichrist cannot be revealed until the Church has been taken away, and even then none may point out the Lawless One until the last head of Roman power has been seen to arise from comparative obscurity

[1] Matt. xxiii. 34, 35.

by overcoming three of the Ten Kingdoms, and establishing himself as emperor over all of them ; has been heard denying the Father and the Son ; and is known to have made a covenant with a majority of the Jewish nation for seven years. While these things remain unaccomplished, whatever may be our suspicions, we have nothing more than possibility, or at the most probability, on which to rest, and must not forget how little we really know, how eager we, unconsciously, are to translate prophecy into the history of our own times, and how easily we may be deceived.

With this preface we will mention some reasons which make it probable that the first Napoleon was the seventh king, and seem also to point to his family as being that from which the eighth is likely to arise. These reasons are briefly as follows.

I. Napoleon effected an important change in the Roman Empire by putting an end to the line of emperors which had come down in direct succession from Augustus.

II. He transferred the imperial dignity from Germany to France ; and, since the latter kingdom, by the revolution of 1789, began to spread the principles of that anarchy out of which Antichrist will arise, it does not seem improbable that the great king himself may be a French monarch.

III. He aimed at the restoration of the Roman Empire, under his own sway, in the precise manner in which it is predicted that Antichrist will restore it.

IV. He tampered with the Jews, and suffered them to flatter him in such terms as to provoke the suspicion that he would eventually have declared himself to be their Messiah, if he had retained his sovereignty.

V. He displayed the names of blasphemy, and desired to be thought more than human.

VI. His Greek origin may possibly satisfy the prophecy contained in the eighth chapter of Daniel.

VII. His name is remarkable, and his insignia are such as would well suit the pretensions of the last head of Roman power.

In fine, the ideal of the first Napoleon clothed him with a startling resemblance to the Antichrist of Scripture ; but he failed to realize it. Now the tenacity with which his family cling to their traditions is well known: it does not, therefore, seem impossible that one of them may succeed in carrying out the gigantic scheme of their much-revered founder. And should this happen, the event need not in any way clash with what has been previously said respecting Nero. For it is only the spirit of Nero which could ascend from the abyss ; the body in which it would take up its abode is not indicated.

We will now in a few words explain the reasons just enumerated.

I. Napoleon put an end to the succession of emperors which had descended in a direct line from Augustus. To understand this we must briefly trace the vicissitudes of the Empire, which for three centuries was united under one head. The first to divide it was Diocletian, who gave up the Western territories to Maximinian, the joint emperors assuming respectively the names of Jovius and Heraclius. But even this partition of the cares of government did not sufficiently lighten them ; and so two other associates, Galerius and Constantius, were also appointed, but at the same time were considered to be inferior to Diocletian and

Maximinian, the latter taking the title of Augusti. while their younger colleagues were called Cæsars. This division was effected in A.D. 292, and while each of the four emperors was supreme in his own district, their united authority extended over the whole Empire.

About thirty-two years later the government was again centred in one man, Constantine: at his death it was divided among his three sons. Then Julian, and after him Jovian, were sole emperors; but Valentinian, who came next, bestowed the East upon his brother Valens, retaining the West for himself. And from that time, if we except the reigns of the Theodosii, there were always two emperors until A.D. 476, when the Western Empire fell, and the Eastern alone remained to support the dignity of Rome.

But in A.D. 799, the West, which had hitherto owned allegiance to the East, revolted, and the Holy Roman Empire was formed. The primary cause of alienation was the Iconoclast controversy; and when a woman, the Empress Irene, was permitted to usurp the throne of the East, the indignation of the West rose to its climax, and Charlemagne was crowned Emperor of Rome. Thus there were again two distinct Empires until A.D. 1453, when the Eastern was overthrown by the Turks. And from that time, unless the claim of Russia be admitted, the Western Sovereign remained the sole representative of Rome; until, in A.D. 1806, Napoleon compelled Francis II. to renounce the title of King and Emperor of the Romans, and formed some of the countries.

[1] "Of those who in August, 1806, read in the English newspapers that the Emperor Francis II. had announced to the Diet his resignation of the imperial crown, there were probab'y few

which had constituted the Holy Roman Empire into the Confederation of the Rhine, of which he made himself Protector.

Thus, according to the interpretation which regards the heads of the Beast as forms of government,[1] he destroyed the sixth head and established the power of the seventh—an achievement which seems to point to him as being also the seventh king.

II. In the manner just related the headship of the Roman Empire was transferred for the second time to France. Now that country is the mother of modern democracy, and frightful were the birth-throes when she was delivered of her child; for in the revolution which commenced in 1789 no less than two million persons were slaughtered, so that at one time the very rivers ran with blood, and even stained the waves into which they flowed. Then out of the sea of raging anarchy arose the great emperor. But the prophecies of God indicate that these scenes will shortly be repeated on a far larger scale: it may be, then, that the crown of Rome has been given to France because she, who has hitherto played her part so well, is also destined to be the centre of the greater movement.

III. Napoleon wished to restore the Roman Empire in the precise manner in which it is predicted that Antichrist will restore it. On the 2nd of December,

who reflected that the oldest political institution in the world had come to an end. Yet it was so. The Empire which a note issued by a diplomatist on the banks of the Danube extinguished, was the same which the crafty nephew of Julius had won for himself, against the powers of the East, beneath the cliffs of Actium," Bryce's "Holy Roman Empire."

[1] See p. 144-5.

1804, he caused himself to be crowned emperor of the French at Nôtre Dame, the ceremony being performed by Pope Pius VIII., whom he had induced to visit Paris for that purpose. His idea of his Empire is revealed in the fact that he had procured the iron crown of Charlemagne for the coronation, although at that time a large portion of the dominions of Charlemagne owed allegiance to the emperor of Austria. But in 1806 he made use of his victory at Austerlitz to wrest these provinces from the protectorate of Austria, and to unite them to his own sway under the title of the Confederation of the Rhine. At the same time he was arranging to establish some of his brothers and generals as vassal kings over other countries of Europe. His intentions in so doing are thus explained by one of his latest biographers.

"He proposed to make a radical transformation in the whole European system. When, at the commencement of the empire, he was heard to evoke the name and memory of Charlemagne, he had been thought to make a fanciful comparison, using words for the sake of effect—words which had no real connection with the facts. After Austerlitz, it was evident that he had meant something else than a mere chance expression. Not that the federation of kingdoms, by which he had wished to surround himself, had in reality anything in common with the ancient Carlovingian federation. What he had in view under the name of federation was the strictest and most absolute unity. The vassal kings were to be nothing more than the humble instruments of his own domination. They were a disguise to which he had recourse, because the pure and simple acknowledgment of his projects would have made him too many enemies in the actual state of European conquest. . . . But under the imposing titles of kings, princes, dukes, grand and petty feudatories, all these men were mere servitors subservient to an iron centralization."[1]

Thus far, then, Napoleon aimed at the restoration of the Western Empire in the form in which Antichrist will hereafter effect it, that of confederated kingdoms under himself as emperor. In a despatch to the Pope during the same year he thus expresses himself;—"Your Holiness is the sovereign of Rome, but I am her emperor." In 1809 he annexed the Papal States, and styled Rome the second city of the Empire; and in 1811 he chose the title of King of Rome for his infant son.

But his ambition aspired to yet greater power. Since the division of Rome into the Eastern and Western Empires, her standard had been the two-headed eagle, still borne by some of the European countries which formerly belonged to the Western Empire, and by Russia, whose Czar, or Cæsar, claims to be the head of the Eastern. But Napoleon boldly resumed the single-headed eagle, and thereby revealed his design of once more uniting the divided Empire under his sole sway. And Alison, in speaking of the Russian invasion, remarks;—

"The principal reason which directed the mighty conqueror to Moscow, instead of St. Petersburg, was the secret project which he entertained of turning his victorious arms, after the subjugation of the Muscovites, to the Southward, and placing on his brow the diadem of the *Eastern Empire*."

[1] Lanfrey's "Napoleon," vol. ii. p. 531

This project he had in view from very early times, and is said, when only a subaltern officer of artillery, to have nourished the hope of being *king of Jerusalem*. Strange that he should have wished for that which Heathen soothsayers predicted as the destiny of Nero. Satan will never rest until he has insulted and profaned the city of the Great King by making it the throne of the Beast. And at last he will succeed; but his success will fill up the measure of his iniquities.

Napoleon appears to have accepted the command of the Egyptian army in the hope of establishing an Oriental dynasty, and, after the failure of one of his assaults upon Acre, delivered himself to his secretary Bourrienne in the following extraordinary terms;—

"That miserable fort has indeed cost me dear; but matters have gone too far not to make a last effort. If I succeed, as I trust I shall, I shall find in the town all the treasures of the Pasha, and arms for three hundred thousand men. I shall raise and arm all Syria, which at this moment unanimously prays for the success of the assault. I will march on Damascus and Aleppo; I shall swell my army, as I advance, with the discontented in every country through which I pass; I will announce to the people the breaking of their chains, and the abolition of the tyranny of the Pashas. Do you not see that the Druses wait only for the fall of Acre to declare themselves? Have I not been already offered the keys of Damascus? I have only lingered under these walls because at present I could derive no advantage from that great town. Acre taken, I will secure Egypt; on the side of Egypt cut off all succour from the Beys, and proclaim Devaix general-in-chief in that country. I will arrive at Constantinople with armed masses, overturn the empire of the Turks, and establish a new one in the East which will fix my place with posterity; and, perhaps, I may return to Paris by Adrianople and Vienna, after having annihilated the house of Austria."

In this exposition of his vast schemes, it is interesting to mark how the thoughts of Napoleon centre upon Constantinople, the ancient seat of the Eastern Empire, and the house of Austria, which at that time held the titular headship of the Western. But the bravery of the Turks under English guidance, and the plague which his troops had brought with them from Jaffa, cut short his purposes, and forced him to retreat with the conviction that he was relinquishing a throne, and, as he often afterwards remarked, that Sir Sydney Smith had made him miss his destiny.

But it was not only in his gigantic project for uniting the whole Roman Empire under himself, and governing it by means of vassal kings, that Napoleon developed the scheme which Antichrist will yet carry out: he also felt the need of a prophet—like the second Beast—to strengthen his power, and endeavoured to supply the want. He forced the Pope and his cardinals to move to Paris, conveyed thither the archives of the Vatican, the tiara, and all the insignia and ornaments of the Pontifical state, and attempted to settle the Papacy in France. His purpose in so doing is thus explained by Lanfrey;—

"It was to be a sort of Oriental patriarchate, in which the Pope, swearing allegiance to him, paid and inspired by him, would be nothing but a grand functionary of the empire, a colleague of Cambacérès, a species of ecclesiastical arch-chancellor. 'What a lever!

what a medium of influence over the rest of the world!' he afterwards enthusiastically exclaimed, when reviewing his favourite ideas of that period on the subject of the Church. 'I should have made an idol of the Pope; he should have remained near me. Paris would have become the capital of the Christian world, and I should have governed the religious as well as the political world. . . . I should have had my religious sessions as well as my legislative sessions. *My councils* would have been the representation of Christianity, of which the Popes would have been only the presidents.' All the notes, letters, and acts, of Napoleon at this period prove that this was, in fact, the ultimate aim of his projects in the matter of religious organization. The Church once the slave of his will, disciplined like a regiment, and the two powers merged in the person of the Emperor—there is no doubt, considering the infinite perfection to which he had already brought his despotism, that this system would have produced the most absolute tyranny the world has ever seen; a scourge compared to which the abuses of the temporal sovereignty were as nothing."[1]

It thus appears that, if any member of the Buonaparte family should be able to realize the ideal of the first emperor, he would, in regard to the extent and arrangement of his dominion, civil and religious, exactly fulfil the conditions of Antichrist, provided that his vassal kingdoms should be ten in number.

IV. Napoleon made overtures to the Jews, and took them, to some extent, under his protection. In July, 1806, he invited them to hold their Sanhedrim in Paris; and in March, 1807, seventy-one doctors and leading

[1] Lanfrey's "Napoleon," vol. iii. p. 563

men of the nation assembled in that city, and formed themselves into a national council, the like to which had not been held for more than seventeen hundred years—not, indeed, since the destruction of Jerusalem by Titus. The immediate cause of his interest in them may, no doubt, be found in his desire to conciliate the wealthy Jews of Old Prussia, Poland, and the Southern provinces of Russia. But they looked upon him as their deliverer, and styled him "the Lord's anointed Cyrus"; and since we know his designs in regard to the East, we may be quite sure that he had also some ulterior plan for utilizing them in their own country.

V. He displayed the names of blasphemy. When he was in Egypt he openly regretted that he could not, like Alexander, give himself out to be the son of Jupiter Ammon.[1] But what he could do he did, as may be seen by the following proclamation, issued after the suppression of a revolt at Cairo.

"Sheiks, Ulemas, Orators of the Mosque, teach the people that those who become my enemies shall have no refuge in this world or the next. Is there any one so blind as not to see that I am the Man of Destiny? Make the people understand that from the beginning of time it was ordained that, having destroyed the enemies of Islam, and vanquished the Cross, I should come from the distant parts of the West to accomplish my destined task. Show them that in twenty passages of the Koran my coming is foretold."

Throughout the whole of his career he showed a desire to be considered something more than human, and while many of the addresses presented to him recognised him as a sort of divinity, it is not on record

[1] Lanfrey's "Napoleon," vol. i. p. 283.

that he ever imitated the noble conduct of Canute. On the contrary, he excused many unscrupulous and outrageous proceedings by the assertion that he was acting as the arm of God; he loved to be addressed by the title of Vôtre Providence; and Lanfrey, after quoting one of his letters to the Pope, remarks;—"These singular expressions show that Napoleon already considered himself as something more than the Pope's suzerain; for he went nearly so far as to dispute with him his title of Vicar of God."

In the hall in which the Sanhedrim met at Paris, the cipher of Napoleon's name and that of Josephine's were blended with the name of God, and placed over the Ark of the Covenant! But a still more fearful instance of blasphemy is given by Madame de Remusat, in her "Memoirs."[1]

"Some years later, at another *fête* given by the city of Paris to the Emperor, the repertory of inscriptions being exhausted, a brilliant device was resorted to. Over the throne which he was to occupy were placed, in letters of gold, the following words from the Holy Scriptures: 'I am That I am.' And no one seemed to be scandalized!"

Surely the miserable man, by permitting so appalling a crime, denied both the Father and the Son, and showed a disposition to exalt himself above all that is called God, or that is worshipped.

VI. We have already shown that Antichrist must, in some way, spring from one of the four kingdoms into which the Third Empire was divided; and the origin of the Buonapartes may, perhaps, satisfy this condition. In the "Memoirs" of the Duchess of

[1] Vol. i. p. 336

Abrantes their genealogy is traced back to the noble family of the Comneni, who "upheld for a while the sinking fate of the Eastern Empire," and of whom six ascended the imperial throne at Constantinople.[1] After the capture of that city by the Latins, they attempted to found a new empire at Trebizond, where they ruled until David II. surrendered to the Turks in A.D. 1461. Some of his family subsequently migrated from the shores of the Bosphorus to Mania in the neighbourhood of Mount Taygeta. But, after a lapse of two centuries, civil discords in Greece compelled them to fly from their country, and seek an asylum in Italy.

On the 1st of January, 1676, three thousand refugees under the leadership of Constantine Comnenus, who had been tenth Protageras of Mania, landed at Genoa. The Senate of the Republic received them with cordiality, treating the Comneni as persons of distinction, and, under certain conditions, ceded three districts of Corsica to them. The title of "Privileged Chief" was conferred upon Constantine, and the clergy were ordered to offer incense to him on his arrival, apparently as a recognition of his imperial lineage.

Of the sons who accompanied him, one named Calomeros[2] was subsequently despatched to Florence on a mission to the Grand Duke of Tuscany. But, upon the death of his father Constantine soon after his departure, the Grand Duke, who was greatly fascinated with the young man, persuaded him to renounce Corsica and fix his abode in Tuscany. After an

[1] One in the eleventh, and five in the twelfth century.
[2] That is, καλὸν μέρος, the exact Italian equivalent of which is *buona parte*. The first member of the compound appears in Calo-Johannes, the name given to Napoleon's ancestor the Emperor John Comnenus (A.D. 1118).

interval, one of his descendants returned to Corsica, and became the founder of the Emperor Napoleon's family. He was received as a kinsman by the Comneni, who, however, in speaking of his line, always retained the Greek form of their name, calling them Calomeri or Calomeriani.[1]

Doubtless it was the knowledge of this genealogy which inspired Napoleon, even in his youth, with a hope of reviving the Eastern Empire, and had he succeeded in establishing himself in the West, we should, perhaps, have heard more of his imperial descent.[2]

VII. Lastly; the name and insignia of Napoleon would seem to agree with what we are told of Antichrist. The name will at once become Greek—the

---

[1] Of the correctness of the genealogy given above there can be little doubt, so far as the Comneni are concerned. Towards the close of the eighteenth century Demetrius Comnenus applied to the French Government for the restoration of his property, which had been appropriated by the Crown, and of his rank of "Privileged Chief," which had been abolished. The justice of his claims was admitted, provided he could prove his extraction. And "after an investigation before the king's council, a direct filiation from David II., last Emperor of Trebisonde, who was killed by order of Mahomet II., to Demetrius Comnenus was acknowledged, and confirmed by letters patent of Louis XVI., dated September 1st, 1783" (Madame Junot's "Memoirs").

[2] If it seems to any that this connection with Greece is too slight to satisfy the prophecy of the little horn which springs from one of the four, the writer has no wish to oppose them. Time alone can show the certainty of these things, and it is quite possible that the eighth monarch may be wearing the crown of Greece, or of either of the other three kingdoms of Alexander's successors, when he first appears upon the stage of Christendom. Yet the fact that the Napoleons are a Greek family is certainly somewhat significant, and of course a scion of the family might hereafter be chosen as sovereign of the land of his origin. It should be noticed that the eighth king has no necessary connection with the seventh; and, consequently, that any objection to the arguments of this book respecting the former does not affect the identification of the first Napoleon with the latter.

language of the New Testament—by a mere change of the letters (Ναπολέων), and its meaning will then be "the lion of the thicket." This may be no more than a coincidence: nevertheless, it harmonizes very remarkably with the great prophecy of Jeremiah ;—" The lion is come up from his thicket, and the destroyer of the Gentiles is on his way: he is gone forth from his place to make thy land desolate ; and thy cities shall be laid waste, without an inhabitant."[1]

But a still graver mystery seems to be hidden in this name when we discover that its dative case—Ναπολέοντι —the case which expresses dedication or devotion to, yields the exact number of the Beast, the ominous six hundred and sixty-six.

The emblems of the Napoleonic dynasty are equally remarkable. They are the eagle, the violet, and the bee, which were all included in one of the presentations made at Chislehurst to the late Prince Imperial, when he attained his majority. It consisted of an inkstand shaped like a beehive, surmounted by an eagle, and set around with amethysts, which are used to represent the violet. And the meaning of these devices seems to be as follows :—

The single-headed eagle puts forth the union of the whole Roman Empire, Eastern and Western, as the traditional aim of the family.

The violet—usually represented by the Oriental amethyst, or violet sapphire, which is said by Pliny to have in perfection the very richest shades of purple— may be intended to mark the Napoleons as the imperial family of the Roman Empire.

[1] Jer. iv. 7. The Septuagint does not, however, use the word νάπη, or νάπος, in rendering this verse.

But there is far more significance in the colour than at first appears. In the directions given for the preparation of the Tabernacle, we find frequent mention of "blue and purple and scarlet," and it will be noticed that the middle colour is produced by the blending of the two outer. Now the blue seems to symbolize the heavenly origin of the Lord Jesus, and the scarlet His human nature of flesh and blood; while the purple signifies the blending of these natures in Christ Incarnate, the God-man. A similar meaning appears to attach to the imperial purple, the wearers of which were styled "divi," and adored as deities. During the early persecutions the test usually proposed to Christians was that they should offer frankincense on the altar before the emperor's bust. And God's revelation of the future tells us that in this matter also history shall repeat itself, that "the thing that hath been, it is that which shall be."

In regard to the last symbol, the same noun is used in the Chaldean language to signify both "a bee" and "a word." Consequently, the bee was adopted by the initiates as an emblem of "the Word," or "the Revealer of the Godhead." And hence the god Mithras was sometimes represented in Persian mythology as a lion with a bee in his mouth. The lion distinguished him as the sun-god, the lion being the astrological house of the sun; while the bee in his mouth indicated that he was the Word of God, the Enlightener. How well this device would suit the pretensions of Antichrist is sufficiently obvious.

Such, then, are some of the reasons for regarding the first Napoleon as the seventh head of the Beast, and for supposing that the eighth may also arise in his family.

They do not amount to an absolute demonstration of the second point, though it must be admitted that even there they are not to be lightly thrust aside. But in regard to the first Napoleon, we confess that the testimony of history appears to us complete and decisive.

And if this be the case, the inference is most grave ; for then the seventh head has fallen, and the eighth may appear at any time. But, as we gathered from the twelfth and thirteenth chapters of the Apocalypse, before the latter can ascend from the abyss, the summons, the voice of the archangel, and the trump of God must be heard, and the waiting believers, whether living or dead, be conveyed from the doomed earth into the presence of their Lord.

XIII.

THE RE-BUILDING OF GREAT BABYLON.

THE Woman called Mystery Babylon represents, as we have already seen, that great Society founded in connection with Nimrod, which has ever played a leading part in the drama of mankind, and has done so during the Christian era, and in the West, chiefly by manipulating the Church of Rome.

But in the eighteenth chapter of the Apocalypse we find something quite different: there a literal city is depicted, the commercial centre of the world. And the error of those who attempt to identify it with the Woman will appear from the following considerations.

I. The subject of the seventeenth chapter is "Mystery, Babylon the Great."

That of the eighteenth is simply "Babylon the Great," or, "that great city Babylon."

II. Mystery Babylon is to be destroyed by the Ten Kings, "because God hath put it into their hearts to fulfil His will, and to agree and give their kingdom unto the Beast."[1] Thus the Woman is put out of the way in order that her power may be transferred to the Beast: her end must, therefore, precede the reign of Antichrist.

But the great city Babylon meets with its doom under the seventh vial, which is poured out at the close of Antichrist's career.[2]

It thus appears that the catastrophes are distinct, and that there is an interval of not less than three and a half years between them.

III. The Woman is hated by the Ten Kings, who make her desolate and naked, and eat her flesh, and burn her with fire.[3]

But these same kings—for they are "the kings of the earth" at the time—bewail and lament for the fall of the city.[4]

IV. The human agency of the Ten Kings works the ruin of the Woman, and, apparently, by a lengthened process.

The city, on the contrary, perishes by some frightful and instantaneous judgment, is engulphed in a moment, like a mill-stone cast into the sea, and disappears amid the flames vomited forth by the yawning earth.[5] And

---

[1] Rev. xvii. 17.
[2] Rev. xvi. 17-19.
[3] Rev. xvii. 16.
[4] Rev. xviii. 9. In chap. xix. 19 the Ten Kings are again called "the kings of the earth."
[5] But, besides the earthquake of the seventh vial (Rev. xvi. 18, 19) and the burning (xviii. 8); plagues of "death"—that is, pestilence—"mourning and famine" are said to come upon her in one day (xviii. 8). These are, perhaps, induced, under the sixth vial,

THE RE-BUILDING OF GREAT BABYLON. 171

so unexpected, so signal, so appalling, is her end, that it causes the sailors and merchants, who are on their way to her, to halt at a safe distance in consternation and despair.

If, then, we find so many differences in the details given of them, it is clear that we cannot absolutely identify the Woman and the city. At the same time there is doubtless a close connection between them, the probable manner of which we will endeavour to describe.

In past time, as the reader already knows, the strange power which had affected the world from Babylon was transferred to Rome. In the future, and possibly in the near future, it would seem that Rome, or at least the Romish system, will be destroyed, and the centre of wickedness restored for a brief season to its earliest seat on the banks of the Euphrates.

For the predictions concerning Babylon are not yet accomplished. She has never been suddenly destroyed, "as when God overthrew Sodom and Gomorrah";[1] nor has she, up to the present time, known complete desolation without an inhabitant.[2] Captured but not razed, or even seriously injured, by Cyrus, the city was retained as a royal residence during the whole period of Persian rule. Alexander designed to lift it from the decay into which it had fallen, to restore its wondrous temple of Belus, and to make it again the capital of the world. Josephus and Philo tell us that

by the drying up of the great river into which her sewerage flows, by a water-famine, and by the sudden cutting-off of the water-transit by which she obtains the supplies necessary for her vast population.

[1] Isa. xiii. 19.
[2] Isa. xiii. 20.

in their time it contained the homes of many Jews: and, consequently, we are not surprised to find that Peter, the apostle of the circumcision, visited it, and dated his first Epistle to the "strangers of the dispersion" from the city of Nebuchadnezzar.[1] Five hundred years after Christ it still reckoned large numbers of Jews among its inhabitants, and was the place from which the Babylonian Talmud was sent forth to blind still more the eyes and harden the hearts of the Lord's kinsmen in the flesh. And even now the flourishing town of Hillah occupies its site with a population of some ten thousand souls, and is surrounded with pleasant gardens and date-groves.

Thus the prophecies of the sudden and utter destruction of the wicked city, and of its perpetual desolation, do not appear to have been as yet fulfilled; and we should further notice that both in Isaiah and Jeremiah its unlooked-for catastrophe is closely connected with the final restoration of Israel. It would seem, then, that Babylon must be rebuilt, and become again the centre of the world and the glory of kingdoms, as we have it represented in the eighteenth chapter of the Apocalypse.

Now, in connection with its restoration, there are three questions of deep interest, on each of which we must dwell for a few minutes.

I. Can we discern, in the revelations given to us, any cause which would impel Satan to instigate the rebuilding of Babylon?

II. Is there a probability of such a restoration from a purely human point of view?

III. Does Scripture contain any intimation that the

[1] 1 Peter v. 13.

THE RE-BUILDING OF GREAT BABYLON. 173

centre of wickedness will be removed from Rome, and conveyed back to its original location on the banks of the Euphrates?

I. Now, in regard to the first question, it is God's Kingdom in mystery which is now on earth, and to this Satan opposes Mystery Babylon. The Spirit is still present in Pentecostal power: therefore, the worst manifestations of evil are restrained, and the Adversary is compelled to carry on his operations with craft and more or less of secrecy. Hence his great organization in the past has been a counterfeit Church, which he has not guided to an open denial, but to a pretended confession of the Father and the Son. With such a hypocritical creed the Babylonian Harlot, already settled at Rome, was disguised and tricked out as the Church of Christ. But she retained all her abominations, and especially her goddess, the Queen of Heaven, to whom, under the new name of the Virgin Mary, the worship due to the Father and Son was secretly diverted, until the time should arrive for an open denial of their Godhead.

Such has been the state of things in the past. But before the Ten Kings give their power to the Beast, the Church will be removed from earth, and the Spirit, Who now hinders the manifestation of evil, will also depart, and so be taken out of the way.[1]

All restraint being thus removed, Satan will immediately raise the standard of open rebellion, for which the world is already prepared. His false Church will be of no further service; nay, will even prove an obstacle to his changed plans. Therefore, he will turn the hearts of the children of disobedience against it,

[1] 2 Thess. ii. 6-8

and incite them to the violent and cruel destruction of its organisation and its honest or prejudiced devotees.

But those who have secretly manipulated it for his purposes, and all who adhere to it from selfish considerations, he will move to change their front, to make international commerce and worldly prosperity the basis of their system, in place of religion, and to rebuild Babylon as the seat of their power.

For the return of the Jews, and other signs, will be testifying that God, having removed His Kingdom in mystery, is about to restore the manifested Kingdom to Israel; and Satan, on his part, will again have need of the old enemy of Jerusalem, the wicked city of the Euphrates.

II. As to the second point, the revival of the East is one of the most remarkable phenomena now before us; so many of its countries are awakening from their lethargy, and seem ready to open communications with the West. And there is, perhaps, no place more suitable for a central mart than the site of Babylon, with its great advantages, and its navigable river. Ever since 1850 a Euphrates Valley Railway has been in contemplation, nor is it likely to be much longer delayed. In speaking of the probable results of such an enterprise, W. P. Andrew remarks;—" It brings two quarters of the globe into juxta position, and three Continents—Europe Asia and Australia—into co-relation. It binds the vast population of Hindustan by an iron link with the people of Europe; it inevitably entails the colonization and civilization of the great valleys of the Euphrates and Tigris, the resuscitation in modern shape of Babylon and Nineveh,

THE RE-BUILDING OF GREAT BABYLON. 175

and the reawakening of Ctesiphon and Bagdad of old."[1]

In 1850 the British Government thought so seriously of the project that they sent out General Chesney to survey and explore the river Euphrates, at a cost of over £30,000. Nor is England the only nation which has appreciated the value of this district: for the writer has lately received a letter from Mr. W. Greene, C.E., containing the following interesting information.

"About the year 1851, I was engaged by some eminent Parisian Bankers to examine the country between Madrid and Seville with a view to the construction of a Railway then in contemplation between the two cities. Since there was at that time, as indeed there is at the present, a great scarcity of good maps and surveys of the district, access was procured for me to the Department of the War Office in which were deposited all the valuable surveys made by order of Napoleon the First for the movements of his armies in Spain. With the assistance of a French draughtsman, who copied whatever I thought likely to be useful, I examined many documents prepared for the requirements of the great Emperor, and among them found a survey of the river Euphrates. It contained a plan for a new Babylon, with quays, river walls, and other arrangements necessary for a large commercial city. Evidently the vast schemes of Napoleon comprehended the Eastern as well as the Western side of the old Roman Empire, and especially that wonderfully fertile portion of the Euphrates valley in the neighbourhood of the site of Babylon."

From this it would seem that the mind of Napoleon

[1] "Memoir of the Euphrates Valley Route to India.'

was set on the restoration of great Babylon, the capital city of Nebuchadnezzar and of Cyrus, the chosen seat of Alexander, and, in all probability, the destined royal residence of the Fourth Empire's mightiest king.

And thus both England and France have formed, in connection with the Euphrates valley, projects which, if they had been carried out, would have resulted in the rebuilding of Babylon; while the newspapers have lately circulated a rumour of a Russian intrigue to obtain the Porte's permission for the construction of a Railway through the same district. Surely a spot which possesses such attractions for the nations is not likely to remain long in the condition in which it is.

If, however, Babylon is to be rebuilt, we must not allow its restoration to clash with other predictions of Scripture by placing it between present time and the coming of the Lord for His Church; but must remember that the enterprise need not, necessarily, be taken in hand until after the first translation of the saints.

And with what rapidity it might be accomplished we are, perhaps, now able to understand. European Congresses are becoming more and more frequent; and, in connection with the present mania of the Great Powers for annexation, they seem to indicate that the separated parts of the Roman Empire are beginning to draw together again, and to assume the sovereignty which they must ultimately possess over the whole earth.

When they are more completely united, and more accustomed to act together, it is by no means unlikely, even from a human point of view, that some grand scheme of world-commerce may induce the Ten King-

THE RE-BUILDING OF GREAT BABYLON.

doms to rebuild Babylon as an international mart, situated, as it is, just between the civilized West and the fast reviving East. In such a case the construction of its own quarter of the city would probably be assigned to each country, and there would be a realization of Bunyan's Vanity Fair.

"Here is the Britain Row, the French Row, the Italian Row, the Spanish Row, the German Row, where several sorts of vanities are to be sold."

Undoubtedly the rivalry of the nations would stimulate them to set in motion the whole machinery of their vast resources, with a view both to rapidity of building and magnificence of architecture. And when we also remember that the attention of Satan and the whole Kingdom of Darkness would be concentrated upon the work, and all their power exerted to forward it, we may fairly suppose that the result would in some degree approach to the poet's fancy ;—

> "Anon out of the earth a fabric huge
> Rose like an exhalation."

Thus, just as Babylon—Satan's centre of the earth as opposed to Jerusalem—was originally built by a cosmopolitan effort upon which the judgment of God fell ; so it would be resuscitated amid still grander displays of human power and pride, but only to be speedily and finally destroyed by the high hand and the outstretched arm of the Almighty.

III. Proceeding now to the third question, we seem to have a Scriptural intimation that the seat of wickedness will be transferred from Rome to Babylon in the fifth chapter of Zechariah. The prophet had been made to see three visions of the night, in the first of which the Lord showed him that Jerusalem, although at the time humbled, even as the myrtle bushes in a hollow, was, nevertheless, guarded by His angels and reserved for His purposes of mercy which were already beginning to work; in the second, that four hostile kingdoms must arise against Israel, but that God would find agents to terrify and cast them out; and in the third, that prosperity should finally return to Israel, so that Jerusalem should be inhabited as towns without walls for the multitude of men and cattle therein, while the Lord would be unto her a wall of fire round about, and be the glory in the midst of her.

But the mind of Zechariah may have sought to know how the daughter of Zion could be cleansed and made fit to receive blessings so great; and an answer was vouchsafed to him in the following visions.

He was transported in spirit to the Holy of Holies, and there beheld the High Priest, Joshua, standing before the Mercy-seat on the great Day of Atonement. Instead, however, of the usual robes of pure white, Joshua was clad in filthy garments, which set forth his own and his nation's sin; and Satan was there to resist him. But the Lord, after rebuking the Adversary, both pardoned His people in their representative, and provided a righteousness for them.

Thence the prophet seems to have passed into the Holy Place, where he saw the result of the favour which had just been granted: for the Jewish candlestick was burning brightly through the ministration of the Spirit by the Two Witnesses.[1]

Thus he learnt in what way God would cover the

[1] Compare Zech. iv. 11-14, and Rev. xi. 4.

iniquity of the remnant of His people, according to the words of the angel to Daniel. And in the following visions of the Flying Roll and the Ephah, corresponding respectively to the two which precede them, he was made to understand the sin of the corrupters of the earth, its final development, and its punishment.

For, proceeding, apparently, into the outer court, he beheld a Flying Roll,[1] passing over the face of the whole earth, in order that it might enter the houses of sinners, and destroy themselves and their dwellings. And the sinners are classified as thieves and false swearers, offenders against the second and the first tables.

Again Zechariah lifted up his eyes, and saw an Ephah "going forth." Now the Ephah, which is the largest of Hebrew dry measures, is often used as a symbol of commerce, and such is doubtless its meaning in the vision. When, therefore, the angel explains, "This is their appearance in all the earth," he means that the thieves and false swearers who will be destroyed by the Roll, are those who are dishonest and perjured in commerce, and that, at the time of the vision's fulfilment, the world will be full of such men. Just as Babylon of old made all the nations drunken so the corruption wrought by this Ephah of iniquity will be universal. Its principles have already been adopted by the false Church which has made merchandise of everything—of sacraments, of masses for the dead, and of the souls of men—but now it is " going

[1] Perhaps its dimensions, since they are the same as those of the floor of the Holy Place in the Tabernacle, indicate that the prophet saw it issuing from thence. Or they may signify that it punishes according to the measure of the Sanctuary

THE GENTILES.

forth." The expression is peculiar, and is more tnan once used in the Old Testament of those who are forced by the pressure of foes to quit their own city.[1] And a similar meaning may attach to it here: the calamity at Rome, and the destruction of the Romish Church, has compelled those who were directing the system of wickedness to flee from their city and to change their tactics. Accordingly, the prophet sees the Ephah coming from the West and proceeding to the Euphrates in the East.

As he looked on, its leaden cover was removed, and lo! a Woman was sitting in it, who seems to have immediately raised herself. "This," said the angel, "is Wickedness;" and, as he spoke, he thrust her back into the Ephah, and cast the leaden cover upon her. She was to be conveyed in secrecy to Babylon: none should know that she was the spring of the new system, until in changed form she should be manifested in the land of Shinar, and the Ten Kings, who hated and destroyed her as the Church of Rome, should love her again as the Babylonian Harlot of Commerce.

Again the prophet lifted up his eyes, "and behold there came out two women, and the wind"—or "the spirit"—"was in their wings; for they had wings like the wings of a stork: and they lifted up the Ephah between the earth and the heaven." He inquired its destination, and was told that it was being borne to the land of Shinar, where a house should be built for it, and it should be established, and set upon its own base.

What the women represent is not easily determined. But the work in which they are engaged is that of Satan, and since the execution of God's judgments by

[1] Jer. xxxix. 4; l. 8.

THE RE-BUILDING OF GREAT BABYLON.

spiritual powers from His presence is set forth in the next vision,[1] it may be that these women are the spiritual agents of Satan who will bring about the transit of the Ephah. At least there is something very ominous in the description of their wings, if we remember three characteristics of the stork mentioned in the Bible.

For according to the Mosaic law it is an unclean fowl. And yet the name—*chasid*—by which it was known among men signifies "the pious bird." Hence it seems to symbolize something which is good in the eyes of men, but abominable to God. May we thus find a hint that, in the conveyance of the Ephah, the angels of Satan will so act that men will suppose them to be angels of light? And is there a similar meaning in the lifting up of the Ephah between the earth and the heaven? It is quite possible that there may be some flaunting of pious principles while Wickedness still lies in concealment, but, upon her manifestation, they will quickly disappear.

Again; we are told of the stork that "the fir trees"— or rather, "the cypresses," that is, the tall towering trees—"are her house."[2] That which she represents rests upon the established powers of earth. She is as those fowls of the air which devoured the good seed, but found shelter in the mustard plant when, by a monstrous and unnatural growth, it had become a tree.[3]

Lastly; "the stork in the heaven knoweth her appointed times . . . but My people know not the judgments of the Lord."[4] Even the children of this world

Zech. vi. 5.   [2] Psalm civ. 17.
See Part III. chaps. iii. and v.   [4] Jer. viii. 7.

are wise for their generation, much more so are the spirits of evil. They are well aware when they may act, and understand their seasons, so that even while they believe and tremble they are yet able to say;— "Art Thou come to torment us before the time?" Accordingly, they recognise their opportunity, and at the fitting moment carry back the Harlot enclosed in the Ephah to her own place.

Thus the women may represent the Satanic agencies by which the relics of the system destroyed at Rome will be conveyed to the land of Shinar. And by its new development the last universal rebellion will be brought about on the very spot where men first conspired against God

PART II.

THE JEWS

I.

The Purpose of God concerning Israel.

WE have thus traced out the whole line of Gentile prophecy, which flows in an unbroken stream from Nebuchadnezzar to the last great head of the Fourth Empire.

And we have found that we are now in the clay-iron times of the feet of the image, and that the world is soon to see the revival of the Roman Empire under the form of ten confederate kingdoms, the brief but memorable course of which will be cut short by the fall of the stone from the mountain—that is, by the descent of the Lord Jesus from the height of His power.

But while earth was bending to the sway of the Babylonian monarch, or shuddering beneath the tread of Persian myriads; while men were wondering at the lightning-rapidity and irresistible bravery of the legions of Alexander, or saluting Cæsar as lord of the world and a present deity; when the crown was placed on the brow of Charlemagne, and the majesty of Rome again hovered over Europe; while the Eastern Empire was being destroyed by Moslem hordes; or while the armies of Napoleon were spreading like a prairie-fire over the surface of Christendom—what, during these long times of commotion and change, was the counsel of God in regard to the Jew? Had He cast away His people? God forbid! He had not cast away His people whom He foreknew.

Through all the turmoil of Gentile times His purpose concerning Israel has remained sure. And although the children of Abraham have long been a nation scattered and peeled, a nation meted out and trodden down, whose land invaders, like overflowing rivers, have spoiled; yet when the iniquity of the Gentiles is full, and God's patience with them exhausted, Israel shall come into remembrance and be again gathered. Great Babylon shall fall, and Jerusalem shall arise and shine as the true city of the great King, and the joy of the whole earth.

Now the key to the future of Israel is to be found in the ninth chapter of Daniel. If we understand that portion of God's Word, our difficulty with the remainder of Hebrew prophecy will be greatly diminished, and we shall easily see how to arrange other predictions each in its own place.

Nor is this all. The closing verses of the chapter, by marking out the times of God's dealings with the Jews, instruct us also in regard to the position of the Church in the grand progress of His purposes; and show us that, although her members will hereafter reign with Christ, she, nevertheless, at present occupies a mere parenthesis in the world-history.

Believers often fail to realize this fact practically, even when they agree to it in theory. They are eager to apply the prophetic Scriptures directly to themselves; can spare but little for the Israelite; nay, will sometimes even speak of his history as though the great object of his existence were to supply a type of the Church of this age.

To counteract such views, Paul wrote the eleventh chapter of the Epistle to the Romans, in which he shows that the Gentiles are merely as the branches of a wild olive tree which are at present grafted on the Jewish stock, but shall shortly be broken off to make way for the restoration of the natural branches. He warns the Gentiles not to be ignorant of this mystery, lest they should grow wise in their own conceits; and reminds them that God has a covenant with Israel, and that His gifts and callings are without repentance. Therefore the glory of earth must return to the children of Abraham, and "if the casting away of them be the reconciling of the world, what shall the receiving of them be but life from the dead!"

The Church has indeed a glorious destiny; but her calling is heavenly, while the Israelites shall be the Kings of the Earth. Since, therefore, prophecy mainly refers to earth, the Israelite has by far the greatest share of it. For those who are strangers and pilgrims here, and who are commanded not to mind earthly things, require to know but little of the world's history; those whose Saviour, whose home, and whose city, are in heaven, are not much concerned with the course of events below. Those who are warned that at any moment, even in an hour when they think not, the King's messengers may announce, "The Master is come and calleth for thee," have no need to know the times and the seasons.[1]

The Lord has, consequently, given but two continuous prophecies of the Church, while the prophetic

[1] 1 Thess. v. 1

Scriptures abound with details of the time when He will resume His covenant relations with Israel

II.

THE PERPLEXITY OF DANIEL.

IN the fourth year of the reign of Jehoiakim, just before Nebuchadnezzar came to Jerusalem for the first time, God foretold the impending trouble by the mouth of Jeremiah, and also set His limit to it. Judah should be a desolation, and should serve the king of Babylon seventy years; at the close of which time Babylon should be punished, and the land of the Chaldeans destroyed.[1] The prophet did not, however, add anything respecting the restoration of his countrymen.

But shortly after the departure of the second band of captives—Jehoiachin and those who were taken with him—the false prophet Hananiah declared that, within the space of two years, the Lord would break the yoke of Nebuchadnezzar from off the neck of all nations, and bring back to Jerusalem the vessels of the Lord's house which had been carried away to Babylon.[2] The same strain was taken up among the captives by Ahab, the son of Kolaiah, and Zedekiah, the son of Maaseiah:[3] the hope of the exiles was raised, and many of them contemplated an immediate return to Judæa.

But this was forbidden by a letter from Jeremiah, who directed them to settle in Babylonia, since God would have them to do so until the end of the Seventy

[1] Jer. xxv. 8-14.   [2] Jer. xxviii. 10-17.   [3] Jer. xxix. 20-23.

Years, and would then visit them and permit them to return to their own country.[1] Apparently the people obeyed this command, and remained where they were.

At last, however, the empire of the Chaldeans fell, and in the first year of the reign of Darius the Mede, Daniel, who had been promoted to the place of prime minister, became perplexed and anxious, probably from a twofold cause. He had carefully studied the prophecies of Jeremiah, and found that permission had been given to return to Jerusalem within two years from that time; for it was then about the sixty-ninth year of the captivity. Yet when he considered the disposition of his people, he saw that their exile had not led them back to God, that they were not chastened and humbled by affliction, and were, therefore, by no means in a condition to receive mercy at the hand of the Lord.

And again; he was well aware that there would be a gathering of all Israel from the nations among which they had been scattered, when the Messiah would rule over them in their own country; and he seems to have looked upon this grand restoration as identical with the return at the end of the Seventy Years. Hence a great perplexity; for he knew by former revelations that four Gentile empires must run their course before the sovereignty could be transferred to Israel. And as yet only one of these had fallen. there were still three to fulfil their destiny and the last of them must pass through three phases; while for all these great events there remained but a little more than one year!

Such seems to have been Daniel's perplexity, and

[1] Jer. xxix. 4-11.

he was quite unable to solve the enigma. His procedure was, however, characteristic. The difficulty in regard to the empires he left, not doubting that God would find a way to accomplish His own purpose; but remembering that, in the terrible prediction of Moses respecting the captivity,[1] confession is mentioned as that which will cause the Lord to return to His people, he set his face unto the Lord God, to seek by prayer and supplication, with fasting and sackcloth and ashes, and made humble confession for himself and his people, earnestly entreating the Lord to turn away His anger and fury from them and from Jerusalem for His great mercies' sake.

III.

The Prophecy of the Seventy Weeks.

An answer was speedily vouchsafed to the prophet. While he was yet speaking his prayer was interrupted by a gentle touch, and looking round he saw the man Gabriel, who had interpreted his previous vision, again standing near him. This heavenly messenger had been despatched from the Throne to assure the greatly beloved one that his petition had been heard, and should ultimately be granted; but that God must for a while defer the removal of His anger and fury from Jerusalem. Daniel must patiently wait and endure, even as the Lord did when the cup He so much dreaded might not pass away; or as Paul, when it was signified to him that the thorn in the flesh, from which he had thrice besought the Lord for

Levit. xxvi. 40-43

deliverance, must still be a messenger of Satan to buffet him.

But just as an angel descended to strengthen the Lord in His agony, just as Paul was told that God's grace should be sufficient for him, so Gabriel was sent to Daniel to give him skill and understanding, and to reveal the matter to him, and make him know the purposes of God. Thus the prayer of the prophet opened a channel of blessing, and called forth a great revelation upon which all other prophecy appears to hinge, and without a clear knowledge of which it seems vain to attempt to understand anything. And intensely concentrated as this wondrous utterance is, it, nevertheless, presents no great difficulty, provided we begin with a good translation. The following is a literal rendering :—

Dan. ix. 24. "Seventy Weeks have been severed off upon thy people and upon thy holy city, to shut up the transgression, and to seal up sins, and to cover iniquity, and to bring in everlasting righteousness, and to seal up vision and prophet, and to anoint a Holy of holies."

Ver. 25. "Know, therefore, and understand:—From the going forth of a command to restore and build Jerusalem unto an Anointed One, a Prince, shall be Seven Weeks, and Sixty and Two Weeks: the street shall be restored and built, and the wall, even in the pressure of the times."

Ver. 26. "And after the Sixty and Two Weeks the Anointed One shall be cut off, and there shall be nothing for Him. And the city and the sanctuary shall the people destroy of a prince that shall come : and his end shall be in the overflowing " (that is, of God's wrath), "and until the end there shall be war, that which is determined for desolations."

Ver. 27. "And he" (that is, the prince that shall come) "shall confirm a covenant with the majority" (that is, of the Jewish people) "for One Week: and in the midst of the Week he shall cause sacrifice and offering to cease: and upon the wing of abominations shall be the desolater, even until the consummation, and that which has been determined shall be poured upon the desolate."

We must now examine these verses minutely.

Seventy Weeks. Literally, *Seventy Sevens.* The word "week" is retained, because we have no exact equivalent for the Hebrew original,[1] which signifies a period of seven, but does not decide whether the seven are hours, days, months, years, or any other measure of time. That point must always be determined by the context; and in the present passage periods of seven *years* each are doubtless intended, because Daniel's mind is dwelling on the Seventy *Years* of Jeremiah.[2] The meaning of the angel seems to be— The Seventy Years of probation will not suffice; nay, after them must come seven times seventy other years. We should remember that the Sabbatical years and the Jubilee made the idea of a week of years very familiar to Israelites.

Have been severed off. That is, from the times of the Gentiles, from the age during which their four World-empires should hold sway.

Upon thy people and upon thy holy city. This prophecy, then, is concerned with Israelites, and not with Christians. Seven times seventy, or four hundred

[1] Some commentators use "heptad," or "hebdomad"; either of which words would do, if it could be considered English.
[2] If Christians be suspected of bias in interpreting "the sevens" as weeks of years, because the end of the sixty-ninth seven is thus made to synchronize with the time of Christ's death, it is impossible to bring such a charge against Jews. And yet, until the Middle Ages were far advanced, the Jews invariably adopted the same explanation, although by so doing they convicted themselves of rejecting the Messiah, and placed a formidable weapon in the hands of their Christian opponents.

THE PROPHECY OF THE SEVENTY WEEKS.

and ninety years are to be taken out of the times of the Gentiles for the special dealings of God with the Jews and Jerusalem ; that is, of course, with the Jews at Jerusalem : for the people must during the time be dwelling in their own country.

The Four Hundred and Ninety Years of God's pleadings with His people shall be made to produce six results, which are named as follows.

I. To shut up the transgression.

II. To seal up sins.

III. To cover iniquity.

IV. To bring in everlasting righteousness.

V. To seal up vision and prophet.

VI. To anoint a Holy of holies.

We may divide these six consequences into two classes : for the first three are concerned with the taking away of sin, and the last three with the bringing in of righteousness. And the latter will be found to correspond, each to each, with the former.

To shut up the transgression. That is, to arrest and restrain it, so that it can no longer work and spread. The article probably indicates the whole course of Israel's transgression, or " breaking away " from God.

To seal up sins. The figure of sealing is connected with that of shutting up in prison or restraining. So Darius seals the stone, which is put at the mouth of the lions' den, with his own signet and with that of his lords.[1] And in the book of Job, God is said to seal up the stars, so that they do not shine ;[2] and is also described as sealing up the hand of every man, when by the frost and rain of winter He prevents the continuance of daily labour in the fields.[3] The sealing

[1] Dan. vi. 17. [2] Job ix. 7. [3] Job xxxvii.

up of sins consequently signifies their restraint under safe custody.

There is a good illustration of both figures, and probably a clue to the interpretation of the passage, in the twentieth chapter of the Revelation, where an angel, after binding Satan and casting him into the abyss, shuts him up and sets a seal upon him, that he may deceive the nations no more.

To cover iniquity. That is, according to the well-known scriptural figure, to make atonement for it. While the previous clauses seem to refer to the two-thirds of the Jewish nation which will perish during the refining process, and have their part with Satan and his angels, these words speak of another way of getting rid of sin, and point to the one-third which shall be saved.[1]

We now come to the second group of results.

To bring in everlasting righteousness. When the transgression is shut up and sins are sealed, then everlasting righteousness shall be brought in. This will be done by the introduction of the new covenant, in accordance with which God will no longer write upon tables of stone, but put His law in the inward parts of His people and write it in their hearts.[2]

To seal up vision and prophet. When sins are sealed up, vision and prophecy shall also be laid aside as being no longer needed. For it was only after sin had come into the world that prophecy was introduced as a great instrument of God in the war against it; and so, when sin is put away, prophecies also shall fail.

To anoint a Holy of holies. Lastly, in the place of the Tabernacle and former Temples, in which the

[1] Zech. xiii. 8, 9.   [2] Jer. xxxi. 33.

THE PROPHECY OF THE SEVENTY WEEKS. 195

covering, or atonement, was wont to be typified, a new Holy of holies shall be anointed. There is great significance in this announcement; for although the Tabernacle of Moses was anointed, there is no mention of such a ceremony in the consecration of the Temple of Solomon, the latter being regarded as a mere continuation of the former. And it is doubtless for a similar reason that we hear nothing of an anointing in the case of the Temple of Zerubbabel. But the Holy of holies of this prophecy, the grand Temple described in the latter chapters of Ezekiel, will be no mere continuation of former Sanctuaries : the fact that the great Sacrifice has already been offered once for all, and that sin—as regards Israel at least—will then be shut up and sealed, will doubtless cause great changes in the ordinances and service. And, moreover, this Temple, which Messiah Himself shall build,[1] will also be the place of the manifestation of His glory during the Millennial reign, and the anointing will, perhaps, specially consecrate it for that purpose.

Such, then, will be the results of God's dealing with the Jews, at the close of the Four Hundred and Ninety Years. The trangression will be restrained and sins sealed up, so as no longer to affect them—for the stumbling-blocks will then have been consumed with the wicked ;[2] their iniquity will be expiated, and the new covenant of their God will bring them everlasting righteousness; all promises will then have been fulfilled ; the law of God will be written on the heart of every Israelite, so that there will be no further need of the exhortations, rebukes, warnings, and threatenings, of the prophets ; and Mount Zion will be crowned with

[1] Zech. vi. 12, 13.   [2] Zeph. i. 3.

a Temple, of which the building of Solomon was but a very faint type, and to which—as we are elsewhere told—the Cherubim and the Glory will return, to be a cloud and smoke by day, and the shining of a flaming fire by night.[1]

But what sign would mark the commencement of the Four Hundred and Ninety Years? And, when they had commenced, would their course be unbroken to the end of the period, or would it be interrupted? These questions the angel now proceeds to answer.

The appointed time would begin at the going forth of a command to restore and build Jerusalem—not the Temple, of which there is no mention, but the city, the street and the wall.

The prophecy did not, therefore, take as its commencing date the decree of Cyrus, which had reference only to the rebuilding of the Temple; nor that of Darius Hystaspes, which was no more than a confirmation of the permission granted by Cyrus. And again, the edict issued in the seventh year of Artaxerxes Longimanus merely empowered Ezra to carry on the Temple services.

But in the twentieth year of Artaxerxes, certain men of Judah came to Shushan, and, in answer to Nehemiah's inquiries after his brethren at Jerusalem, replied;—"The remnant that are left of the captivity there in the province are in great affliction and reproach; the wall of Jerusalem also is broken down, and the gates thereof are burned with fire."[2] Over this intelligence Nehemiah mourned, and, like Daniel, made humble confession before God for the sins of his people.

[1] Ezek. xliii. 1-5; Isa. iv. 5, 6.   [2] Neh. i. 3.

THE PROPHECY OF THE SEVENTY WEEKS. 197

Shortly afterwards, in the month Nisan, he went into the royal presence to perform his duty as cup-bearer, and the king observed that his countenance was changed with sorrow. Interrogated as to the reason, Nehemiah replied;—" Let the king live for ever: why should not my countenance be sad, when the city, the place of my fathers' sepulchres, lieth waste, and the gates thereof are consumed with fire?"[1] Sympathizing with his distress, Artaxerxes immediately issued a decree for the rebuilding of the city and the wall, and sent Nehemiah to Jerusalem to superintend the work. It is clear, therefore, that the Four Hundred and Ninety Years commence from some day of the month Nisan in the twentieth year of Artaxerxes Longimanus.

From this date until the appearance of an Anointed One Who should also be a Prince—that is, a Royal Priest—Seven Weeks and Sixty and Two Weeks were to elapse; or, in other words, there should be Forty-nine and Four Hundred and Thirty-four, or Four Hundred and Eighty-three Years between the edict and the coming of Messiah as a Prince.

The Forty-nine Years are probably separated off as being the period taken up by the restoration of the city and the wall.[2] Of the pressure of the times we may find some account in the book of Nehemiah.

The Anointed One, Who should also be a Prince, can be none other than the Lord Jesus, of Whom it was said;—" Thou art a Priest for ever after the order of Melchizedek." [3] And again;—" Even He shall

[1] Neh. ii. 3.
[2] The wall is said to have been finished in fifty-two days (Neh. vi. 15): but this must have been merely a temporary work for present exigencies. Moreover, the city also was to be rebuilt.
[3] Psalm cx. 4.

build the Temple of the Lord; and He shall bear the glory, and shall sit and rule upon His throne; and He shall be a Priest upon His throne."[1]

But at what period of our Lord's life can He be said to have presented Himself as Priest and King? Not at His birth: for He was then only known as the carpenter's son. Not during the greater part of His ministry: for, although He was anointed by the Spirit, and quickly revealed Himself as the great Priest by teaching the people, by cleansing lepers, and by forgiving sins, He, nevertheless, would not put Himself forward as King. On the contrary, He forbade His disciples to disclose His real nature; and when the crowd, excited to enthusiasm by His wondrous words and works, would have set the crown upon His head, He refused it, and sent them away.

But at His entry into Jerusalem, four days before His death, His manner changed, and He suffered the whole multitude which followed Him to break forth into the cry;—"Blessed be the King That cometh in the name of the Lord."[2] And when the Pharisees urged Him to rebuke His disciples, He replied;—"I tell you that, if these should hold their peace, the stones would immediately cry out." In other words, He chose at that time to have Himself openly proclaimed King, and Matthew informs us that He did so to fulfil the prophecy of Zechariah;—"Tell ye the daughter of Zion, Behold, thy King cometh unto thee, meek, and sitting upon an ass, and a colt the foal of an ass."[3] This prophecy reveals the significance of the event, and shows us that the day indicated was that of the appearing of Messiah as the Prince.

[1] Zech. vi. 13.   [2] Luke xix. 38.   [3] Matt. xxi. 5.

Thus, then, the commencing-point of the Four Hundred and Ninety Years was the promulgation of the edict in the month Nisan of the twentieth year of the reign of Artaxerxes Longimanus; and the Four Hundred and Eighty-third Year ended on the tenth day of the month Nisan, when Christ entered Jerusalem as the King of the daughter of Zion. Both starting-point and goal are so clearly indicated in Scripture that, as believers, we have no need to trouble ourselves with the uncertainties of human computation, but may at once assume that the interval was exactly four hundred and eighty-three years.

If, however, the prophecy can be verified chronologically, its influence will be greatly extended: it will then become a powerful testimony to unbelievers, as well as a guiding light to the people of God. And of all attempts so to verify it, the solution lately proposed by Dr. Anderson seems the most satisfactory. We will, therefore, summarize it, recommending the reader to seek further details in the pages of "The Coming Prince."

Now the first point to be settled is the length of a prophetic year. And the Bible furnishes evidence that such a year was not reckoned according to the Julian system, but contained only 360 days. Even in the history of the flood we find that the five months, from the seventeenth day of the second month to the seventeenth of the seventh, are reckoned as 150 days.[1] And in the Apocalypse the same period is described as $3\frac{1}{2}$ years, as forty-two months, and as 1,260 days. Evidently, therefore, twelve months of thirty days each, or 360 days, are assigned to a year.

[1] Gen. vii. 11, 24; viii. 3, 4.

Consequently, 483 prophetic years would contain 483 × 360, or 173,880 days.

Again; the starting point of the prophecy, as we have just shown, is some day of the month Nisan, in the twentieth year of Artaxerxes the king," that is, in B.C. 445. And by proving that Nehemiah must have commenced his journey to Jerusalem very early in Nisan, Dr. Anderson makes it probable that the decree was given on the first of the month, which in that year would correspond with the 14th of March.

On the other hand, the close of the 483rd year is signalled by the Lord's entry into Jerusalem four days before His death. To find the date of this occurrence, we must remember that His ministry commenced in the fifteenth year of the reign of Tiberias, that is, in the year which began on the 19th of August, A.D. 28.

Hence the first Passover of our Lord's public ministry must have been in the Nisan of A.D. 29. And since He appears to have kept four, the last would have been in the Nisan of A.D. 32. Now the Passover was on the fourteenth of the month: therefore our Lord must have entered Jerusalem on the 10th of Nisan, or the 6th of April, A.D. 32.

Thus then——

The edict of Artaxerxes was promulgated, March 14th, B.C. 445.

Christ presented Himself in Jerusalem as King, April 6th, A.D. 32.

"The intervening period—according to the Julian reckoning—was 476 years and 24 days (the days being reckoned inclusively, as required by the language of the prophecy, and in accordance with the Jewish practice).

THE PROPHECY OF THE SEVENTY WEEKS.

But 476 × 365	173,740 days.
Add (14th March to 6th April, *both* inclusive)	24 ,,
Add for leap years	116 ,,
	173,880 days."[1]

But it has been shown above that 69 of Daniel's weeks, or 483 prophetic years, contain just 173,880 days.

Therefore, the first part of this great prophecy was exactly fulfilled *to the very day*.

Now the Jews of our Lord's time doubtless retained a copy of the famous edict which restored their national existence; or, at least, its date must have been well known to them. And thus, with very little trouble, they might have calculated the precise day on which their Messiah was to present Himself as King; while the prophecy of Zechariah would have instructed them as to the manner of His entry into the city. With such exactness, and in so literal a manner, are the predictions of God brought to their fulfilment!

At the close, then, of the appointed interval, Messiah the Prince moved towards Jerusalem; and after halting to weep over it from the heights of Olivet, passed under the gates and through the streets which were so soon to be levelled with the dust, and offered Himself as her King to the daughter of Zion. But, alas! she saw no beauty in Him that she should desire Him: He was despised and rejected, and, only four days later, the fickle multitude which had enthusiastically cried, "Blessed is the King that cometh in the name of the Lord!" was rending the air with discordant shouts of "Crucify Him! Crucify Him!"

[1] "The Coming Prince," 2nd edition, p. 128.

And so, after enduring the horrors of that night whose beginning saw Him basely betrayed by one of His own disciples, and during the dark watches of which He gave His back to the smiter and His cheek to them that plucked off the hair, and hid not His face from shame and spitting; after that mocking trial, in which the judges bribed false witnesses, but did not even then succeed in obtaining coherent testimony; after He had been further dragged, once before Herod and twice before Pilate, and none could find aught against Him—then at length the Anointed One was cut off.

And there was nothing for Him; none of those glories which were to surround the person of the Messiah. Instead of appearing as the King of kings and Lord of lords, He was found in the form of a servant. And so far was He from possessing a kingdom above all, and an everlasting dominion, that He had not, during His life, where to lay His head, and was soon cut off altogether from the land of the living.

In place of that Divine beauty and appalling majesty, the first glance of which struck the persecuting Saul helpless to the ground, and which caused even the beloved disciple John to fall at His feet as dead, lo! His visage was marred more than any man, He had no form nor comeliness, nor was there any desirable beauty seen in Him.

For His painful mission in those days was to bear our griefs, and carry our sorrows; to be wounded for our transgressions, and bruised for our iniquities; to receive the chastisement which should bring peace to us, that by His stripes we might be healed. He came to make His soul an offering for sin, to pour out His soul unto death, to be numbered with the transgressors, to bear the sins of many.

He was cut off, and there was nothing for Him.

But the crucifixion of our Lord took place four days after His appearance as the Priest-King—that is, four days after the close of the Four Hundred and Eighty-third Year—and yet it is not said to have happened in the Seven Years which still remained to be fulfilled. At this point, therefore, it seems that there is a gap separating the Four Hundred and Eighty-third Year from the last Seven. For God had given up the sinful nation which rejected His Son: His covenant was suspended, so that they were no longer His people: and, consequently, the course of the Four Hundred and Ninety Years had ceased to run on.[1]

The prophecy then speaks of vengeance which should follow for the cutting off of Messiah: the city and the Sanctuary, Jerusalem and the Temple, should be destroyed. This was fulfilled by the Romans under Titus, about forty years after the death of Christ: but still there is no mention of the missing Seven Years; the interval continues.

Lastly; we are told that, after the destruction of the city and Sanctuary, there should be wars and desolations until the end, during a period fixed indeed by God, but unknown to man. Terribly has this been verified; and so frequent have been the captures of Jerusalem by Roman, Persian, Saracen, and Turk, that the city of our Lord's time has become deeply buried beneath successive layers of ruin and *débris*, and is now found from fifty to eighty feet below the level of the

[1] For the principle on which this explanation is based, see the chapter on Mystic Chronology in the Prolegomena.

soil. All these destructions are included in the words, "And until the end there shall be war, that which is determined for desolations"; and yet there is no mention of the final Seven Years.

Thus, from the appearing of Messiah the Prince, there occurs an undefined interval, a great interruption in the progress of the Seventy Weeks, which, as we shall presently see, is not unnoticed in other parts of Scripture.

But, to retrace our steps for a moment, the city and Sanctuary were to be destroyed by the people of a prince that should afterwards come; and since it is added that this prince will meet his doom in the last great outpouring of God's wrath, it is manifest that he cannot have appeared in past time. Now the Romans destroyed the city and Sanctuary: so far, therefore, we gather that the prince will be a head of the Fourth Empire; but the time of his end shows us further that he will be the last head—that is, the Antichrist.

In the final verse of the prophecy we are told that he will confirm a covenant with the majority of the Jewish people for One Week. And so at length we find the missing Seven Years, the Seventieth Week.

Now the Jews must by this time have settled again in their own land, because the prophecy is expressly connected with the people and the city. Possibly the prince may himself have restored them: but, at any rate, he will find them in some trouble, or terrified by some impending danger, and will undertake their protection in Palestine for seven years. The compact may, perhaps, be similar to that by which Napoleon III. promised to maintain Maximilian as emperor of Mexico for a fixed time. But whatever the covenant may be, it will only be accepted by a majority of the people, and not by the whole nation: God will again leave Himself a remnant which shall not bow the knee to Baal.

Thus restored and settled in their own land, the Jews will rebuild their Temple and renew the sacrifices and services; but, probably, in a proud and atheistical spirit, and certainly in a way very displeasing to God. The last chapter of Isaiah represents them as engaged in these works not long before the appearing in glory of the Lord Jesus, a description of which begins with the fifteenth verse. But their efforts will spring from national pride, and will not be stimulated by love to God; therefore He declares;—"Thus saith the Lord, The heaven is My throne, and the earth My footstool: where is this house that ye build unto Me? and where is this place of My rest? For all these things—that is, the visible world—My hand hath made; then all these things came into existence, saith the Lord; but to this man will I look, even to him that is poor and contrite in spirit, and trembleth at My word."

Then, in reference to the sacrifices which are again being offered, the Lord adds;—"He that killeth the ox is as the slayer of a man; he that sacrificeth the sheep as one that breaketh the neck of a dog; he that offereth an oblation, it is swine's blood; he that causeth incense to rise up as a memorial is as one that blesseth an idol." That is, the offerings will be as offensive to God as if men were insulting Him by sacrificing what He has declared to be unclean, or by paying adoration to false gods.

But the Jews will go on in their own ways during the first half of the Seven Years, and then there will be a change. In the middle of the Week—that is, at the end of Three Years and a Half—Antichrist will cause the sacrifices to cease, and transfer the worship of Jehovah to himself, exalting " himself above all that is called God, or that is worshipped ; so that he as God sitteth in the Temple of God, showing himself that he is God."[1]

The words, " upon the wing of abominations shall be the desolater," are difficult ; but we must remember that " abomination " was a common term among the Hebrews for a false god. So, in the first book of Kings, we find " Milcom, the abomination of the Ammonites," " Chemosh, the abomination of Moab," and "Moloch, the abomination of the children of Ammon."[2] And again ; the false gods are declared in both Old and New Testament to be real existences.[3] " The things which the Gentiles sacrifice, they sacrifice to demons, and not to God."[4]

If, then, abominations may here be taken to mean demons, the reference may be to some blasphemous imitation of the chariot of the Cherubim, produced by Satanic power, and perhaps similar to that on which Satan might have conveyed our Lord from the pinnacle of the Temple, could he have bent Him to the temptation. Possibly the appearance of Antichrist thus borne aloft by the agency of demons may be that which will finally determine the world to worship him as God ; while the apostate Jews may regard it as the expected sign from heaven, and as the return of

[1] 2 Thess. ii. 4.
[2] 1 Kings xi. 5-7.
[3] See " Earth's Earliest Ages," 2nd edition, pp. 245-9.
[4] 1 Cor. x. 20.

THE PROPHECY OF THE SEVENTY WEEKS.

the Glory to their Temple. For when another shall come in his own name, him they will receive. And immediately after this will commence the terrible persecution of all who refuse to worship the Beast and his image.

In such a mockery of Godhead the prince will continue, until the hour allotted to the Powers of Darkness has come to its full end. Then that which has been decreed will have been poured upon the desolate city of Jerusalem, and the time of the consummation will have arrived. Down from heaven will the flood of God's indignation be poured: the blasphemous pretender will be confounded by a brightness —far above that of the sun—which, lighting up the whole globe with the speed of the storm-flash, will proclaim the long-expected advent of the King of kings.

Such, then, is the great revelation granted, in answer to Daniel's confession and prayer, as a key to all Hebrew prophecies. Until he had received it, he could not understand his own previous visions. After that of the Four Wild Beasts we find him saying ;—" As for me, Daniel, my cogitations much troubled me, and my countenance changed in me."[1] And at the end of the eighth chapter also, he remarks ;—" And I Daniel fainted, and was sick certain days; afterwards I rose up and did the king's business; and I was astonished at the vision, but none understood it."[2]

But the disclosure of the Seventy Weeks, which was vouchsafed to give him skill and understanding, enabled him to comprehend the purposes of God; and, consequently, in his preface to the next revelation

[1] Dan. vii. 28.   [2] Dan. viii. 27.

he tells us that "he understood the thing, and had understanding of the vision."[1]   Surely that which enlightened Daniel is of the greatest importance to us also, upon whom the ends of the ages are come; nor should we forget those pregnant words;—"And none of the wicked shall understand; but the wise shall understand."[2]

IV.

The Interval foretold by Zechariah.

From the words of Gabriel we have gathered that the course of the Four Hundred and Ninety Years was to be interrupted just before the cutting off of Messiah: are there any other notices in Scripture of the setting aside of His covenant with the Jews at that time? We shall find one in the eleventh chapter of Zechariah, of the contents of which the following is a slight sketch.

The prophet begins with a description of terrible destruction,[3] the reason for which is given in the subsequent verses.

Then Judah is set before us as a flock destined for slaughter, whose rulers are swayed only by selfish motives: their possessors the Romans, their sellers the Herodians, and their shepherds the Pharisees and Sadducees, all join in oppressing them.

But the Lord undertakes to feed them, especially distinguishing the poor of the flock; and as Moses had his rod, so Christ takes two staves significant of His office, one of which He calls Beauty, or rather Favour, and the other Bands. By the first the full

[1] Dan. x. 1.   [2] Dan. xii. 10.   [3] Zech. xi. 1-3.

THE PROPHECY OF THE SEVENTY WEEKS.

outpouring of God's love was secured to the nation, according to the prayer of Moses;—"And let the favour of the Lord our God be upon us; and establish Thou the work of our hands upon us; yea, the work of our hands establish Thou it."[1] By the second, even if they lost for a time the favour of God, they would still be held together as a covenant people.

Having Himself undertaken to be Shepherd, the Lord proceeds to cut off in one month three hireling shepherds whom His soul abhorred. These were probably the Pharisees, Sadducees, and Herodians, the silencing of whom we may find in the twenty-second chapter of Matthew. Our Lord Himself points them out as false teachers when, on one occasion, He warns His disciples against the leaven of the Pharisees and Herodians;[2] on another, against that of the Pharisees and Sadducees.[3]

Then because their soul abhorred Him, He declared that He would no longer feed them, and broke His staff called Favour, giving as His reason, "That I might break My covenant which I had made with all the peoples"—that is, the covenant which He had made with the Gentiles to restrain them from injuring the Jewish nation.[4] This withdrawal of the light of His countenance was foretold by the Lord on the Mount of Olives, when He wept over the doomed city: and it was speedily carried into effect—as soon as

[1] Psalm xc. 17.
[2] Mark viii. 15.
[3] Matt. xvi. 6.
[4] In Hosea ii. 18, God promises to make a similar covenant, in favour of Israel, "with the beasts of the field, and with the fowls of heaven, and with the creeping things of the ground." Compare also Job v. 23, and Ezek. xxxiv. 25.

the rulers of the people had refused to recognize Him as the King of the daughter of Zion—at a time exactly corresponding to the prophecy of the Seventy Weeks.

Nevertheless, the poor of the flock, as many as believe on Him, continue to wait on the Lord, and He still feeds them; but of the rest of the nation He demands the wages of His service in anticipation of His betrayal, and is priced at thirty pieces of silver.

Then the second staff, Bands, is broken; for the Jews go on to smite the Judge of Israel with a rod upon the cheek, and can, therefore, no longer be held together as a covenant nation at Jerusalem, but are given up to be scattered from their city, until the time that she which travaileth hath brought forth.[1]

Such is an outline of the prophecy to the end of the fourteenth verse, after which comes the interval revealed to Daniel; and, consequently, we are at once carried from the betrayal of the Messiah and the dispersion of the Jews to the idol shepherd, the Antichrist, who will destroy the flock in the last Week, and be himself overthrown "when the chief Shepherd shall appear."[2]

V.

The Interval recognised by Matthew.

A similar outline may be traced in the dispensational Gospel of Matthew.

For both the Fore-runner and the Lord Himself begin their ministry with the cry, "Repent, for the Kingdom of the Heavens has come nigh." The Four Hundred and Eighty-three Years were drawing to a

[1] Micah v. 1, 3.   [2] 1 Pet. v. 4.

THE INTERVAL RECOGNISED BY MATTHEW.

close; but the dreary interval would not be necessary if Israel could at that time repent and receive the Anointed Prince.

In the fifth sixth and seventh chapters, the laws of the Kingdom are delivered by the King, Who speaks throughout on the authority of His own word, and finally reveals Himself to the astonished multitude as the future Judge of the quick and the dead.[1]

But it was reasonable to expect that such claims should be supported by proofs of no ordinary kind; nor was the expectation disappointed. A leper, hopelessly stricken with the sacred disease which none but Jehovah could heal, was listening at a distance; and, convinced by the wondrous words of the Speaker that He must be the Son of God, ran boldly to Him, and said;—" Lord, if Thou wilt, Thou canst make me clean." This simple faith, and unreserved acknowledgment of Jesus as Lord, soon proved that all things are indeed possible to them that believe.

The Saviour put forth His hand, and, as He touched the pale sufferer, uttered the word of power;—" I do will; be thou clean." In an instant the disease had fled: a warm flow of blood thrilled the stagnant veins of the leper, and flushed into his white face, and he stood healed and sound in the presence of the awe-struck multitude.

Yet this was only the beginning of the mighty works by which the Lord showed that He was in very truth the Son of God: the eighth and ninth chapters contain accounts of other stupendous miracles testifying to His absolute sovereignty over disease, the elements, the spirits of evil, and even death itself.

[1] Matt. vii. 21-23.

The leaders of Israel did not, however, hail Him as the long-expected Messiah, but disliked His teaching, and became more and more determinedly opposed to Him as He multiplied the signs of His power. Consequently, He soon began to hint that there must be delay in the restoration of the Kingdom, and spoke of a future absence of the Bridegroom, during which the children of the Bride-chamber should mourn.[1]

Nevertheless, when He looked on the multitude, He was moved with compassion, "because they were harassed and scattered abroad, as sheep having no shepherd."[2] And so He renewed His offer, and, by sending out His twelve disciples, again appealed to the hearts of the people with the stirring proclamation, "The Kingdom of the Heavens has drawn nigh."[3] But there was no adequate result: for He presently began to complain of the waywardness of His generation, and to upbraid those cities wherein most of His mighty works had been done, because they repented not.[4]

In the twelfth chapter, the malice and opposition of the rulers is still more marked; and, unable to deny His acts of power, they dare to say;—"This fellow doth not cast out demons but by Beelzebub the prince of the demons." Then at length He began to show that His soul also abhorred them: His mouth spoke terrible things, and He declared that their despised privileges should bring down the thunder of God's judgment upon their heads.

He concluded His discourse with the prophetic parable of the man out of whom the unclean spirit

---

[1] Matt. ix. 15.
[2] Matt. ix. 36.
[3] Matt. x.
[4] Matt. xi. 16-24.

had gone, and predicted that their cloak of hypocrisy should yet be torn away, and their real apostasy from God discovered. The spirit of avowed idolatry had indeed been exorcised for the time by the Babylonian captivity, and its grosser manifestations they had swept out of their hearts. Nor was this all: they had also garnished the house; but with a cold and formal religion which, though professing to honour God, was of no avail save for purposes of self-glorification. For the Spirit of God had not taken possession of them; therefore the foul demon should return to the empty dwelling with seven others worse than himself, and the last state of the Jews should be more openly idolatrous than the first. They had rejected the Lord of glory; but they should be moved to worship a man, even that Lawless One who will oppose and exalt himself above all that is called God, or that is worshipped.

The Lord ceased to speak; and immediately there ensued a significant incident, pre-arranged by His power to show that no tie of the flesh, however strong, would be recognised before Him, unless it were accompanied by faith and obedience. His mother and her sons had come to the outskirts of the crowd wishing to see Him, and a bystander said;—"Behold, Thy mother and Thy brethren stand without, desiring to speak with Thee." But He replied;—"Who is My mother, and who are My brethren?" Then, stretching forth His hand towards His disciples, He said;— "Behold My mother and My brethren! For whosoever shall do the will of My Father Which is in heaven, the same is My brother, and sister, and mother." The mere earthly relationship could not avail to stay judgment: even the seed of Abraham according to the flesh, and the Lord's kinsmen, must perish if they continued in unbelief: He would mark for mercy only those who did the will of His Father. And this will was that they should believe on Him Whom the Father had sent: but they were rejecting Him, and should, therefore, be also themselves rejected.

Having thus predicted the fate of the Jews, the Lord then proceeded, *on the same day*,[1] to foretell what should follow; to speak of the branches of the wild olive tree which should be grafted in after the breaking off of the natural branches; to reveal, though as yet only in parable, something of the great mystery which had been hidden from past ages. And by so doing He is said to have fulfilled the prophecy;—"I will open my mouth in parables: I will utter things which have been kept secret from the foundation of the world."[2] For until the disposition of the Jews toward the Lord had made it evident that they must be cast off for a season, God would not reveal what should take place during the time of their rejection. It is as though He had left it open to them to decide, by their obedience or disobedience, whether the last of Daniel's Weeks should be fulfilled immediately after the Sixty-ninth, or whether there should be a wearisome interval of discipline.

Henceforth the character of our Lord's preaching was changed, and we find from Luke that, as He drew nigh to Jerusalem for His death, He spoke a parable to show that the first offers were withdrawn, and that the Kingdom of the Heavens could not now immediately appear.[3] A little later, probably in the same hour, He was standing on the brow of Olivet, and,

[1] Matt. xiii. 1.   [2] Matt. xiii. 35.   [3] Luke xix. 11.

while gazing from thence at the fair scene spread out before Him, wept as He uttered the memorable lamentation ;—" If thou hadst known, even thou, at least in this thy day, the things which belong unto thy peace ! But now they are hid from thine eyes. For the days shall come upon thee that thine enemies shall cast a trench about thee, and compass thee round, and keep thee in on every side, and shall lay thee even with the ground, and thy children within thee ; and they shall not leave in thee one stone upon another ; because thou knewest not the time of thy visitation."[1] For Messiah was about to be cut off, and afterwards both city and Sanctuary should be destroyed.

Nevertheless, He entered into the city on this last day of the Four Hundred and Eighty-third Year of Daniel's period, and he did so "riding upon an ass and upon a colt the foal of an ass," that, by the simultaneous fulfilment of two great prophecies, He might make a last appeal to the rebel Jews. But it was all in vain : the enthusiasm of the populace was only momentary, while the malice of their rulers was greatly intensified.

Then the covenant was broken, and the barren fig tree cursed as a sign ; the parable of the vineyard was uttered with its terrible conclusion—"Therefore, I say unto you, the Kingdom of God shall be taken from you, and given to a nation bringing forth the fruits thereof";[2] and the Temple was given up with the words, "Behold, your house is left unto you desolate."[3]

In the prophecy which He immediately afterwards delivered on the Mount of Olives, the Lord fills in that part of Daniel's outline which was yet future,

[1] Luke xix. 42-44.   [2] Matt. xxi. 43.   [3] Matt. xxiii. 38.

even mentioning the prophet by name. He hints at the destruction of the city and Sanctuary after His own decease,[1] and then passes on to notice what should happen in the days immediately preceding the fulfilment of the times of the Gentiles and the simultaneous completion of the last Seven Years of God's dealings with the Jews in Jerusalem. And thus, in the New Testament also, the great interpreting revelation given to Daniel is found to be the key of all prophecy which concerns the Jew.

VI.

The Interval in other Visions of Daniel.

We will now endeavour to trace the scheme of the Seventy Weeks in the other visions of Daniel: for, in accordance with our previous conclusions, we expect to find these also concerned at first with events not later than the destruction of the city and Sanctuary, and then passing over the interval in silence, and resuming their detail in the last Week.

But of course this expectation does not extend to the vision of the image: for that was granted, not to the Hebrew prophet, but to the first head of Gentile dominion. Naturally, therefore, it takes in the whole period of that dominion, revealing its condition during the cessation, as well as during the progress, of God's dealings with the Jews. Hence, in the two legs of the image, it discloses the division of the fourth World-power into two Empires, an event which is not mentioned in Hebrew prophecy, because it was to take place during the interval.

[1] Matt. xxiv. 6.

On the other hand, the first of the visions seen by Daniel, that of the Four Wild Beasts, entirely ignores the events of the interval. For the Fourth Beast represents the Roman Empire in unity, as it was at the time of the destruction of Jerusalem, and the first part of the description well applies to it up to that period of its history. Then follows the clause, "And it had ten horns," referring to the Ten Kingdoms in which it will ultimately be arranged. Thus the division of the Empire into two parts is omitted, and we are carried on from the destruction of Jerusalem by Titus into the last Week.

Again; the vision of the Ram and the He-goat begins to find its fulfilment in the days of the prophet, although the angel affirms that its main reference is to "the time of the end"—a fact which seems to identify the little horn of this revelation with that of the Ten-horned Beast. The horn of the He-goat, we are told, is Alexander the Great; while the four, which spring up after it has been broken, are the four kingdoms into which the Macedonian Empire was subsequently divided, and the last survivor of which—that is, Egypt—was absorbed into Rome after the battle of Actium, in B.C. 31. The interval, therefore, occurs between the four horns and the little one, and is plainly intimated by the angel, who prefaces his description of the king of fierce countenance with the words, "And in the latter time of their kingdom, when the transgressors are come to the full." Thus the prediction passes on at once from about B.C. 31, which is within the Sixty-nine weeks, to the appearance of Antichrist in the Seventieth.

The last revelation to Daniel, contained in the tenth,

eleventh, and twelfth chapters, also begins its disclosures from the times of the prophet, and notices the reigns of Cambyses, Pseudo-Smerdis, Darius Hystaspes, and Xerxes.[1] From the last-mentioned king it passes on to Alexander, and speaks of his great dominion; but at the same time predicts that none of his posterity should retain his power, and that his empire should be divided into four kingdoms.[2] Then it traces out the fortunes of two of these kingdoms, Syria and Egypt, because their policies and wars affected Palestine which lay between them. With occasional detail of wonderful minuteness it foretells the conflicts of the Seleucidæ and Lagidæ, especially dwelling upon the doings of Antiochus Epiphanes.[3] Afterwards there is an evident reference to the Maccabees in the words, "But the people that do know their God shall be strong, and do exploits."[4]

In the next verse it mentions the rise of a very different class of agents, "they that understand among the people," who do no exploits, but "instruct many." This is a description in which we cannot fail to recognize the appearance and work of the Lord Jesus and His disciples. But the instruction would be rejected by the mass of the people, and would not, therefore, avail to forefend the approaching judgment; for the prophecy continues;—"Yet they shall fall by the sword and by flame, by captivity and by spoil, many days."[5]

This is an evident reference to the destruction of the city and Sanctuary by Titus, and the consequent

[1] Dan. xi. 2.
[2] Dan. xi. 3, 4.
[3] Dan. xi. 5-32.
[4] Dan. xi. 32.
[5] Dan. xi. 33.

dispersion of the Jews; and our Lord uses similar language in foretelling the same events.[1] He expresses the "many days" of Daniel by saying that "Jerusalem shall be trodden down of the Gentiles, until the times of the Gentiles be fulfilled."

Thus we are again brought down to the same crisis as in the prophecy of the Seventy Weeks, and then immediately carried on to the doings of Antichrist: for the thirty-sixth verse introduces the Wilful King. And so the same scheme may be detected in all the great revelations given to Daniel.

VII.

The Scheme of the Seventy Weeks is the Key to all Prophecy.

We have thus found from the prophecy of the Seventy Weeks—as well as from other parts of Scripture, in which the Lord is represented as breaking His covenant with Israel just before His death—that there has now been for more than eighteen hundred years an entire cessation of God's dealings with the Jews as a nation. A great gap extends—as we understand by the words of Daniel, Zechariah, and the Lord Himself—from Messiah the Prince to the false prince that shall come; from the good Shepherd, Whom the flock abhorred and rejected, to the idol shepherd, whom the majority of them will follow to their own destruction; from Him Who came in His Father's name to that other who shall come in his own name.

And during the interval between the true Messiah

[1] Luke xxi. 24.

and the false, Hebrew prophecy is almost entirely in abeyance, and there remain in present operation only one or two fearful utterances which stretch, as it were, here and there across the whole width of the chasm.

Such is the cry of Hosea, which startled the prosperous and haughty times of Uzziah with the fateful words ;—" For the children of Israel shall abide many days without a king, and without a prince, and without a sacrifice, and without an image, and without an ephod, and without teraphim."[1]

Such is the mournful burden of Micah that, because of the smiting of the Judge of Israel upon the cheek, God would give up His people, until the travailing woman should bring forth.[2]

And such, especially, are the terrible fulminations in Leviticus and Deuteronomy, those words of fear ;— " And the Lord shall scatter thee among all people, from the one end of the earth even unto the other ; and there thou shalt serve other gods, which neither thou nor thy fathers have known, even wood and stone. And among those nations shalt thou find no ease, neither shall the sole of thy foot have rest : but the Lord shall give thee there a trembling heart, and failing of eyes, and sorrow of mind : and thy life shall hang in doubt before thee ; and thou shalt fear day and night, and shalt have none assurance of thy life. In the morning thou shalt say, Would God it were even ! and at even thou shalt say, Would God it were morning ! for the fear of thine heart wherewith thou shalt fear, and for the sight of thine eyes which thou shalt see."[3]

[1] Hosea iii. 4. [2] Micah v. 1, 3. [3] Deut. xxviii. 64-67.

With the exception of such passages as these, and the few predictions respecting the Gentiles, all Old Testament prophecy—which invariably refers to the literal Judah, Jerusalem, and Israel—centres upon the events immediately connected with the two advents. For, as Peter tells us, the Spirit through the prophets "testified beforehand the sufferings of Christ, and the glory that should follow"[1]—that is, the first coming to suffer and die, and the consequent rejection of the Jews; and the second coming to rule with power, and the consequent restoration of all Israel.

The knowledge of this fact is indispensable to a right understanding of prophecy; for events connected with the two great, but now widely separated eras, are often mentioned together, even in the same sentence. Nor is there any confusion in such an arrangement: for had the Jews received Christ at His first coming, John the Baptist would have been Elijah to them,[2] the

[1] 1 Pet. i. 11.

[2] It has been supposed by many that John exhausted the prophecy in Mal. iv. 5. But nothing less than the personal appearance of "Elijah the prophet"—or "Elijah the Tishbite," as the Septuagint has it—can fulfil that utterance. Moreover, his coming must be just before the *second* advent, "the great and dreadful day of the Lord." When the Saviour speaks of this subject it is with an ambiguity which can only be dispelled by a knowledge of the Seventy Weeks. On one occasion He says of John;—"And if ye are willing to receive him, this is Elijah which is to come" (Matt. xi. 14). That is, "If you will allow John to do the work of Elijah, he shall be Elijah to you; the Seventieth Week shall follow immediately upon the Sixty-ninth, and then the Kingdom shall be restored to Israel." But the preaching of the Baptist did not turn the hearts of the Jews; and accordingly, *after his death*, when the opportunity had passed, the Lord said, "Elijah indeed cometh, and shall restore all things; but I say unto you that an Elijah came just now (ἤδη ἦλθε), and they knew him not, but did unto him whatsoever they listed" (Matt. xvii. 11, 12). Here the coming of the personal Elijah is affirmed to be

last Seven Years would have followed immediately, and then the Kingdom would have been restored to Israel. But the unbelief of the Jews separated those things which might have been joined together, and, consequently, the marvellous events of the last Week have not yet begun to take place.

Lest, however, we should feel any perplexity in regard to the interpretation of Old Testament prophecy, the Lord Himself has given us a clue. In the fourth chapter of Luke we may find an account of His visit to the synagogue at Nazareth, where He read a passage from Isaiah, and declared that it was fulfilled on that day in the ears of His audience. The passage runs as follows;—"The Spirit of the Lord is upon Me; because He hath anointed Me to preach the Gospel to the poor; He hath sent Me to heal the broken-hearted, to preach deliverance to the captives, and recovering of sight to the blind; to set at liberty them that are bruised, to preach the acceptable year of the Lord."[1] When He had read so much, He closed the book; and if we turn to the sixty-first chapter of Isaiah, we shall see in what manner He extracted the passage. He ceased reading in the middle of a sentence, because

still in the future; and we are told that he will do what John might have done but did not, and will bring back Israel from apostasy. In the words which follow, the allusion to John shows that his appearance "in the spirit and power of Elijah" was a tentative fulfilment of Malachi's prophecy, preparatory to the offers of the Kingdom which Christ made in the beginning of His ministry, but never repeated after the death of John. For although His entry into Jerusalem marked the time when He would have allowed Himself to be recognised as King, had He not been already rejected; yet His lamentation over the doomed city, before He passed its gates, proves that this was no real offer, because the Jews were irremediably hardened.

[1] Luke iv. 18, 19; Isa. lxi. 1, 2.

its next clause leaps the wide chasm between the first and second advents, and speaks of "the day of vengeance of our God." Unless, therefore, He had closed the book when He did, He could not have said, "This day is this Scripture fulfilled in your ears."

Before, however, we deduce a canon of interpretation from our Lord's method of procedure, we should be careful to notice that prophecy must always, when it is possible, be taken literally. The Bible is not a riddle, but a revelation. Written to suit the mean capacities of our race while still in the flesh, it is easily intelligible to those who surrender themselves to the guidance of the Spirit. It presents but few difficulties, if we are willing to receive it just as it has been delivered to us, and do not wish to avoid that which is supernatural. And with a few avowed exceptions—such as when the mind that hath wisdom is challenged, or when he that hath ears to hear is bidden to hear—if it does speak figuratively, it employs plain and obvious figures, the purpose of which is to illustrate and make clear, and not to mystify.

That what we affirm is true may be seen by the prophecies of the first advent, which, fulfilled as they were with a wonderful literality, should make us wise in regard to the future. Let the following serve as examples.

The messenger.	Mal. iii. 1 ... Mark i. 2-8.
The virgin mother.	Gen. iii. 15 ;
	Isa. vii. 14. ... Matt. i. 18-23.[1]

---

[1] In the prophecy of Isa. vii. 14, the Authorized Version obscures the meaning by omitting the article; for we should read, "Behold, the virgin conceiving." The same mistake occurs in the quotation in Matt. i. 23, but is corrected in the Revised Version. We scarcely need to say that the article is of

224　　　　　　*THE JEWS.*

The other children of the Lord's mother.	Ps. lxix. 8. [1] ... Matt. xii. 46, John vii. 5
The riding into Jerusalem.	Zech. ix. 9. ... Matt. xxi. 1-11.
The thirty pieces of silver.	Zech. xi. 12. ... Matt. xxvi. 15.
The potter's field.	Zech. xi. 13. ... Matt. xxvii. 7.
The smiting and spitting.	Isa. l. 6.　　... Matt. xxvi. 67.
The piercing *with nails*[2].	Psa. xxii. 16. ... Matt. xxvii. 35; John xx. 25-27.
The piercing *with the spear*[2].	Zech. xii. 10. ... John xix. 34, 37.
The garments and vesture.	Psa. xxii. 18. ... John xix. 23, 24.
The vinegar and the gall.	Psa. lxix. 21. ... Matt. xxvii. 34.
The unbroken bones.	Psa. xxxiv. 20 ... John xix. 33, 36.

The list might be greatly extended, and there is no reason to doubt that the prophecies of the second advent will be fulfilled as literally as those of the first.

From this consideration, and from the example given

the utmost importance, since it points back to some particular virgin who must have been indicated by a previous revelation, and so connects Isaiah's words with the primeval utterance respecting "the seed of the woman." For that unusual expression evidently implies that, just as sin came into the world through the woman alone, so far as earthly agencies were concerned, so the Deliverer should be introduced by the woman alone; in other words, that our Lord should be born of a virgin.

[1] In this prophecy—the next verse of which is applied to Christ in the New Testament (John ii. 17; Rom. xv. 3)—the expression, "My mother's children," precludes all attempts to show that the Lord's brethren were either His cousins or His half-brothers. Without doubt James and Joses and Simon and Judas (Matt. xiii. 55) were the literal brethren of the Lord, and it would never have occurred to any one to deny so plain a fact, had it not been for the wish to substantiate idolatrous theories respecting His mother, and to identify her with Isis, the mother of Horus, and yet the ever-virgin. See the note at the end of the present chapter.

[2] In the passage of the twenty-second Psalm—"They pierced My hands and My feet—the word כָּאֲרִ (akin to בּוּר כָּרָה) is found, which signifies to dig or bore through, and is, therefore, most appropriately used of nails. But in Zech. xii. 10, the verb is דָּקַר, which means to pierce with a sword or spear.

above of our Lord's way of dealing with Scripture, we would suggest the following method of interpretation

In any prediction of the Old Testament, regard that which has been exactly fulfilled at the first advent as already past.

Apply all else to the times of the second advent, as literally as the case will allow.

By way of example we may cite the words of Isaiah; —"For unto us a Child is born, unto us a Son is given; and the government shall be upon His shoulder." Now the Child was born, and the Son was given, at the first advent; but the government did not then devolve upon Him, for He was cut off and there was nothing for Him. He left our world as a nobleman going into a far country to receive for himself a kingdom and to return. At the second advent, therefore, will the government be placed upon His shoulder. It is only *after* the Fourth Beast has been slain, and his body destroyed and given to the burning flame, that the Son of man shall be brought to the Ancient of days, and invested with dominion, and glory, and a Kingdom.[1]

So in the thirteenth chapter of Zechariah, the seventh verse refers to the first advent,[2] but the eighth and ninth to the second; for the destruction of Jerusalem by Titus resulted in the dispersion of the whole Jewish nation, not in the deliverance of one-third of them.

If, then, we apply this process, of which our Lord Himself gives us an example, the Bible becomes a plain revelation, and is no longer a tissue of enigmas. Its every page sparkles with glory, and it is found to be filled with disclosures and instructions which Paul might well compare to gold, silver, and precious stones.

[1] Dan. vii. 11-14.   [2] Matt. xxvi. 31.

Note on the Brethren of the Lord.

The actual blood-relationship of our Lord to those persons who in the New Testament are called "His brethren," and are usually mentioned in connection with His mother, is a truth of great importance. It bars the way against that doctrine of Paganism which has ever corrupted the nominal Church more powerfully, perhaps, or, at least, more persistently, than any other. And just as it was vehemently assailed in the early centuries of our era, so now it is either ignored or opposed by many, because the causes which first rendered it distasteful are once more working actively among us.

For Mariolatry is gaining ground in those countries which have hitherto been termed Protestant; while that which it really represents, namely, the worship of the female principle in nature, has of late found favour with many Secularists—such as Strauss, Comte, and John Stuart Mill—and prevails extensively among Spiritualists and Theosophists.

Now this wide-spread error, which may, ultimately, prove a bond of union to men of very diverse opinions, is at once deprived of all the support which it pretends to draw from Christianity if the Lord's brethren can be shown to be the veritable sons of His mother. For the universal Heathen goddess of many names, with which men have ever sought to identify her, was the mother of a divine son, and yet a virgin. Hence the importance of the question.

But to an unprejudiced mind there could be no question at all. Were we without interest in the controversy, we should, upon reading of the Lord's "mother and His brethren," instinctively understand the brethren to be related to Him in the flesh in the same literal sense in which His mother was. And if any feeling within us forbids so obvious a conclusion, it certainly does not spring from the Scriptures, which contain nothing that could possibly suggest it.

On the contrary, the simple command to Joseph, "Fear not to take unto thee Mary *thy wife*,"[1] is sufficient to show that the usual conjugal relations subsisted between the pair after our Lord's birth. And the plain narration, that Joseph "took unto him *his wife*, and knew her not till she had brought forth her firstborn Son,"[2] affords conclusive evidence that Matthew, at least, had no wish to guard against the legitimate meaning of his words.

Again ; the significant but much neglected fact that, in Scripture, Mary is never called a virgin after the birth of her firstborn Son, is in itself fatal to the purely Heathen doctrine of her perpetual virginity.

And lastly ; it cannot have been without design that, in a Psalm repeatedly applied to Christ in the New Testament, and immediately preceding a verse both the clauses of which are cited by inspired writers as referring to Him,[3] we should find the words ;—

> "I am become a stranger unto My brethren,
> And an alien unto My *mother's children*."[4]

It is unnecessary to say more : the Bible certainly assumes the brethren of the Lord to be the actual sons of His mother, upon whom—with two memorable excep-

Matt. i. 20.
Matt. i. 24, 25.
Psa. lxix. 9. Compare John ii. 17 and Rom. xv. 3.
Psa. lxix. 8.

tions, of which we shall speak presently—it always represents them as being in attendance. So carefully did He Who knows the end from the beginning anticipate the attempt to identify the Saviour's earthly parent with Isis the ever-virgin mother of Horus—just as also, in the plans of the Tabernacle and the Temple, He directed that the Holy of holies should be set in the West, and so at once distinguished His worshippers from the multitudinous votaries of nature and the sun, who turned towards the East.

But in this case, as in many others, human corruption quickly made the Word of God of none effect. In very early times the wish to assimilate Christianity to Paganism by furnishing it with a virgin-goddess, together with the prevailing tendency to asceticism, resulted in a theory that Joseph was a widower when he espoused Mary, and that the "brethren" were his sons by his first wife.

The origin of this theory is betrayed by the sentiments of its supporters. Not a particle of evidence can be adduced in its favour: for there is no historical mention of a previous marriage of Joseph, nor do the fictitious elder half-brothers appear in the few incidents of the Lord's birth and childhood which are revealed to us. Even Jerome taunts those who believe in it with "following the Apocryphal writings, and inventing a wretched little woman, Melcha, or Escha."

But, in order to Paganise Christianity, it was not enough to dispose of these brethren: it was also necessary to show that Mary *could* have had no other children besides her Firstborn. Accordingly, about the middle of the second century, the Protevangelium Jacobi represented Joseph as being, at the time of his second marriage, a very old man with adult children. Unfortunately, however, for the reputation of that work, it allowed him no daughters, although the New Testament mentions the Lord's sisters [1] as well as His brothers. But the idea of Joseph's extreme age became very popular in Apocryphal writings, and is worked out from them, with grotesque extravagance, in the Coventry Miracle Plays which are preserved in the British Museum. And while the doctrine of Mary's virginity was being thus disseminated, the name of Theotocus, or Mother of God, was also assigned to her and led to the natural inference that the Godhead of Christ as well as His human body proceeded from her and, therefore, that she must herself have been a goddess.

Towards the close of the fourth century, a number of female devotees, who had migrated from Thrace to Arabia, gave out that they were priestesses of Mary, and commenced an idolatrous worship which, by the form it assumed, seems to point to an identification of her with Ceres. On appointed festival days they conveyed about in chariots—such as the Pagans used in their religious processions—certain cakes, or wafers, consecrated to her and called *collyrides*, from which they derived their own name of Collyridians. After presenting these cakes as offerings, they then ate them. The ceremony was, perhaps, an adaptation of the harvest festival of Ceres, known as the Thesmophoria; or, possibly, of the *mizd*, or round wafer used in the worship of Mithras.[2] This last is the prototype of the

[1] Matt. xiii. 56.
[2] From the Paganised Christian point of view this would, of course, be a transfer of the Lord's Supper to the worship of Mary.

host, and the origin of the Roman Catholic term *missa*, the mass.

Of course so open a deification of the Lord's human mother was not carried on without considerable opposition. It was, however, defended with fanatical violence by Epiphanius, Bishop of the Cyprian Salamis, who invented a name for the opponents of his idolatry, calling them Antidicomarianites or "Adversaries of Mary."

Among those who objected to the new goddess was one Helvidius, a lawyer of Rome. This man, shocked by Jerome's extravagant praises of celibacy, undertook to confute the obnoxious views, and, in the course of his argument, maintained that, after the birth of the Lord, Mary had become a wife and the mother of children.

To this statement Jerome, who was greatly the superior of Helvidius in learning and dialectics, and who either disliked or distrusted the theory of Joseph's previous marriage, replied that the brethren of the Lord were not the sons of His mother, but merely His cousins. The spirit in which he put forth this opinion may be gathered from his boast that he claimed virginity, not for Mary only, but also for Joseph. The argument by which he supported it is a worthless tissue of errors, and may be stated as follows:—

In the list of the Twelve there are two apostles bearing the name of James. And we also read of James the Lord's brother.

This last must, however, have been one of the Twelve, or, otherwise, there would have been three persons of the same name.

And in such a case how could one of them be called

"James the less," a term which implies that there was but one other?

Moreover, in writing to the Galatians Paul narrates, "But other of the apostles saw I none, save James the Lord's brother,"[1] thus classing the latter with the Twelve.

This argument, the basis of Jerome's whole theory, may be disposed of without much trouble.

For such an expression as "James the less" is not to be found in the original of the New Testament: the apostle is called "James the little"—ὁ μικρός.[2]

And the words of Paul may be rendered, "I saw no other apostle—that is, no other save Peter who has just been mentioned—but only James, the Lord's brother. Moreover, even if we admit that this James was an apostle, it by no means follows that he was one of the Twelve. For the title was conferred upon others also, as for instance upon Barnabas.[3] Indeed in one passage Paul appears to distinguish between "the Twelve" and "all the apostles."[4]

Such, then, was the false foundation upon which Jerome was content to build the subjoined theory.

Since James the Lord's brother is mentioned after the death of James the son of Zebedee, he must be identified with James the son of Alphæus.

Now the latter had a brother named Joses, and, in the Gospels of Matthew and Mark,[5] there is record of a Mary the mother of James and Joses being present at the crucifixion. She must, therefore, have been the wife of Alphæus.

[1] Gal. i. 19.
[2] Mark xv. 40.
[3] See Acts xiv. 4, 14.
[4] 1 Cor. xv. 5, 7.
[5] Matt. xxvii. 56; Mark xv. 40.

But in the fourth Gospel, in place of the mother of James and Joses we read of a Mary of Clopas, the sister of the Lord's mother, standing by the cross.[1] This must, therefore, be the same as the wife of Alphæus,[2] who is thus proved to be the sister of the Lord's mother.

Hence her children were His cousins, and they are called His brethren merely because that term is often applied to any near relations.

This elaborate superstructure is as worthless as its foundation, and a single fact will suffice to prove our assertion. James the Lord's brother *could* not have been the son of Alphæus, for the latter was one of the Twelve; whereas of the Lord's brethren we are told, without reserve, that they did not believe on Him.[3] But although there is no necessity for further discussion, we will, nevertheless, add one or two remarks which will help the reader to a still clearer view of the standing of Jerome as a teacher.

And, first, Mary the wife of Clopas is not to be identified with the sister of the Lord's mother. For the passage in John should be read as follows:—"Now there stood by the cross of Jesus His mother and His mother's sister, Mary the wife of Clopas and Mary Magdalene." Not three only, but four women are mentioned, and they are arranged in couples, just as the apostles are in lists of the Twelve.[4] And by so understanding the passage, we avoid an absurdity: for, according to Jerome, both the Lord's mother and

---

[1] John xix. 25.
[2] The two names Clopas and Alphæus might be identified, since both forms could be derived from the same Aramæan original. Jerome was not, however, aware of this fact.
[3] John vii. 5.   [4] Matt. x. 2-4; Luke vi. 14-16.

her sister must have borne the same name of Mary. Indeed, some supporters of his theory are bold enough to affirm that the Jews frequently gave the same name to sisters; but, so far as we are aware, they offer no evidence of the prevalence of so irrational a custom.

The argument from the names James and Joses is also valueless; since there were but few names in common use among the Jews at that time, as indeed we might gather from the frequent recurrence of certain appellations in the New Testament. Hence it is probable that many women in Judea might have been called mothers of James and Joses.

Lastly; the assertion that "cousins" may be styled "brothers" is scarcely true, in an absolute sense at least. The instances adduced by Jerome[1] occur in affectionate or rhetorical appeals: he is unable to cite any from plain matter of fact history such as that of the Gospels. His theory is rendered still more improbable by the mention of the Lord's sisters, and there is yet another difficulty. If the "brethren" were the cousins of the Lord, why are they found in continual attendance upon His mother while their own parent was still alive? It could not have been from any feeling of veneration on account of her Son; for in Him they did not believe.

Such, then, is Jerome's attempted explanation, the most remarkable fact in connection with which is that learned men should ever have admitted so faulty and preposterous a theory within the range of their theology. Its author was less tenacious of it than some of his disciples; and in the Epistle to Hedibia, which belongs to his later years, he evinces a complete change of

[1] Gen. xiii. 8; xxix. 15.

mind by disowning the identification of the mother of James and Joses with the sister of Mary. Since this is the citadel of his position, it is clear that he must have discovered its untenableness, and so have deliberately abandoned it.

Bishop Lightfoot, in the essay appended to his Commentary on the Epistle to the Galatians, decides peremptorily against Jerome; but, after wavering between the literal theory and that of the half-brothers, finally inclines, like Hilary of Poitiers, to the latter for the subjoined reason. He conceives it to be impossible that our Lord, when on the cross, "would have snapped asunder the most sacred ties of natural affection" by commending His mother to the care of John if she had had four sons of her own living at the time.

But while it is always dangerous to substitute our own theories for the plain and literal sense of Scripture, there is in this case no reason whatever for such a course. Provided we be content to waive tradition and hold to revelation, the alleged difficulty may be very easily removed.

In the single passage of the Gospels in which our Lord's brethren appear without their mother,[1] they display a strong spirit of opposition, and we are told that they did not believe on Him. Hence the reason why the mother is no longer with them: she had kept the sayings of Jesus in her heart, and, therefore, had faith to follow Him to the cross; she had once attempted to interfere with His actions, and had learnt her lesson from the rebuke which she received.[2]

[1] John vii. 3, 9.
[2] Thus our latest glimpse of the brethren, before the crucifixion,

But if the brethren were unbelievers, and were even then angry with the Lord because He refused to seek popularity, what must have been their feelings as they saw His ministry becoming more and more opposed to the prejudices of their nation, and perceived that the consequent hatred to His person was increasing every day? Is it not more than probable that their growing dislike to Him, now heightened by the fear of family disgrace, would alienate them from His mother who persisted in her faith? And thus, neglected by her own sons in her time of deepest trouble, she would be in sore need of temporary protection, which the Lord graciously provided.

So far there is surely no difficulty; but at this point tradition steps in and adds a story, opposed to all reasonable inference from Scripture, that Mary remained under the protection of the apostle John for the rest of her life. There can be no doubt that this is a pure fiction devised to support the theory of her virginity; for the Bible plainly indicates that she returned to her sons after their conversion.[1]

The tender heart of the Lord yearned for His brethren in the flesh, and, accordingly, after He had appeared in His resurrected body to Peter, to the Twelve, and to the five hundred brethren, He presented Himself to his brother James. Who can doubt the effect of the glorious sight? The eyes of James were opened, and he beheld no longer the carpenter's son of Nazareth, the executed malefactor, but the Con-

reveals them separated for the first time from their mother and casting reproaches upon the Lord; whereas at the cross the mother is seen deserted by her sons. It is impossible to deny the significance of such a fact.

[1] Acts i. 14.

queror of Death, the Lord of all power, the only begotten Son of the Father. By his testimony, or, it may be, by special revelations to themselves, the other brethren were also converted before the Lord left the confines of earth.

We can readily understand how such a change of mind would affect them in regard to their neglected mother, who seems to have been at once removed from the temporary protection of John to the loving care of her own family. And so it happens that in the list of those who continued in prayer in the upper room, waiting for the promised power from on high, we find the mother of Jesus and His now believing brethren again united.[1]

VIII.

THE RETURN OF THE JEWS TO PALESTINE.

SUCH, then, is the outline of God's dealings with the Jews, as it was revealed to Daniel. For four hundred and eighty-three years His Spirit strove with them in their own land, and, at the close of that appointed time, Messiah the Prince appeared, and they rejected Him. He came unto His own, and His own received Him not. Then He also rejected them, and cast them out to endure the curse uttered by Moses.

Anon they will return, and place themselves under the protection of the last head of the Fourth Gentile Empire. And when he makes his covenant with them, then may the world and Satan know that but seven short years remain for the indulgence of unbridled sin. At that time the great body of the nation will be in

[1] Acts i. 14.

THE RETURN OF THE JEWS TO PALESTINE. 237

unbelief, and will, therefore, share in the madness of the world, and wonder after and worship the Beast. And of the small number who do fear Jehovah, few, if any, will know the Lord Jesus as the Lamb of God, however they may recognise Him as their Messiah and King; for, according to Zechariah, neither the house of David, nor the inhabitants of Jerusalem, will find out the fountain that is opened for sin and for uncleanness, until they have actually beheld the face of Him Whom they pierced.[1]

That they will rebuild the Temple is implied, as we have already seen, in the eighth and ninth chapters of Daniel, and so it is also in the sixty-sixth of Isaiah. But the latter passage reveals to us the spirit in which the restored exiles will undertake the work, and the Lord's indignant rejection of that which is done by proud and self-willed sinners, who choose their own ways, and know nothing of the broken and contrite heart in which alone He delights.

At the same time there is a recognition of some few who will tremble at the word of the Lord, and whose brethren will hate them and cast them out for His name's sake, while they hypocritically say;—"Let the Lord be glorified." These afflicted ones are strengthened for their brief trial by the significant words;—"But He shall appear to your joy, and they shall be ashamed."[2]

When the Temple has been thus erected by the unsuspecting Jews, all will be ready for the fearful scenes which are to close the dispensation, and which are especially foretold in the sermon on the Mount of Olives, and in some of the chapters of the Apocalypse.

[1] Zech. xii. 9—xiii. 1.   [2] Isa. lxvi. 5.

And with a brief comment on the first of these prophecies, or rather, on that part of it which concerns our subject, we will conclude what we have to say respecting Hebrew predictions.

IX.

THE SERMON ON THE MOUNT OF OLIVES.

CAREFUL readers will have noticed considerable variation in the reports of this memorable discourse as given by Matthew and Luke. Such differences are, however, perplexing only at first view: to those who can search out their meaning, they are not merely intelligible, but deeply instructive; for we have but to keep in mind the main object of each Evangelist, and all will be clear. Now Matthew wrote his Gospel especially for Jews, and to set forth the Lord Jesus as their King; while Luke points out Christ as the Son of man, and is the Evangelist of all converts who, being in Christ, are neither Jews nor Greeks.

Many traces of these diverse aims may be discovered. For instance, the object of the genealogy in Matthew is to prove our Lord's title to the crown of Israel. It, therefore, first shows Him to be a genuine son of Abraham, the father of the nation; and then gives His official pedigree, exhibiting the successive heirs to the crown from David to Christ. But Luke, in placing Him before us as the Son of man, unfolds His natural descent, and that, too, from Adam, the common parent of all men.[1]

[1] This consideration, together with two others, will be found to explain all the apparent discrepancies in the genealogies of Matthew and Luke, which, it must be remembered, are both

Again: our Lord's description of the evil spirit going out of a man is in Matthew concluded with the special application, "Even so shall it be also unto this wicked generation." For, as the context itself shows, it is there to be taken as a prophecy of the Jewish people. But Luke gives an entirely different context,

expressly said to be pedigrees of Joseph. See Matt. i. 16, and Luke iii. 23. The other two points are—(1) that, if a man's direct line became extinct, the Jews were accustomed to enter his heir upon the record as his son; and (2) that they were in the habit of abbreviating genealogies by the simple process of striking out names; so that a man would often appear as the son of an ancestor who had died a century or more before he was born.

Keeping these facts in mind, we will glance at the lists of the two Evangelists, which, although they agree from Abraham to David, are entirely different from David to Jeconiah. The reason is, however, very simple. David was succeeded by Solomon, whose line occupied the throne until it became extinct in the childless Jeconiah (Jer. xxii. 30). Then the right of the succession passed over to the family of Nathan—another Son of David, from whom our Lord was actually descended—and Salathiel, the son of Neri, became heir to the throne, and, according to Jewish custom, was transferred to the royal genealogical tables as "the son of Jeconiah." After Jeconiah the lists appear to coincide for four generations: for each of them has Salathiel and Zorobabel; Rhesa (רֵישָׁא=the prince) is merely a title of Zorobabel, which seems to have slipped into the text from the margin; Joanna is omitted by Matthew, according to the practice mentioned above; and Abiud and Juda are identical. Abiud had two sons, Eliakim and Joseph. The line of the former ceased with Eleazer, and, consequently, Matthat, of the house of Joseph, became heir to the crown. Matthat had two sons, Jacob and Heli. Jacob died without issue—or, at least, without male issue; for it is very probable that Mary was his daughter—and so Joseph, the son of his younger brother, Heli, became his heir, and was placed on the official genealogy as "the son of Jacob."

It may easily be proved that names are omitted from the record by Matthew in order to square the numbers, and this is a sufficient explanation of the fact that he only mentions twenty-eight generations from David to Christ, while Luke has forty-two. If Mary was Joseph's cousin, married by him, according to Jewish custom, because he was his uncle's heir, the genealogies will of course belong to her as much as to her husband.

and omits the concluding words, because in his Gospel the warning is written for general and individual application.

It is just so with regard to the prophecy on the Mount of Olives. Whatever may be our historical exegesis, the fact remains that the Lord has spoken through the two Evangelists with special reference to two distinct bodies of His people respectively. Matthew writes to convince Jews, and for those unready believers who will have to share much the same fate as Jews by continuing on the earth during the last Week. Therefore, he follows the usual line of Jewish prophecy—that is, he notices very briefly the course of events till the destruction of Jerusalem by Titus; and then, passing over the long interval in silence, concentrates our attention upon the last Seven Years, when God will again resume His dealings with His people and their holy city. And, consequently, his warnings and directions apply, not to the siege by Titus, but to the far graver woes of the future, when all nations shall be gathered against Jerusalem to battle.[1]

On the other hand, Luke is writing for believers, who might indeed be concerned in the siege by Titus, but who ought to be standing before the Son of man when Antichrist is revealed, and, consequently, require to know but little of the last Week.

In his Gospel the question put to our Lord is simply, When shall this Temple, upon which we are now gazing, be destroyed; and what shall be the signs accompanying its destruction? Therefore his report of the answer enters into particulars of the times

[1] Zech. xiv. 2.

immediately following the ascension, and speaks of the temptations, persecutions, and sorrows, which believers would then have to endure; nor does he forget to note that the *synagogue* would be a principal cause of their trouble.[1] He also gives them a sign by which they might know when to leave Jerusalem, and so escape the horrors of her supreme agony.[2] Then he

[1] Luke xxi. 12. Compare Matt. xxiv. 9.
[2] Luke xxi. 20, 21. The sign was, "When ye see Jerusalem compassed with armies, then know that her desolation is at hand"; and most clearly was it set before them at the critical time, as we may learn from Josephus (Bell. Jud. ii. cap. xix.). For Cestius Gallus surrounded the city in the autumn of A.D. 66, and on the sixth day succeeded in undermining the Temple, had all but taken it, and so alarmed the Jews that a large number of them were preparing to open their gates. At this crisis he suddenly recalled his soldiers from the place, and retired, as Josephus says, "without any reason in the world." "Had he," the historian remarks, "but continued the siege a little longer, he had certainly taken the city; but it was, I suppose, owing to the aversion God had already to the city and the Sanctuary, that he was hindered from putting an end to the war that very day." This may have been one reason, but there was also another, and the Christians recognized the sign which the Lord had given them: they had seen Jerusalem compassed with armies. And with the signal for flight came also its opportunity. In ordinary circumstances the insurgents at Jerusalem would never have permitted the departure of a numerous body of Christians; but the retreat of Cestius so raised their courage, and inflamed them with such ardour, that they poured out of the gates of the city, pursued their enemies vigorously for more than forty miles on the road to Cæsarea, slew five or six thousand of them, and had almost effected a capture of the whole Roman army. While Jerusalem was thus emptied of its leading spirits, the Christians seem to have quietly fled in the opposite direction, towards the Jordan, and so made good their escape.

It is worthy of notice that, while the sign promised in Luke was so plainly given before the legions of Titus closed in upon the devoted city, the same cannot be said of that which is mentioned in Matthew. For the idea that the Roman eagles, and not the image of the Beast, are "the Abomination of Desolation," is untenable; and if it were not so, the Roman eagles never stood in the Holy Place—that is, in the Temple.

describes the days of vengeance in which she should be destroyed, and adds that from thenceforth she should be trodden down of the Gentiles, until the times of the Gentiles should be fulfilled. The close of this long period should be announced by signs in the sun and in the moon, and by convulsions of nature and distress of nations upon the earth; and then the Son of Man should come with power and great glory.

Nothing could be clearer, or more easy of comprehension, than the grand utterance of the Lord as thus presented to us; but since we are considering the future of the Jewish nation, we are just now more nearly concerned with the account given by Matthew.

X.

THE TWENTY-FOURTH CHAPTER OF MATTHEW.

THE sermon on the Mount of Olives, as it appears in the Gospel of Matthew, is closely connected with the preceding chapter, the contents of which are, therefore, included in the question, "Tell us, when shall these things be?" We must understand the disciples to be asking, How shall the Jews fill up the measure of their fathers? When will prophets and wise men and scribes be sent, and be persecuted to the death? At what time will all the righteous blood shed upon the earth come upon this generation? When will the Temple be destroyed, and Jerusalem left desolate? And when will the people be willing to cry, "Blessed is He that cometh in the name of the Lord"? These questions are all Jewish; we may, therefore, be sure that the answer will also point to Jews.

But the disciples go on to ask, "And what shall be the sign of Thy presence, and of the end of the age?" Now the taking up of the Church will be the sign that Christ is present in the air; while His judgment of the living Gentile nations will be the closing act of the age. Hence the answer to the three questions involves the fate of the Jews, the Church, and the Gentiles, respectively; and the Lord accordingly proceeds to unfold the manner in which the present state of things will end to each of these three great divisions of the world.[1]

Beginning with the Jews, He shows, in response to the first question, that these things shall not be finally accomplished until the last Week, just before His appearing;[2] and adds that, when He appears, He will send forth His angels to gather together His elect of the Jews.[3]

We will, then, attempt a slight sketch of this part

---

[1] The whole discourse may be simply divided into three parts, corresponding to the three questions asked by the disciples. The first part (xxiv. 4-35) concerns the Jews, and answers the question, "When shall these things be?" The second (xxiv. 36—xxv. 30) discloses the sign which will make known the presence of Christ in the air; and since it is to be the sudden removal of those who are looking for Him, He adds some instructions and warnings respecting this solemn subject. The concluding section (xxv. 31—46) is a response to the inquiry, "What will be the sign of the consummation of the age?" And the Lord replies that His last act in regard to it will be the judgment of the quick, of those nations which, being without the circle of Christendom, have not heard His fame nor seen His glory (Isa. lxvi. 19), and which will, therefore, be judged with regard to the way in which they have obeyed the law of mercy written upon their hearts in their treatment of the dispersed Jews.

[2] Matt. xxiv. 4-30.

[3] Matt. xxiv. 31. The remnant of the Church will have been previously removed at the sounding of the Seventh Trumpet. On this subject the reader will find a chapter in Part III.

of our Lord's discourse, which wholly belongs to our present subject.

The first words, to the close of the sixth verse, refer to the immediate future. There would shortly be events and signs and troubles in connection with Judæa, similar, on a small scale, to those which shall precede the close of the age. False Christs would arise—and we have historical proof that this was the case—and would deceive many, though they would be unable to support their pretensions by miraculous power, such as Antichrist and the False Prophet will exhibit hereafter. Again, there would be wars and rumours of wars in Judæa, commotions which would result in the destruction of Jerusalem and the Temple. Nevertheless, the disciples were not to be troubled; for all these things must come to pass, but the end would not be yet.

By the significant words, "the end is not yet," the Lord indicates the interval so invariably marked in Jewish prophecy, and then passes on to the Seventieth Week. He had spoken of the signs which would make some think that the end had come, when God's purpose was merely the dispersion of the Jews, that they might undergo a long sifting among the nations: now He reveals what will be the beginning of the actual end,[1] the throes or birth-pangs—for so the

---

[1] The following paraphrase may, perhaps, explain the connecting force of "for" at the commencement of the seventh verse. "These disturbances, caused by false Messiahs in Judæa and local wars and troubles, must happen, but will not be signs of the end; *for* before that can come there must be general wars and famines, pestilences and earthquakes in many quarters of the world. Such will be the character of the events which will herald the time of the end."

word translated "sorrows" should be rendered—of earth just before the appearing of the King.[1]

At this time the Jews will, of course, be again in possession of their own land, having been restored, it may be, by Antichrist, or, perhaps, by some other power. Or, possibly, they will return gradually, and fill their country as they are driven out from among the nations by a hatred which seems to have already commenced in Russia, Germany, Austria, the independent States between Russia and Turkey, Italy, and along the north coast of Africa. But by whatever means they re-occupy Palestine, they will certainly be found there at the commencement of the last Week, and will be in league with Antichrist by the provisions of the seven years' covenant. Then the signs foretold by the Lord will begin to appear, following each other in rapid succession.

The first birth-pang is war; but war universal, and no longer local: for "nation shall rise against nation, and kingdom against kingdom."[2] This corresponds to the opening of the second seal in the Apocalypse, when the red horse went forth, "and power was given to him that sat thereon to take peace from the earth, and that they should kill one another; and there was given unto him a great sword."[3] While our Lord deals solely with the visible events, John appears to have seen the spiritual agency which will cause them. And who that considers the present state of the world, teeming as it is with ever-increasing hosts of armed millions, can fail to see on all sides a preparation for this beginning of sorrows?

The second sign will manifest itself in local famines.

[1] Matt. xxiv. 8. [2] Matt. xxiv. 7. [3] Rev. vi. 4.

This corresponds to the black horse of the third seal, whose rider causes scarcity in the necessaries of life, the wheat and the barley; but not in its luxuries, the oil and the wine.[1] Do we not seem to have already had a rehearsal of this sorrow in the late severe famines in various parts of the world—famines which have impoverished many countries, and rendered them less able to face the severer troubles which may be close at hand?

The third sign is pestilence, which is also the woe inflicted by the rider on the livid horse, who appears when the fourth seal is broken, and whose name is Death.[2] This would most certainly be the result of universal war and local famines: and indeed all these earlier throes are troubles which have frequently occurred in the world's previous history; but they will shortly be repeated with unusual and appalling severity.

Then follow earthquakes, the most terrible of which will doubtless be the great shock at the opening of the sixth seal.[3] The increasing frequency and ubiquity of earthquakes during the last few years must have been noticed by every one. And although thus far the majority of the shocks have been comparatively slight,[4] yet their great number has caused many to suppose that we are entering on a period of terrestrial commotion, a time, possibly, of terrific physical con-

[1] Rev. vi. 5, 6.
[2] Rev. vi. 7, 8.
[3] Rev. vi. 12.
[4] We have remarked in a previous note that this was written before the occurrence of the earthquakes at Agram, Casamicciola, Chios, Ischia, Java, Colchester, and Andalusia. For the Scriptural theory of earthquakes, see Moses' description of the subterranean fire kindled in God's anger (Deut. xxxii. 22).

vulsions similar to those which by their traces seem to have ended some of the geological ages.

The succeeding verses, to the end of the thirteenth, describe to us the condition of God's people during these times of wrath and trouble. Probably the faithful Jews, who will be afflicted and killed by their own people, and hated of all nations, will be, in great part, those who have been roused by the preaching of the Two Witnesses; and if so, this would account for their persecution. For the world will regard the Witnesses as its tormentors, and, in its anger and excitement against them, will be likely to show but little love to their followers.

This persecution is doubtless the same as that which is indicated at the opening of the fifth seal.[1] And the martyrs there mentioned are clearly distinguished as belonging to the last Week, and not to the present time: for, in the spirit of the old dispensation, they cry for vengeance, a thing which no Christian of this age may dare to do.

The effects of the persecution will not, however, be confined to the true worshippers; it will also bring the whole Jewish nation to the test. Those who are not sincere will be offended by it, and will hate and betray their faithful relations and friends: for to this time belongs the counsel of Micah;—"Trust ye not in a friend, put ye not confidence in a guide: keep the doors of thy mouth from her that lieth in thy bosom."[2]

And in the midst of the prevailing excitement, while the pure worship of Jehovah is hated, many false prophets will arise, and by their lying suggestions lead

[1] Rev. vi. 9-11.   [2] Micah vii. 5.

multitudes astray. Nor will this be all: for, owing to the dreadful immorality and lawlessness which will everywhere abound, the love of many, who bid fair to run well, will gradually lose its light and warmth, and grow cold even as that of other men. These, however, will not be the elect: for only he who is enabled to withstand all the trials and temptations, and to endure till the end, shall be saved.

But by what means will faith be nourished and strengthened during this time of terror, so that it shall finally overcome? Evidently in that way in which it always is both manifested and sustained, by works. If any man have not the Spirit of Christ he is none of His; but he that is joined unto the Lord is one Spirit, and is, therefore, constrained, in however humble a way, to co-operate with his Saviour in letting the new light which is placed in him shine before men, and in offering salvation to the world. That which avails is the faith which worketh by love, and the command to all believers is, "Ye are My witnesses, saith the Lord."

Accordingly, in the present passage, the mention of those who shall endure to the end, and be saved, is at once followed by an account of their work. "This Gospel of the Kingdom shall be preached in all the world, for a witness unto all nations." What zeal and energy, what a spending and being spent, do these words imply! But the servants of Christ will all learn to be earnest when they know by the promised sign that He has come out of His place, that His presence is an actual fact, that human society has assumed its last form of evil, and that the pillars of the world are trembling for their fall. Happy are those who, through the favour of the Lord, will not require the stimulus of that fearful time, but whose simple faith is sufficient to rouse them from sloth, so that they shall be accounted worthy to escape all the things that shall come to pass, and to stand before the Son of Man. To them in a special sense do those words apply;—" Blessed are they that have not seen, and yet have believed."

The Gospel of the Kingdom is not, of course, the same as the Gospel of grace; for, while the latter is the good news that Christ Jesus has died for sinners, the former is the glad tidings that His Kingdom of peace and joy is just about to be manifested upon earth, so that His servants will no longer need to pray, "Thy Kingdom come." Such a Gospel could, therefore, be preached only on the eve of the Lord's appearing.

But not even this thrilling proclamation will draw men to God. It will, indeed, be made known throughout the habitable, or at least the civilized, world; but will for the most part serve only as a witness to the nations, and vindicate God's righteousness in the judgments which must immediately follow.

Possibly the Two Witnesses will be the leaders of this preaching; and, from the next sentence of our Lord's discourse, it seems not unlikely that Antichrist will strive to wrest it to his own advantage by giving out that he is the great King Who is to sit on the throne of His father David.

For the Lord seems to suggest some such connection by immediately passing on to speak of the setting up of the Abomination of Desolation in the Holy Place. The meaning of these terms is readily discovered by

Hebrew usage: for the Jew recognized no holy place save the Temple;[1] and the word "abomination" was commonly used to signify an idol, or false god.[2] And in regard to their application, the Lord bids us search the writings of Daniel the prophet, who has thrice spoken of "the Abomination of Desolation," or "Abomination that causeth desolation."

In his eleventh chapter,[3] it had been declared that "the Abomination that maketh desolate" should be set up in the Sanctuary by Antiochus Epiphanes, and the fulfilment of the prophecy may be found in the first book of Maccabees,[4] and in the history of Josephus.[5] For Antiochus himself entered into the Sanctuary, and, after carrying away the sacred furniture and treasures, built an idol altar upon the altar of God—doubtless setting up the idol also in its proper place—and sacrificed swine upon it. This gives us a hint of what the future Abomination of Desolation will be.

Whose image will then be set up we may learn from the second passage of Daniel, which we have already considered, and in which it is said of Antichrist, that "upon the wing of abominations shall be the Desolator."[6]

Lastly, in the twelfth chapter,[7] the taking away of the daily sacrifice, and the setting up of the Abomination that maketh desolate, are mentioned as marking the commencement of the Great Tribulation.

Subsequent utterances of Paul and John throw a stronger light upon our Lord's words, and confirm

---

[1] Acts vi. 13; xxi. 28.
[2] 1 Kings xi. 5-7; 2 Kings xxiii. 13.
[3] Dan. xi. 31.
[4] 1 Macc. i. 54.
[5] Joseph. Antiq. xii. 5. 4.
[6] Dan. ix. 27. See pp. 206-7.
[7] Dan. xii. 11.

their allusion to the placing of the image of the Beast in the Temple, to the middle of the last Week, when the Lawless One shall cause the sacrifice and oblation to cease, and publicly deny the Father and the Son by exalting himself "above all that is called God, or that is worshipped; so that he, as God, sitteth in the Temple of God, showing himself that he is God."[1]

It is possible, as we have already remarked, that this new era will be inaugurated by a travesty of the return of the Cherubim as foretold by Ezekiel, and that the prophecy in the ninth of Daniel refers to the blasphemous scene. If so, the pretended descent from heaven would explain the fact that the sign will be seen from the housetops and the fields.

But, however this may be, the people of God who are in the neighbourhood of Jerusalem will be able to recognize the signal, and will know that it is a warning to betake themselves to instant flight. For an imperial edict will be quickly issued, compelling all men on pain of death to worship the Beast and his image. And this will be Satan's scheme for the destruction of the elect, the Dragon's endeavour to devour the Woman, after her Child has been transported far beyond his reach.

Without a moment's delay, then, all those inhabitants of Judæa who are at the time guided by God's word must fly in circumstances of great anxiety and suffering. Woe to the pregnant, and to the mother with infant in arms! Yet the distress may be mitigated if those who are to endure it will only pray before the time come. And this the Lord exhorts them to do, that their troubles may be aggravated, neither by natural causes,

[1] 2 Thess. ii. 4.

nor by human arrangements. They are directed to entreat that their flight may not be in the winter; for then the days would be short, the weather inclement, the ground, on which they must often lie, damp and cold, and they would find no food either upon the trees or in the fields. They must pray, too, that it may not be on the Sabbath day; for, if it were, they could not, as conscientious but unenlightened Jews, travel more than the Sabbath day's journey, and would, therefore, certainly be overtaken. For they will doubtless be pursued; the figure of the Dragon casting out of his mouth, after the Woman, water as a river, would seem to indicate an expedition sent forth in hot haste. And, possibly, what follows, the earth helping the Woman by opening its mouth and swallowing up the river, may point to the destruction of the pursuing column by an earthquake, just, perhaps, as they are in sight of their intended victims.

This flight will be the commencement of the Great Tribulation, in which judgment must begin at the house of God, and will then fall upon the renegade Jews, who have consented to worship the Beast and his image, and upon the world. It is described as "great tribulation, such as was not since the beginning of the world to this time, no, nor ever shall be." These words show that there can be but one such time of distress; therefore, it must be the same as that which is also mentioned in the last chapter of Daniel, where the prophet says;—"There shall be a time of trouble such as never was since there was a nation even to that same time; and at that time thy people shall be delivered, every one that shall be found written in the book."[1]

[1] Dan. xii. 1.

Since, then, both the prophet and the evangelist must be speaking of the same tribulation, the latter clause of the verse from Daniel proves that we are right in referring the passage under our consideration to the times of Antichrist, and not to the overthrow of Jerusalem by Titus. For the prophet adds, "And at that time thy people shall be delivered," a statement which would be notoriously untrue were we to apply the prophecy to the past siege, but which exactly agrees with what Zechariah tells us of that which is still to come.

And it is remarkable that Luke, in describing the trouble of the immediate future, avoids the stronger expressions of Matthew and Daniel, and merely says, "There shall be great distress upon the land, and wrath unto this people."[1] For the tribulation of which he speaks, though great, was not unparalleled, and was only local; but this which is to come will be universal, and more terrible than any which ever has been, or ever shall be; so that, unless its days should be shortened, no flesh would be saved. Its details may be found in many a passage of the prophets and in the Apocalypse, and should be carefully studied, that we may learn what shall be the end of this present age and all who cast in their lot with it.

In times of distress which baffle their own powers of foresight and calculation, men have ever been prone to turn to the supernatural. It was so with the polished Athenians, and other Greeks, at the commencement of the Peloponnesian war, when, as Thucydides tells us;—

"Many prophecies were being continually repeated,

[1] Luke xxi. 23

and oracle-mongers ceased not to recite them, both in those states which were on the point of engaging in war and in the others."[1]

And so, in our own days of uncertainty, perplexity, and fear, when all old faiths are disappearing, and not merely one kingdom, but the whole world is filled with rumours of war, and seems to be on the eve of a revolutionary explosion, the result of which no one can forecast—at this time of excitement, a craving for the supernatural is once more returning in the forms of Spiritualism and Theosophy, and in the revival of what was supposed to be an ancient superstition, the art of astrology.[2]

These movements will probably continue to spread and extend their influence, and from the twenty-fourth verse we find that they will powerfully affect the Jews in the Great Tribulation, when their minds have become excited by the general distress, the strange plagues, and the fear of what may be coming next.[3] Perhaps, too, they will by that time have begun to distrust the prince with whom they made their covenant, and to

---

[1] Thuc. ii. 8.

[2] There are at the present time millions of Spiritualists who, with the aid of a copious literature, are everywhere influencing society, and preparing it for the leadership of an avowed spirit from the dead. Of their apostasy, important as it is, but little is said in this volume, since it is very fully discussed in another of the author's works, "Earth's Earliest Ages, and Their Connection with Modern Spiritualism and Theosophy," published by Messrs. Hodder and Stoughton. As to astrologers, letters from and concerning them frequently appear in the daily newspapers, and Zadkiel is fast becoming an authority.

[3] Hence we may understand the meaning of Zech. xiii. 2;—"And it shall come to pass in that day, saith the Lord of Hosts, that I will cut off the names of the idols out of the land, and they shall no more be remembered; and also I will cause the prophets and the unclean spirit to pass out of the land."

feel his tyrannous oppression. And so they will be longing for deliverance; not, however, in a spirit of meekness and submission toward God, but that they may be avenged of their enemies, and be exalted in the world. Satan will not fail to take advantage of this temper, and will raise up false Messiahs to deceive still further the miserable people who would not have the Lord Jesus to reign over them.

But there will be a notable difference between the false Christs of the last days and those which clustered around the first advent. The latter were supported only by their own testimony, and could display no supernatural marvels; but the former will have their prophets to testify to them, be filled with Satanic power, and show forth great signs and wonders; so great, indeed, that, were it not for the special grace of God, the very elect themselves would be deceived.

Their adherents will be vigorous in their endeavours to make disciples, and will be continually saying, "Christ is in the wilderness," or, "He is in the chambers"; that is, He is in the solitary wastes, in the secret places far away from the haunts of men; or, He is hidden somewhere in the great cities where only His disciples may see Him. But neither of these statements can ever be true of the Lord Jesus. For instead of appearing in secret to a few, the manifestation of His presence will be as the lightning flash which in a moment sweeps the heavens from East to West. Nor will He seek the desert places; but wherever the great crowd of them which are corrupting the earth is to be found, thither will He descend with the ministers of His vengeance, even as the eagles swoop down from the sky upon the fallen carcase.

Immediately following upon the Great Tribulation —toward the close of which, if not earlier, all nations will come up against Jerusalem and besiege it—there will be convulsions of nature premonitory of the approaching end. The sun, moon, and stars, hitherto used chiefly for light, and for seasons, and days, and years, will now be made to serve the first-mentioned purpose of their creation, and be for "signs" that the Lord is at hand.

The word "immediately" contrasts strongly with what follows the account of the days of trouble in Luke. There, after the destruction of Jerusalem, we are told that the holy city "shall be trodden down of the Gentiles, until the times of the Gentiles be fulfilled." And only at the close of these times, which have already continued for more than eighteen hundred years, will there be "signs in the sun, and in the moon, and in the stars." Even if there were no other proof that the Evangelists refer to different tribulations, this in itself would be decisive.

The sun, then, shall be darkened, the moon shall not give her light, the stars shall fall from heaven, and all the celestial machinery be deranged : and at this awful moment the sign of the Son of man will appear.[1] What this sign will be does not seem to be distinctly revealed ; nor is much light thrown upon the obscurity by the conjecture of a flaming cross, in which ancient and modern writers have delighted. Apparently our only Scriptural basis lies in the Lord's previous saying, that the manifestation of His presence will be as the lightning which flashes from the one end of heaven to the other. It may be that this will

[1] Matt. xxiv. 30

occur while men are horrified with the unnatural darkness, and that it will be caused by a sudden and momentary cleaving of the black heavens, so that the glory of the Lord will break through, and He will for an instant be revealed in close proximity to earth. Thus the Jew may at last receive his sign from heaven.

That which follows, and which should be rendered, "Then shall all the tribes of the land mourn," points to the connection of this verse with Zechariah's prophecy;—"And I will pour upon the house of David, and upon the inhabitants of Jerusalem, the spirit of grace and of supplications: and they shall look upon Me Whom they have pierced, and they shall mourn for Him, as one mourneth for his only son, and shall be in bitterness for Him, as one that is in bitterness for his firstborn."[1]

And again; the manner in which Zechariah's prophecy is quoted in the Apocalypse may, perhaps, afford some slight argument in favour of the explanation suggested above, that the sign of the Son of Man is Christ Himself seen for a moment through a rift in the clouds. For John says;—"Behold He cometh with the clouds: and every eye shall see Him, and they also which pierced Him: and all the tribes of the land shall mourn because of Him."[2]

Thus the Jews, although they may not as yet understand all, will at least know that it was the Messenger of Jehovah Whom they slew, and that in so doing they pierced Himself. And they will mourn with no feigned lamentation, but as one mourns for his firstborn, nay, his only son. All their pride will have

[1] Zech. xii. 10.   [2] Rev. i. 7.

broken down; for the word will then have been fulfilled, " I will take away out of the midst of thee them that rejoice in thy pride, and thou shalt no more be haughty because of My holy mountain. I will also leave in the midst of thee an afflicted and poor people, and they shall trust in the name of the Lord." [1]

And so God will look down upon the stiff-necked and rebellious people, whom long centuries of chastisement could not subdue, and lo! a remnant, broken-hearted and contrite, humbly confessing that they are all as an unclean thing, that all their righteousnesses are as filthy rags, that they are all fading as a leaf, and that their iniquities like the wind have carried them away. They long for the personal interposition of God their Father, and cry, "Oh that Thou wouldest rend the heavens, that Thou wouldest come down!" They are ready at last for their Messiah. Christ has become precious to them: there is no need that He should longer refrain Himself. He had indeed said, "Ye shall not see Me henceforth till yĕ shall say, Blessed is He that cometh in the name of the Lord." [2] But that word withholds Him no longer; for now their eyes are waiting for the Lord their God, until that He have mercy upon them: their souls are watching for Him more than they that watch for the morning. And, as we find from the last chapter of Zechariah, they are also in evil plight, and are all but swallowed up by their enemies.

At this crisis He will suddenly come forth from His pavilion of clouds, the whole earth will be lighted with His glory, and the sons of Abraham, looking up, will behold the despised Jesus of Nazareth descending

[1] Zeph. iii. 11, 12.   [2] Matt. xxiii. 39.

toward Jerusalem, with power and great glory, for the utter destruction of their enemies.

The manner in which He will preserve the Jews, while He is destroying the myriads of Antichrist, is foretold by the prophets. Isaiah gives a hint of it in the words, "Come, My people, enter thou into thy chambers, and shut thy doors about thee: hide thyself as it were for a little moment, until the indignation be overpast. For, behold, the Lord cometh out of His place to punish the inhabitants of the earth for their iniquity: the earth also shall disclose her blood, and shall no more cover her slain."[1] Zephaniah, again, says, "Seek ye the Lord, all ye meek of the land which have wrought His judgment; seek righteousness, seek meekness: it may be ye shall be hid in the day of the Lord's anger."[2] And by comparing Zech. xiv. 4, 5, with Mal. iv. 1-3, we may, perhaps, see what these mysterious utterances mean. For in the former passage we find that, when the Lord descends, the Mount of Olives will be cloven into two mountains with a very great valley between them, and that into the valley the Jews will flee with haste out of the all but captured city. Such will be the chamber, the hiding place in which they will be safely sheltered while the lightnings of the Lord are doing their work of destruction.[3] And at the close of this day, "which shall burn as an oven," they shall "go forth, and skip"—not "grow up," a meaning which does not belong to the Hebrew root—"as calves of the stall."[4] That is, just as calves come forth skipping with glee from the dark winter stalls into the pleasant meadows of

[1] Isa. xxvi. 20, 21.
[2] Zeph. ii. 3.
[3] Rev. xix. 20, 21.
[4] Mal. iv. 2.

spring, so shall the Jews issue from their gloomy shelter into the fair Millennial morning; the Sun of Righteousness will arise upon them with healing in His wings; and they will find the innumerable armies of the dreaded foe reduced to ashes beneath their feet.

So will He preserve the people that remain in the all but captured city. And then, with a great sound of a trumpet, He will send forth His angels, and they will gather to Him at Jerusalem the elect of Israel[1] from all places whither they have been scattered; and He will make Himself known to them, as Joseph made himself known to his brethren, forgive them, comfort them, and say;—" God sent Me before you to preserve you a posterity in the earth, and to save your lives by a great deliverance." [2]

It is probably at this time that the Throne of Glory will be set up, before which the angels will gather the nations for the judgment of the sheep and the goats, while the Lord's Jewish brethren stand by.

Then will follow the establishment of the Kingdom at Jerusalem, and the Lord's feast to all peoples on Mount Zion. And so at length the enemy and the avenger shall be stilled, and the great King shall rule in righteousness. The feverish dreams of men shall vanish; the restlessness, the strifes, the agonies, the universal suffering, of this age be over, and the glorious words realized, " The whole earth is at rest, and is quiet: they

---

[1] The elect will probably be those Israelites who will at the time have turned to Christ, so far as to be expecting Him as the Deliverer. Possibly the formation of this body has already commenced in the wonderful movement in South Russia, under Joseph Rabinowitch. But the scattered ones who are still alienated from Christ will be subsequently gathered and conveyed to their land by the Gentiles. See Isa. lxvi. 20.

[2] Gen. xlv. 7.

break forth into singing."[1] And in that day the Lord will destroy "the face of the covering cast over all people, and the veil that is spread over all nations. He will swallow up death in victory ; and the Lord God will wipe away tears from all faces ; and the rebuke of His people shall He take away from off all the earth : for the Lord hath spoken it."[2] And "the earth shall be full of the knowledge of the Lord, as the waters cover the sea."[3]

XI.

THE PRESENT CONDITION OF THE JEWISH NATION AND LAND.

SUCH, then, is a bare sketch of the line of prophecy which concerns the Jew up to the time when the Lord will restore the Kingdom to Israel. The design of this book, and the consequent need of brevity, forbid any reference to the interesting details in which the Scriptures abound; but we must add a few words on the present condition of the Jewish nation and land.

It is clear that the first great sign of the end must be the return of the exiles in considerable numbers to their own country, and the subsequent rebuilding of the Temple. Now this return has actually commenced, and various causes already in operation seem likely to favour it, some of which we propose to notice.

And, in the first place, we may mention that Jerusalem itself is gradually becoming a centre of civilization, and is assuming the appearance of a modern city : villas are being erected in its neighbourhood, and no

[1] Isa. xiv. 7. [2] Isa. xxv. 7, 8. [3] Isa. xi. 9.

less than three exclusively Jewish building societies have been for some time carrying on their work.

Again : during the last ten years the Jewish population has doubled itself, so that at the present time it outnumbers the remainder of the inhabitants. Such a condition of things has not previously been known in Jerusalem since its destruction by Hadrian.

Various causes have contributed to bring about this result, and seem likely to extend it. Among them are the following :

In 1840, at the request of Sir Moses Montefiore, the Sultan issued a firman for the relief of his Jewish subjects. After stating in the preface that the various accusations—such as that of sacrificing a human being to make use of his blood at the Passover—which were popularly brought against the Jews were pure calumnies, he declared that thenceforth the Israelitish nation should be protected and defended, and should possess the same advantages, and enjoy the same privileges, as the numerous other nations under his sway. Thus one great obstacle to the return of the Jews to Palestine was removed.

In 1867, the Turkish Government made an important concession in regard to their land laws, and gave permission to the subjects of foreign powers to purchase land in their own name. It is easy to see how favourable this change is, indirectly, to immigration, since any rich European Jew can now buy up property in Palestine, and let it as he chooses to families of his own nation. And not a few have availed themselves of the opportunity.

In 1874, Russia—in which vast empire there are between two and three millions of Jews—adopted the

German military system, so that all Hebrews became liable to service in the army. This was very distasteful to them; and about the same time they were subjected, especially in Poland, to divers persecutions, such as are frequently raised by the Greek Church. It is reported that, for these reasons, nearly the whole of the Jewish community has resolved to leave Russia, family by family, as each may be able to extricate itself; and certainly a steady emigration is continually going on, stimulated at intervals by fierce assaults and cruel outrages, from which the Government seems by no means anxious to protect its alien subjects. Many families have arrived in Palestine, to the great increase of the Hebrew population: others escaped to America, where they found the people strangely unwilling to receive them: still larger numbers have poured into Germany.

In the latter country, however, they find no ease, neither rest for the sole of their foot; but seem likely to be driven on to seek another home, and possibly even to cause the departure of their brethren who had previously settled there. For, within the last few years, the ancient hatred of the Jews has been revived in Germany, their wonderful prosperity and rapidly increasing power having excited jealousy and prejudice, and induced a persuasion that many of the ills of the country are to be referred to their presence in it. An agitation—commenced by Herr Stöcker, the court chaplain—was lately set on foot under the auspices, strange to say, of the Liberal party. It was taken up with enthusiasm by all ranks of society: vast meetings were held, and anti-Semitic associations formed throughout the country. The object of the agitators was to check the further immigration of foreign Jews, and to deprive those who were already resident of many of their civil rights, by excluding them from state or judicial office and from the legal and educational professions.

Just now there is a lull in the violence of the persecution, interrupted, however, now and then by local outbreaks, more especially in Russia and Austria. But unless the strong anti-Semitic feeling quickly subsides, all Jews will be compelled to leave the countries which we have mentioned; nor does it seem certain that they would find a welcome among other nations of Europe. A London newspaper recently remarked upon the matter as follows ;—

"This feeling is not, of course, expressed in the same crude manner among ourselves, nor in anything like the same measure; but we know from our own correspondence that it would be going too far to say that Englishmen themselves have got rid of it completely. . . . The truth undoubtedly is, that the Jews are more or less an object of jealousy in every country in Europe. The antagonism they excite is, no doubt, partly an antagonism of religion, yet more an antipathy of race; partly, also, it is the survival of an age far less humane and much more ignorant than our own. Mainly, however, it is due to the fact that during the present century they have made an extraordinarily rapid advance in enterprize and prosperity. On this point there is little exaggeration in the talk of their enemies. Even when trammelled by every kind of restriction, they were in some departments of commercial activity more than a match for their rivals; and since their emancipation they have vastly extended the scope of their energy. And why they should have done so is clear enough: they possess in a high degree the qualities which it was to be expected that centuries of oppression would develop—patience, tact, industry, and resource."[1]

Such is a competent opinion upon the state of European feeling toward the Jews. And Russia, Germany, and Austria, are not the only countries in which the sentiment has already ripened into open hostility; for the new states liberated by the Berlin Treaty are, doubtless through the influence of the Greek Church, showing a strong disposition to persecute the Hebrew race. This is no new feeling, as may be seen by a significant appeal from the Jews of Bucharest[2] which appeared, some time ago, in the *Jewish Chronicle*. The subjoined clauses are extracted.

"The troubles which the Jews of Roumania are compelled to suffer are well known to you. It is a land whose princes are like the wolves of the forest in their endeavours to annihilate the children of Israel. With fearful zeal they seek to persecute us; one day they pursue us under the name of religious enthusiasm, and on the morrow they abandon the cry which is so disgraceful to them. But then they conceal their hatred under the name of economy, alleging that the state of trade and the mercantile prospects of the country compel them to act oppressively to the Jews who absorb the substance of the Roumanians, and many other such excuses. Thus are we constantly and severely attacked, and our powers of endurance are exhausted. We have, therefore, resolved, after

[1] *St. James's Gazette*, Nov. 19th, 1880.
[2] Dated Aug. 20th, 1880.

mature deliberation, to leave the country. With this view we have formed ourselves into a Society for the Colonization of the Holy Land, consisting of a hundred families. Every one of the members is experienced in the work of cultivating the soil, and it is our intention to journey to Palestine to 'till the ground and to guard it.'"[1]

"God," says Mr. Friedländer,[2] "has sent a feeling of homelessness into the hearts of many thousands of Jews, and that feeling is spreading far and wide. The handful of well-to-do Jews in England and Germany will not admit it, but the fact remains all the same. Wherever the spirit of persecution is prevailing, there the Jews begin to think of Palestine as the only safe home which this world can give them. *The thought is a new one, and is forced upon them by very remarkable occurrences.* That America, open to all the world, should send back Jewish refugees from her shores is so extraordinary an experience that all intending emigrants are feeling themselves shut up to the one idea, that in order to found a new home they can go nowhere but to Palestine."

Even so: for who can withstand the will of the Almighty, or who shall change His purposes? And the set time for their fulfilment seems now to have come.

[1] I have never had the opportunity of speaking to Roumanians about their feelings in reference to the Jews. Though I would fain hope that they have some conscientious reasons for doing what they do, it is very hard to understand them. With a finesse worthy of a better cause, they pass law after law to deprive Jews in Roumania of the means of making a livelihood, and the result is ever-increasing emigration."—H. FRIEDLÄNDER, Oct. 15th, 1884.
[2] In his interesting report of Oct. 15th, 1884.

Just before the commencement of the anti-Semitic agitation in Germany, the Jews appeared to be comfortably settled in most parts of Europe, except Russia. Their wealth and influence were continually increasing: and, probably, their satisfaction and confidence in the future had never been so great since the destruction of Jerusalem. Their prevailing sentiment was well illustrated at the time by an article in the *Jewish Chronicle*, the writer of which made merry with the Christian idea of the destiny of his nation. He affirmed that they were far too much at home in the luxurious cities of Europe to think of returning to a barbarous Asiatic country, and quoted with approval the saying of a well-known Jew, who, when the prophecies of the restoration had been mentioned to him, replied ;—" Well, if we have to go back to Palestine, I know what I shall do. I shall petition his Judaic Majesty to send me as ambassador to Paris."

At last, then, the thought had arisen in the hearts of the children of Abraham, that they would forget their own land, and be as the nations; and at the same time the hour for God's interference was approaching.

A furious persecution was being arranged in Russia: the Jews perceived the rising of the storm, and intimations were conveyed to them from the highest minister of the Government, that, by paying a vast sum of money, they might avert it. They refused to do so, and a series of cruel outrages followed, involving great destruction of life and property, besides other sufferings of a terrible nature. And immediately afterwards the Germans, who had long been regarding with envy and anger the riches and influence of the Jews in Germany, also began to give open proof that their hatred of the devoted race had revived.

Could there be a more signal and literal fulfilment, in its first stage, of the vivid words of Ezekiel?

"And that which rises up in your mind shall not be at all, in that ye say, We will be as the nations, as the families of the countries, to serve wood and stone.

As I live, saith the Lord Jehovah, surely with a mighty hand, and with a stretched-out arm, and with fury poured out, will I rule over you.

And I will bring you out from the peoples, and will gather you out of the countries wherein ye are scattered, with a mighty hand, and with a stretched-out arm, and with fury poured out.

And I will bring you into the wilderness of the peoples, and there will I plead with you face to face."[1]

The last verse contains a terrible threat which may be now in process of fulfilment, but is not yet completely realised. We sometimes speak of the solitude of London; and few circumstances are more depressing than to suffer need and distress amid vast crowds in which we can perceive no glance of compassion, nor find a helper. But the Jews seem likely before long to suffer something worse than this, and, wherever they turn, to find themselves encompassed with faces lowering, menacing, and cruel. The wilderness of the nations will prove far more dreadful to them than the waste howling desert in which Moses was their leader.

But the jealousy and hatred of those among whom they sojourn will be God's means of driving them back to the place where He will deal with them; just as, in

[1] Ezek. xx. 32 35.

the days of old, their hard bondage made them glad to leave the flesh-pots of Egypt, and to turn their faces toward Canaan.

And it may be that He is already beginning to set His seal upon the elect remnant of which the prophets so often speak, the one-third which He will guide safely through the time of trouble into the Millennial glory: for a very startling and significant movement is now going on among a portion of the Jews.

During the persecution in South Russia, a lawyer of Bessarabia, named Joseph Rabinowitch, became impressed with the thought that his harassed kinsmen could find rest only in their own land. Meeting with much sympathy from the Jews around him, he turned his mind to the ways and means of carrying out his idea, and, in order to obtain full information, undertook a journey to Palestine. During his stay there, he was deeply moved as he realised the great discrepancy between God's description of the country, as a good land flowing with milk and honey, and its present actual condition.

Had he been imbued with the spirit of the Nineteenth Century, he would have quickly solved his difficulties by giving the lie to revelation. But he believed in the God Who made the heavens and the earth and the sea and the fountains of waters, and, therefore, proceeded, on the spot, to inquire how those things could be, by diligently searching the Old Testament Scriptures. His faith was rewarded by the discovery that Jesus of Nazareth was the Messiah and only hope of Israel, and that the curse had fallen upon the children of Abraham and their land because they rejected Him.

Having so far apprehended the truth, from an exclusively Jewish point of view, he returned to Bessarabia and set it forth in the synagogues, with the result that a separate community has been formed which already numbers some eight hundred persons. Its members hold that the Lord Jesus is the Messiah, and the only One Who can restore His nation to their own land and to peace. They do not, however, recognise Him as the only Begotten Son of the Father, and probably will not do so, as a body at least, until they behold Him with their eyes. But they call themselves "The National Jewish New Covenant Congregation," and have adopted a new liturgy for their Passover service, in which the Lord is recognised as their Redeemer, and as the Subject of the fifty-third chapter of Isaiah and other prophecies.

Thus, then, it would seem that the cry, "Blessed is He that cometh in the name of the Lord," is at last beginning to ascend from Jewish hearts; and, if it continue and increase, the separation between themselves and their King will be removed, and He will fulfil His promise by coming to them again without fear of a second rejection. Truly the purposes of God are speeding to their end!

And while the Jews are harassed in many other lands, the finger of God seems to be revealed in the comparatively friendly attitude of the present owners of Palestine toward them, and their appreciation of it. This appreciation they showed very manifestly, during the late difficulties between England and Russia, by their vigorous support of Lord Beaconsfield's policy. And when they were taxed by the Opposition with their preference for Turkey, a letter appeared in the

Times admitting their bias, and justifying it on the ground that they had always received better treatment from the Mussulmans than from the Latin and Greek Churches; so much so, indeed, that for centuries they had used the proverbial saying, "The children of Ishmael are more merciful than the children of Edom."

It is not unlikely that these friendly relations may continue, and that the Jews may be re-settled in their land with the approval and good-will of the Turks, who have once before received them as outcasts from Christendom, and who have never exhibited toward them that systematic hatred which has at all times characterized the Catholic Churches.

But even if the Turkish empire should have fallen apart into its four ancient divisions—as it must do at the time of the end—before Palestine is re-peopled, the Jews will, nevertheless, have little cause to complain of the governing power, whatever it may then be, in Syria. For the great prophecy of Ezekiel[1] proves that they will be able to establish themselves in peace and security, and to dwell with all their wealth in unfortified towns,[2] until the Prince of Rosh, Meshech, and Tubal, comes down upon them. It is thus sufficiently indicated that the instinct of the Jews is correct, and that Russia, and not Turkey, is the great enemy of Israel.

Such are some of the influences which are powerfully affecting the exiles of the Two Tribes. Their operation may continue, or may not; but certainly, so far as we can read the present signs of the times, God seems to have cast up a highway for the return of the Jews, and

[1] Ezek. xxxviii. and xxxix.   [2] Ezek. xxxviii. 11, 12.

to be both driving and alluring them toward their own land.

Meanwhile, the general interest—and especially that of British Christians—which is awakened in regard to Palestine, the frequent journeyings of Europeans and Americans through the length and breadth of it, the exploring and surveying expeditions, and the exertions of Sir Moses Montefiore and other Jews, have done much to ameliorate the condition of the country, and remind us of the prophecy—

> "Thou wilt arise, and have mercy upon Zion;
> For it is time to favour her;
> For the set time is come.
> For Thy servants take pleasure in her stones,
> And favour the dust thereof." [1]

Among the many striking incidents of the last few years, we may mention the proposal for the colonization of Eastern Palestine suggested by Mr. Lawrence Oliphant,[2] who, in common with the majority of thoughtful and unprejudiced Englishmen, has viewed with alarm the rapid southward advance of Russia, and felt the necessity of checking it before the British route to India becomes seriously endangered. For the results of the late war have placed some important military positions in the hands of the Czar, and have extended the Russian empire into Armenia; while Turkey, owing to her continued mal-administration, which is ceaselessly fostered by Russia, can no longer be regarded as a reliable barrier, and indeed, unless reforms be introduced, must soon collapse, and leave

[1] Psa. cii. 13, 14.
[2] This scheme is explained in Mr. Oliphant's interesting book, "The Land of Gilead."

for the Muscovites an open road to Jerusalem and to the Suez Canal.

With such a prospect into the future, it occurred to Mr. Oliphant that, by placing a large colony of Jews in the land of Gilead, the finances of Turkey might be increased, and an example of good government displayed which would probably be imitated by other provinces of Asia Minor; while, if the colony could be developed, a powerful Hebrew community, with all the influence of the race, might in course of time be interposed between Russia and the Red Sea.

Accordingly, he drew up the outline of a scheme which received the private approval of Lords Beaconsfield and Salisbury, and also of M. Waddington, who was at that time French Minister of Foreign Affairs, and in which the Prince of Wales and the Prince and Princess of Schleswig-Holstein evinced a warm interest. Shortly afterwards he started for Syria, and made a careful survey of the country in which he proposed to establish the colony, and which he found to be fertile, admirably adapted for cultivation, and at the same time practically uninhabited.

He received the cordial support of Midhat Pasha, the governor of Syria, and then proceeded to Constantinople with his completed scheme. There the Grand Vizier, Khaireddin Pasha, regarded the project with great favour, quickly perceiving the advantage which would accrue to the Turkish empire by a course which might easily be made to procure for it an alliance with the whole of the wealthy and powerful Jewish race. But at this critical time the Turkish ministry was overthrown; and its successors were suspicious of every proposal which emanated from a foreigner.

All hope of an immediate carrying out of the plan was therefore checked: but the delay may be merely temporary; for the political importance of Palestine is daily increasing. The Congress of Berlin has for the present placed a bar to the advance of Russia in Europe; but that restless power, which seems destined to be a great disturber of the world, is thereby rendered the more free for operations in Asia. And, owing to the late war, her Asiatic frontiers are now as near to the Mediterranean as her European; while in the countries bordering upon the former there is nothing to hinder her progress, except the Convention of Cyprus, which she is likely, owing to the present mood of the British people, to regard as a cancelled document. And if she should thus reach her goal, the shores of the Mediterranean, by way of Asia Minor, and establish herself at Alexandretta, an easy march through Palestine would give her the command of the Suez Canal, Egypt, and the Red Sea; and the British passage to India would be closed.

But although the command of two seas and the interception of British communication with India would be advantages sufficient in themselves to stimulate Russia to the most desperate exertion, there is, nevertheless, another motive which would urge her still more powerfully along the route which we have mentioned. Her fanatical population has always longed for the possession of the holy places in Palestine; so much so that even during the Crimean war their martial feelings were excited and sustained by the promise that Jerusalem should be their ultimate goal. Nor does the intervening time appear to have cooled their ardour. "Every year," says Mr. Oliphant, "about four thousand Russian pilgrims, composed largely of discharged soldiers, make painful and laborious journeys to visit the sacred shrines. One comes in contact with them in crowds during the Holy Week, and it is impossible not to be struck by the air of fanatical superstition which characterizes them."[1] Such a nation might easily be incited to a crusade which, while it would satisfy the superstitious desires of the people, might also be made subservient to the insatiable ambition of their leaders.

Should the English discover—before their opportunity has passed—the necessity of opposing a barrier to Russian advance into Palestine, it is not improbable that the establishment of a large and influential Jewish colony would form a part of their plan. That such a project has received much consideration may be inferred from the fact that a second gentleman, Mr. Cazalet, elaborated a scheme similar to that of Mr. Oliphant, which was published about the same time as the latter.

When, however, we consider the present condition of this country, it is difficult to avoid the conclusion that she may be in the decrepitude of old age: for on every side we see a waning of patriotism, a preference of party to imperial interests, a general indifference to the colonies and frontier lines, an unsteadiness in foreign policy and neglect of allies, and a false security which insists that the empire can be defended by thousands, though her ambitious neighbours are beginning to reckon their armies by millions. Unless all this be quickly changed, England will prove unequal to the struggle which she cannot avoid, and in that

[1] "Land of Gilead," pp. 517, 518.

case another nation is ready to step into the arena
The ceaseless vigilance of France in every matter which
concerns Egypt, and her known designs upon Syria,
point to her as the power which will then confront
Russia. And the idea of the restoration of the Jews
as an aid to French policy in the East is not new: it
has been already suggested by the first Napoleon, and
seems, indeed, to be a part of the traditions of his
family.

Possibly, therefore, we may now be able to discern,
in dim outline, the manner in which the nations will
unconsciously work out the will of Him Who knows
the end from the beginning; but whether this be the
case or not, certainly the progress of events has at
last made Palestine the centre of the great Eastern
question.

Nor are signs wanting that its soil is destined before
long to be the battle-field of the nations, though not,
probably, until the Jews have been settled in it. Then
the conflicts of opposing armies, like the ancient struggle
of the kings of Syria and Egypt, may, perhaps, form
no small part of the discipline through which the kinsmen of the Lord have yet to pass during the time of
Jacob's trouble. And what deep shadows these coming
events are already casting before them may be seen
by the following extract from a daily newspaper, in
which the writer is commenting upon the delay in the
publication of the one-inch map of Palestine, made in
the late survey. After an historical sketch to prove
the strategical importance which has ever attached to
the Holy Land "as the gateway between the East
and the West, or rather, as the barbican which commands the two avenues of the Euphrates and Red

Sea lines of communication," he concludes with the words;—

"It is probable that the power which, from the date of the inroads of Thothmes III. to the present time, has made the most advance towards a permanent acquisition of Palestine, is Russia. 'Standing on the approximate site of the old tower of Psephinus,' says the author of 'Tent Work in Palestine,' 'the Russian hospice commands the whole town (of Jerusalem), and is thought by many to be in a position designedly of military strength.' Nor is this the only place on which the grip of the Czar has been laid. If the contest between the civilization of the West and the autocratic barbarism of the North be ever committed to the arbitration of arms, nowhere is the contest so likely to be decided as in the region which guards the two roads from the Mediterranean to the Indian Ocean. Nor is it needful to wait for that time to become aware of the strategical value of the one-inch map of Palestine."[1]

It would seem, then, that we may be very near to the times of which it is written, "And it shall come to pass in that day that I will make Jerusalem a burdensome stone to all the peoples; all that lift it shall be wounded; and all the nations of the earth shall be gathered together against it."[2]

The grand swoop of the Russian eagle appears to be described in the thirty-eighth and thirty-ninth chapters of Ezekiel, in which it is now almost universally admitted that the name and titles of the Northern king should be rendered, "Gog of the land of Magog, prince of Rosh, Meshech, and Tubal." The

[1] *St. James's Gazette*, Sept. 15th, 1880. [2] Zech. xii. 3.

kingdom of this leader can be identified in no dubious manner with the present dominions of the Czar, and, as Dean Stanley remarks, "this early Biblical notice of so great an empire is doubly interesting from its being a solitary instance. No other name of any modern nation occurs in the Scriptures."

The Scythian, or Tartar, tribe of Ros—mentioned by Byzantine writers of the tenth century as being located to the north of Taurus, and by Ibn Foszlan, an Arabian of the same age, as dwelling on the banks of the Rha, or Volga—has been recently acknowledged by a consent of Russian ethnologists to be the origin of their name and people.

Meshech was another Scythian tribe, known to Classical writers as the Moschi. Of these Rawlinson says;—" They are frequently mentioned in Scripture under the name of Meshech, and occur as Muskai in many of the Assyrian inscriptions. . . . There is reason to believe that they ultimately took refuge in the Steppe country, where they became known as Muscovs, and gave their name to (Moscow) the old capital of Russia."[1]

The clans of Tubal, a third Scythian tribe, are, under the name of Tuplai, associated with the Muskai in Assyrian inscriptions; while in Classical authors they are called Tibareni, or the people of Tubal, and are usually coupled with the Moschi. The Assyrian records place them in Lower Cappadocia, on the Southern flanks of the Taurus; but, after a few centuries, we find them driven up to the South-eastern coast of the Black Sea; and they seem to have subsequently continued their Northward wanderings

[1] Rawl. "Herod," vol. iv. p. 180.

until they settled in Western Siberia, where they have given their names to the river Tobol, and also to the city and government of Tobolsk.

Thus these three Scythian tribes of Asia Minor, which appear in olden time to have lived in close proximity, and two of them at least on terms of friendship and alliance, were gradually forced away from their pleasant habitations and fertile lands into the cold and inhospitable region of the Steppes, and are now united as Russians, Muscovites, and the people of Tobolsk, in the great empire of the Czars. And if we keep their history in mind, it will, perhaps, give a peculiar significance to the words addressed to Gog, "I will cause thee to return,"[1] which may have meant that in the latter times these Scythians should make their way back again to the country from whence they came: that they should burst the "Iron Gates," which they did when they annexed the Trans-Caucasian provinces, and should stream on through Armenia, which they have already begun to do, until, having re-crossed the ridge of Taurus, they have reached the plains of Mesopotamia and the banks of the Euphrates, where we first hear of them in the times of the old Assyrian empire. And then they will not be very far from the borders of the Holy Land, upon which they shall come as a storm, and shall cover it like a cloud.[2]

There is, then, bitter tribulation awaiting the sons of Abraham in the immediate future. The curse which the miserable people called down upon their own heads is not yet exhausted: the blood of Him Whom the

[1] Ezek. xxxviii. 4. This rendering is better than that of the English Version, "I will turn thee back."
[2] Ezek. xxxviii. 9.

Father sent is still upon them and upon their children : there is no fountain as yet opened to the house of David and the inhabitants of Jerusalem for sin and for uncleanness ; they are still bearing every one his own iniquity. But the hour of decision is approaching, when that which can be saved shall be saved, and that which will perish shall perish : the time is near when the people shall be gathered in unbelief into their own country, as men " gather silver, and brass, and iron, and lead, and tin, into the midst of the furnace, to blow the fire upon it, to melt it : "[1] the day is not far distant in which the inhabitant of Jerusalem shall indeed say, " I am sick," and all the cities and fields of the devoted land shall be anguished with pain, and sorrow, and crying, and death. For the last end of the indignation, like the closing trouble of Joseph's brethren, shall be the worst suffering of all. But its fruit will be the broken and contrite heart ; and then mercy will take the place of judgment, and He shall appear Who is able to save to the uttermost, and Who " turneth the shadow of death into the morning."[2]

[1] Ezek. xxii. 20.   [2] Amos v. 8

PART III.

THE CHURCH OF GOD

I.

The Mystery hidden from the Ages.

In the previous section we have seen that, at the first advent, our Lord broke His covenant with the Jews, because they rejected Him; and that a suspension of the fulfilment of Jewish prophecy has, consequently, supervened—a long interval which seems, however, to have almost exhausted its term.

But what were God's plans for this interval? Would He during its course remain without witnesses, and without a people upon earth? Not so: while the glory of Israel was tarrying, Christ should be a light to lighten the Gentiles, and thus reveal, in its appointed season, another purpose of the Almighty.

It was late in the evening of that memorable day on which the Lord ate the last Passover. He was still sitting at the table with eleven of His disciples: the supper was ended: the bread had been broken, and the wine drunk. The traitor Judas—though he had been suffered, like many others who shall never sit down with Christ in the Kingdom of the Heavens, to eat of the bread and drink of the wine—could not be permitted to share the great secret which was about to be disclosed. Therefore he had been dismissed, that the Lord might speak in peace the farewell words of love and hope to those whom He had chosen.

They had just been partaking of the joyous feast of deliverance, but there were no signs of joy upon their features: deep sorrow, nay, the very shadow of death, seemed to have fallen upon the little company, and every face had gathered gloom.

For they had heard strange and terrible things that night: their security had been dispelled, and their hopes utterly destroyed. There was, indeed, no excuse for their surprise: for in past time the Lord had more than once foretold the impending trouble. But they had neither heeded, nor cared to understand, His warnings; and were, therefore, entirely unprepared for the events which He had just declared to be then actually confronting them.

His first remark, before supper, must have excited their alarm: for He spoke of the intensity of His desire to eat that Passover with them *before He suffered*.

Then He announced that one of their number was a traitor, and would betray Him.

That Satan had demanded and obtained all of them, that he might sift them as wheat.

That Peter, who had been so loud in expressing his devotion, would deny his Lord three times in the course of that very night.

And, saddest of all, that He Himself was just about to leave them, and that whither He was going they could not then follow Him, though they should do so in after-time.

This last-mentioned disclosure must have struck a death-blow at all their hopes. For as yet they knew nothing of the purposes of God: they talked only of Palestine and the earthly Jerusalem, and never dreamt that they were appointed to a higher destiny, that heaven was their home, and the Jerusalem which is above their mother-city. According to their conceptions, Christ should have set up His royal standard, and summoned all Judæa to follow Him; should, after the Roman legions had been destroyed, have caused Himself to be crowned at Jerusalem, and then have placed them upon the promised tribal thrones. And now He spoke of going away; of leaving them, and abandoning the land promised to Abraham's seed! All their expectations were shattered in a moment, and they were as those who see the beauteous forms of some fair dream breaking up and dissolving into the cold grey mist of morning.

But not only had their high hopes fallen; there was something even worse: for, if their Lord should depart, what would become of them in the world! He had been their support and stay, their guide, their help and defender in all danger, the One Who was never without resource to deliver them from every snare, to ward off every assault of their enemies. He had also been their joy; and if the Bridegroom should be taken away, what could the children of the bride-chamber do, but weep and lament for ever! Now they began to comprehend His dark saying;—" The days will come when ye shall desire to see one of the days of the Son of Man, and ye shall not see it."

Who would thenceforth be able to comfort them in times of distress; to speak words which could make their hearts burn within them, and lift them to hope from the lowest despair? Who would give them succour in every perplexity, create bread for them in the desert, and command the fishes of the sea to bring them the tribute money?

Who, if their ship were again sinking beneath the storm, would bid the boisterous wind be still, and command the white-crested billow to fall back ere it broke? Who, if the Pharisees should excite a tumult against them, would stand forth and expose the hypocrisy of their adversaries with such clear and incisive words of power that the surging crowd would melt away, until there remained but a few awe-struck sinners, no longer threatening, but crying out with emotion, "Never man spake like this man!"?

And if any among them should lie ill, who could rebuke the disease, and in a moment heal the sick? Or if the death of a beloved one should rend their hearts with anguish, who would turn their mourning into joy by commanding, even at the door of the sepulchre, with a voice which neither Death nor Hades could resist, "Lazarus, come forth!"?

And who could supply His tender affection? For He had not been with them those three years without entwining Himself around their hearts, and making them feel that in Him they had a Friend indeed, Whose love passed the love of women, and Who was nearer to them than a brother. And yet He had just predicted that all of them would, on that very night, forsake Him in the hour of trial; nay, that one would betray and another deny Him!

We can imagine their despair: we can conceive the confused thoughts raging in their minds, like the wild waves of a tempestuous sea. Yet they could not disburden themselves: no sound escaped their lips, and a gloomy silence possessed the room.

At length the Lord opened His mouth, and broke the oppressive stillness with soothing words which shed hope upon their hearts, even as His command, "Let there be light," had once gone forth over the shoreless ocean of earth, and dispelled its darkness.

"Let not your hearts be troubled," He said. "Believe in God, and believe in Me. In My Father's house are many abodes: if it were not so, I would have told you; for I go to prepare a place for you. And if I go and prepare a place for you, I am coming again, and will receive you unto Myself, that where I am, there ye may be also."

It is difficult for us to comprehend the surprise which these words must have occasioned to the disciples—if, at least, they understood them at the time. They had thought only of peace and glory in connection with the Jerusalem which is on earth, and such a vision would have been their sole consolation in the present distress; but the Lord removes this stay, gives them no hope of anything better than tribulation in the world, and at last reveals in plain terms the great secret of God's purpose.

He bids them resign their privileges and expectations as Jews; for He has called them to a higher destiny. Because they have received Him, He will give them power to become the sons of God; and they shall dwell, not at Jerusalem, but with Him where He is, that they may behold His glory. And though He is about to leave them for a season, it is that He may prepare abodes for them in His Father's house; and, as soon as they are all gathered in and ready, He will return, and take them unto Himself for ever.

A few weeks later, when the apostles and some other faithful believers were assembled in an upper room, the Holy Spirit descended to baptize them into one body, and to found the Church of Christ. And from that time God began to seek out for Himself a people from all flesh;[1] not, however, to rob the Israelite of his future dominion over the earth, but to sit in the Heavenly Places with the Lord Jesus, and in association with Him to become the spiritual rulers of the world.

Thus the present age commenced, but there is no prophecy which will enable us to discover the exact length of its course. We must, however, remember that, although dispensations may overlap, and a short transitional period be the result, yet God cannot, with this exception, have two peoples of different callings upon earth at the same time. Such a law is implied in the prediction of Micah, that, because of the smiting of the Judge of Israel on the cheek, the Jews should be given up for dispersion until the travailing Woman should bring forth—that is, until the number of believers should be completed. And when this point is taken up in the Book of Revelation, we are further instructed that, as soon as the Man-child is born, he shall be caught up to God and to His Throne; so that the way will then be cleared for the resumption of dealings with the Jews. Precisely similar is the teaching of Paul: for he affirms that "a hardening in part has befallen Israel, *until the fulness of the Gentiles be come in*"; and that, afterwards, all Israel shall be saved.

Thus the first sign of the end of this age will be the sudden translation of all waiting saints: and until that event has happened, there is no place for calculation. For, as we have before observed, the times of the Church are not properly a part of the Fifth Dispensa-

[1] Joel ii. 28.

tion, but a parenthesis fixed in it on account of the perversity of the Jews; an inserted period, unknown to Old Testament prophecy, and set apart for the preparation of a heavenly, and not of an earthly people.

It was, as we are told, "at the end of the world," or rather, "of the ages," that Christ appeared, and put away sin by the sacrifice of Himself. For when the Son of Man bowed His head in death upon the cross, there remained but seven short years for the course of this world. Mercy had been rejected; the time of forbearance was exhausted; and the terrific agents described in the Revelation were awaiting the command to speed forth upon their deadly missions, and execute the last indignation. But the wrath which had been gathering burst upon the Lord Jesus; the righteous sword of the Almighty was turned against the Man Who was His Fellow: and then God granted a respite to the world for which Christ died: then He checked the rapid flight of events, and, as it were, stayed the wings of the fleeting age, until a time shall have passed the duration of which is known only to Himself.

For if the Church inquires when her Lord will return, she receives but the answers;—"At an hour when ye think not;" "Surely I come quickly;" "Be ye therefore ready." The great apostle of the Gentiles warned her of the futility of attempting to compute the length of her stay upon earth. "But of the times and seasons, brethren," he said, "ye have no need that I write unto you. For yourselves know perfectly that the Day of the Lord so cometh as a thief in the night." The duty of the Church is to keep herself in readiness and to watch, not to reckon times. But, as soon as she is removed, all will be changed. The Fifth Age will finish its intercepted course; the Seven Years will quickly commence; there will be the Time, Times, and Half a Time, the Three Years and a Half, the Forty and Two Months, the Twelve Hundred and Sixty Days: all periods will then be capable of exact calculation.

But, if we cannot accurately compute the times of the Church, we are by no means without intimation of the present nearness of Christ's coming. For we see Christendom beginning to assume its last form, and the Mystery of Lawlessness daily gaining strength; while the Jewish prophecies seem to be on the point of fulfilment. Since, therefore, the Church must be taken away before any of these things is consummated, we may be well assured that the Lord is at hand, and should exhort one another so much the more as we see the Day approaching.

Moreover, besides other revelations in the New Testament, there are two great prophecies from the mouth of Christ Himself, the interpretation of which appears to intimate that the acceptable year of the Lord is almost ended. These prophecies are the Seven Parables in the thirteenth chapter of Matthew, and the Seven Epistles in the second and third chapters of the Apocalypse, both of which we propose now to examine.

The number of Parables and of Epistles is seven, that number being significant of dispensational completeness; and, in each of the two prophecies, we apparently have set before us seven successive phases, or characteristic epochs, of the Church, which embrace the whole of her career upon earth. These epochs commence in the order in which they are given; but any of them may overlap that which succeeds it or even extend its influence, in a greater or less degree, to the end of the age.

II.

THE SEVEN PARABLES.

IT is usual to treat these Parables as if they merely contained matter for what is called practical application. This, however, as we hope to show, is by no means the case; they are a continuous prediction of the whole career of the Church between the two advents. Undoubtedly they will also yield an abundant supply of more general instruction; but in this context, at least, the prophetic is the primary meaning.

We have previously sketched the plan of the earlier chapters of Matthew, and pointed out the manner in which they lead up to and introduce the Parables as a revelation of a new order of things then about to be brought in. For, on the one hand, they relate the repeated offers of the Kingdom to the Jews, the proclamation of its laws by the King, and the exhibition of His marvellous credentials; on the other, the ever-increasing hatred of the Jewish leaders, and their refusal to recognize the Lord's authority—a refusal prompted by so bitter a spirit that, when they are unable to deny His mighty works, they even dare to accuse Him of doing them by the aid of infernal power. By this blasphemous assertion their true condition is revealed: their immediate salvation is proved to be impossible; and, at the end of the twelfth chapter, the Lord intimates that they are about to be rejected of God, and delivered into the hands of Satan for a season.

A crisis in the history of the nation had arrived, similar in some points to the time when Jerusalem was given up to Nebuchadnezzar, but involving a far deeper degradation.

For the earlier chastisement merely deprived the Jews for a while of their right to be "the Kings of the Earth upon the earth." God still retained them as His people, though He sent them into captivity, and caused them to be bound in affliction and iron. Consequently, at that time it was only necessary to appoint temporary World-rulers, until the Kingdom could be restored to Israel; and this was done by the transfer of the sovereignty to the Gentiles. And, since the secret of the Lord is always revealed to them that fear Him, His purposes in regard to the change were disclosed to the godly Jews by the pen of Daniel.

Such were the circumstances connected with the assumption of the supremacy by Nebuchadnezzar, and the plan of the Gospel of Matthew is in strict analogy with them. But, in this second crisis, the Jews, by the rejection and murder of the Son of God, brought upon themselves a far more grievous punishment than the mere loss of their earthly dominion; for the covenant of Jehovah was now altogether suspended, and they were no longer recognized as His people. Yet it was necessary, during the interval which followed, that some witnesses should be chosen to maintain a testimony for Him upon the earth —without, however, infringing the power already granted to the Gentiles—and, accordingly, from that time He began to raise up a new band of believers who received a heavenly calling. And since the

THE SEVEN PARABLES.

Father would again, as in the days of Daniel, have some knowledge of His purpose revealed for the guidance of the humble, the Lord Jesus proceeded, on the very day in which He announced the rejection of the Jews, to unfold the mystery which had been hidden from the ages, and to foretell in parables what should befall the people of God during the interval between the Sixty-ninth and Seventieth of Daniel's weeks.

That His discourse contained an entirely new revelation, we are informed by the Evangelist, who observes that, in delivering it, Christ fulfilled the prophecy;—" I will open My mouth in parables; I will utter things hidden from the foundation of the world."[1] Indeed, we are more than once reminded in the New Testament that the purpose of God in regard to the Church and the heavenly calling had been kept secret, until the Lord Himself disclosed it.[2]

Thus the Seven Parables were similitudes of the Kingdom of the Heavens, intended to foreshadow the varying conditions under which those who shall hereafter reign with Christ have been, and are still being, gathered out of the present age. And the main burden of the prediction was that this body would, during its stay upon earth, be continually liable to become clogged and corrupted by admixtures of evil; that it would be interpenetrated, surrounded, and even altogether concealed, by a far greater multitude who would profess to belong to it, while they were in reality the children of the Wicked One.

The prophecy is, therefore, concerned with the whole

[1] Matt. xiii. 35.
[2] Rom. xvi. 25, 26; 1 Cor. ii. 7; Eph. iii. 5, 9; Col. i. 26.

number of nominal believers throughout the world, with every Church or sect which professes to derive its doctrines from the word of God, and in any way acknowledges His Son Jesus Christ. This vast and motley crowd spreads over the whole extent of Christendom in the largest sense of the term; while here and there in the midst of it, and ever acting more or less as a check upon the corruption around them, stand the scattered children of God, unable to extricate themselves from the press, and destined to continue unable, until heaven shall ring with the cry;—"Gather My saints together, those that have made a covenant with Me by Sacrifice!"

Now the whole of this great mixed multitude of Christendom is, for the time, called the Kingdom of the Heavens, because it holds within it—and so entangled that none but God can separate them—the true heirs of the Kingdom. Hence each of the Seven Parables appears to foreshadow some characteristic of the nominal Church especially prominent at a particular time. And they seem to be arranged in chronological order; for, to pass by details which we shall presently consider, they begin with the sowing, or first preaching, of the word, and end with the separation of good and evil at the close of the dispensation.

Yet, although they indicate the true succession of the phases which they represent, it does not, of course, necessarily follow that the period of one Parable must be completely ended before another commences: on the contrary, as we before remarked, it may overlap, and be contemporaneous with, that which follows it. We will now proceed to examine them separately.

III.

THE PARABLE OF THE SOWER.

THE first scene which opens before us is a large field already ploughed and prepared for the sowing. On one side of it runs a road, the wayfarers and waggons travelling by which have passed so heedlessly that they have trodden down and pressed the bordering ploughed land, until it has become well-nigh as hard as the highway itself. Extending underneath a considerable portion of the field lies a slab of rock, with but little soil above it; so that this part is quickly dried up by the sun. A third portion has rich and deep mould, but abounds in thorn-roots and seeds: the remainder of the field consists of soil both clean and good.

Presently the sower comes, and scatters his seed broadcast over the furrows. Some of it falls upon the trodden ground near the highway, and lies exposed upon its hard and smooth surface. Possibly it might yet sink into the soil, if it could be left untouched till heavy rains set in; but there is no chance of that. Multitudes of little birds are on the watch, and, as soon as the sower's back is turned, snatch up and devour every grain.

Some seed, again, falls upon the rocky soil, and, being unable to sink far beneath the surface, quickly sends forth blades of promise. But the sun arises in his strength, and they soon wither and die; for the thin-spread mould is speedily reduced to dust.

Other seed is scattered over the place already occupied by the thorn-roots: it comes up well, but the thorns also appear with it. It is not injured by the sun, for it has depth of soil; but the ever-increasing weeds draw away its nourishment and take up its room, until, almost concealed by their luxuriant growth, it becomes sickly and thin, and cannot bring its fruit to perfection.

But the seed which falls upon good ground puts forth its blades in due time, and grows and produces much fruit, though in varying quantities; some grains a hundredfold, some sixtyfold, and some thirtyfold.

This Parable exhibits the first period of the Gospel dispensation. The ploughed field is the world prepared for the reception of Christ by previous dealings of God: the untilled highway is the bordering Kingdom of the Air, tenanted by those fallen angels and spirits to whom the offers of Christ were not extended; so that their realm is neither ploughed nor sown. The Sower is, first and principally, the Lord Jesus Himself, and, afterwards, those who succeeded Him in the work of carrying on all that He began to do and to teach. The seed is the glorious word of the Gospel: the various conditions of soil represent the four classes of hearers which are found among men. And the fact that but one of these brings forth the desired fruit is a hint, at the very outset of the discourse, that all expectations of the universal success of the Gospel in the present age are false; that the way of the strait gate will remain narrow, and only a few, comparatively, find it, until a change be brought about by the advent of the King.

The first class of hearers are those who live so nigh to, and in such close communion with, the Powers of Evil, that they have become similar to them, and almost as hopelessly callous. For if men, like demons, do not care to retain God in their hearts, He gives them over to a reprobate mind, so that they have no further thought of Him. His Spirit is grieved, and ceases to strive: the sentence is pronounced, "Ephraim is joined unto idols, let him alone"; and henceforth they become more and more hardened. Therefore, the seed cannot penetrate their hearts, but lies on the surface, whence it is immediately picked off and devoured by the watchful spirits of the air, lest something unforeseen should cause it to sink in and quicken. And these agents of evil have countless devices whereby they can steal away the word—such as frivolous thoughts, idle conversation, pleasure-excitements, business-cares, and many other things. And so they destroy the germ of good from off the earth, that it may benefit neither him in whom it was sown, nor any of those around him.

There are other hearers, again, who have hearts as hard as the nether millstone, but overspread with a thin layer of sentiment. These receive the Gospel, or anything else, with an eagerness and a gushing enthusiasm which give hope of abundant fruit. But if, perchance, persecution appear on the horizon, or they be called to deny themselves an indulgence or convenience, they will straightway cast off their faith, and, by their unyielding obduracy to all subsequent appeals, show how stony their hearts really are beneath the soft envelope. Such people will weep in their comfortable rooms over the miseries of others, but will rarely bestir themselves to aid the objects of their compassion. They delight in talking of what they mean to do; but, if any opportunity for action should obtrude itself, usually find that they have need to attend to some private care, or social duty, which must take precedence of the Lord's business. These are they which spring up on all sides in times of revival, and cast the greatest dishonour upon Christ by their apparent conversion and ostentatious zeal: for they quickly fall away, and practically, if not avowedly, disown the faith for which they had professed themselves ready even to die. Their inner selfishness is firm as a rock; but, unstable as water in all other things, they cannot excel, and will be found at last without the gates of the Golden City.

The mind of the third class of hearers is of a different order. These can think and feel deeply; but they can do so in regard to other matters besides the love of God in Christ. In their heart the word lies amid various seeds and roots, which will presently spring up into the deceitful pleasure-seekings of early life, the cares of middle age, and the desires of other things rather than God. Nor is the range of the last-mentioned temptations confined to such spheres as ambition, political power, intellect, love, hatred, or covetousness, can afford; they may be discovered in very unsuspected quarters. In some cases, for instance, they war against the soul by inducing a quiet indulgence of appetites, to which many yield, by no means so far as to provoke the rebuke of their fellows, but just so much as to incline their bodies to an apparently well-meaning indolence and complacency, which, while it lasts, most effectually bars out the powers of the World to Come. But, whatever their individual bent, the wheat and thorns grow up together in persons of this class. They would be Christ's, but will not give up the world: they persist in striving to serve two masters; and, since they cannot hate the one, find themselves quite unable to cleave to the other: they do not follow the Lord with a whole heart; therefore He will not accept them, and, at last, altogether withdraws the pleadings of His Spirit. Then the thorns choke the word, and cover its withering remains with their luxuriant growth. Fruit may have begun to appear, but it is never brought to perfection: these are they who are almost saved, but lost.

Lastly, there are some who, humbled and brokenhearted through a sense of their own sinful condition, receive the word with gratitude. These, realizing the horrors from which they have been rescued, are willing to give up all things for the love of the Lord Who redeemed them; to deny themselves daily, to take up their cross and follow Him; to count not their lives dear, if they may but finish their course with joy. In the hearts of such the word grows by the power of the Holy Spirit, so that they are enabled to be witnesses for their Saviour, and to do works which shall be their joy and crown in the day of His appearing.

A solemn thought is suggested by the mention of the rates of increase—"some a hundredfold, some sixty, some thirty." Less than thirtyfold the Lord does not recognize: it is for every true Christian to ask himself whether the seed sown in him can yet have borne this minimum of fruit in the conversion and edification of others; nay, whether he has had any proof whatever that he is in the faith by the fulfilment in him of the Lord's saying;—"He that believeth on Me, as the Scripture hath said, out of his belly shall flow rivers of living water."[1]

[1] John vii. 38.

To these four classes of hearers the Gospel began to be preached, first by the Lord Himself, and afterwards by His disciples. The latter commenced their labours at Jerusalem, and added three thousand souls to the Church on the very first day of their mission. So active, indeed, were they and their converts in spreading the knowledge of the Lord Jesus, that, in less than thirty years, Paul could speak to the Colossians of the hope of the Gospel, "which ye heard, which was preached in all creation under heaven."[1] And to the truth of this statement even Heathen writers bear ample testimony. For example, Tacitus mentions the arrest of a "vast multitude" of Christians at Rome only a year or two later than the date of the Epistle to the Romans. And about seventy years after the Crucifixion, Pliny, in his famous letter to Trajan, affirms that "the contagion" of Christianity had then seized, not merely on the cities of Bithynia and Pontus, but even on the villages and country places.

Thus was the world sown in the first age of the Church: and during this time the prominent characteristic of the followers of Christ was an earnest propagation of their faith in every land; though, after all, their efforts were baffled by the generally unfavourable conditions of the human heart, and achieved but a very partial success.

IV

The Parable of the Tares.

In the second Parable there is also a Sower of good seed; but he is followed by a malignant enemy, who

[1] Col. i. 23.

comes while men are sleeping, scatters tares upon the wheat, and then steals away unperceived. The tares used for this evil purpose are still too well known in Palestine, and so nearly resemble good wheat in their growth, that it is almost impossible to distinguish them from it until the ear begins to ripen, when their fruit becomes black instead of yellow. In due time this proof of the admixture appears, and the servants of the lord of the field inform him of it, and ask if they shall go and pull up the noxious weeds. But he, after explaining that an enemy has done the mischief, tells them that the crops are now so inextricably mingled that they must be left to grow together until the harvest, when the reapers shall separate them, and shall bind the tares in bundles to burn them, and gather the wheat into the garner.

This Parable is also interpreted by the Lord Himself. The field is the world, and the enemy the Devil : but the meaning of the seed is not the same as in the first Parable ; for it no longer signifies doctrines, but persons. " The good seed are the children of the Kingdom ; and the tares are the children of the Wicked One." The latter are those hypocrites who are found to be suitable instruments for developing the deep and treacherous designs of Satan ; who, though they know not Christ, will foist themselves among Christians, and make it the business of their lives to spread corruption, either in doctrine or behaviour.

Many such men crept into the Church even in apostolic times ; but it is the history of the second and third centuries which affords the most terrible proof of the Lord's foreknowledge. During that period multitudes of grievous wolves entered stealthily into the fold, not sparing the flock; and many arose speaking perverse things to draw away the disciples after them. Then heresies began to spring up on all sides, heresies of every imaginable form and hue, and resulting in sects which in manifold ways weakened or altogether destroyed the power of the word of God, and provided an attractive but useless religion for every kind of intellect and disposition. The universal Church became corrupt, and has never thrown off the taints of this epoch: to the present day every Christian sect bears traces of them upon its tenets or ritual.

Only those who are acquainted with the literature of the second and third centuries can form any adequate conception of the multitude of tares which during that time were manifesting themselves by their black fruit: but the study of two works, which have come down to us, will give some idea of the principal errors with which Satan was then bewildering the Church. One of these, put forth in the last quarter of the second century, is a volume "Against Heresies," from the pen of Irenæus of Lyons, a disciple of Polycarp who had himself listened to the apostle John. The other is "A Refutation of all Heresies," written by Hippolytus of Portus, a pupil of Irenæus, in the first half of the third century.

From these books we learn that, at their early dates, the seed of nearly all subsequent errors had been imperceptibly sown in the churches, with a resulting crop of heresies, sects, and schools, so numerous that it would be tedious even to mention their names. And these heresies were of all degrees, beginning with a slight admixture of evil, and going on to such a pitch of madness that some even declared the accursed serpent, the beguiler of Eve, to be the true Messiah, and actually styled themselves Ophites, or Serpent-worshippers. Another sect held that the Scriptures did not emanate from the Supreme God, but from a lower and malignant deity, whom they called the Demiurge, and who, as they affirmed, had caused the sacred history to be distorted, so that the righteous in it—such as Cain, Esau, the men of Sodom, and Korah —were made to appear wicked, and the wicked righteous. Hence they regarded Cain as the first saint mentioned in the Bible, and from him named themselves Cainites.

During the whole period included by this Parable violent persecutions were occurring at intervals, and in the other continuous prophecy of the Church we shall find them specially noticed. Here, however, there is nothing more than a very obvious allusion. The Lord feared lest His Church should take a lesson from their oppressors, and, if at any time they had the power, put to death obstinate heretics. Hence the servants are ordered not to root up the tares out of the field—a commandment which may be easily understood if we remember that "the tares are the children of the Wicked One," and that "the field is the world."

In regard to the harvest, a difficulty has arisen in the minds of many, because the command, "Gather ye together first the tares," seems to imply that Christ will execute judgment upon the wicked before He deals with His Church. It is, however, impossible that such a sequence of events could be intended, or this passage would stand alone, and oppose itself to the general testimony of Scripture.

As an example of that testimony, we may quote the

fourteenth chapter of the Apocalypse, in which three classes of men affected by the Lord's return are represented as Firstfruits, Harvest, and Vintage. And, in accordance with the order of nature, the Firstfruits, as we may see by the context, are those who will be "redeemed from the earth" before the Tribulation; the Harvest follows at its close; and still later comes the Vintage, the grapes of which answer to the tares of the Parable.

And again, in the nineteenth chapter, it is after the Marriage Supper that John sees heaven opened and the Lord appearing, with the whole Church in His train, to destroy them which corrupt the earth.

Indeed, if we turn to the last of this very series of Parables, we shall find the apparent order of the second reversed: for the good fish are first picked out of the net and placed in vessels, and then the bad are cast away.

Now a right understanding of Scripture quickly dispels all supposed inconsistencies: how, then, can we explain this seeming discrepancy in parables of the same series? Probably by the following considerations.

In the original of the command to the reapers there is no word—such as "then," or, "afterwards"—to mark the apodosis to "Gather first." We must, therefore, supply one, and may do so in the next clause. For the "but" ($\delta\acute{\epsilon}$) which follows is often used adversatively, and may merely indicate an antithesis or contrast of destiny, without any reference to order of time. Thus the command will read;—"First collect the tares, and *then* bind them in bundles to burn them: but as to the wheat, gather that into My barn."[1]

[1] The reason why the Lord, in His description of the harvest, speaks first of the tares is sufficiently obvious: since they are the subject of the Parable.

We may, perhaps, add that a farmer would not be likely to trouble himself about the tares, provided they were carefully picked out of the wheat, until he had safely conveyed the latter to its receptacle.

Again ; we must remember that the two Parables are elementary and general : they are by no means intended to furnish details of the end, but only to lay down the broad principle that Christ will throughly purge His floor. The inevitable mingling of evil and good in the present age, and the certainty of ultimate judgment and separation, are the great lessons which they teach.

A peculiar Greek word, signifying " to gather by picking out," is used of *the tares* in one Parable and of *the good fish* in the other ; so that the meaning may be clear from both sides. Satan must sow his tares, and they will grow up with the wheat, and become inextricably entangled with it until the harvest. But before the Lord gathers in His own, He will not fail to pick out from their midst all the children of the Evil One. And again ; while the Gospel net is lying in the sea of the nations, the nominal Church must needs include multitudes of merely intellectual, of sentimental, and of hypocritical members, as well as real believers. But as soon as the net is drawn to shore, just as fishermen carefully select the good fish to put into their vessels and then cast the rest away, so the Lord will take every soul of His own out of the great masses of spurious worshippers before He consigns the latter to their doom.

In passing on to interpret the remaining Parables, we must keep one point clearly in mind. We have just seen that wheat and tares are to grow together until the end; and, accordingly, in the seventh and last Parable we shall find good and bad fish mingled in the same net. It is manifest, therefore, that all the intervening Parables must also represent the Church in conditions more or less corrupt.

V.

The Parable of the Mustard Tree.

In the third similitude, a grain of mustard—proverbial in Palestine as being the smallest of familiar seeds—is sown by a man in his field: and, with a solemn significance, the Lord tells us that this plant, although really belonging to the class of pot-herbs, or garden vegetables ($τὰ\ λάχανα$), grows, nevertheless, into a tall tree.[1] This is an evident intimation of something wrong: for God would have every seed to develop according to the limits of its kind.

In becoming a tree the mustard throws out great branches,[2] so that the fowls of the air, which in the first Parable caught up and devoured the good seed, are able to come and lodge under its shelter. Here, then, is another very ominous hint, which, had it been duly weighed, would have checked the frequent, and undoubtedly mistaken, use of this Parable for missionary sermons.

The grain represented the principles of the Church

[1] Thomson remarks that he has seen the wild mustard as tall as the horse and his rider, and suggests that there may have been a perennial kind which grew into a tree, just as the castor bean sometimes does. See "The Land and the Book," p. 414. Very possibly there is no exaggeration in the assertion of R. Simeon Ben Chalaphta, who says;—"A stalk of mustard was in my field, into which I was wont to climb as men climb into a fig tree."

[2] Mark iv. 32.

THE PARABLE OF THE MUSTARD TREE. 307

as sown by Christ in the world: the description of its unnatural growth signified that those principles would be abandoned as the age rolled on—a prediction which was very manifestly fulfilled.

For the Lord charged His disciples to learn of Him, and be meek and lowly in heart during their sojourn upon earth; to cast aside every high thought, and follow their despised and rejected Master. But Satan, by means of false teachers and errors stealthily introduced during the period of the tares, prevailed on the great body of professing Christians to turn from the words of golden hope, "Behold I come quickly"—inscribed, as it were, by the Lord upon the blue veil of heaven through which He ascended—and to fix their eyes upon earthly things. He taught them to think of the cessation of human enmity, and of their own growing importance; and so allured their community in the direction of an eminence to which they could attain only by forsaking Christ and serving Mammon. Then, when the fitting moment had arrived, he approached them, and offered the present favour of earthly kings in exchange for the hope of the King from heaven. And, forgetful of their Lord's example, they accepted the offer: like Eve, they were beguiled, and blindly consented to receive their power and influence from the Prince of this World.

The phase represented in the Parable began to be developed in the early part of the fourth century, when Constantine was carried to the imperial throne upon the shoulders of his British legionaries, the great majority of whom were Christians, and a nominal Christianity became the state religion of the Roman Empire.

Now it had been a frequent custom of the polytheistic Romans to acknowledge all the gods, while they selected one of them as a special patron and object of adoration. And, accordingly, Constantine, in deference to the feelings of his soldiers, placed Christ in the Pantheon, and adopted Him as his favourite god; though, at the same time, he continued to worship the Heathen deities, giving the preference to Apollo.

For his religion was dictated by motives of policy, and his desire was to weld his Christian and Pagan subjects into one people. To promote this end, a set of double-meaning symbols was carefully prepared, or rather, a number of recognized Pagan symbols were so adapted that those who wished might interpret them of Christ, while others continued to explain them from their own mythology.

Among these symbols was the mystic Tau,[1] the famous but obscene "sign of life," known from the earliest antiquity throughout the whole circle of Heathendom, and marked in baptism upon the foreheads of those who were being initiated into the mysteries.[2] This was brought into greater prominence, and for Christians was made to signify the cross of Christ, while among the Pagans it retained its previous meaning.

[1] The great Phallic emblem. "It is high time that Christians should understand a fact of which sceptics have long been talking and writing, namely, that the cross was the central symbol of all ancient Paganism. What it represents must remain untold: but it was probably made the medium of our Lord's death through the crafty devices of the Wicked One, into whose hands He was for a while delivered, with a view to the future corruption of Christianity, and the carrying on under its name of all the abominations of the Heathen."—"Rome: Pagan and Papal," by Mourant Brock.

[2] Another form of this symbol was the Egyptian *crux ansata*, the well-known sign of the goddess Venus.

Just in the same manner the device on the standard of Constantine, which he was reported to have seen in his vision, the Chi-Rho, was set before the Christians as the monogram of Christ; but the Heathen easily recognized it as a slightly altered form of the sign of Osiris, or Jupiter Ammon.[1] Besides which, it was usually set upon the top of the pole; while on the purple-silk field of the banner below were the heads of the emperor and his sons, which might be worshipped by the Pagans according to their custom.

Another instance of Constantine's policy is worth mention. The Christians of that time were scrupulous in keeping holy the first day of the week in remembrance of their risen Lord. Perceiving that this was in itself sufficient to distinguish them from their fellow-citizens, and to promote a party spirit, he issued an edict that the Pagans should observe the same day in honour of Apollo, the Sun-god, and should call it Dies Solis, or the day of the Sun. Very soon Christ and Apollo began to be more or less identified, and from this unseemly origin comes our modern term "Sunday."

It was probably at the same time that the custom of turning to the East was introduced into the Church. For, however this ceremony may be explained, it is altogether Pagan, and is connected with the worship of the Sun-god. Its extreme antiquity may be known from the fact that, when God gave directions for the arrangements of the Tabernacle and Temple, He caused the Holy of holies in both cases to be set in the West,[2]

[1] Jennings' "Rosicrucians," pp. 147, 180.
[2] The longer sides of the Tabernacle were to face the North and South respectively, so that they extended from East to West (Exod. xxvi. 18-20). The West end was to be completely boarded, like the sides, because the Holy of holies was to be there

in order that His people might be clearly distinguished from the idolaters around them.

It is only by bearing this in mind that we can understand the deep significance of a passage in Ezekiel. That prophet, when relating how he was caught up by the Spirit and conveyed to Jerusalem to see the abominations which had provoked God to doom both city and Sanctuary to destruction, thus describes the last and greatest of them ;—" And He brought me into the inner court of the Lord's house ; and, behold, at the door of the Temple of the Lord, between the porch and the altar, were about five and twenty men, with their backs toward the Temple of the Lord, and their faces toward the East ; and they worshipped the sun toward the East."[1]

The confusing and corrupting effects of Constantine's policy may be easily imagined : Christianity was transformed into a kind of Paganism with new names, and the world ceased to view it with disfavour. And, meanwhile, the private conduct of the emperor, inasmuch as it had to be condoned by the Church, must have greatly contributed to laxity of morals ; for, among other crimes, he put to death his eldest son and his own wife, listening in each case to accusations which he afterwards discovered to be false. This caused his enemies to say, that he had become a Christian because no other religion offered pardon for such atrocities as he chose to commit.

(vv. 22-3). But the East end was the entrance to the Holy Place, and was covered with a curtain. The passage quoted from Ezekiel in the next paragraph shows the position of Solomon's Temple, since the men who were worshipping the sun towards the East had their backs turned to the Temple of the Lord.

[1] Ezek. viii. 15, 16. The number of the men seems to indicate that they were the High Priest and the heads of the twenty-four orders (1 Chron. xxiv.).

Certainly, when the Church accepted the alliance of such a man, it might well have been said of her, as of Jerusalem, "How is the faithful city become a harlot!" She had, indeed, grown great upon the earth ; but instead of the presence of the Holy Spirit, the Comforter, the foul and rebellious spirits of the air came and lodged in her branches, took possession of her, and directed her ; so that she ceased, as a visible body, to be a witness for Christ, and became a mighty instrument in the hands of Satan

VI.

THE PARABLE OF THE LEAVEN.

IN this Parable we see before us a woman hiding leaven in three measures of fine meal ;[1] so that the process of fermentation commences, and silently proceeds, until the whole is leavened. The interpretation of the scene depends, of course, on the meaning to be given to leaven, which has been commonly supposed to represent pure Christianity. But such an explanation could only have originated in the minds of men who had determined it by their own preconceived ideas of what the future should be, and not by patient investigation : for leaven is an unmistakable symbol of sin and corruption, as will appear from a consideration of the following points.

I. The nature of the leaven used by the ancients, and its consequent figurative meaning in the Heathen as well as the Jewish world.

[1] The measures are probably seahs, three of which were contained in an ephah ; while the latter seems to have been a full measure for baking. See Gen. xviii. 6 ; Judg. vi. 19 : 1 Sam. i. 24.

II. The apparent basis of the Parable in the Old Testament.

III. The *invariable* use of leaven as a symbol of evil in the Bible.

IV. And the fact that, if a contrary meaning were given to it in this instance, such an interpretation would involve a doctrine not to be found elsewhere in Scripture.

I. In regard to the first point, the only leaven known to the ancients was something sour; and the effect which it produced was incipient corruption spreading through the dough and rendering it sour, and, unless baked at the right time, positively corrupt. Hence, in speaking of bread, the Hebrews used "sour" for leavened, and "sweet" for unleavened. And hence, also, leaven became a symbol of corruption both to the Jews and to many Heathen nations.

In the Talmud it is a frequent figure for "evil affections and the naughtiness of the heart," and, among other instances, we find the following prayer;—" Lord of ages, it is revealed and known before Thy face that we would do Thy will; but do Thou subdue that which hinders, namely, the leaven which is in the lump." One of the Rabbis also says;—" Trust not a proselyte till twenty-four generations; for he holds his leaven."

At Rome, the Flamen Dialis, or High Priest of Jupiter, was forbidden to touch it; and Plutarch, the Greek historian, explains the prohibition on the ground that "leaven is both itself generated by corruption, and also corrupts the mass with which it is mingled."

II. Our Lord, Who frequently founds His sayings upon something written in the Old Testament, appears to have taken the present Parable from the description of the meat-oblation in the second chapter of Leviticus. That offering, which seems to represent the devotion of Christ, our Substitute, in service, was of fine flour ; and, if the flour were in any way baked, there is an express injunction that no leaven should be in it. Moreover, this special command is immediately followed by the general precept ;—" For ye shall burn no leaven, nor any honey, in any offering of the Lord made by fire."[1] Thus the woman, by putting leaven into the fine flour, was rendering it unfit for an offering to the Lord.

III. We are directed to interpret Scripture by comparing spiritual things with spiritual, and leaven is, without a single exception, used as a familiar and well-known figure of corruption in both Old and New Testaments.

The Israelites were to put it away from their houses at the Passover ;[2] God would have none of it offered upon His altar ;[3] and it is expressly contrasted with salt, the symbol of purity.[4] Accordingly, when Amos, in bitter irony, bids the people multiply their transgressions and provoke God still further, he tells them that this may be done by offering a sacrifice of thanksgiving with leaven.[5]

But, perhaps, the most striking instance of the figurative significance of leaven is to be found in the description of the Feast of Pentecost.[6] On that occasion two ordinary leavened loaves, made of the corn of the year, were to be brought forth from the habitations of the

---

[1] Levit. ii. 11.
[2] Exod. xii. 15, 19, 20 ; xiii. 6, 7 ; Deut. xvi. 3, 4.
[3] Levit. ii. 4, 5, 11 ; vi. 17 ; x. 12.
[4] Levit. ii. 11, 13.
[5] Amos iv. 4, 5.
[6] Levit. xxiii. 15-21.

Israelites to the altar, as the firstfruits unto the Lord. But, because there was leaven in them, they could not be burnt upon the altar and ascend from it as a sweet savour, and were, therefore, set down before it. These loaves, perhaps, symbolized the Church—which was called into existence on the day of Pentecost by the descent of the Holy Spirit, as a kind of firstfruits of creation [1]—presented before God, but unacceptable to Him on account of the sin which is in it.

Then seven lambs without blemish, a young bullock, and two rams, were offered for a burnt offering, as a type of the whole devotion of our Substitute Christ, even to the death. Each of these sacrifices was followed by its appropriate meat and drink offering, pointing to His perfect and willing service in daily life, His fulfilment of the second table of the Law for us. Then a kid of the goats was slain as a sin offering, a shadow of Christ putting away sin by the sacrifice of Himself. Lastly, two lambs were brought to the altar for peace offerings; to set forth Christ reconciling us to God, and restoring us to communion with Him.

And so, after the whole work of the Saviour had been thus represented, the two loaves were taken up and waved before the Lord, and—although they could not, indeed, be placed upon the altar, on account of their leaven—were, nevertheless, accepted and passed on for the use of the priest—a wondrous type of the Church, which, spite of all her faults, shall also be accepted in the Beloved.

The sin, then, which cleaves to us, and renders us unfit for the presence of God, unless we be cleansed in the blood and clothed in the righteousness of Christ, is

[1] James i. 18.

THE PARABLE OF THE LEAVEN. 315

symbolized by leaven; and, in the New Testament, the Lord gives some hints respecting special forms of this evil by warning His disciples to beware of the leaven of the Pharisees,[1] the Sadducees,[2] and the Herodians[3] —three Jewish sects which are never without their counterparts in the professing Church.

Passing on from the Gospels to the Epistles of Paul, we shall find other examples of the symbolic meaning of leaven. On two occasions the apostle, when exhorting churches to put away evil, remarks;— " A little leaven leaveneth the whole lump."[4] And to one of these admonitions he adds the significant words;—" Purge out, therefore, the old leaven, that ye may be a new lump, even as ye are *unleavened*. For our Passover also hath been sacrificed, even Christ : wherefore let us keep the feast, not with old leaven, neither with the leaven of malice and wickedness, but with the *unleavened* bread of sincerity and truth."[5] It is, then, an entire absence of all leaven which God desires in the Church ; and we cannot consent to set aside the emphatic and oft-repeated meaning of the symbol in the single instance in which it has been disputed.

IV. Again ; were we in this passage to interpret leaven of a good influence, the Parable could only mean that all evil would be overcome by a gentle, gradual, and almost imperceptible process; and it would thus be made to contradict the whole testimony of the Bible. For the inspired writers repeatedly affirm that wickedness will increase, until at length it

[1] Luke xii. 1.
[2] Matt. xvi. 6.
[3] Mark viii. 15.
[4] 1 Cor. v. 6 ; Gal. v. 9.
[5] 1 Cor. v. 7, 8

shall be forcibly checked by the interference of the Lord Himself. The mystery of lawlessness had begun to work like leaven even in apostolic times, and it must go on until its true nature be revealed in the person of the Lawless One. It is needless to multiply passages which speak of evil men and seducers waxing worse and worse, deceiving and being deceived, of love growing cold, and faith waning; passages which predict that the world will again become corrupt and filled with violence as in the days of Noah, will be reeking with the foulest crimes, like the cities of the plain, so that the Lord will come forth out of His place to shake terribly the earth, and to punish its inhabitants for their iniquity.

Even in this series of Parables we are taught that wheat and tares must both grow together to the end of the age; that the children of the Wicked One will be left undisturbed, until the Son of Man sends forth His angels to gather out of His Kingdom all things that offend, and them which do iniquity; and that, after the net has been drawn to shore, the wicked shall be severed from among the righteous, but not made like to them.

There is, therefore, no doubt in regard to the Scriptural significance of leaven, and if it be accepted, the Parable falls easily into its place. The agent in the scene is a woman—the usual symbol of a system or Church; and the fact that she is secretly corrupting the fine flour, acting like the enemy who sowed tares upon the wheat, proves her to be the Harlot, and not the true Church.

The leaven is corrupt doctrine, and is explained for us by Matthew in the words;—" Then understood they

THE PARABLE OF THE LEAVEN.

how that He bade them not beware of the leaven of bread, but of the teaching of the Pharisees and Sadducees."[1]

In the previous chapter we have attempted to describe the manner in which Christianity began to be Heathenized. The process of transformation continued, until the truths of revelation were entirely changed by the gradual admixture of human traditions and philosophies, which, like leaven, were not merely corrupt in themselves, but had also the property of imparting their own nature to that with which they were mingled. The earthly agency by which this strange result was achieved became more and more powerful under the name of "the Catholic Church." And so effectual was its organization, and so vigorous its action, that in a short time the whole society of the Roman world was interpenetrated with its influence, and men regarded themselves as Christians when they were really polytheistic idolaters who had changed the names of their gods.

The three kinds of leaven mentioned by the Lord may be easily distinguished in this apostasy. In both the Greek and the Latin communities there has ever been a sufficiency of Pharisees, those who have, perhaps, some kind of faith in what they teach, but who put their trust in outward forms, in the traditions of men, and in the authority of their own Church; while they look down, sometimes with pity, but more frequently in a spirit of contempt and persecution, upon all who venture to differ from them.

And again; there is always a plentiful sprinkling of Sadducees, men who decline, more or less, to believe

[1] Matt. xvi. 12.

anything which they have not experienced, or cannot understand; who disparage revelation, avoid all mention of the supernatural, and are ever unwilling to speak of the atonement; who dream that the new birth can be effected by education, human philosophy, and the practice of virtue and philanthropy; and who, while apparently acquiescing in the doctrines and practices of their Church, are in their hearts altogether indifferent to them; nay, are often possessed with a bitter spirit of scepticism which resents the very suggestion of a God. When the false religion is growing old in a land, and its authority is becoming relaxed, these men are the fungi which draw life from its decay: they multiply in numbers and increase in boldness, until at length they throw off all disguise, and openly avow their real sentiments, and their hatred of every form of worship. Such are the dregs which Romanism invariably leaves behind it when all else has evaporated.

Of Herodians, who would support religion by the arm of secular power, and who consider political intrigue a fitting means for advancing the interests of Christ's Kingdom, it is needless to speak. Men of this class have ever been conspicuous in the communities of apostate Churches, and in none more than that of Rome.

But there are also many misguided believers, of more orthodox views, who so mind earthly things that they are often found to be practically regarding the political questions of the day as more important than the far weightier matters of the heavenly Kingdom. And they persuade themselves to such a state of mind by the false assumption that the present work of Christ is to improve the world, forgetting that He bids us rather co-operate with Him in gathering His elect out of it.

Such, then, was the period of the leaven; nor have reformations or revivals, however great their partial success, been able to free Christendom from its pernicious influence. It is still found, to a greater or less extent, and in one or other of its forms, in every Church and sect: it continues to work in the whole mass of professing Christians, though sometimes one of its developments may be more powerful, sometimes another. Hitherto the Pharisean and Herodian elements have usually been the most prominent; but for a long time the Sadducean has been rapidly increasing, and this will probably be the chief agent in forcing the mystery of lawlessness to its climax. All three will, however, remain active until the end, and, in their final development, are possibly represented by the three unclean spirits of the Sixth Vial, which will drive men on to the last extreme of rebellion, and "gather them to the battle of that great day of God Almighty."[1]

VII.

THE PARABLE OF THE TREASURE IN THE FIELD.

There is now a pause in our Lord's discourse, and the remaining Parables are spoken to the disciples alone. Some turning-point is indicated, and possibly a more confined area, as though the action of this scene would, in the main, be restricted to a few favoured countries of Christendom. And so we seem to recognize the results brought about by the Reformation. The ceaseless working and rapid progress of the leaven is checked; but that is all: the leaven is not itself purged away. Only that which had been

[1] Rev. xvi. 13, 14.

active for evil now settles down into a cold inert mass; so that the outward appearance of the nominal Church is that of a field. Nevertheless, hidden beneath its unpromising surface lies the heavenly treasure.

The description is wonderfully true when applied to the times of Protestant deadness which, quickly following the Reformation, lasted on with but few signs of life to vary their monotony until it was broken by the preaching of Wesley, Whitefield, and others. For after the enthusiasm of the conflict with Rome had passed away, men speedily settled down to a mere form of godliness, while they denied its power. They thought it a duty to go through their heartless services, but love had grown cold: they boasted of their pure faith, but failed to show the works which it should have produced. And a mournful proof of this may be found in the fact that two centuries had elapsed before they roused themselves to any general missionary effort.

Soon the peoples of Christendom among whom the Reformation had triumphed were divided off into sharply-defined sects, like fenced fields. Each of these sects held the life-giving doctrine of the atonement: but it was often concealed more or less by other teachings, which in some cases seemed to have been very imperfectly purged from the leaven.

During this period the number of believers was usually increased in the manner indicated by the Parable. A man would, as it were by chance,[1] hear

---

[1] The husbandman *found* the treasure: while he was engaged in ordinary work, his ploughshare or mattock, perhaps, struck upon something which proved to be valuable. It was, then, an instance of what we call treasure-trove. And, consequently, the interpretation of those who see Christ in the husbandman, and His people in the treasure, leads to very strange results. Surely

the Gospel of Christ, and, having received it, would in his joy buy the whole field, that is, accept, at any cost to himself, all the doctrines of the community of Christians in which he had found his treasure. This was a very characteristic feature of the times from the Reformation to the middle of the present century : the generality of good men, after finding the heavenly treasure in some professing body, while holding firmly, indeed, to fundamental and vital truths, would in other matters thenceforth read the word of God, not independently, but by the light of, and to prove the correctness of, the doctrines which they had adopted. And the various Protestant Churches, while conceding salvation to all believers in Christ's atonement, were wont, nevertheless, to preserve strongly-marked lines of separation, and to remember their distinctive tenets.

VIII.

THE PARABLE OF THE PEARL OF GREAT PRICE.

IN this similitude the scene again changes : the solid field breaks up into the ever-shifting waves of the sea, and the secret of the Kingdom is found as a pearl in its lowest depths. This points to times like those on which we seem already to be entering ; times in which the narrow boundaries of sect are becoming indistinct, and are little noticed, while almost every man holds his own peculiar opinions. And, just as the pearl lies far beneath the restless surface of the waves, so, in no

our Lord did not accidentally light upon His Church, while He was about some other business in the world ! And His people can scarcely be called treasures at the time when He finds them : they become so afterwards, by His grace, as new creations in Him.

distant day, will the word of God be hidden beneath the many waters of perpetually changing confessions, creeds, sects, opinions, and philosophies; and still later, at the culmination of the great apostasy, its very existence will be almost forgotten. The truth of God will be no more found, as it were, accidentally—as a man unexpectedly stumbles upon treasure-trove—but only by means of earnest inquiry.

For in this case a merchant, who knows the value of pearls, is seeking for them; and the reward of his diligence is the discovery of the pearl of great price, to obtain which he gives up all that he has. The Lord thus signifies that, even in the perilous times of the end, those who are really desirous of truth will be guided to the great truth. But, as we learn from other prophecies, their sincerity will be sorely tested; they will have to turn away from that which is exciting the enthusiasm of the whole world in order to begin the search; and, when they have been successful, may be required to surrender family, position, property, and even life itself, if they would possess the prize.

Since, however, the merchant is able to find the pearl, we are taught that God will not leave Himself altogether without witnesses while the Lawless One is reigning: there will yet be fishers, blessed of Him, who will be empowered to bring up His truth from beneath the troubled waters of human opinions, and to offer it to those who are honestly seeking for "glory and honour and immortality."[1]

[1] We must carefully bear in mind that the merchant does not dive to bring up the pearl from the deep, but merely purchases it from one who has previously procured it. Great, therefore, is the mistake of interpreters who find in this Parable a representation of Christ seeking and saving His Church.

If we look around us, we cannot but suspect that we are living in the transitional period between the previous Parable and that which we are now considering. Already, on every side, the fields of dogma are breaking up, and where one distinct and unalterable law was wont to prevail, there is nothing but uncertainty and innumerable opinions—opinions, too, which rarely claim to be derived from the revelation of God, but are avowedly based upon human authority, whether ancient or modern, whether ecclesiastical or secular.

The Protestant sects, as communities, attracted by human traditions and philosophies, are ceasing to hold fast the Head, and becoming less and less able to withstand the powerful influx of corruption. Those principles which used to characterize them are, like houses surprised by an inundation, already tottering, and threatening every moment to fall through the violence of the floods; so that shortly nothing will be seen but the tumultuous waters out of which Satan will evoke the last great enemy of Christ.

Some twenty or thirty years ago, the first slight advances of Secularism were viewed with alarm wherever they were discovered, and the seven Essayists and Bishop Colenso regarded as strange teachers in the National Church. But it is not so now: almost all popular magazines and reviews teem with scepticism, and it is openly taught by those who might have been expected to act as barriers against it. Nor is the spread of Romanism, especially in covert forms, less remarkable.

The scarcely noticed summer stream has swelled into a broad and foaming river, and is bringing destruction with it from the mountains. We cannot hope to stay its rapid tide ; for it will prevail, until He appear unto Whom all power is given. But we must not, therefore, remain idle all the day : nay, we are exhorted to greater exertions as the difficulties increase and the end approaches, lest the Lord coming suddenly should find us sleeping. We can stand by the rushing torrent, and pull out many a one, who is being carried away by it, before his spirit is quite extinguished : we can warn others, so that they may avoid it altogether. And by the mercy of God there are still large numbers of His people thus employed. The energy of evil is for the present provoking some little corresponding energy of good ; but of this we shall hear in our Lord's second continuous prophecy. For in the Parables He deals more especially with the general outward appearance of that which claims to be the Church

IX.

The Parable of the Net Cast into the Sea.

The Lord has now completed the sad story of the mingling of Satan's tares with the wheat of God : it only remains to speak of the final separation, which shall once more make it easy to discern between the righteous and the wicked, between him that serveth God and him that serveth Him not. And this time of judgment is depicted in the Parable of the net.

The sea here, as often in Scripture, represents the world in agitation. So the Psalmist says of the Lord ; —" Which stilleth the noise of the seas, the noise of their waves, and the tumult of the peoples."[1]

[1] Psa. lxv. 7. So, too, in Daniel's vision, the four Gentile World-powers are seen to emerge from the raging sea.

The net is the circle of the visible Church, all the Christian sects which are used for the gathering in of God's people. We may, however, remark that nets do not catch all the fish of the sea, nor is even a mere profession universal. Also that, although fish of every kind are caught, there are at last but two sorts: all are either good or bad.

The net is not brought to the shore, which is the end of this age of restless confusion, until it is full: for God has fore-ordained how many of the human race shall come within the circle of the Gospel during the times of the Gentiles. And the first indication that it has been drawn up will be the removal of a number of believers into the presence of their Lord: then the separating process will be continued by a second ascension of saints, at the sounding of the seventh trumpet; and finished by the appearing of the Lord in glory and the destruction of the wicked. Thus the good will first be gathered into vessels, and then the bad will be cast away.

X

Summary of the Seven Parables.

Such, then, is the first great revelation in regard to the career of the nominal Church. The Lord sows good seed; but the bad soil of human hearts renders it for the most part unfruitful. And where it is growing well, an enemy causes disastrous confusion by stealthily introducing disguised children of the Wicked One among the children of the Kingdom. Changed by this evil admixture, the professing Church casts off her humility, and, ceasing to wait for the Lord from heaven, strives to establish herself upon earth. Throwing aside the cross, she desires to say, " I sit a queen, and am no widow "; and, in order to gratify her ambition, enters into a shameful alliance with the great ones of earth, and suffers the Powers of Darkness, the devourers of the word, to take shelter in her branches. With such counsellors and helpers she organizes herself, and so corrupts the whole word of God by the teachings of demons that it can no longer be recovered, any more than fine flour can be again purified from that which has once leavened it. After a while there follows a time of partial revival, corresponding to the reformation of the Jews under Zerubbabel and Joshua, but also resembling that movement in its speedy subsidence to apathy and deadness. During this period, however, the word is able to be separated from the field, though it could not be recovered from the leaven, and many a one comes upon it unexpectedly, and receives it with joy as a great treasure, although in order to obtain it he must needs buy the whole field. Then the word is again hidden ; not, however, at this time by fixed and rigid dogmas, but by opinions of perplexing variety which are ever shifting like the waves of the sea. Yet the agitated and threatening state of the world moves some to search earnestly for Divine revelation and truth, and those who do so find the pearl of great price, and if they are willing to give up all else, may possess and enjoy it. At the close of this period the Lord suddenly begins to pass in review the whole of Christendom, all the nations who have heard His Gospel, and by taking those who have accepted it to Himself, and casting the obstinately rebellious into a furnace of fire, at length effects the separation which His servants are not permitted to attempt, and finishes the mystery of God.

Who can thoughtfully consider these Parables and refuse to admit their striking fulfilment, thus far, in the history of the professing Church, together with the grave inference that the days of this dispensation are numbered ?

XI.

THE PLAN OF THE APOCALYPSE.

Before we examine the prophecy contained in the Epistles to the Seven Churches, it will be necessary to have some idea of the general scheme of the Apocalypse —that last gift of the Lord Jesus to His people, that book without a little understanding of which it is unlikely that any Christian will be kept from the delusions, religious and political, which are now overspreading the earth. "Blessed is he that readeth, and they that hear, the words of the prophecy, and keep the things which are written therein : for the time is at hand."

The beloved apostle was suffering affliction, on the barren island of Patmos, " for the word of God, and for the testimony of Jesus Christ," when the revelation was made to him.

He was, as he tells us, "in spirit on the Lord's day," that is, according to the majority of interpreters, "in spirit on the first day of the week." But by such an explanation John is made to introduce a term unknown to the New Testament in place of the invariable designation of the Christian Sabbath. Moreover, the sense thus educed is weak and inadequate, having no apparent connection with the revelations which follow.

To us, then, although we admit a slight grammatical difficulty,[1] the rendering, "I was in spirit in the Day of the Lord," seems far more probable, and by adopting it we both secure a vigorous sense which bears upon the whole Book, and at the same time preserve for the expression, "the Lord's day," or the day belonging to the Lord, that meaning which, however much subsequent usage may have departed from it, is always retained in the Old and New Testaments.

By the words "in spirit" John explains his own condition: he was not, like Paul on a similar occasion, uncertain in regard to it, but fully aware that he was out of the body and on the plane of spirit. "In the Day of the Lord," on the contrary, has reference to the external surroundings in which he found himself, and furnishes us with a general clue for the interpretation of the visions. A strictly analogous description may be found in the second verse of the fourth chapter, where he says;—"And immediately I was in spirit; and, behold, a Throne."

If the clause be thus understood, it contains an announcement that the vision is for the time of the end, dealing first with Christ's judgment of the whole career of His Church, and then passing on to the last of the Seventy Weeks in which He will have His great

[1] We speak of it as slight, because the Greek of the Apocalypse is by no means severe Attic, and John may have had in mind rather the fact that he found himself in the Day of the Lord than that he was projected thither. In that case there would be little difference between the construction of this sentence and the ἐγενόμην ἐν τῇ νήσῳ of the preceding verse.

A good parallel to ἡ κυριακὴ ἡμέρα, in the sense of the Day of the Lord, may be found in Paul's use of ἀνθρωπίνη ἡμέρα for "man's day" in opposition to it. See 1 Cor. iv. 3—5. The E. V. has "man's judgment," which is, however, an exposition, not a translation.

controversy with Jew and Gentile. Such a meaning will be in exact accord with the nineteenth verse, and also, as we shall presently see, with the whole structure of the Book.

While, then, in spirit, and disengaged from earthly things, John suddenly heard behind him a great voice, like that of a trumpet, saying ;—" What thou seest, write in a book, and send it to the Seven Churches ; unto Ephesus, and unto Smyrna, and unto Pergamos, and unto Thyatira, and unto Sardis, and unto Philadelphia, and unto Laodicea."

At the sound of this voice John turned, and beheld a vision which, at first, may have suggested to him the Holy Place of the Temple. But it was not the Temple: for he quickly perceived an absence of familiar objects ; there was neither altar of incense, nor table of shewbread. Nor was he gazing upon any of those heavenly realities which were shown as a pattern to Moses on the Mount ; for, in place of a single seven-branched lampstand, seven distinct lamps were set before him.

What he saw was the heavenly Sanctuary arranged for the present parenthetical dispensation. And, consequently, all that had formerly represented Christ was now removed, because He was present in His own person : John beheld nothing save the Lord and the symbols of the Church for which He had died. There were seven separate lamps of gold, connected only by their association with a glorious Priestly Figure walking in the midst of them.

But why this change from the one seven-branched lamp of Israelitish times ?[1] The Lord Himself presently

[1] It will, perhaps, occur to the reader that there were ten lampstands in the Temple of Solomon (1 Kings vii. 49 ; 2 Chron. iv. 7).

gives the reason: each lamp represents the Church of a particular place; so that they indicate locality, and not, as some have supposed, the human divisions of sect, which could never be recognized in the heavenly Sanctuary.

In the previous dispensation there had been one earthly and visible centre of worship; and, to signify this, the lamp of the Tabernacle was in one piece. But now there is no Jerusalem to which men must go: true worshippers must worship the Father in spirit and in truth. And the Church of Christ is defined for us as consisting of "all that call upon the name of our Lord Jesus Christ *in every place*, their Lord and ours."[1] Therefore in every locality the whole body of believers, to whatever outward denomination they may individually belong, collectively form the lamp of that place.

Alas! that Christians should so often ignore this fact of their unity; or, if their lips confess it, convict themselves of hypocrisy by their deeds! Yet, even though they be born again, God can only delight in them while they are walking as brethren; for they are members of Christ's body, of His flesh and of His bones. The

But we are not told what became of the original light which had stood in the Tabernacle, and may, therefore, probably conclude that it occupied its proper place in the Temple, and understand, with the Rabbis, that the ten were additional to it and distinct in meaning. For in the reign of Abijah we still find mention of a single lampstand of gold which it was the priest's duty to keep burning throughout the night (2 Chron. xiii. 11).

In the Temples of Zerubbabel (1 Macc. i. 21; iv. 49) and Herod, also, we hear of but one, which, upon the destruction of its last resting place, was carried to Rome, and, after having graced the triumph of Titus, was deposited in the Temple of Peace. According to one legend it was finally lost in the Tiber, having fallen into the water from the Milvian bridge during the headlong flight of Maxentius from Constantine.

[1] 1 Cor. i. 2.

distinctions of sect, however impossible it may be to get rid of them in this present distress, owe their existence to human sin and lack of love. Consequently, they will altogether disappear when the Church is glorified, and should be kept as much as possible out of sight in the Church militant.

Standing, then, in the midst of the golden lamps was the majestic form of the High Priest Who has entered into the heavens, now to appear in the presence of God for us. John did not, however, see Him in the heavenly Holy of holies turned toward God in intercession, but in the Holy Place watching the lamps, that is, directing and judging His Church. He was not yet clad in the robes of glory and beauty: for His dress apparently corresponded to the linen garments which were used in ordinary priestly service, and especially by the High Priest on the great Day of Atonement. Then, after the sin-offerings had been sacrificed, the atonement in the Holy of holies accomplished, and the scape-goat sent away, Aaron put off the garb of service in the Holy Place, and, clothing himself in his splendid array, lifted up the veil, and appeared to the waiting people in token that their iniquity was covered. But Christ's intercession was not yet ended: it was not the time for Him to fulfil this type by appearing to them that look for Him without sin unto salvation.

He was clad in a garment reaching down to the feet, and girt with a golden girdle. His head and His hair were white and lustrous; His eyes like flames of fire; His feet as brass glowing in the furnace; and an effort is made to give some idea of the fulness and majesty of His voice by the glorious comparison that it was as the sound of many waters. In His right hand—held, perhaps, as a garland—were seven stars; and out of His mouth went a sharp two-edged sword; while the face, in which there was once no beauty to be desired, the visage, which was so marred more than any man, was now resplendent as the sun shining in his strength.

And although even this was far from being the fulness of His glory, yet the beloved disciple was unable to bear it, and fell at His feet as dead.

Then the Lord touched him, and again John heard the loving words, "Fear not," and was strengthened to receive the command;—"Write the things which thou sawest, and the things which are, and the things which shall come to pass after these."[1] It was thus evidently implied that the revelation to be written by the apostle would consist of three distinct parts: unless, therefore, we can so divide the Apocalypse, it is useless to think of interpreting it.

Now in regard to the first division there can be no difficulty: "the things which thou sawest"[2] can only refer to the vision of the heavenly Sanctuary, by which

[1] Dean Alford strongly supports a different rendering of this verse;—"Write the things which thou sawest, and what things they signify, and the things which are about to happen after these." The change is scarcely necessary, and, if it be preferred, does not affect our interpretation. For the exposition of what John saw must still reveal the things that are, or the present Church-period as symbolised by the lampstands in the Sanctuary. And the first verse of the fourth chapter still marks the transition from this dispensation to that which shall follow it.

[2] The aorist tense εἶδες, which should be rendered, "thou sawest," and which is repeated in the following verse, seems to imply that the vision had already passed away. In the fourth and succeeding chapters the Sanctuary is altogether different. The laver, the altars, and, finally, the ark of the covenant, reappear, showing that the prophecy is then concerned with the Jews of the last days.

the difference between the Christian Church and the Jewish system had been exhibited, and the solemn fact revealed that the Lord's eyes of flame are ever upon those who profess to be His.

"The things that are"—or a prophetic outline of the phases of the nominal Church, which were to succeed each other during the present age—naturally follow in the next chapter. They are also continued in the third, but no further: for, in the first verse of the fourth chapter, John sees a door opened in heaven, and hears a voice saying;—" Come up hither, and I will show thee the things which must come to pass after these."

Then the scene is shifted from earth to heaven; and the ascent of the apostle is doubtless a type of that translation of believers which will close "the things that are," and announce the approaching resumption of the suspended covenant with Israel. Henceforth the Church disappears from the prophecy; and the very name occurs no more till we come to the sixteenth verse of the twenty-second chapter, where "the Churches" are indeed mentioned, but merely as those to whom testimony is given, and not as having any part in the scenes of terror which shall characterize "the things that must be after these." This fact is in itself a most significant hint of the removal of believers from earth before the judgments of the seals, trumpets, or vials, begin; and there is yet stronger evidence of a change of dispensation in the fourth and following chapters.

For we must not forget the difference between the previous age and the present time of grace, in that God had then a visible Kingdom upon earth, which is not the case now. Consequently, during that period, judgment was to be executed upon those who broke His law: vengeance, as we so often find in the Psalms, was imprecated upon all who feared Him not; and it was right to destroy His enemies with the sword.

But the Spirit descended upon our Lord in the form of a harmless dove: and, accordingly, we discover nothing in His teaching or example analogous to the slaying of the firstborn, or the overwhelming of Pharaoh and his host in the Red Sea; nothing like the extirpation of the Canaanites, or the calling down of fire from heaven to consume the adversaries. On the contrary, when His disciples would have had Him imitate Elijah, He replied;—"Ye know not what manner of spirit ye are of. For the Son of man is not come to destroy men's lives, but to save them." Hence any desire of vengeance is unlawful for believers of our age: we are required to love our enemies; and even if we should be persecuted to the death, have for our prayers only such models as, "Father, forgive them; for they know not what they do"; or, "Lord, lay not this sin to their charge."

The Spirit will, however, in His dove-like form, ascend with the translated Church; and, therefore, in the fourth chapter His influence is very differently represented as "seven torches of fire burning before the throne"—an appearance which corresponds with Isaiah's prophecy that God will, in the times of the end, purge "the blood of Jerusalem from the midst thereof by the Spirit of judgment, and by the Spirit of burning."

And this change in the form of the Heavenly Power soon manifests its solemn meaning: for, in the sixth chapter, the plagues of God begin to trouble the world, and the martyrs beneath the altar are heard crying for vengeance. Nor does their petition seem strange when, in the seventh chapter, we discover that Israelites are again the people of the Lord, and that those who are sealed for preservation are of the Twelve Tribes. And, a little later, the commission given to the Two Witnesses to destroy those who would hurt them, and the terrible severity with which they exercise their power, prove that they also are not subject to the laws now in force, but are connected with the dispensation of Moses and Elijah.

It will thus be seen that the plan of the Apocalypse presents no serious difficulty, provided that we remember its threefold division, and interpret it by means of the great clue, the prophecy of the Seventy Weeks. We may sum up its contents as follows.

Chap. i. is a vision of the heavenly Sanctuary prepared for these present times.

Chaps. ii. and iii. reveal the whole career of the visible Church, from the close of the Apostolic period until the Lord comes.

Chaps. iv. and v. exhibit the preparations in heaven for the judgments of the Last Week.

Chaps. vi.—xviii. describe the appalling culmination of wickedness in the last seven years : they also foretell the judgments by which those who corrupt the earth shall be destroyed, while the remnant of Israel is being purged and delivered from the oppression of the world by such fearful signs, and wonders, and plagues, that it shall no more be said ;—" The Lord liveth, that brought up the children of Israel out of the land of Egypt ; but, the Lord liveth, that brought up the children of Israel from the land of the North, and from all the lands whither He had driven them." These chapters are generally consecutive : we have first the seals, the seventh of which includes the seven trumpets ; and then the last trumpet is developed into the seven vials, the final plagues by which the wrath of God is completed. Chaps. xi.—xv. seem to be a parenthesis inserted for the purpose of supplying details of the times of the seals, trumpets, and vials. The seventeenth chapter is partly concerned with the previous history of the Woman and the Beast, in order that the last scene in their joint history may be better understood : the eighteenth describes the fall of Babylon the Great.

Chaps. xix.—xxii. treat of the appearing of the Lord, of the destruction of His enemies, and of the setting up of His Kingdom. Then there is a brief notice of a rebellion which will follow the loosing of Satan from the abyss at the end of the thousand years, and also of the last judgment ; and the prophecy closes with a description of the heavenly city.

If it be thus interpreted, the Revelation is no longer a sealed book. Those portions of it which have already become history may be explained without difficulty ; while the remainder is, in general outline at least, sufficiently easy of comprehension.

XII

The Epistles to the Seven Churches.

THERE can be no doubt that these letters were primarily intended for the communities to which they are inscribed, and deal with actual circumstances of the time. But, since they are also called "the things that are," as distinguished from those which shall be hereafter in a different dispensation, it seems equally clear that the Churches addressed must have been selected on account of their representative character. And the arrangement was probably made to serve a double purpose.

In the first place, because, when taken together, they exhibited every phase of Christian society which would ever be found in the various parts of Christendom, and so enabled the Lord to give comfort, advice, exhortation, warning, and threatening, from which something could be found to suit any possible circumstance of His people till the end of the age.

And secondly, because, in the order in which they were given, they foreshadowed the successive predominant phases through which the nominal Church was to pass, from the time when John saw the vision until the Lord should come.

We have thus two reasons for the selection of these particular Churches to the exclusion of others of equal or greater importance, and also for the mystical number seven, which here, as elsewhere, signifies dispensational completeness.

At present we are, of course, mainly concerned with the Epistles as prophetically foreshadowing the great changes which should succeed each other in the condition of the visible Church. This they do in a striking manner; and, indeed, the mere names of the Churches, when their meaning is understood, suggest seven ecclesiastical epochs. These names we now subjoin, before going into details in regard to the Epistles themselves, adding their significations, and the periods of Church history in which they seem to find their fulfilment.

Ephesus = relaxation. The waning of love at the close of the apostolic period.

Smyrna = myrrh, bitterness. The Ten Persecutions.

Pergamos = a tower. Earthly greatness of the Church from the accession of Constantine.

Thyatira = she that is unwearied in sacrifices. The Church of Rome with her perpetually repeated sacrifice of the mass.

Sardis = renovation. The results of the Reformation.

Philadelphia = brotherly love. The gathering out of those who think the love of Christ a stronger bond of union than any ties of sect, and who will be caught up to meet Him when He comes.

Laodicea = the judgment of the people, the Church in which the people constitute themselves judges of what is right. The self-confident body which goes its own way, and is thoroughly satisfied with it, but is rejected of the Lord.

Thus the bare names of the Churches furnish a sketch of the history of Christendom until the end of the age; and the outline, as we shall presently see, is filled in by the Epistles themselves. Nor is it difficult to understand why the Lord chose so peculiar a form for His revelation. For while these chapters have been at all times most useful for reproof, correction, instruction, or encouragement, their prophetic import could scarcely have been discovered, or even suspected, until they were all but fulfilled. And so they would never, by suggesting events that must first happen, cause the Church to say, "My Lord delayeth His coming." And, on the other hand, when, at the time of the end, the Spirit should unveil their hidden meaning, it would bring deep conviction of the nearness of the advent to every thoughtful and reverent mind.[1]

XIII.

EPHESUS.

THE believers in Ephesus had, as a Church, enjoyed the greatest privileges; and stirred by the ministry of Paul, Apollos, Aquila and Priscilla, Timothy, Tychicus, and others, they had so far advanced in holiness and the knowledge of our Lord Jesus Christ, that Paul, in his Epistle to them, is able to speak in terms of high commendation. But the letter which we are now to consider was dictated some thirty years later, and then the symptoms of a deadly decay were just beginning to appear. Another generation had arisen, still holding fast the tradition of earnest devotion to Christ, but having lost much of the motive power of that

[1] We must not forget that in this prophecy, as in that of the Seven Parables, a phase may be continued, though with contracted area, far beyond the time of its predominance, even, indeed, until the Lord's return. There is a plain intimation that this will be the case with Pergamos—for the Lord has not yet fought against the Balaamites with the sword of His mouth; with Thyatira—for the remnant are bidden to hold that fast which they have until He come; with Sardis—for she is told that, unless she watches, He will come upon her as a thief; and with Philadelphia—for He promises her that He is coming quickly, and charges her to hold fast that which she has, that no one take her crown. Indeed, the nominal Church will, doubtless, in its last as in its first days embrace communities which, taken together, will exhibit all the characteristics mentioned by Christ; so that each of these Epistles will retain its directly practical value until the end. But at that time the prevailing phase will be the Laodicean.

devotion. And so this Church, with its suggestive name of Ephesus, or "relaxation,"[1] could aptly represent the waning of love at the close of apostolic times.

To the Ephesians, then, the Lord presents Himself as the One Who holds in full control the seven angels of the Churches, and walks continually in the midst of the lamps: for believers who had lost their first love were likely to have forgotten these solemn facts. The result of His ceaseless inspection is, that He knows, not merely every word and deed, but even every thought of the Church; and, most graciously, He first mentions what is deserving of praise.

Their works and labour and patience, in regard to all who were within the pale of the professing body, have not escaped His notice. He has observed their hatred of that which is evil, and their carefulness in testing and detecting the false apostles of whom they had been forewarned.[2] He has seen, too, their attitude towards them that are without, their steady patience in endeavouring to lead them to Him, and their willingness to bear persecution for His sake; and He has marked that, spite of all hindrance and opposition, they have not grown weary in well-doing.

He has, therefore, no complaint to make in regard to doctrine or work. There is both orthodoxy and energy, and, moreover, a praiseworthy determination to be separate from evil. And yet all this cannot avail. Upon the seemingly perfect Church there is a slowly-spreading plague-spot which causes Him suddenly to change His tone. The praise He has

---

[1] Ἔφεσος from ἐφίημι, which often means "to let go," or, "loosen the rein."

[2] Acts xx. 28-30.

given is deserved, but He adds;—" Nevertheless, I have[1] against thee that thou hast left thy first love." The teaching, labour, and zeal, of Ephesus were blameless; but her love was waxing cold, and, therefore, she was fast becoming as sounding brass or a clanging cymbal.

But the Lord would not abandon her to ruin. He calls upon her to remember; to look back upon what she was, that she may mourn for what she is, and cry, " Oh that I were as in months past!" For, after all, this Church, which to the eyes of men seemed perfect and wanting in nothing, is found to be " fallen."

A threat follows. Unless Ephesus repents, and does the first works—not merely feels the first feelings, but does the works which should spring from them— the High Priest will remove her candlestick: she shall be His witness no longer. This chastisement does not involve everlasting destruction, but only the withdrawal of power to bear effectual testimony. Many an unfaithful and worldly-minded believer is smitten by it, and walks the earth deprived of all power of speaking for his Saviour. He may utter words, but they carry no weight: the influence of the Spirit does not accompany them. For the sin of his covetousness, for his selfishness, and because his soul cleaves to the dust of earth, he has been deprived of the gifts which he abused: he is losing the precious seed-time of life: there is no reward laid up in the heavens for him. Such a one can scarcely hope to have boldness in the

---

[1] The " somewhat " of the Authorized Version is not found in the Greek, and its introduction conceals the severity of the reproof.

Day of Judgment, when he stands before the Throne of Christ to give an account of the things done in the body: he must expect to suffer loss, and to be saved only "so as through fire."

So searchingly has the Lord used His eyes of flame; and in laying bare the condition of Ephesus, He reveals to us the earliest symptom of decline which appeared in the universal Church, the wane of love. But what depths of His tenderness are disclosed by this Epistle! He first speaks at length of those things which He could commend; and then, after a very few words of censure, again reverts to praise. Yet He does rebuke: He will not overlook our faults for the sake of our virtues.

The last thing for which Ephesus may be praised is that she hates the deeds of the Nicolaitans, which Christ also hates. Possibly those to whom reference is made were a sect of the day in Ephesus; yet nothing is known of their history, all notices in early writers being manifest conjectures framed to explain our Lord's allusion. But, whatever they may have been in the literal Ephesus, it is clear that something more than an unknown party or sect is indicated in a great prediction of the whole Church. And so, in the prophetic interpretation of the Epistle, the name Nicolaitan is doubtless typical—like Jezebel, Sodom, and Egypt, in other parts of the Apocalypse—rather than historical. It signifies "subduers of the laity," or "people,"[1] and its introduction seems to intimate

---

[1] Νικολαιτοί, from νικάω "to conquer," "overpower," and λαός "people." From the latter word comes the English term "laity," through the adj. λαϊτος. The name Balaam, which is brought into connection with the Nicolaitans in the Epistle to Pergamos,

that the apostolic arrangements for the government of the Churches were beginning to be abused; that some were already striving to act as lords over the charge allotted to them, endeavouring to establish a hierarchy, a clerical caste which should be distinguished from and superior to the great body of believers. No authority for such a scheme could be found in the New Testament, and those who were guided by the word and Spirit of God must have foreseen how disastrous its results would be. For, if successful, it would turn away the eyes of the Church from her great High Priest to human leaders: it would quickly arouse party feelings, cause schisms, and tend to secularize that which should be purely spiritual: and it would thus soften, and finally obliterate, the line of demarcation between the Church and the world, and induce the former to use the tactics, and desire the aid, of the latter.

Paul anticipated Nicolaitanism in his farewell address to the Ephesian elders, when he said;—"For I know this, that, after my departing, shall grievous wolves enter in among you, not sparing the flock. Also of your own selves shall men arise, speaking perverse things, to draw away the disciples after them."[1] And these men, since the Ephesian Church had not yet yielded to them, are probably to be identified with those who said they were apostles, but upon trial were detected and found to be liars.[2]

Peter also throws out a hint that the evil was

---

has a still stronger meaning, and signifies "devourer of the people."

[1] Acts xx. 29, 30.
[2] Rev. ii. 2.

spreading in other Churches, when he entreats the elders to whom he is writing not to exercise the oversight of their flocks as if they were lords over the charge allotted to them.[1] And John refers to a particular case, and speaks of one Diotrephes, who loved to have the pre-eminence, and was casting out of the Church those who would not submit to him.[2]

But all this mischief had been foreseen and reprobated by the Saviour Himself in the memorable words;—"Ye know that the rulers of the Gentiles lord it over them, and their great ones exercise authority over them. Not so shall it be among you: but whosoever would become great among you shall be your minister ; and whosoever would be first among you shall be your servant."[3]

The significant manner in which the Lord notes the rejection, for the time, of the Nicolaitans by Ephesus, coupled with the emphatic addition of the words, "which I also hate," is, perhaps, a hint that, although the Church was still standing in that particular, she had need to take heed lest she should fall. For if any Church is losing its love to Christ, how can it avoid becoming a mere earthly organization under human leaders?

Some twelve years after the dictation of this letter, Ignatius addressed an epistle to the Ephesians which contains unmistakable evidence that a hierarchy was then being established among them. Ignatius supports it, and gives the most extravagant injunctions respecting obedience to the bishop, which culminate in the words;—"It is manifest, therefore, that we ought to look upon the bishop even as we would look upon

[1] 1 Pet. v. 2, 3.   [2] 3 John 9, 10.   [3] Matt. xx. 25-27.

the Lord Himself."[1] The subject appears to have been attracting general attention at the time; for Ignatius often alludes to it, and in his Epistle to the Magnesians, allows himself to say;—"As, therefore, the Lord does nothing without the Father—'For I can,' He says, 'of Mine Own Self do nothing'—so also do ye nothing without the bishop; whether ye be presbyters, or deacons, or laymen?"[2]

Thus, then, the signs of decadence among professing Christians of the first age were the waning of deep and heartfelt love to the Lord Jesus, and a consequent discontent with Him as the only Head of His body the Church—a feeling similar, perhaps, to that which prompted the Israelites to demand a king who should go before them. And so men began to form human organizations, which, whatever their nominal sovereignty, soon proved by their deeds that they owed allegiance, not to Christ, but to His adversary, the Prince of this World.

In the last portion of the Epistle, the promise to

[1] Ignat. Ad. Eph. vi.
[2] Ignat. Ad. Magn. vii. Ignatius is the first writer who uses the term "bishop" in the modern, rather than in the apostolic, sense. For the apostles instituted only two orders of ministers—elders, or presbyters, and deacons: but as soon as Churches began to be organized among the Hellenists, the Greek term "bishop" ($\dot{\epsilon}\pi\dot{\iota}\sigma\kappa o\pi o\varsigma$—that is, "overseer") was frequently substituted for "elder." The two words were, however, strictly synonymous, as we may see by examining the following passages;—Acts xx. 17 and 28; Titus i. 5-7; 1 Peter v. 1, 2. In Phil. i. 1, Paul salutes the bishops and deacons: he would not have left out the presbyters if they had been another order. So, in 1 Tim. iii. 1-7, he speaks of bishops, and then, in vv. 8-13, goes on at once to deacons. Clement of Rome uses bishop and presbyter as interchangeable terms, and the recently discovered "Teaching of the Apostles" contains the command;—"Appoint, therefore, for yourselves bishops and deacons worthy of the Lord."

the overcomer, the Lord addresses those individual members of the Church who are so guided by the Spirit that they are able to discern even the deep things of God. There is a similar promise at the close of each of the other letters, and they are all drawn from the Old Testament, and arranged in historical order. And so, in this first case, the reward offered is the Tree of Life, which is in the midst of the Paradise of God.

The allusion is singularly appropriate. The parents of our race were created in innocency, and should have eaten of the Tree of Life; but were commanded by God not to touch the Tree of the knowledge of Good and Evil. Then another being, the Tempter, appeared upon the scene, and induced them to break God's commandment on the ground of expediency.

Thus they turned from Jehovah and obeyed Satan: they ate of the forbidden fruit, and were, consequently, driven out of the garden, and far away from the Tree which would have made them live for ever.

So, in these early days of the Church, Satan craftily enticed her aside from her Lord; and, as her love towards Him began to wax cold, suggested that His spiritual presence was no sufficient connecting bond for the assemblies of His people upon earth, and that believers must, therefore, endeavour to weld themselves into societies by adopting such forms of government as are usual in the world.

To these seductions she yielded, and, despising the wisdom which is from above, chose rather to be led by that which is earthly, soulish, and demon-like. So her early purity became as the morning dew: she was quickly, as a corporate society, thrust out of the

Heavenly places into which she had been called to sit with Christ: her organization began more and more nearly to resemble those of this world: and she was soon fain, by minding earthly things, to seek consolation for the loss of that spiritual power which now remained only with some of her individual members.

XIV.

SMYRNA.

WE have seen that in the first, or Ephesian period, the Church was losing the fervour of her love to the Lord Jesus. In the second, we may discern the correction of this declension, the severe chastening which followed closely upon the early symptoms of corruption. And this is foreshadowed in the Epistle to Smyrna, the very name of which is deeply suggestive:[1] for its root-meaning is "bitterness;" and it then comes to signify "myrrh," an unguent commonly used in connection with death.[2] The love of the Church for Christ is diminishing, therefore the world which is attracting her must be made bitter: she must be cast into affliction and suffering even unto death. But the loving sympathy of the Lord shines forth in this painful crisis. He stayeth His rough wind in the day of the East wind, and has no censure for the persecuted Church, but only gracious words of praise and encouragement, and a tender exhortation to His own to be faithful unto the end, that He may give them a crown of life.

[1] Σμύρνα is used for μύρρα—that is, myrrh. It is connected with a Hebrew root which shows that "bitterness" is its primary meaning.
[2] John xix. 39.

He describes Himself to them as the First and the Last: and how comforting is the thought conveyed by this title to those who are suffering and depressed. For at times, when hope has been long deferred, it seems to sickening faith as if God had departed from our world, and none were left to check the cruel power of the enemy. But it is not so: whatever may happen in the meanwhile, He that was the First, and gave the promises, will also appear with irresistible power as the Last to see that they fail not in the very least particular. So that every fainting believer may revive himself with the glorious—though in our version somewhat obscure—words of Job;—"I know that my Redeemer liveth, and that He shall arise as the Last One over the dust of my grave."

But the Lord also reminds His troubled people that He is the One "Which was dead and lived again." "When He putteth forth His own sheep, He goeth before them." All their sufferings He has endured in His own person; therefore, He knows how to succour them: His path of death had led to everlasting life; and as it had been with Him, so should it be with His faithful disciples.

With the conditions and trials of this Church also the High Priest is fully acquainted: He has marked her tribulation, and the patience with which she endured it. Whenever affliction has altogether ceased, it is to us much as waters that have flowed by: but He remembers in what spirit we bore it, and will by no means forget our trustfulness, if we have been enabled to commit ourselves into His hand as unto a faithful Creator.

SMYRNA.

The believers in Smyrna were bowed down by oppression, and were also in great poverty; but they had taken joyfully the spoiling of their goods. And the Lord declares that in the meanwhile their treasure in heaven has been augmenting, and that they will presently find themselves exceedingly rich, and a notable example of the word;—" There is that scattereth, and yet increaseth."

But He not only knows the afflictions of His people, and puts all their tears into His bottle: He also sees the cruelty and blasphemy of their oppressors. In the literal application of the Epistle, those " which say they are Jews, and are not," were probably actual Jews according to the flesh, who in early times were always on the side of the enemies of the Church. And it is worthy of notice that, in the account of Polycarp's death at Smyrna, certain Jews are mentioned as being active in providing the wood for his martyrdom. It may have been one of the peculiar trials of believers in those days to find the children of Abraham invariably ranged with the Heathen against them. Satan may have plagued many with the suggestion; —" Can you possibly be right? The chosen people themselves are opposed to you, those to whom the oracles of God were committed. The nation which for so many centuries was set forth by God as His witness upon earth, and from which you confess that your Messiah sprang, declares that you are deceived." But the Lord here intimates that those who were once His people are no longer so, but have become a synagogue of Satan; just as He had previously told them to their faces;—" Ye are of your father the Devil."

In the prophetic application of the Epistle, those "which say they are Jews, and are not," represent the multitude of false teachers who at this time entered the Church, and of whom we have already spoken in our interpretation of the Parable of the Tares. Many of the so-called Fathers were among them; and they strove, under a false pretext of Old Testament authority, to introduce the Babylonian priestcraft. Their plan was to magnify the importance of outward forms, and then to affirm that none but initiated priests could rightly administer them, a doctrine which the Heathen would well understand. And so, Baptism and the Lord's Supper were conveniently modified; and then, although they are but seldom mentioned in the New Testament, they were made the foundation of the false Christianity.

But the Church in Smyrna was not only suffering from the curses and revilings of Jews, it had also known what it was to be despitefully used and persecuted, and there were yet worse troubles to come. Satan was about to cast some of the disciples into prison, and would even move his agents to slay them. But while the Adversary would do this for their harm, God would turn it into good: it should prove to be that trial of their faith and patience which, after it had finished its work, should leave them perfect and entire, wanting nothing. And although men might take away their lives, the Lord would turn the shadow of death into a glorious and everlasting morning. Ten days were doubtless the exact time of the hottest persecution in the case of the literal Smyrna: in the prophetic interpretation we may, probably, find a reference to the ten great persecutions which began with Nero's cruelties at the close of the apostolic times.

The promise with which this Epistle concludes is pregnant with meaning. There is an evident allusion in the words, "He that overcometh shall not be hurt of the second death," to the entrance of death into the world, after the revolving flame had cut off all access to the Tree of Life. Now of the first martyr, Abel, we are told that by faith he offered a more excellent sacrifice than Cain, and that God testified to his righteousness by accepting him, while He rejected his brother.[1] But the latter "was of that Wicked One": his envy was excited, and he slew Abel, because his own works were evil and his brother's righteous.[2] This was the first outburst of enmity from the serpent's seed, and from that time until now, he that is born of the flesh has ever persecuted him that is born of the Spirit. It was not long before the Church discovered this truth, and she had bitter experience of it in the Ten Persecutions.

But she is comforted with the promise that, if she remains faithful, she shall suffer nothing worse than the first death, and shall never be hurt of the second, which is the Lake of Fire and Brimstone.[3] And so the Lord here repeats in another form the solemn warning;—"And I say unto you My friends, Be not afraid of them that kill the body, and after that have no more that they can do. But I will warn you Whom ye shall fear: Fear Him Which after He hath killed hath power to cast into Hell; yea, I say unto you, Fear Him."[4]

[1] Heb. xi. 4.
[2] 1 John iii. 12.
[3] Rev. xxi. 8.
[4] Luke xii. 4, 5.

XV.

Pergamos.

In examining the third Epistle, we shall find it expedient to consider first its practical bearing as addressed to the literal Pergamos,[1] in order that we may the more clearly understand its prophetic import.

To this Church the Lord is " He that hath the sharp two-edged sword." Against Smyrna the sword of man had been lifted up : but now the sword of the Lord is drawn, and He stands confronting those who are moving toward the world, even as His angel stood in the way of Balaam.

Pergamos, as we have already mentioned, had once been the centre of Paganism, and still retained much of its prestige. It was said to be more devoted to the worship of the deities than any other city of Asia, which is no marvel when we remember how long it had been the head-quarters of the Chaldean priest-king. "It was," says Mr. Blakesley, "a sort of union of a Pagan cathedral city, a university town, and a royal residence embellished, during a succession of years, by kings who had a passion for expenditure and ample means of gratifying it." Its inhabitants were styled νεωκόροι πρῶτοι τῆς 'Ασίας, a title which it is difficult to translate, but which indicated that they were entrusted with the maintenance of some important religious worship on behalf of Asia. What kind of

---

[1] This name would be more correctly written " Pergamum ' ' but we have not altered the customary form. It is connected with πύργος, " a tower." Hence Πέργαμος, or the plural Πέργαμα, was the name of the citadel of Troy, and was afterwards used for any citadel.

PERGAMOS.

worship it was, we have no means for determining; probably it was connected with the history which we have already sketched. But, however this may be, the Bible does not leave us in uncertainty as to the supreme importance of Pergamos to Heathendom, since it reveals the fact that Satan's throne was still there. In such a city outbursts of fanatical zeal would be likely to occur, and the Epistle intimates that the followers of Christ had recently suffered from them. Satan had presented himself as a roaring lion: he had torn some of the Pergamean believers, and driven others into great distress; but had effected nothing. The Church had held fast the name of her Lord, and would not deny His faith.

And now the Adversary was changing his tactics: he had lulled the storm of persecution, and was working by means of "false apostles, deceitful workers, fashioning themselves into apostles of Christ." Nay, he was fashioning himself into an angel of light, and using seductive flatteries; so that the Church which could brave his fury was yielding to his fascinations. She had ceased to cast out the false teachers, and they were rapidly bridging the chasm between herself and the world.

And this is the charge which the Lord had to bring against the Pergameans, though He would not utter it until He had first commended their faithfulness in the hour of trial. But ease and prosperity were now rendering them so careless that they were allowing the doctrine of the son of Beor to prevail among them, and did not eject those who held it. This was a symptom of fearful declension: for Balaam, though called of God to be a prophet, had taught Balak, one of the kings of this world, how to cast a stumbling-block before the children of Israel, by inducing them to eat things sacrificed to idols, and to commit fornication. And that which had been done to the mischief of Israel was now being repeated in order to effect the ruin of the Church at Pergamos.

The first part of Balaam's story is too well known to need repetition : it is sufficiently clear that, had he been permitted, he would have been willing, for the sake of gain, to abuse the powers entrusted to him, and to curse the people of God. In this, however, he was checked by the interposition of the Almighty; but even while the Divine influence was upon him, he continually wavered, and, as soon as it was withdrawn, appears to have given the rein to his covetousness. Through his greed for the wages of the Gentile king, he became anxious to assist him by reducing Israel to the level of Midian, and with this object tendered the fiendish advice, that all open resistance to the pilgrim-nation should be waived, that the hand of friendship should be extended to them, and the pleasures of sin set before them. If by such means they could be drawn into idolatrous abominations, there would no longer be any reason why the special favour of God should rest upon them, or why He should destroy the kingdoms of the world for their sake.

This guileful plan was speedily carried out, and idol festivals, with all their sensual attractions, were held within easy distance of the camp in the wilderness. The curiosity of the Israelites was excited : the feeling which had prompted them to eat and drink and play before the calf was again aroused. Many of them went to see the sight ; and, perhaps to their surprise, were received as friends by the Midianites, and invited to join the revel. Surely they could do so—just as they had often been present at the orgies of Egypt—and yet neither worship Baal nor provoke Jehovah. And, after all, Jehovah and Baal were but different names for the same Supreme Being, and the Midianites were serving Him according to their light. By such thoughts, it may be, Israel was enticed within the circle of Heathen abominations, and entered the fatal precincts surrounded—as the people of God always are, if they wilfully approach temptation—by hosts of evil spirits watching for an opportunity of hurling them over the precipice as soon as they could see them near the brink. Perhaps, for a short while, they thought they would only look on; but the allurements of sin quickly overcame them: they were soon feasting at the rich table of Baal, and becoming fascinated with the seductions of the daughters of Moab. Meanwhile, the Lord in the heavens was whetting His glittering sword, bending His bow, and preparing His arrows upon the string against His own rebellious people.

This history seems to have been repeated at Pergamos; for, after a bitter persecution, the Pagans were changing their tactics, and endeavouring under a friendly guise, and by the attractive sensuality of their worship, to lure away those believers whom they had failed to move by fear. And, doubtless, the Gnostics, unwearying mediators between Paganism and a careless Christianity, had crept in among the disciples, and were so bewildering them by skilful blendings and explanations, that they were gradually yielding, and allowing themselves to be drawn into the snare. Their own leaders, too, already accustomed to make a selfish use of their influence, were beginning, like Balaam, to run greedily after the gain which could be secured by conciliating the great ones of earth. And so, as the Church was leaving her appointed camp of separation, the Lord suddenly appeared in the way, and sternly commanded those who were His own to repent, and cast out the Balaamites, lest He Himself should be compelled to use His flashing sword.

Such, then, appears to have been the condition of the Christian community at Pergamos; and, with this knowledge of it, we may proceed to consider the prophetic meaning of the Epistle, as setting before us the third period of the universal Church.

The times of fiery persecution had now passed by. The slaughtered apostles were resting with their Lord; and the ashes of the flaming bodies used to illuminate the gardens of Nero had now lain cold for more than two centuries. The cruelties of Domitian, Trajan, and Adrian, were almost forgotten. Lyons had long ceased to shudder at the pains of Blandina and Pothinus; nor would Perpetua be any more worried by the savage beasts of the amphitheatre, or pierced by the sword of the gladiator. Maximus and Decius were dead: the African lime-kiln and the worship of Jupiter were no longer alternatives. The bloody reign of Diocletian and Maximian was ended: Sebastian had endured his second martyrdom, and the last sigh of Timothy and Maura had ascended to God from their crucified bodies. A new era had commenced: Satan had stayed the persecutions which had proved so ineffectual, and was now trying for better success by means of flattery and corruption, and by tempting the Church to accept worldly power.

PERGAMOS.

For this change he had been long preparing through the agency of the false teachers—those tares which he had stealthily sown among the wheat in the times of trouble, when hypocrisy was little suspected. By their influence Nicolaitanism had become an almost universal rule; so that the Churches were being governed, in much the same manner as earthly communities, by those whose intellectual power, or rank, or wealth, or intrigue, brought them to the front. And, as a natural consequence, many of these leaders were craving an extension of their influence, and manifesting a desire for worldly pre-eminence which soon caused a change in doctrine.

In the earliest times, believers were taught by the apostles to live in daily expectation of the Lord's return, and recognized no other way of permanent deliverance from the troubles of this world; but now ideas of a very different kind began to be ventilated. It was suggested that Christ could not return to a world so unprepared; that persecution would presently cease, and God might then be expected to give great power to His Church, and enable her to convert all men by her preaching. In this way the Millennium would be introduced without the need of any personal interference on the part of Christ. And since some Scriptural support was required for the new doctrine, it was obtained by affirming that the Jew had been cast off for ever, and then misapplying the prophecies of Israel's future glory to the body of nominal believers upon earth. Thus the disciples were induced to say with the slothful servant, "My Lord delayeth His coming"; and a spirit of worldliness continued to prevail in the Church until, when the fatal hour of prosperity arrived, she altogether ceased to wait for the Son from heaven, and proudly thought, "I sit a queen, and am no widow, and shall see no sorrow."

While these opinions were being disseminated, the great majority of Christians were manifesting a disposition to become conformed as much as possible in outward appearance to the world; and, as an example of the tendency, we may note that during this period various festivals were instituted at the times of the great Heathen festivals, because the Christians did not like to appear singular. And although they gave their own names to these holy-days, nevertheless, in order to attain their end, they were forced to imitate many of the Heathen customs. We will give one specimen of this kind of adaptation.[1]

According to Mr. Greswell, who supports his proposition by very able reasoning, our Lord must have been born on the fifth of April. But whether this date be exactly correct or not, it is sufficiently evident

[1] Many would be disposed to say, "Why not suffer the curtain of oblivion to rest for ever upon these lamentable facts? Now, at least, the days are honestly kept as Christian festivals: is it well to disturb men's minds by tracing such observances back to their Pagan origin?" There is, alas! a very urgent reason for doing so. Already there are in circulation among the educated classes infidel books, of considerable ability, in which the Pagan robes of certain forms of Christianity are powerfully and convincingly exposed. And then, since much which they have been taught to deem sacred is demonstrated to have been brought to them from Heathen sources, Christians are invited to believe that all other doctrines and observances of their faith are also of a similar character. It seems, therefore, absolutely necessary that we should henceforth accustom ourselves to discriminate between those things which, being ordinances of men, are justified only by their value in the war against the world and Satan, and those which, being direct commands of the Lord and His apostles, must be firmly retained in spite of all opposition and of every actual or possible consequence.

that the twenty-fifth of December could not have been the day. For shepherds would not have been "abiding in the field, keeping watch over their flock by night," at that cold season of the year, since they are not accustomed to do so later than October. Besides which, our Lord's mother would scarcely have been able, just before the birth of her Son, to travel from Nazareth to Bethlehem in the very depth of winter. "But pray ye that your flight be not in the winter," is His own injunction in the sermon on the Mount of Olives.

How is it, then, that the festival of Christ's birth is always kept on the twenty-fifth of December? To understand the mystery we must glance at a passage of Tertullian, in which he remonstrates with Christians of the end of the second, or beginning of the third, century as follows.

"But if we have no right of fellowship in such matters—that is, in Heathen festivals—with aliens, how much more sinful is it for brethren to assort together therein! Who can endure or maintain this? The Holy Spirit reproacheth the Jews for their feast days. 'Your Sabbaths,' saith He, 'and your new moons, and your ordinances, My soul hateth.' And do we, to whom these Sabbaths belong not, nor the new moons, nor the feast days once beloved of God, celebrate the feast of Saturn, and of January, and of the Winter Solstice, and the feast of Matrons? For us shall presents flow in; new year's gifts jingle; sports and banquets roar? O truer fidelity of the nations to their own religion, which claims for itself no solemnity of the Christians! No Lord's day, no Pentecost, even if they had known them, would they have shared with us! For they would be afraid lest they should be thought Christians: we are not afraid lest we should seem to be Heathen!"[1]

This passage exposes, generally, the origin of many of the so-called Church festivals, which were unknown to earlier times, and were adapted from Paganism because the Christians had grown cowardly, and were no longer willing to bear testimony to Christ by entire separation from the world. They would not remain on the top of the hill, where they could not be hid,[2] and so came half-way down towards the valley.

Now—to leave generalities and return to the subject of Christmas—the twenty-first of December is the shortest day of the year, the time when the sun has reached his lowest point; and it is not until the twenty-fifth that he begins to lengthen the duration of his light. Hence, throughout the whole Heathen world, the twenty-fifth was regarded as the birthday of the Sun-god, and a high festival, which was celebrated at Rome by the "Great Games" of the Circus. And, for obvious reasons, the Christians determined to commemorate the birth of Christ at the same time.

In his thirty-first homily, Chrysostom, after quoting the directions from the Pagan Calendar, remarks ;— "On this day, also, the birthday of Christ *was lately fixed at Rome*, in order that, while the Heathen were busied with their profane ceremonies, the Christians might perform their holy rites undisturbed."[3] He seems, however, to be conscious that the proceeding required some further apology, besides the excuse

[1] Tertull. De Idol. xiv.   [2] Matt. v. 14.

contained in the latter part of his sentence, and presently adds ;—" But they—that is, the Pagans—call this day the birthday of the Invincible One :[1] who, then, so invincible as the Lord that overthrew and vanquished death? Or because they style it the birthday of the Sun? He is the Sun of righteousness." This is a species of argument which has contributed much to the corruption of Christianity. What confusion of thought was produced by it in the particular matter before us, we may, perhaps, discover by a Christmas sermon of Leo the Great, who flourished about the middle of the fifth century. In it the prelate blames certain Christians for causing offence to their weaker brethren by reverencing the festival, not so much on account of Christ's birth, as on that of the "Rising of the new Sun."[2]

This instance will suffice to show in what manner the Christians were gradually induced to make compromises, until at last they fell, almost without suspicion, into the snare which Satan had prepared. For the process of blending Christianity and Paganism was carried on until a compound religion had been manufactured, of which we may say, generally, that Christianity furnished the nomenclature, and Paganism the doctrines and rites. The other great festivals of the "Catholic Church" will be found, like Christmas, to depend upon celestial phenomena, and this was detected by Sir Isaac Newton, who suggested that they were determined upon an astronomical basis. They were, in fact, arranged by the astrologers of Babylon for the worship of the host of heaven, and

[1] A common appellation of the Sun-god.
[2] Serm. II. See King's "Gnostics," pp. 49, 50.

having been received by the Romans, as we have already explained, were afterwards passed on to the nominal Church, as soon as she had been sufficiently corrupted to accept them.

Such, then, was the condition of things when the last persecution commenced. Constantine, who, after the death of his father Constantius, became emperor of the district to the west of the Alps, did not sanction the cruel treatment of the Church: for his own countries of Britain and Gaul were filled with professing Christians, and his legions were recruited from them. Consequently, when he had overpowered his colleagues in the Empire and gained the whole for himself, he showed especial favour to the followers of Christ. Such a patronage caused large numbers of insincere persons to join the Church: the real Christians were swamped, and the pastors and bishops were elected by nominal believers. But Constantine found that this mixed multitude was divided by the Arian controversy; and, regarding the Church merely as a political instrument, he saw the necessity of healing the breach, and determined upon summoning a council of bishops to discuss the question at issue, and decide it by their votes. The bishops assembled at Nicæa, or Nice, in Bithynia, and the orthodox party triumphed; not, however, without purchasing votes by dangerous concessions, one of which is said to have introduced into the Church the worship of Isis under the name of the Virgin Mary. But the proceedings were finally unsuccessful, and though Arius was banished at the time, the emperor quickly recalled him.

Of Constantine's real opinions, of his attempts to

blend Christianity and Paganism from motives of policy, and of his moral behaviour, we have spoken in the remarks on the Parable of the Mustard Tree. He wished to make the Church the handmaid of the State, and the Christians had been so prepared by the craft of Satan, and had among them so many merely nominal believers, that they seemed only too willing to run greedily after the error of Balaam for reward.

And so a new community began to spread over the Roman earth, professing to be Christian, but denying one precept at least of its supposed Founder, in that it openly acknowledged two masters: for, while claiming to receive its authority from the Lord of heaven, it was willing, whenever its interests could be served, to wield that authority according to the bidding of the emperors of Rome. Everywhere it indicated its presence by the rise of stately edifices, by gorgeous rites and ceremonies, and by an adoration of heroes and martyrs somewhat difficult to distinguish from the Polytheism which it was understood to have supplanted.

The Balaamites who brought about this change have never yet been cast out of the visible Church, and are still found, in some form or other, professing heavenly, but minding earthly things: for the Lord has not yet come to fight against them with the sword of His mouth. But when the measure of their iniquity is full, He will appear to their dismay, and in answer to their frantic appeal, "Lord, Lord, have we not prophesied in Thy name?" will sternly reply, "I never knew you: depart from Me, ye that work iniquity."

In the promise to him that overcometh, there is again a reference to the times in which Balaam lived.

The idea of the hidden manna is not taken from that which formed the daily food of the Israelites, and which became corrupt unless it was immediately eaten ; but from the pot of incorruptible manna, which, having been laid up for the generations of Israel, was enclosed within the Ark, and never seen. It represents, perhaps, the nourishment of the resurrection body, laid up in store for those who, during their sojourn here, abstain from things offered to idols, and who refuse to change the ways of God in order to please the world, and obtain its good things. If we can turn from the dainties with which the god of this age tempts us, we shall eat angels' food, and sit down to the marriage supper of the Lamb. The great High Priest after the order of Melchizedec will meet us as we return from our warfare with the kings of this world, and will bless us, and bring forth bread and wine, the royal dainties which He reserves for them that love Him.

The promise of the white stone seems to belong specially to those who keep themselves from spiritual fornication, from sinful communion with this world. There has been much dispute in regard to the metaphor ; but we may at once dismiss those explanations which are founded upon Classical allusions as altogether irrelevant.

The word translated "white" is often used of a bright and dazzling whiteness, as, for instance, that of a sunbeam: hence the white stone may be a glittering gem ; perhaps, a diamond. Now the mysterious implement by which the High Priest was enabled to obtain an answer from the Lord, and which was called the Urim and Thummim, or "Lights and Perfections," was probably a diamond ; and it is likely that the name of the Lord was inscribed upon it. The breastplate of the High Priest formed a sort of pouch into which it was placed; but, precious as the case was, that which was enclosed would reasonably be even more so. Hence, the Urim may have been a diamond, most costly of gems. The Lord will, therefore, give to him that overcometh a glittering stone inscribed with His own name, like that which the High Priest bore in the breastplate of judgment; so that the possessor will be enabled to know His will at all times, will have the privilege of continual communion with Him. So glorious a recompense is there for him who can renounce the fleeting and insincere friendship of this world, and who, turning from the luring phantoms that beckon to him, sets his face as a flint to follow by the way which the Master trod, and to watch with Him during the one short hour of life.

XVI.

Thyatira.

Next in order comes the Church which is ever offering sacrifices,[1] and to her the Lord presents Himself as the Son of God, thus solemnly vindicating His despised majesty against her idolatries, and the claims of the false prophetess. For, without any formal rejection, He has been virtually denied by the introduction of other objects of worship, and the heed given to spirits

[1] Θυάτειρα, that is, Θυῶν ἀτειρής, she that is never weary of presenting sacrificial offerings.

of darkness. And since Thyatira imagines that she has concealed her Heathenism under a cloak of Christianity, He speaks of His eyes of flame which can penetrate the inmost secrets of man, and detect all the depths of Satan; and intimates that He is shortly coming to trample down His foes beneath the feet which glow like brass in a furnace.

In this Church the great multitude of individual members are children of the adulterous Jezebel, and only a remnant belong to Christ. The latter are sincere, but, owing to the corruption with which they are surrounded, in great ignorance; and to them exclusively the Lord addresses Himself. He sees much to commend in them, abounding works, love, faith, ministry, and patience: nay, these good fruits are ever increasing. But their affection is unbalanced, and their power of resisting evil consequently weakened. They are better than the Ephesians in that their love, far from waxing cold, is becoming warmer; but inferior to them in that they have not learnt to test those who falsely claim to be apostles, and to find them liars.

Foremost among these pretenders was a woman, perhaps of noble extraction, certainly of great influence; but a worshipper of idols, a sorceress and harlot, who, while she seems to have borne the name of Jezebel, also resembled the infamous wife of Ahab in her character and actions. To understand what she was doing in Thyatira, and more especially what is her prophetic antitype, we must briefly consider the history of the Israelitish queen.

Jezebel was not by birth a daughter of Abraham, but a princess of idolatrous Tyre at a time when its

THYATIRA.

royal family was famed for cruel savagery and intense devotion to Baal and Astarte. Her father Ethbaal, a priest of the latter deity, murdered the reigning monarch Pheles, and succeeded him. Her nephew, whom Virgil calls Sychaeus, afterwards became king and priest of Baal, and was the husband of Dido. He was assassinated by his brother Pygmalion, who ascended the throne in his stead, and through fear of whom the widowed Dido fled to Africa and founded the city of Carthage. Born of a family so distinguished for fanaticism and crime, Jezebel proved herself in every way worthy of her lineage, and found the condition of her husband's realm most favourable to her plans.

For the first monarch of Israel had disregarded the law of God on the ground of expediency, and had set up the golden calves at Bethel and Dan, incurring thereby so terrible a guilt that it is repeatedly said of later kings;—"He walked in all the ways of Jeroboam, the son of Nebat, and in his sin; wherewith he made Israel to sin." By acquiescing in this act the Israelites of the Ten Tribes were completely cut off from their brethren; nor was this the end of the mischief. Within their own borders, all true servants of Jehovah refused to be separated from His Temple, and, therefore, left their homes and migrated to Judah; so that the land was forsaken by the godly.[1] And restraints having been thus removed, the Israelites naturally inclined more and more to their Heathen neighbours, to whom, indeed, they had become assimilated in religion by

[1] 2 Chron. xi. 13-17. This migration sufficiently accounts for the presence of a few families of the Ten Tribes among the Jews in New Testament times.

the setting up of the calves, since they were now themselves image-worshippers, or idolaters.

But the lesser sins are pioneers of the greater. By thus adoring Jehovah under the form of an image, they were preparing their hearts for a still worse crime, the avowed worship of other gods; and, just at the right moment, Satan presented the temptation in the person of Jezebel. Aided, probably, by her youthful beauty, her winning fascinations, and popular manners, she propagated the religion of the Phœnician deities with fierce determination of character and fanatical enthusiasm; and the success attending her efforts was so great, that a temple with an altar and image of Baal was erected in Samaria, and Ahab also made "a grove"—which is not a plantation of trees, but an obscene symbol of Astarte. In fine, the gorgeous and lascivious worship of the Pagans was appreciated to such an extent that it soon became the national religion, completely obliterating the old faith; so that Elijah actually supposed himself to be the only God-fearing man left in Israel. For no voice of remonstrance was raised, although the altars of Jehovah had been broken down, and His prophets slain with the sword, and replaced by the four hundred and fifty prophets of Baal and the four hundred prophets of the grove, that is, of Astarte. Elijah did, indeed, by calling down fire from heaven, make the renegade people fall on their faces and cry out for the moment, "Jehovah, He is the God!" Yet the influence of Jezebel was so powerful, that on the very next day he was flying for his life. And this influence she exercised, not only while her husband was alive, but also during the reigns of her two sons, Ahaziah and Jehoram. Moreover, the marriage of her daughter Athaliah to Jehoram, son of Jehoshaphat king of Judah, supplied her with a lever by which to move that country also. Nor did Athaliah disappoint her mother's hopes, for she caused a house of Baal to be built in Jerusalem itself;[1] while her sons broke up the House of the Lord, and bestowed its dedicated things upon the Baalim.[2]

We may conclude our sketch of Jezebel's character by citing the words of Jehu to her son;—"What peace, so long as the whoredoms of thy mother Jezebel and her witchcrafts are so many?"

Returning to the Jezebel of Thyatira, we find the charges brought against her to be, that she falsely called herself a prophetess, and that she taught and seduced the servants of Christ to commit fornication, and to eat things sacrificed to idols. When we remember that the Christians of those days were even more closely surrounded by Heathenism than the Israelites of old, we may easily understand the process of corruption to which this lying prophetess was subjecting them. Time had been given to her to repent, but she repented not: therefore judgment was near. She had chosen the bed of sin: it should be changed into a bed of anguish: her paramours should be thrown into great tribulation, and her adulterous children slain. And their fate should cause a fear to fall upon the Churches, like that which men felt when they saw Ananias and Sapphira smitten with death in the midst of the assembly.

Having thus pronounced sentence, the Lord turns to His own, whom He calls "the rest"—for even in

[1] 2 Chron. xxiii. 17. [2] Ibid. xxiv. 7.

Thyatira He had much people scattered amid the throng of idolatrous professors; just as there were seven thousand in Israel who had not bowed the knee to Baal, though Elijah was ignorant of them. These were, indeed, standing in rank side by side with the corrupters, but without consciousness of their real position: they were deceived by their seducers, and knew nothing of the depths of Satan and his dark plans.

The Gnostics, as their name implied, boasted of a deep insight into the things of God, and the mysteries of evil; and under the guise of assumed knowledge, led their followers step by step into an abyss of wickedness and uncleanness. But the remnant were guileless of this great iniquity; and, although they had occasional scruples which they sometimes boldly avowed, were, nevertheless, honestly disposed to look upon the evil around them as more than counterbalanced by the good, and did not at all perceive the intention of the whole system of doctrines presented for their acceptance. And so in His treatment of them, ignorant and bewildered as they are, the Lord is full of consideration and tender love. They have no power to fathom the Satanic depths; therefore, He will lay upon them no other burden than that they hold fast what little truth they have until He come.

It will be noticed that this letter deals with a far more settled state of wickedness than that which existed at Pergamos. The latter Church had, indeed, committed fornication with the world; but in Thyatira the children of the adulterous connection appear.

For the present Epistle foreshadows the career of Ecclesiasticism, that mysterious power which was dominant during the period of the Dark Ages, and continues even in our days to exercise a baleful influence. The body of nominal Christians first attached themselves to the Heathen World-kingdom, which was under the influence of Mystery Babylon; and then suffered the Mother of Abominations to lay hold of them, and use them for her own purposes. For the initiated, having once begun to profess Christianity, diplomatized so skilfully that they presently succeeded in procuring the bishopric of Rome for one of their own leaders. This was effected in the years 366-367 A.D., when—after his faction had engaged in a bloody conflict with that of his rival Ursicinus, and had on one occasion stormed a church [1] out of which they dragged some hundred and fifty corpses—Damasus found himself in secure possession of the episcopal chair, and forthwith proceeded to complete the union of the Christian and Heathen communities. In the year 378 A.D., the emperor bestowed upon him the title and office of Pontifex Maximus,[2] and means were then taken for subordinating the universal Church to the See of Rome, just as the whole Heathen world was subject to the Grand Master of the initiated. And all who refused to acknowledge Astarte under her new name of the Virgin Mary, or who would not deny the second coming of Christ in His glorified flesh, were regarded as heretics.

In 381 A.D., the second general council met at Constantinople, and by its decrees the Pontifex

[1] Then called Liberius, now St. Mary Major
[2] This title is still retained by the Pope.

Maximus was recognized as Head of the universal Church, while the Bishop of Constantinople was to rank as second to him. The amalgamation thus became an accomplished fact, and before the year 400 A.D., "the tonsured priests of Isis, sworn to celibacy," were being received as the ministers of Christ. Just as in Israel the prophets of Baal and Astarte replaced those of Jehovah, so the false Church, the new Jezebel, introduced the hierophants of the very same deities, under changed names, among the followers of the Lord Jesus. Then all the doctrines of Paganism began to be preached, with a little change in the nomenclature, and were declared to be Christian—baptismal regeneration, justification by works, the sacrifice of the mass, extreme unction, prayers for the dead, and many others. The mystic *tau* was everywhere prominent as the sign of the cross; the wafer of Astarte was substituted for the broken bread; the bishop retained the crooked staff of the Roman augur, but called it a crosier; and wore on his head the fish-head mitre of the priests of Dagon.[1] Everything was Pagan except the bare names. The vast conspiracy to convert Christianity itself into Heathenism had succeeded, so far as the bulk of professing Christians was concerned.

To those who were not aware of this fearful mystery, and still clung to the visible Church in ignorance of the change which had taken place, the Lord speaks of knowing their works, and love, and faith, and

---

[1] Many curious illustrations of this mitre may be found among the Assyrian and Babylonian antiquities in the British Museum. It bore no resemblance whatever to the so-called mitre of the Israelitish High Priest; for the latter was a turban of fine linen, and its name מִצְנֶפֶת is derived from צָנַף to roll.

THYATIRA.

patience. For to these points the preaching of the innovators was mainly directed, in order that they might draw off the minds of Christians from doctrine, and so retain their influence over them. The sincere acted upon this preaching, and many wonderful deeds of love, labour, and self-denial, resulted. These works did not escape the Lord's notice : His grace rested upon the but partially enlightened Christians who did such things out of a pure heart ; and His Spirit taught them, so that they often detected error, and resisted it even to the death. For the Roman Jezebel, like the Phœnician princess, soon began to slay the prophets of God. The latter should have had sufficient perception to discover that Rome had no part or lot with Christ, and so have disowned her. But they were blind : they suffered the woman to teach and seduce, looked upon her as the true Church, and strove only against particular errors, which they did not associate with the general system. Yet, after a while, some began to see the name "Mystery Babylon" upon the forehead of the Harlot.

The words, " till I come," seem to be an intimation that this apostasy will not altogether disappear until the Church has been summoned to meet her Lord. Indeed, we have already seen that the great ecclesiastical system will be broken up and destroyed by the Ten Kings, in order that they may give all power to the Beast ; and that the latter does not arise out of the troubled waters until the Man-child has been safely conveyed to the Throne of God.

In this Epistle only the Lord adds something to the description of the one who shall obtain the reward, and designates him as " he that overcometh, and he that keepeth My works unto the end." For there would be strong temptation to keep other works, to serve the Church rather than Christ; and if any one were so influenced, however pious he might seem, he would not ultimately be found among the overcomers.

Again the promise is strikingly appropriate. After the toils of the wilderness, the Israelites were, if they remained faithful, to subdue the Canaanitish nations and possess their land. So shall the Church hereafter subjugate and rule over the world with Christ, as soon as the last weary traveller of her long procession shall have passed out of the desert of this life. In the present age, we are individually priests unto God, and should take heed that we do not neglect the priestly duties of interceding for and instructing the people; but, when the great King shall have gathered together into one the children of God that are scattered abroad, then will the time have come for the Saints of the High Places to possess the Kingdom.[1] The Roman Church wishes to reign now, without the presence of Christ, without His apostles, and without the countless members of His body who have already crossed the stream; but those who resist her seductions, and are willing to be esteemed as nothing in this world, shall, when the Lord comes, enjoy to the full that after which she is vainly striving. And so completely does the Lord identify Himself with His own that He gives

[1] It is, then, not without deep meaning that we find, in Rev. i. 6, the remarkable expression, "a Kingdom, priests"—such is, doubtless, the correct reading—applied to the Church. The difference of number points to the fact that, immediately after conversion, every member of Christ is a priest individually; but that believers can only become a Kingdom when all have been gathered together to the Lord.

to them the very same power over the nations which He has received from His Father.

"Faithful is the saying: For if we died with Him, we shall also live with Him: if we endure, we shall also reign with Him."

But there is something more for the overcomer: he shall have the morning-star—a promise differing from that which was given to the pious Jew, upon whom the Sun of righteousness shall arise. The explanation is, perhaps, as follows. Those who anxiously wait for the dawn know its welcome harbinger, the silver planet, which emerges in the glimmer of early twilight, bright and conspicuous at first, and then growing fainter and fainter in the gradually increasing light, until at last it dies "on a bed of daffodil sky." But sometimes it is swept away in very different fashion; it may be that it has scarcely appeared when the storm-cloud comes on, obliterates it in a moment, shuts out the hope of day, and brings back the darkness of midnight. Yet, after a while, the roar of the tempest is hushed, the angry lightnings cease, the clouds part and float away, and lo! the sun has arisen, and is looking down upon the earth in all the splendour of his might.

Such a daybreak as this must, it would seem, be in our minds when we consider the promise of the morning-star. Those servants of Christ who are ever looking for His coming will see Him when He calls His own to Himself. But this manifestation, of which the slumbering world may be altogether unaware, will be but momentary, and then the storm-clouds of the Great Tribulation will bring back midnight darkness upon the earth. At the close, however, of the time of trouble, the Messiah will appear in all His glory to deliver the children of Abraham, and, as the clouds part, will be found to have arisen as the Sun of righteousness, with healing in His wings, over them that fear the name of the Lord.[1]

XVII.

SARDIS.

WE now pass on to a Church of knowledge, indeed, and comparative orthodoxy, but withal to one which is fast sinking from the Heavenly Places into the world, and losing all its spiritual power. The word "Sardis" is not Greek: hence some have derived it from a Hebrew root, which would give it the meaning of "remnant"; and this they refer to "the rest in Thyatira" mentioned in the preceding Epistle. But such a derivation is unfair: for the word is no more Hebrew than it is Greek. It is a Lydian name; and, therefore, in a Lydian root we must seek its interpretation, which will then be "new," "new-born with the year," "renewed."[2] This at once suggests the Churches originating in the Reformation, which have been generally distinguished as orthodox on the whole, but very seldom as showing a spiritual power in due proportion to their privileges. For, as we have previously remarked, when the enthusiasm occasioned by their delivery from the thraldom of Jezebel had subsided, instead of gathering in one loving circle around the Saviour, they fell apart into antagonistic sects, which, so far as the great crowd of their members was con-

[1] Mal. iv. 2.
[2] See Stier's "Words of the Risen Saviour"

cerned, soon lapsed into a state of spiritual deadness. And few, indeed, were the exceptions which proved this rule, at least until the efforts of Wesley, Whitefield, and their contemporaries, began to excite some symptoms of returning life.

To the professing Christians of this period the Lord presents Himself as "He that hath the seven Spirits of God," a title which is full of meaning for them. They lack vitality, and He appears as the Possessor of the Spirit in all the sevenfold plenitude of His power: whatever may be their intellectual force and activity, they are little moved by Divine energies, and He comes with gracious purpose, that they may have life, and may have it abundantly.

In His hand He holds all the seven stars which are the angels of the Churches. This seems to be, as it were, a solemn repetition of His claim to be Head over all, and to indicate the critical time of a new beginning, a fresh departure, analogous to the return of the Jews from captivity and the rebuilding of the Temple.

Again the Lord knows: He has no need that any should witness to Him of this Church, and it is useless for special pleaders to defend her. His eyes of flame pierce through every covering of hypocrisy: therefore, void as she is of spiritual power, it will not avail her to have a name to live. She may deceive men, and may even, like the more advanced Laodicea, go on to deceive herself; but she cannot hide her real condition from Him. Against the Church which preceded her, she boasts that she holds to the pure word of God; nevertheless, her vitality is at so low an ebb, that she is spiritually almost as a person in a swoon is physically: it might be said of her, as Paul says of the woman who lives in pleasure, that she "is dead while she liveth."

It is not without deep significance that, whereas adversaries are found assailing five of the Churches either from within or from without, there is no mention of any foe in the Epistles to Sardis and Laodicea. For these two have ceased to be effectual witnesses, and, therefore, Satan has no quarrel with them: they do not in any way torment those who have settled down as dwellers upon the earth; why, then, should anger be excited against them? They have a tacit understanding with the world that, although their opinions may differ upon some points, there is nothing to hinder a mutual friendship.

The first admonition of the Lord points directly to the source and root of all this deadness to spiritual things and conformity to the world. "Become watchful," He commands; and, if we interpret this verse by the next, we shall see that He is not speaking of general watchfulness, but of waiting for His return. Yet such a waiting certainly includes watchfulness in all things; for he who lives in the daily expectation of seeing Christ as He is will surely not be deficient in zeal to purify himself even as He is pure. But, after the Reformation, the Protestant Churches seemed to have little love for their Lord's appearing: they rarely mentioned it, and persuaded themselves that, although it was an event which must assuredly take place at some far-distant time, it, nevertheless, could not happen for a long season; not, indeed, until after the whole world had been converted and changed by means of their exertions. And so they made the fatal mistake, from which the Scriptures should have saved them, of saying in their heart, "My Lord delayeth His coming," and soon fell into the idle slumber from which He now calls upon them to arise, lest coming suddenly He should find them sleeping.

"Strengthen," He continues, "the things which remain, that are ready to die"—for life was not quite extinct. And in this warning we may probably discern a reference to teaching, as well as to work: the thought of the Lord's appearing had been cast aside, and all other doctrines were becoming indistinct. The great disclosure, which impresses upon us, more powerfully than any other revelation, the fact that we are strangers and pilgrims here, was "spiritualized," and whatever else seemed burdensome was deprived of its meaning in a similar way. The literal presence of Christ was not desired; therefore, His person was no longer a constant subject of contemplation. Compared with the multitude who had the responsibility of knowledge, but few gazed fixedly upon Him; and, consequently, but few were changed from glory to glory into the same image. And since the Church had no apprehension of being suddenly called away, she found it easy to do much the same as the world, and, settling down upon earth, began to lose all the heavenly gifts. Gradually it became the custom to bring everything to the test of intellect and human philosophy; so that, as time went on, the very foundation-doctrine of the Atonement began to disappear from the sight of those who were unaffected by the Philadelphian revival, and large numbers of professing Christians are now denying the Lord Who bought them.

But the waning of faith speedily changes outward

conduct, and so the Lord goes on to say;—" For I have found no work of thine fulfilled before My God." The works are deficient in quality: it is not the *pure* love of Christ which constrains the doers, but lower motives. They are wanting in quantity: the daily tale which God has appointed is not accomplished. " Suffer it now: for thus it becometh us to fulfil *all* righteousness," said the Lord: but the Sardians, if they coldly perform some part of their duty, are satisfied that they have thereby compounded for the neglect of all the rest. This, however, will not suffice. " And say to Archippus, Take heed to the ministry which thou hast received in the Lord, that thou fulfil it."[1] For God reviews, not merely the things that are done, but also the things that are left undone.

That she may realize her present lifeless condition, Sardis is exhorted to remember how she received the word which was sent to her; with what heartiness of joy, which is now gone; with what warmth of love, which has now grown cold; with what demonstration of the Spirit and power, which is no longer felt! And, at the same time, she should call to mind the substance of the instruction, reproof, and correction, which she has heard; the earnest appeals, the teachings of the Spirit, and the great responsibilities which they involve.

She has received and heard, and, consequently, there is no excuse for her, as there was for the remnant in Thyatira. " If ye were blind, ye would have no sin: but now ye say, We see: therefore your sin remaineth." And so a solemn appeal is made to her; she is urged to observe and keep what she has heard, and to repent quickly: but if she refuse to respond, the time of

[1] Col. iv. 17.

visitation is passing: there is a limit even to the forbearance of God. The faithless Church must share the fate of the world which she has loved, and That Day come upon her unawares. At an hour when she thinks not, unexpectedly, as a thief in the night, He will arrive in the air to beckon away all who are watching for Him; and, as Enoch vanished from among his fellows, they will depart, or as Lot was hurried through the streets of slumbering Sodom. But those believers who dare to sleep as do other men, who suffer their God-consciousness to grow drowsy, so that they become apathetic, and the powers of the World to Come lose their hold upon them—such foolish ones must be left for a while among the wicked, to experience the full development and unrestrained nature of that lawlessness which they have not been sufficiently careful to avoid.

But there are, the Lord says, a few names in Sardis which did not defile their garments. How sweeping the charge implied in these words! What! in professing Christendom only a few with whom the Lord is satisfied! Even so: for alas! we may flatter ourselves now, but shall shortly be subjected to a very different kind of judgment, and shall discover how fearful a mistake it is to confound privileges with the use made of them. "And thou, Capernaum, shalt thou be exalted to heaven? Thou shalt go down unto Hades: for if the mighty works had been done in Sodom which were done in thee, it would have remained until this day. Howbeit I say unto you, that it shall be more tolerable for the land of Sodom in the day of judgment than for thee." We have ever before us, in the case of the Jews, an awful instance of the severity of God towards those who have proved faithless in spite of abounding grace and long forbearance; of how much sorer punishment shall they be judged worthy who could grow cold and worldly, who could be disobedient and self-willed, even while Jesus Christ was being openly set forth crucified before them!

There are, however, a few in Sardis whose garments are not spotted by the flesh; for if at any time they have stained them, they have gone at once to the fountain, and made them white in the blood of the Lamb. They have escaped the contamination of the leaven, and preserved purity of doctrine; they have esteemed Christ in all things as the First and the Last; and if urged to conduct which was not in the strictest accord with His commands, they have replied, "We ought to obey God rather than man," and have not hesitated to stand firm, even when they were but two or three against the great multitude. Nor will God forget their faith and patience: when others are in anguish, when the whole earth is writhing and throbbing beneath the repeated strokes of the Almighty in the days of terror, they shall be walking with Christ in the heavenly places, clothed in the white robes of righteousness: they shall be far removed from all trouble and alarm, even as Abraham was when, from the mountains of Canaan, he looked down upon the smoking ruins of Sodom.

In this promise there is probably an allusion to the procession of priests and Levites who, clothed in white linen, followed Solomon on his way to dedicate the newly built Temple.[1] And certainly the psalm of

[1] 2 Chron. v. 11, 12.

praise, which at that time ascended to God, will well suit the happy throng which shall hereafter cluster round the Lord Jesus, never again to leave Him. With heart and lips will they rejoice to cry;—"For He is good; for His mercy endureth for ever."

But they shall fare thus because they are *worthy*. Let not Christians of our times dare to shrink from that word uttered by Him Who is the same yesterday, to-day, and for ever. The light of the glorious Gospel must, indeed, first shine into our hearts by the command of God alone; but after the darkness has been dispelled, though all the power must still come from Him, He, nevertheless, expects a co-operation of hearty will on our part. When we know His promise to give His Holy Spirit to them that ask Him, it becomes our duty to ask; and if we ask, we shall receive, and shall then be enabled to do "those good works which God afore prepared that we should walk in them."[1] But if we are careless in this matter, we shall fail in power, our work will be left undone, and we shall not gain the prize which is set before us for patience in the race, and self-denial in the fight. It is possible for a Christian to suffer loss, and to be saved only so as through fire,[2] instead of having an entrance richly supplied into the eternal Kingdom of our Lord and Saviour.[3] And one way, at least, of suffering the loss and passing through the fire seems to be the being left upon earth in the days when the Lawless One shall be unveiled.

In the words to the overcomer, the promise of white raiment is repeated; and we are, moreover, told that those who are thus arrayed will have passed beyond

[1] Eph. ii. 10.   [2] 1 Cor. iii. 15.   [3] 2 Peter i. 11.

all tests, and will never be in jeopardy again; for the
Lord will in no wise blot their names out of the Book
of Life. The expression is difficult: it seems to imply
that all who are brought under the sound of the Gospel
are graciously written in the Lamb's Book of Life;
just as every Israelite at his birth was numbered among
the favoured people. But an Israelite might so neglect
or despise the law of his God that sacrifice could not
be accepted for him; so that he was doomed to bear
his own iniquity, and be cut off from his people.[1] In
like manner, those who have heard the glad tidings
of salvation may, by their disobedience and continued
rebellion, cause their names to be erased from the
Book of Life. They may be within the Gospel-net
when it is brought to shore, but be cast away as bad
fish when the separation takes place.

In Ezra there is a significant verse which careless
professors would do well to ponder. Of certain of the
children of the priests we read;—"These sought their
register among those that were reckoned by genealogy,
but they were not found; therefore were they, as
polluted, put from the priesthood."[2]

The Lord will own the overcomers of this Church
before His Father and the angels, because they have
not been ashamed to confess Him before men. Living
in the midst of a cold and spiritually dead generation,
who regarded any attempt to put faith into practice,
or evince love by obedience, as the act of a troublesome enthusiast, they, nevertheless, remained true to
Him who died for them, and accepted the consequences.
And so He meets them, when the trial is over, with
the gracious acknowledgment, "Well done, good and

[1] Levit. xix. 8; Num. xv. 30, 31; xix. 13.   [2] Ezra ii. 62.

faithful servant." He presents them to His Father as His own, those whom He has chosen to reign with Him, whom He has taken from the dunghill to make them inherit the Throne of Glory.[1]

XVIII.

PHILADELPHIA.

IN the Epistles to Philadelphia and Laodicea we come to the immediate times of the end; for these Churches seem to represent the final result of the Reformation-period, and the two classes which are to be ultimately evolved from it. Philadelphia, which signifies "brotherly love," is the company of the elect upon earth; those who will be chosen when Laodicea is rejected and left to suffer the judgment threatened to Sardis. The present Epistle is, therefore, specially addressed to the people of the Lord in the last days, to those who shall be alive when He comes. And the voice of prophecy agrees with the course of events in pointing to ourselves as being the persons directly concerned, either with this letter, or with that which follows it: so that the solemn question for each of us is, Which of them applies to my case? Am I among the beloved of the Lord who shall be delivered from the hour of temptation? The question is urgent, and must be settled at once while opportunity is still granted: for all things are full of warning that the Lord is at hand. To the reasons which have been already suggested for this expectation, we will here add another, which is connected with the subject of this Epistle.

[1] 1 Sam. ii. 8

On the day of Pentecost, when the Spirit had descended and endued the disciples with His mighty power, great was the astonishment of those Jews who had come from distant regions as they heard, each in his own tongue, the speech of the Apostles. "What meaneth this?" they cried in their perplexity. "Behold, are not all these which speak Galilæans? And how hear we every man in our own language, wherein we were born?" But while some were amazed, others mocked, and said;—"They are filled with new wine." Then, amid the bewildering din, the Twelve stood up, and Peter stepped forward as spokesman. They were not, he said, drunken with wine, as some supposed; but God was bringing to pass that which He had spoken by the mouth of the prophet Joel in the glorious words—

"And it shall be in the last days, saith God,
I will pour forth of My Spirit upon all flesh:
And your sons and your daughters shall prophesy,
And your young men shall see visions,
And your old men shall dream dreams;
Yea, and on My servants and on My handmaidens in those days
Will I pour forth of My Spirit; and they shall prophesy.
And I will show wonders in the heaven above,
And signs on the earth beneath;
Blood, and fire, and vapour of smoke:
The sun shall be turned into darkness,
And the moon into blood,
Before the day of the Lord come,
That great and notable day:
And it shall be, that whosoever shall call upon the name of the
Lord shall be saved."

Now this prophecy of the latter days foretold an outpouring of the Spirit of God upon all flesh—that is, upon all nations without distinction, and not merely upon Israel, to which such influences had been previously confined; and Peter affirmed that the promise was even then beginning to be fulfilled in the eyes of the people. But the words which he quoted go on to speak of signs in the heaven above, and on the earth beneath, which did not then appear, nor indeed will do so, until the close of the dispensation and the eve of the Day of the Lord. Indeed, they are the same as the signs mentioned in the discourse on the Mount of Olives, which will be the signal that the times of the Gentiles are ended. And, consequently, the predicted work of the Spirit extends throughout the whole of the present age. Hence, perhaps, the reason why Peter does not say, "This is the fulfilment of that which hath been spoken," but only, "This is that which hath been spoken"; in other words, "This is a part," or, "the beginning of it." Since, then, there were to be outpourings like those of Pentecost connected with the whole period of the dispensation of grace, in what way were they to happen?

If we keep in mind the fact that the metaphor is that of a refreshing shower of rain, we may find an answer to the question in the following words of James;—"Be patient therefore, brethren, until the coming of the Lord. Behold, the husbandman waiteth for the precious fruit of the earth, being patient over it, until it receive the early and latter rain. Be ye also patient; stablish your hearts: for the coming of the Lord is at hand."[1]

Now in Palestine the normal early, or autumn, rain begins in October, at sowing time; while the

[1] Jas. v. 7, 8.

latter comes on in March, and continues a little way into April. By the middle of April the barley is ready for cutting, and the wheat harvest follows about a fortnight later. At the present time both the rains are usually scanty; and, on the other hand, there is no absolute cessation of wet weather between the seasons. But this is doubtless an abnormal condition of things; for in more than one passage of the Old Testament it was plainly intimated that the rain-supply of the Holy Land would depend upon the obedience of the people. We may cite the following promise as an instance;—" And it shall come to pass, if ye shall hearken diligently unto My commandments which I command you this day, to love the Lord your God, and to serve Him with all your heart, and with all your soul, that I will give you the rain of your land *in its due season*, the first rain and the latter rain."[1]

It would seem, therefore, that we must understand James to be alluding to the regular early and latter rains, the course of which would be after this manner. The first would come on during sowing-time: storms would prevail for a day or two; then there would be a short interval of fine weather succeeded by another series of showers; and so on, until the dry season set in, at the close of which, about six weeks before harvest, the clouds would return, and the latter rains begin.

Accordingly, in applying the figure, we should expect copious outpourings of the Spirit in the early days of the Church, and also toward the close of the age, at

[1] Deut. xi. 13, 14. Compare Levit. xxvi. 3, 4; Jer. iii. 3; Joel ii. 23.

the sowing and just before the reaping, with an intervening period of but little power. And this is precisely what has happened. From the Pentecost which was the birthday of the Church, there were for some three centuries showers of grace in many countries, and multitudes of earnest preachers overspread the world. But in the fourth century, when the persecutions had ceased, and Christianity was becoming corrupt and fashionable, a coldness, worldliness, and laxity of doctrine, set in; the power of the Spirit was withdrawn, and there was a great drought which lasted, without any general intermission, through many weary years, until the close of the Dark Ages.

Then the season of the latter rain seems to have commenced, and the first copious showers resulted in the Reformation. The next remarkable outpouring in this country caused the awakening in the middle of the eighteenth century. Then came a marvellous and abundant rain in the revivals of 1857—59, which affected the whole of the Protestant world; and, lastly, the movement which is still going on.

It will be noticed that the great showers follow at ever-shortening periods. Between the Reformation and the days of Wesley more than two centuries had passed by; but seventy or eighty years spanned the interval between Wesley and the revival which commenced in America; and about fourteen years after the latter, the present movement began.

Another interesting fact is that the former rain lasted about three hundred years, and that it is now rather more than that time since the Reformation. Is the patient waiting for the early and latter rain all but over, and has the season of harvest come at last?

What means the cry which is ever gathering strength among the people of the Lord ;—"Behold, the Bridegroom cometh; go ye out to meet Him!"? Does the eye of faith already discern One like to a son of man seated upon the white cloud with His sharp sickle in His hand, and expecting the message, "Thrust in Thy sickle and reap: for the time is come for Thee to reap: for the harvest of the earth is ripe!"? But if so, how will that harvest affect us? Shall we be gathered into the Master's garner, have an entrance richly ministered unto us into the Kingdom of our Lord and Saviour, and pass through the pearly gates of the city with the rejoicing cry, "'Tis heaven at last!"? Or shall we be left upon the reaped earth, miserably groaning, "The harvest is past, the summer is ended, and we are not saved!"?

Yet one more remark upon the four great revivals: for we may discern in them a very striking and significant progress of doctrine.

In the times of the first, the everlasting foundation-stone, which had been buried beneath the rubbish of centuries, was uncovered, so that it could be seen by all; and once again the apostolic message was freely proclaimed, that man can be saved only through faith in Christ Jesus, and not by his own works or deservings.

In the second, the new point chiefly insisted upon was that conversion is instantaneous and miraculous, being caused by the entrance into a man of the Holy Spirit, by whose indwelling he is made a new creature in Christ Jesus, separated off from the world, and gradually sanctified and prepared for his glorification.

In the third movement, the great truth of the unity of the Church was recovered, and men began to see, as they never had before in modern times, that Christ is the one Centre around which all who believe in Him must cluster; that no human sects or creeds must be allowed to keep Christians apart, because the whole of the real Church has been baptized by the Spirit into one body.

And lastly, during the present outpouring of grace, two things have been brought into unwonted prominence—the doctrine of sanctification with the necessity for a higher spiritual life, and the proclamation that the Lord is at hand. These doctrines are closely connected, and their simultaneous appearance shows that the Spirit is now pressing upon the Church the words, "Therefore, be ye also *ready:* for in an hour that ye think not the Son of Man cometh."

These considerations may be added to what has been previously said, as tending to strengthen the conviction that we are now living in the time indicated by the Epistle to the Church at Philadelphia, the prophecy in which is being manifestly fulfilled around us. For the deadness of Sardis has for some time given place to the warmth of revival; though alas! this accession of energy is by no means confined to the Church of Christ: for all the powers of Satan seem on every side to be starting into activity.

We find in this letter no open mention of blame or rebuke in regard to those who are directly addressed. For Philadelphia is the Church of brotherly love,[1] and when that grace reigns, Christ has little fault to find. We must, however, be careful that we understand the meaning which the New Testament attaches to the term: we must not interpret it of the world's love of

[1] Φιλαδέλφεια, from φιλεῖν, "to love," and ἀδελφός, "a brother."

clansmen, of the feeling which keeps together members of the same sect or society, or of the mutual attraction of minds which have been cast in a similar mould. For it is a yearning toward all true believers, not by reason of any qualities they may possess, nor on account of coincidence of opinion, but because they are the objects of Christ's affection.

To this John refers when he says;—"We know that we have passed out of death into life, because we love the brethren."[1] For if the love of Christ constrains us, so that we are drawn toward those who would naturally be unattractive or even offensive to us, we have proof that we are a new creation in Him, because we no longer know our fellow men after the flesh, but only through the great heart of the Lord Jesus, Who has become our life.[2] And this grace must be manifested in us, if we would belong to the Philadelphian Church, and be saved from the evil that is coming upon a flesh.

To His own people Christ chooses to be known as "He that is holy," thereby intimating to us what manner of persons we also must be, if we would be His at His coming; for without holiness no man shall see the Lord.

But He also presents Himself as "true," and what earnest searchings of heart should that word stir up in each one of us! For how great insincerity, and what confusion of motives, may be found even in our service to God! So natural, indeed, is this condition to us that none can tell how often he offends; and yet the Most High desires truth in the inward parts, and all things are naked and laid open before the eyes of Him

[1] 1 John iii. 14.   [2] 2 Cor. v. 14—17; Gal. ii. 20.

with Whom we have to do. Surely the most advanced believer is ever needing to pray with the Psalmist—"Remove from me the way of lying."

Lastly; the Lord speaks of Himself as having the key of David, an expression of considerable difficulty on account of the purpose for which the key is afterwards used. It seems, perhaps, better not to seek an explanation from the twenty-second chapter of Isaiah —where "the key *of the house* of David" may have a different shade of meaning—but to understand a simple claim on the part of the Lord to the power of the throne of David.

When the heart of Ahaz was moved and the heart of his people, as the trees of the wood are moved by the wind, through fear lest the royal family of Judah should be exterminated, God announced that the root of Jesse should not fail until a virgin should bring forth a Son upon Whose shoulder the government should rest for ever.[1] Now Christ, alone of men, was born of a virgin mother, and He was also the lineal heir to the throne of David; therefore, in Him the prophecy must be fulfilled. Accordingly, He here asserts His claim to that power over the world which is the prerogative of the Davidic crown. He has the right to open, and none dare shut; or to shut, and none may open: He alone can let loose, and He can restrain. This great power He will shortly assume to Himself in the sight of all men; but, even before His time comes, He will anticipate it in favour of the Philadelphians, so as to set for them an open door which no man can shut.

The open door probably means an opportunity for

[1] Isa. vii. 2, 14; ix. 6, 7

testimony. "Withal praying for us also," says Paul, "that God may open unto us a door for the word, to speak the mystery of Christ."[1] And again; "But I will tarry at Ephesus until Pentecost; for a great door and effectual is opened unto me."[2] And in yet another place he relates that, when he came to Troas to preach the Gospel of Christ, a great door was opened unto him in the Lord.[3]

Thus the title, He that hath the key of David, taken in connection with the promise which follows it, may have been intended to signify that the Lord would use His rightful power over the world to restrain opposition to the preaching of His people in the times of the end. In other words, that a testimony should go forth, a last warning cry, like that of Enoch before he was taken away from the doomed earth.

And the promise is now being fulfilled before our eyes. The world is not changed; yet at the present time it suffers the preaching of Christ with a forbearance never before known. Its great and wise men do not indeed conceal their contempt for the Divine revelation, though by their sneers they are ever proving its truth while they cry;—"Where is the promise of His coming? For from the day that the fathers fell asleep, all things continue as they were from the beginning." Its ecclesiastics and sectaries are still as averse to the real doctrine of Christ as the Pharisees and Sadducees were at the first advent. Nevertheless, there is at present no serious interference with the work of Evangelical Christians: for the Lord has opened, and there is none who may dare to shut. How fearful is our responsibility during a time so

[1] Col. iv. 3.   [2] 1 Cor. xvi. 8, 9.   [3] 2 Cor. ii. 12.

graciously given: how earnestly should we strive, if by any means we may save some of those for whom Christ died! Now it is·day; but the day is fast declining, and the night cometh, when no man can work.

The Lord is, however, careful to explain why He has thus opened a door for Philadelphia. She has heeded the warning given to Sardis: she has strengthened the things that were ready to die, so that she now possesses "a little power"; therefore, He is able to fulfil to her His own words;—"Unto every one which hath shall be given." This little power has been shown in the fact that she has not suffered herself to be carried away by any of the currents of the world: she has held fast to the word of Christ, and has yielded neither to the traditions nor to the philosophies of men. And in the present day how hard it is to do this, how few the number of those who follow such a rule! Yet for this the Lord loves Philadelphia, and will save her from the hour of temptation.

O that all true believers would apply the lesson thus presented to them, and begin to prepare for the impending change by a strict comparison of their own doctrine and practice with the revealed laws of the King! How otherwise can we be ready for His coming! And let us not imagine that any supposed service will cover the defects of our obedience. "Hath the Lord as great delight in burnt offerings and sacrifices, as in obeying the voice of the Lord? Behold, to obey is better than sacrifice, and to hearken than the fat of rams."

And we must not forget that, to pass by individual mistakes, there is not a sect in Christendom which has not some errors in its creed. These it is the duty of every Christian to detect and discard; and so all true believers would find themselves drawing nearer and nearer to each other, and would soon be standing, in these last times, as one body, separated from worldly religion, as well as from every other kind of worldliness, and awaiting the summons which shall bid them quit for ever the painful conflicts of earth for the glory which dwells in Immanuel's land.[1]

It is also said of the Philadelphians that they did not deny Christ's name. Such a denial is not necessarily made in express terms: we may put an earthly Church in His place; we may deify human intellect; or, perhaps, the denial may rest in an ignoring of Christ's name, either through a false shame, or because, however willing we may be to speak of Him as a great teacher and philosopher, we do not really believe Him to be the Only Begotten Son of the Father, and the One Sacrifice for sin.

There are many roads by which Satan leads professing Christians far away from the pale of the Philadelphian Church; and yet how easy it is in these

---

[1] We do not mean by this to suggest the formation of a new Church with none but real Christians for its members. Such a scheme has been often tried with the invariable result that another sect, if not more than one, has been added to previous distractions. None but the Chief Shepherd Himself will ever succeed in gathering the harassed sheep into one visible fold. But while Christians remain—so long as conscience permits—in whatever communities they may happen to be, let them be ever ready to join in intercommunions, and let them remember the solemn context of those words;—"Then they that feared the Lord spake often *one to another*." If the distinctions and feelings of sect keep them from these things, they have little hope of being included within the pale of the favoured Philadelphian Church.

times to confess Christ, when the worst consequences which are likely to follow a faithful testimony are nothing more than the derision of the world, the censure of nominal Christians, and, perchance, the loss of some few friends! Very different will it be when liberty is taken away, and the false king sits on his throne: for then, in the case of all who are to be saved, that confession, which love could not call forth in the days of ease, must be extorted by the fires of persecution.

The renewed activity of preaching, caused by the latter rain, moves Satan to repeat the stratagem by which he gradually counteracted the work of the early Church; and, consequently, the false Jews, the synagogue of Satan mentioned in the Epistle to Smyrna, appear for the second time upon the scene. For some years they have been rapidly overspreading the countries in which outpourings of the Spirit have occurred, especially England and America, neutralizing the pure word of God by means of Babylonian ritual and priestcraft, and often guiding men back to Rome itself. Their followers are taught to look down upon believers who hold more Scriptural views, and to arrogate to themselves the place of God's Church, just as the Pharisees did at the first advent.

But all who are really resting upon their Lord may be well content to endure this treatment for a season; for He has here promised to plead their cause in His own person, and to show that He has loved them. And He will do it in such a manner that some of those who have been led blindfold into the false synagogue, through not understanding the depths of Satan, will repent and bow down before them, confessing that after all they were the true Church, and desiring to be joined to them in Christ.

How this change will be effected, and in what way He will put a distinction between the obedient and the misguided, the Lord now proceeds to explain. But, first of all, there must be no mistake in regard to His reason : *because* the Philadelphians have kept the word of His patience, *therefore* He will keep them from the hour of temptation. How great trouble might we spare ourselves did we but keep the word of Christ! It is comparatively easy to receive it : the difficulty is to hold it fast with patience until the end.

The idea conveyed by the Greek noun translated " patience " is that of manly endurance : the verb connected with it is sometimes used of soldiers who, when charged by the enemy, do not give way, but stand their ground. And so the Lord has set each one of us in a position which we must maintain in spite of all the efforts of the Powers of Darkness to dislodge us.

Waiting amid trials and temptations is a chief ingredient in our cup of discipline; for " it is good that a man should both hope and quietly wait for the salvation of the Lord." There is no fruition for us now, except peace and joy in the Spirit : we must live on the future ; we must, like our Master, endure the cross, despising the shame, for the joy that is set before us. For here we have no continuing city, but are strangers and pilgrims, until we are brought into our own city which is in heaven. Hence Paul says to the Hebrews ; —" Ye have need of patience that, after ye have done the will of God, ye may receive the promises." And he commends the Thessalonians because they turned to God from idols, to serve the living and true God, and to wait for His Son from heaven. This patience and willingness to wait for Christ the Philadelphians have, and their reward is that He will keep them from the great hour of temptation.

Now the temptation will not be partial, but universal; for it is to come upon "the whole world": and, consequently, those who are to be delivered from it must needs be taken out of the world, even as Enoch was before the corruption and violence of men had come to their worst in the days of Noah. And that this is what the Lord means is evident from the following words, "I am coming quickly." The Philadelphians will obey the command to watch and pray always, that they may be accounted worthy to escape all the things that shall come to pass, and to stand before the Son of Man; and they will be heard. At a time known only to God, but, as we have previously seen, before the rise of Antichrist, the Lord will descend to the mid-region of the air, and call to Himself all those who are looking for Him. And then the temptation will come upon the whole world, "to test them that dwell upon the earth."

The last expression is doubtless to be understood in a moral sense of all those who have settled themselves upon the earth, with little or no aspiration beyond it; and who must be tested, because there is some wheat even in that vast heap of chaff. For there are many who believe in the Lord Jesus, but do not go much further in His ways; who are careless of pressing on to know Him and the power of His resurrection, being content with things here below, with their Churches and acts of devotion and good works. And so their thoughts are fixed upon earth: they seldom contemplate the heavenly calling, and do not look for that blessed hope and appearing of the glory of our great God and Saviour Jesus Christ.

Such a state of mind must engender worldliness, and cause those who have it to be more or less dwellers upon the earth. And to separate them from the altogether carnal, to make them start back with horror from the things that are seen and long for the advent of the Deliverer, the hour of trial will come: they will be made to experience what the world is when the restraining influence of the Spirit is withdrawn, and the Mystery of Lawlessness unveiled. Then the miracles of Antichrist will bewilder, and his bloody persecutions terrify, them; but, since they are the beloved of the Lord, He will sustain them, and the fearful agitation of the sifting shall prove them to be wheat.

Very different will be the result to the rest of the world. They will yield to temptation: having rejected God and His Christ, they will fill up the measure of their iniquity by bowing before Satan and the Beast; and be, consequently, swept as chaff into the unquenchable fire.

Since, however, the grace of God will have previously separated the Philadelphians from the world and the false Church, they will not need the severity of the last winnowing, and will, therefore, be removed before that terrible purging of the floor commences. Their minds should be fixed on the promise, "I am coming quickly!" for their toil, and testifying, and light affliction, will not last long: Christ will shortly appear, and turn all their sorrow into everlasting joy.

But He adds a caution. Let them be careful and continually watch and pray, that they may retain the grace given unto them. For although His people can never perish, neither shall any one snatch them out of His hand, yet they may be beguiled of their reward. If by yielding to their own inclination, and the words of those who deprecate fanaticism, they lapse into indolence ; if they follow in the way of others and indulge their fleshly appetites ; if they suffer the cares of life to gather around them like a mist beyond which they can see nothing ; if they turn aside either to human philosophy or tradition—they may fail to lay hold of that for which they were laid hold of by Christ, and miss the glory of the Kingdom, though they be saved from eternal death.

The Lord presses His exhortation still further by the promise to the overcomer. When those who are ready shall have been caught up to Him, it will be time to begin the building of the great living Temple. For the chief of the stones will then have been conveyed to the appointed spot, hewn and chiselled and fitted each for its place, so that no sound of hammer, or axe, or any iron tool of affliction, will ever be heard there.[1] And in the glorious erection those who have endured the contempt of men for Christ's sake will be pillars of strength and beauty, fixed on their bases, so that they shall no more go out. For the former things will then have passed away, and those who in previous times have been bidden to come out from the world, or— which is still more painful—to turn their back upon the false Church, and go forth unto Christ without the camp bearing His reproach, will then have reached the abode of everlasting rest, the dwelling of glory.

The mention of the place appointed for them in the

[1] 1 Kings vi. 7.

Temple may intimate that, during the interval between their rapture and the Lord's appearing in glory, He will judge them in regard to the things done in the body, and assign to each the part he is to sustain in the celestial worship.

But there are yet other rewards for the overcomer. The Lord adds ;—" I will write upon him the name of My God, and the name of the city of My God, the new Jerusalem, which cometh down out of heaven from My God, and Mine own new name." There is something very gracious in the expression, " My God," which occurs four times in this verse. We are reminded of a former utterance ;—" Go unto My brethren, and say to them, I ascend unto My Father and your Father, and My God and your God."[1] By so speaking the Lord seems, in both instances, to identify Himself, as the last Adam, with His own people, in accordance with the Scripture ;—" For both He That sanctifieth and they that are sanctified are all of One : for which cause He is not ashamed to call them brethren."[2]

In regard to the significance of the names, Christ will acknowledge His faithful disciples before His Father, Who will then Himself recognise them, and by setting His name upon them seal them as His own. The overcomer will also be marked as a citizen of the Jerusalem which is now above, but will shortly descend to be the light and glory of the redeemed earth. And, lastly, Christ will write upon him His own new name, probably that to which allusion is afterwards made ;— " And He hath a name written, which no man knoweth but Himself."[3] In Immanuel's land a name is no

---

[1] John xx. 17. [2] Heb. ii. 11. [3] Rev. xix. 12.

empty sound, as with us : it declares the real nature of its possessor. Probably, therefore, this new name indicates some glorious mystery of which, by his union with Christ, the believer will be made a partaker in the coming age.

The last words of the Epistle, the exhortation to listen, should fall solemnly upon our ears : for, as we said just now, there is strong probability that they apply to us above all others, that the Lord is even now completing the number of the Philadelphian Church, and will, in the times of the present generation, remove her to the Heavenly Places. "Watch therefore ; for ye know neither the day nor the hour wherein the Son of man cometh."

XIX.

LAODICEA.

IN its prophetic bearing this Epistle depicts the great body of professing Christians in their last phase, and describes that worldly and self-satisfied disposition for which Christ will at length openly reject them. It is also a final warning, summoning all who can hear to leave the dead, though outwardly prosperous, Church, and join the despised Philadelphians, before Laodicea is disowned by Him Whom she insincerely calls Lord, while she does not the things which He has commanded. For her very name points to her lawlessness, since it signifies the Church in which the people are the judges of what is right.[1] And this indicates the deepseated cause of corruption, by which she has been

[1] Λαοδίκεια from λαός, "people," and δίκη, "custom," "usage," "right."

so terribly affected that, while the Lord finds no fault with Philadelphia, He knows of nothing for which He can commend Laodicea.

As Sardis was evolved from Thyatira, being the development of that body which knew not the depths of Satan, so Philadelphia consists of the faithful and true who have come out from Sardis; but Laodicea —to quote the striking words of Stier—is "the great residuum of dead Christianity gathered together at the last time."

To this Church the Lord introduces Himself in a peculiarly solemn way, which intimates that faith in His promises and person has waned and almost disappeared. For, in the first place, He is the Amen, that is, the Truth, the word being the same "Verily" with which He was wont to preface many of His utterances. He thus meets the ever-spreading unbelief, which, in various forms and degrees, we may detect in almost every circle. It is now the time of the scoffers, who are saying;—"Where is the promise of His coming?" Nay, there are not a few who profess to be Christians, and yet eliminate all that is supernatural from their Christianity! And others, like the Pharisees, are so satisfied with their own Church upon earth, that they can see no necessity for Christ's appearing, and dislike all thought of the changes which such an event would occasion. These and similar ideas are destroying the faith of many; so that, while they profess to think much of the Lord's moral teaching, they disregard or explain away His prophetic utterances. But their folly will soon be turned into bitter repentance: for all that He has said shall be yea and amen—a joy to the Philadelphians, but a terrible woe to the Laodiceans.

He is also the Faithful and True Witness: therefore, although He is long-suffering, yet His very faithfulness will presently cause Him to send forth His wrath. And, accordingly, in the eleventh verse of the nineteenth chapter, where He is represented as suddenly unveiled before the affrighted world, He is styled the Faithful and True.

But there is also another meaning to His title ; for Laodicea has failed in her testimony, therefore He must Himself appear. It is recorded of the persecuted Christians at Lyons and Vienne that, during their severe and protracted sufferings, they refused to be called martyrs, or witnesses, affirming that their Lord was the only true Martyr. Self-satisfied Laodicea has no such thoughts of Him ; and so He declares His character before delivering upon her a judgment awfully contradictory of her own. She has vaunted herself to others, but He is the great Truth-speaker : will she dare to support her cause against Him ?

Lastly ; the Lord is " the Beginning of the creation of God," an expression which Arians have interpreted to mean that He was the first of created beings. But revelation teaches us that He was the Only Begotten Son of the Father ; and, moreover, that "all things were made by Him ; and without Him was not anything made that hath been made." Hence, it is evident that He is called " the Beginning of the creation of God," as being the First Cause of all created things. He is thus the Beginning, and He is also the Amen, or the End ; while in the meantime He is the Faithful and True Witness.

As regards those whom He addresses, since they are described as neither hot nor cold, they must be the saved who have allowed themselves to sink back into "the corruption which is in the world through lust," the unstable believers who strive to make the best of both worlds—to serve God and Mammon. Such an attempt can be made only by withdrawing to a distance from Christ, and then the warmth and zeal of first love quickly begins to cool in the chilly atmosphere which surrounds it. So is it with Laodiceans, wherever they are found: they have ceased to be affected by the powers of the World to Come; Christ is no longer in them as the hope of glory; and, since they do not experience His constraining love, they are naturally disinclined to suffer inconvenience for His sake, to spend and be spent in His service.

The cities of Laodicea and Colossæ were very near to each other, so that the Churches were closely connected; and it is interesting to notice that Paul, in his letter to the Colossians, directs them to salute the Laodiceans for him, and to send on the Epistle to be read in their assembly![1] We may, therefore, fairly infer that the proximity and intimacy of these Churches had caused them to be infected with similar errors, and that the faults of the one had become, to some extent at least, the faults of the other.

Supposing this to have been the case, we can get a glimpse of the state of Laodicea by carefully reading the Epistle to the Colossians; and, in doing so, shall find the great charge against them to be, that Christ had been deprived of His honour and glory by their doctrines and the practices evolved from them. Accordingly, in the first chapter, Paul sets forth the power and Godhead of the Lord Jesus in a marvellous

[1] Col. iv. 15, 16.

description, and then comments upon the errors which had caused Him to be slighted.

The converts had not looked for all the treasures of wisdom and knowledge in Him, and were, consequently, allowing themselves to be made a spoil by means of philosophy and vain deceit, after the tradition of men, after the rudiments of the world, and not after Christ.

For they did not walk in Christ Jesus, the Lord, as they had received Him and been taught: they did not consider themselves complete in Him, made full from His fulness: nor did they frankly believe that He had blotted out the handwriting of ordinances which was against them.

And thus they were moved to seek salvation from other sources, as well as from Him; so that their religion consisted largely of distinctions between clean and unclean meats, and of observances of festivals, which God had, indeed, formerly appointed as a shadow of the coming Saviour, but which had lost all their value now that the body which cast the shadow had taken its place. They were also devoting themselves to a self-conscious, and therefore profitless, humility; and were associating other objects of worship with the Lord Jesus, even daring to pray to those angelic beings whom He had created. Thus they had ceased to hold fast the Head, and just as if He had not died for them, were subjecting themselves to ordinances which He had never commanded, and which could only mean that His work was not all-sufficient.

Again; they practised fastings and other neglectings of the body, which Paul declares to be of no value, but merely to serve for the satisfying of the flesh.

And, in fine, instead of the spiritual service enjoined by Christ, they substituted a fruitless worship arranged according to human ideas, and already condemned by the words of the Lord ;—" In vain do they worship Me, teaching for doctrines the commandments of men." They were being beguiled of their reward, and were wasting the time which God had given them upon earth.

After thus sketching out their errors, Paul makes a powerful appeal to them. If they really were risen with Christ, they should look far beyond the meaningless trifles which were occupying their minds. What had " Handle not, taste not, touch not," to do with those who were dead to the world, and whose life was hid with Christ in God ? It was not theirs to be constructing elaborate systems upon earth : they should be setting their affections on things above, where Christ sits at the right hand of God, where is the city of true believers, and whence they should be looking for the Lord Jesus to come and change their vile bodies into the likeness of His glorious body !

But the Epistle which we are considering shows that Paul's words had not availed with the Laodiceans, whatever effect they may have had upon the Colossians. The former had proved themselves worthy of their name : whatever was right in their own eyes, that was also their faith and their law. And, as a natural consequence, their love for Christ had cooled to lukewarmness : their religion was a mere practice of outward rites and customs and a belief of certain doctrines, and not a personal attachment to their Lord and Saviour.

In the prophetic interpretation, these Laodiceans

seem to be identified with, or rather to include those who in the previous Epistle are described as falsely calling themselves Jews. And in all that we can learn of them there will be found solemn warnings against the carnal religionism and human philosophy which are now characterizing Christendom. For the lukewarm are an abhorring to the Lord: He would deal rather with the absolutely cold. The former class by their lack of love and inconsistent conduct cause the adversaries to blaspheme, and so compel God to reject them openly. If any man hold the form of godliness and deny its power, his chastisement must be made manifest to all, that the holiness of God may be vindicated, and men may know that He does not tolerate insincerity.

Therefore the Lord spued[1] out the Laodiceans of old, and so will He do to all whom He finds like them at His coming. These are they who shall be left when others are taken: these shall stand without, vainly knocking, after the Master has risen and shut to the door: these, having practically denied Christ by adopting traditions, teachings, and systems, which did not come from Him, shall feel what it is to be denied by Him, and be taught by the sharp goad of persecution to keep more carefully to the simple paths which He has revealed.

But the worst feature in Laodicean Christians is that they do not realize their sad condition: they think highly of themselves, and say that they are rich

---

[1] The metaphor is taken from the use of lukewarm water as an emetic, and expresses the very strongest abhorrence. So the land of Canaan is said to have spued out its inhabitants on account of their abominations (Levit. xviii. 28).

and have grown rich, setting forth the asserted fact and the process which led up to it in such a way as to imply that their own arm has done it; but the assertion itself is utterly false. They feel—most fatal of symptoms—that they have need of nothing! ordinances and will-worship have completely satisfied the flesh.

Sternly, therefore, does the Lord expose their real condition in the words;—"And knowest not that thou art the wretched one, and miserable, and poor, and blind, and naked!"

How often in this life are men deluded by sensuous dreams and the arts of evil spirits, until the time comes for an awful awakening! The rich man is clothed in purple and fine linen, and fares sumptuously every day; but presently he opens his eyes in Hades, being in torments, and unable to procure a drop of water to cool his tongue. And even among the saved, how many are now walking as the first who will have to change to the place of the last when the King comes! How many are sitting in the chief seat who will hear the humbling command;—"Give this man place"!

In the words, "And knowest not that thou art the wretched one," the article points to the previous Epistle, in which those who are here called Laodiceans are represented as looking down with contempt upon the Philadelphians; while the Lord comforts the latter with the assurance that He will make their despisers to come and worship before their feet, and to know that He has loved them. Not the little flock to whom it is their Father's good pleasure to give the Kingdom, but the self-satisfied professors and will-worshippers, are those who need pity. The Lord knows what is impending, and calls them the wretched and miserable, because He is just about to reject them as unworthy to escape all the things that shall come to pass. And they are also poor, for they have nothing but the riches and influence of this world, which is ready to fade away; blind, for they cannot see their own miserable condition and fearful prospect; naked, for the Lord has not clothed them, so that they may walk with Him in white.

In the following words, "I counsel thee," there is a mournful significance; for they intimate that Laodicea is departing from the Kingdom of God's dear Son, and crossing the boundary line into the realms of Darkness, so that He no longer commands her, as He would His own subjects, but only offers counsel. Indeed, Laodicea has altogether lost the habit of obeying Him, and seeks to traditions, and councils, and canons, and to science, and great men, and no longer to the word of God as the sole authority.

The doctrines of Pergamos and Thyatira are returning, and ominous is the fact that the Lord now finds no extenuating circumstances, as He previously did, and mentions no good works; for this rebellion is against light and knowledge.

Yet He warns the Laodiceans to cease boasting of their fancied wealth, and to buy of Him "gold refined by fire"; that is, a faith which will endure temptation, and be only purified the more when exposed to the fiery trial.[1] Thus, whatever their condition in the world, they would be rich in faith, and heirs of the Kingdom which He promised to them that love Him.

[1] 1 Peter i. 7.

It is the want of this quality which is ruining them : for they who cannot trust Christ for every need and in every perplexity soon begin to put confidence in themselves, or in their Church, and so are enticed away from the One Foundation.

He also bids them come to Him for white raiment, that they may cover themselves with His righteousness, instead of the filthy rags which can never hide the shame of their nakedness. And, lastly, He points out that they need His eyesalve to heal their blindness, and enable them to perceive what they are, and whither they are tending.

There is, however, but little hope that Laodicea can be restored, except by the Spirit of judgment and of burning ; therefore the Lord significantly adds, " As many as I love, I rebuke and chasten "—words which seem to mean as follows. Either you are Mine, or you are not. If you are not, then go your own way, and show the truth of the Scripture which says ;—" The heart of the sons of men is evil, and madness is in their heart while they live, and after that they go to the dead." If, however, you are Mine, prepare for chastisement. But so terrible will be the chastisement of those who are left upon earth during the days of vengeance that the Lord's mercy again exhorts ;—" Be zealous, therefore, and repent."

For even now the acceptable time has not quite gone by : Christ is yet standing at the door. He should, indeed, be in the midst of those who are gathered together in His name ; but their sins have caused Him to depart from His own place, though He still lingers near them. The dispensation is closing, and the scene is, perhaps, similar to that which Ezekiel witnessed when Jerusalem was being given up to destruction. For the prophet beheld the Glory of the Lord withdrawing slowly and unwillingly from the Temple: he saw it halting first on the threshold of the House;[1] then raising itself from the earth, and taking up a more distant position above the East gate;[2] afterwards passing through the midst of the city, and lingering yet once more upon the mountain which is on the East side of it,[3] before the final ascent of the Cherubim and departure of the Keeper of Israel.

So the Lord, unable any longer to endure the disobedience and multiplied abominations of the Laodicean period, is leaving the Church which boasts His name. Yet He also tarries awhile, as did the Glory in its passage from the Temple, and turns again to knock, if perchance any may awake to the consciousness that He Who should be the Centre is without, and may, therefore, run to open to Him.

Perhaps the knocking may refer to two different means which the Lord is using to rouse His people. The first of them is, probably, chastisement; and, while this would seem to include every kind of uncertainty, rebuke, and affliction, there is one sorrow which in a special manner belongs to the present time. For true believers are being continually vexed by the

---

[1] Ezek. x. 4.
[2] Ezek. x. 19.
[3] Ezek. xi. 23. We are not told that the Glory ascended immediately. Perhaps the Lord remained for a while on the Mount of Olives to supervise the judgment which was about to fall upon the city and the Sanctuary. Standing upon the same spot, He afterwards announced the second destruction of Jerusalem (Luke xix. 43, 44), and uttered the great prophecy of its final trouble (Matt. xxiv.). From thence He ascended to heaven, and thither He will return with all His saints (Zech. xiv. 4).

failure, and, still worse, perversion of testimony, in the sects to which they have joined themselves, and by the corruption and lawlessness which surround them. They are thus being deprived of that thoughtless security in which some rest so entirely upon outward organizations, that they seem to differ but little from the dwellers upon earth. They are being warned by manifest tokens that, if the stream with which they have hitherto floated has been turned from its proper channel, they must no longer suffer themselves to be borne along by it, lest they be presently engulfed amid the waves of destruction instead of being carried into the ocean of Christ's love. They are being taught to cling more closely to the person of the Lord, more obediently to His revelation; and to long for His appearing, by which alone the power of evil can be checked, and the present perplexity disentangled.

For, while He is breaking in pieces their earthly rest, He has not forgotten to set that glorious hope before them. His secret has been communicated to them that fear Him: He has not hidden from them what He is about to do; and, consequently, on all sides proclamation is being made that He is at hand. And power has been given to those who seek it to understand the great prophetic utterances of God, which have for centuries lain sealed and comparatively unnoticed: many have read them through and through, and the knowledge of them has been increased.

Such are the Lord's appeals, which, however, He addresses no longer to the whole Church, but only to individual members of it. "If any man," He says, "hear My voice and open the door, I will come in to him, and will sup with him, and he with Me."

LAODICEA.

A few there may be who will listen to these words, but the great multitude of the Laodiceans have no desire to sup with the Lord.

They are feasting with the dwellers upon earth, nourishing their hearts in a day of slaughter, eating and drinking, marrying and giving in marriage; and so they will go on, until the day that the Master of the house rises and shuts to the door. Then, at the sound of the closing portals, their indifference will be changed to feverish anxiety: they will shudder as they perceive that the Hour of Judgment is come.

In these days of luxury too many believers, like the spouse in the Song of songs,[1] have left the work of tending their flocks in the wilderness, and gone into the city of the world: they are slumbering at ease, and stifling conscience with the weak excuse, "I sleep, but my heart waketh;" I make no outward show of work or labour of love, but am right and true within. And so they permit the fear of any slight inconvenience to deter them from rising to open unto their Lord, until at last His hand is seen through the hole of the door, until He manifests His presence by the rapture of those who are looking for Him.

Then the careless ones awake to consciousness: they are smitten to the heart with remorse and returning love: they spring from the sinful couch, and hasten to unbar the door.

But no fair and glorious Form is waiting in the darkness of the night; the Beloved has withdrawn Himself, and is gone: they seek Him, but cannot find Him: they call Him, but no answer peals back through the gloom. They have trifled with warnings too long:

Song of Sol. v. 2-6.

the appointed time has passed, and they writhe in anguish as they perceive that the slighted threat has been suddenly and inexorably accomplished. The Master has knocked: they were not ready to open to Him immediately, and He has departed and left them alone in the midnight of woe.

But if any of the lukewarm Laodiceans can be roused before it is too late, they will be strengthened to overcome, and will yet attain to the dignity of sitting with Christ on the Throne of Glory from which He will judge the Millennial world. And even those who pass through the Tribulation, provided they refuse to worship the Beast or his image, or to receive his mark upon their foreheads or in their hands, will also reign with Christ, but, as we shall presently see, only as subordinates, and not on the Throne.

We have now considered the seven messages of the Lord to His people concerning the things that are. Who is wise that he may understand these solemn warnings, and find grace to act upon them while there is yet time? In his account of Christ's entry into Jerusalem, John remarks;—" These things understood not His disciples at the first: but when Jesus was glorified, then remembered they that these things were written of Him." How great suspense and anxiety would they have been spared if they had studied and applied the Scriptures before the death of their Master, had recognized every incident as it occurred, and known that He must first suffer those things and then enter into His glory! But they did not apprehend until the great crisis, with its days of perplexity and terror, had passed by. Shall we not learn wisdom from their error, and avoid the far more calamitous consequences of a similar mistake at the close of this age? It is toward evening, and the day is now far spent. He, then, that hath an ear, let him hear what the Spirit saith unto the Churches: for the time is at hand.

XX.

The Presence and the Appearing.

We have already, in discussing the Jewish prophecies, commented upon the twenty-fourth chapter of Matthew up to the paragraph in which the Lord speaks of His appearing and the deliverance of His Jewish elect. In the sentences immediately following, He teaches the latter how they may know that He is near at hand, and declares the certainty of His predictions. And then, in the thirty-sixth verse, He proceeds to answer the second question of His disciples;—"What shall be the sign of Thy Presence?"

But before we consider this solemn subject, it will be necessary to avoid confusion by briefly investigating the meaning of the terms "Presence" and "Appearing."

The Greek word $\pi\alpha\rho o \upsilon\sigma\iota\alpha$ is usually translated 'coming': but we render it 'presence,' because the latter is its strict and literal meaning; while the former is derived, subordinate, and never absolutely necessary. For the sense is much the same whether we say of an absent person—"we shall be glad of your presence," or, "of your coming." Moreover, it is most important to retain the literal signification, because the word is used, not merely of the descent of Christ from the

High Heavens, but of the whole period of His sojourn in the air, which will, it seems, occupy at least seven years.[1] During this time His people will be caught up to Him; some immediately upon His descent, others later. But all are included in Paul's description, "they that are Christ's at His Presence."

The taking up of the first company will, as we shall presently see, be the sign that He has come, and that the judgments of the Apocalypse are about to commence. We may thus understand Paul's appeal to the Thessalonians;—"Now we beseech you, brethren, by the Presence of our Lord Jesus Christ, and by our gathering together unto Him, that ye be not quickly shaken from your mind, nor yet be troubled, either by spirit, or by word, or by letter pretending to come from us, as that the Day of the Lord is now present."[2] The Thessalonians had been in much affliction, and, supposing that no sorrow could be greater than theirs, rashly concluded that they were in the last times, and that the Day of the Lord had come. But Paul reminds them that that Day will be brought about by the Presence of Christ in the air, and that the sign of

[1] That is, of course, the last of Daniel's Weeks when the dispensation will again be Jewish. Whether this period will follow immediately upon the removal of the Church, or whether there will be an abnormal interval—similar to that which came between the tenth of Nisan, on which the Jewish covenant was suspended, and the Day of Pentecost—is not revealed.

[2] 2 Thess. ii. 1, 2. The Greek of the last word does not signify "to be at hand," but "to be present." It occurs in Rom. viii. 38, 1 Cor. iii. 22, vii. 26, Gal. i. 4, Heb. ix. 9, in each of which passages the English Version renders it by "present." In 2 Tim. iii. 1, where the future is used, the Translators have "perilous times *shall come.*" In 2 Thess. ii. 2, they have erroneously rendered "is at hand," evidently for the purpose of bringing the meaning into accord with their own dogmatic eschatology.

His Presence, namely, the gathering together of His people to Him, had not then been given.

The second term, ἐπιφάνεια, signifies "appearing," or, "manifestation," and occurs in connection with the first in a passage which should be rendered ;—"Whom the Lord shall slay with the breath of His mouth, and bring to nought by the Appearing of His Presence."[1] Here it is used of the manifestation of Christ to the world, of the flashing forth of His Glory when the time of the unseen Presence is ended. But it may also be applied to the revelation of this Presence to those who are caught up to Him ; so that the reference, in each case of its occurrence, can only be decided by the context.

We will now return to our Lord's discourse on the Mount of Olives. After an admonition, especially designed for the Jewish converts of the last days, to remember that the fulfilment of the things which He had been predicting would show that He was near at hand—just as the budding of the fig-tree proclaims the approach of summer—He proceeds to speak of His Presence, during which the events mentioned between the sixth and twenty-ninth verses will take place. The precise time of His descent cannot be revealed ; for neither men, nor yet angels, may know it. Like other great judgments of God, it is announced again and again : but, were its appointed season declared, it could not become the test which He intends it to be. For those who saw that it was postponed beyond the term of their lives would altogether dismiss the subject ; while those who expected to see it might, when near the appointed day, excite themselves

[1] 2 Thess. ii. 8

to a faith as worthless as that which men have often exhibited in predictions fixing the hour of doom for the world, and which too frequently lapses into a hopeless scepticism.

The Lord will, therefore, say nothing in regard to the day and the hour; but, nevertheless, He gives signs by which we may discover that they are at hand. A memorable period of history shall be repeated, and again it shall be as it was in the time of the flood, when men were eating and drinking, marrying and giving in marriage, until the command went forth, and Noah entered the ark. Then the world suddenly perceived that the door of escape had been closed, and that the execution of judgment had commenced: their thoughtlessness and mirth were quickly changed into agonizing fear, as the vigour of life found itself confronted by inexorable death.

In the parallel passage of Luke, the Lord adduces Sodom also as an illustration of what the world will be on the eve of His coming. Putting together the accounts of both periods as given in the book of Genesis, we find that their general characteristics include intercourse with beings of another sphere, the corruption of all flesh, violence, and unnatural crime; none of which ominous signs is lacking in the world of to-day. But the Lord does not particularize such things; for they belong to unregenerate and demon-driven men, and He uttered His prophecy for the guidance and consolation of His own people, whether Jews or Christians. For this reason, apparently, He specifies only those pursuits in which He may, at His coming, find the saved so heedlessly engrossed that He will be compelled to leave them for discipline.

They are;—
>Eating and drinking.
>Marrying and giving in marriage.
>Buying and selling.
>Planting and building.

Now all these acts and occupations are lawful in themselves; but, if they be permitted to hide eternal realities from our eyes, they become a cause of destruction. The world will be altogether absorbed in them up to the end; and the saved have need to watch and pray, lest they also should fall into the snare, and be taken by surprise.

In regard to their general character, we may notice that the judgments of God usually come upon men after they have made considerable advances in civilization and its vices: for it is then that pride, fulness of bread, and abundance of idleness, generate rebellion; just as was the case with Sodom,[1] and as in olden time Jeshurun waxed fat and kicked.[2]

Luxurious living is a frequent characteristic of those who are ripening for judgment. "Ye have nourished your hearts in a day of slaughter!" is a charge which God has more than once brought against men. And He is especially indignant that those who profess to know Him should be satisfying the flesh, when they ought rather to be sighing and crying for the abominations which surround them.

Even a slight excess may deprive a believer of his crown: for to obtain it he must overcome, and among his besetting sins there may be one of the kind which goeth not out but by prayer and fasting. Or, if he fares every day sufficiently well to induce fleshly con-

[1] Ezek. xvi. 49.　　[2] Deut. xxxii. 15.

tent and love of ease, he will certainly be found among the slothful servants. Any pampering of the body brings weakness and blindness upon the spirit, and solemnly does our Lord recognise the fact in those words;—"Take heed to yourselves, lest at any time your hearts be overcharged with surfeiting, and drunkenness, and cares of this life, and so that Day come upon you unawares."

But there are other insidious snares besides that of luxurious living. There are the social connections, which, pure and honourable as they may be, too often take undue possession of the heart, and monopolize the thoughts to the exclusion of Christ. There is the commercial temptation; the craving to acquire, and heap up treasure in the last days; the covetousness which sometimes seeks to defend itself from the eye of the Almighty by large donations, which, nevertheless, bear but a trifling proportion to the means of the giver, and do not deprive him of a single gratification. And, lastly, there is the disposal of the wealth accumulated; the preparations for a long stay upon earth, the devices whereby life may possibly be gained now and certainly lost hereafter, the erection of imposing mansions which, at the Judgment, will testify to the extravagance, the luxury, and the selfishness, of the builders. "For the stone from the wall shall cry out, and the beam of the timber shall bear witness."[1]

Such were the thoughts and occupations in the midst of which the Antediluvians and the Sodomites perished miserably, with all that had made up their lives. And, in each case, the silent removal of the righteous was the sign that the day of grace had

[1] Hab. ii. 11.

passed.[1] Will there, then, be any similar sign to announce that Christ is in the air, and that the Day of the Lord has come? This question is answered in the next verse, and further explanation may be found in the first Epistle to the Thessalonians.

The world will one day be surprised by the sudden and unaccountable disappearance of many persons in the midst of their ordinary occupations. Two men will be working in the field in the middle of the day: one will instantaneously vanish.[2] His bewildered comrade may still see upon the ground the garment which had been put off for labour, but the man will be gone. Two women will be grinding the daily supply of corn in early morning; the hand of one will fail: her companion will look up, and see that she is no longer in her place.[3] Two persons—the reference is evidently to a man and his wife—will be in the same bed at night: the one will be taken away, and the other will awake to solitude and bereavement.[4] As soon as this sign is given, then woe for the earth and the sea! Those who shall be accounted worthy to escape will have been removed from the world: the Holy Spirit will no longer restrain the Mystery of Lawlessness; nor will the judgments of God be delayed.

With regard to the meaning of the words, "one shall be taken," an error has often been made through ignorance of the original. Comparing the clause with that of the thirty-ninth verse, "the flood came and

[1] Of course only so far as the natural life was concerned. Space for repentance to the saving of the spirit still remained, until the Judgment was actually carried out.
[2] Matt. xxiv. 40.
[3] Matt. xxiv. 41.
[4] Luke. xvii. 34.

took them all away," some have interpreted, "the one shall be taken away in judgment, the other shall be spared in mercy." But an examination of the Greek immediately dissipates this idea. In the thirty-ninth verse the verb used is $αἱρεῖν$, which means 'to take away by destruction.' But in the fortieth and forty-first verses, we find a very different word, $παραλαμβάνειν$, which properly signifies 'to receive,' or, 'take alongside,' and then, sometimes, 'to take with one as a companion.' Thus the word is most appropriately used of those who shall be caught up to Christ, that they may walk with Him in white, that they may follow the Lamb whithersoever He goeth.

In the fourteenth chapter of John, it occurs in a very significant passage;—"For if I go and prepare a place for you, I am coming again, and will *receive* ($παραλήψομαι$) you unto Myself; that where I am, there ye may be also." Here it is used of the very act of which the Lord speaks in Matthew.

Again, in another place, we are told that the Lord "*taketh*" ($παραλαμβάνει$) Peter, James, and John, as His companions to the Mount of Transfiguration.[1] He selects three out of the twelve disciples to behold His glory; while the nine are, in the meantime, left at the bottom of the hill to struggle hopelessly with Satan; and, consequently, to be subjected to the scorn of the world, until at length the Master is seen descending the hill in company with those whom He had taken with Him.

Surely, this scene is typical, and confirms our interpretation of the passage we are considering, that the one is taken to be a companion of the Lord and to

[1] Matt. xvii. 1.

see His glory, while the other is left to agonize with the world and Satan as a further discipline: for the admonition to watch in the next verse seems to imply that both of the two are disciples.

Having thus described the sign of His Presence, the Lord proceeds to urge upon His followers the necessity of watching, and intimates, by the Parable of the Householder and the Thief, that grievous loss will be sustained by those who neglect His directions. Many other such warnings may be found in the Scriptures, and their special object is plainly set forth in the Lord's own exhortation ;—" Watch ye, therefore, and pray always *that ye may be accounted worthy to escape all these things that shall come to pass*, and to stand before the Son of man." [1]

XXI.

THE FIRST RAPTURE, AS REVEALED TO THE THESSALONIANS.

To none of the Churches with which he was connected did Paul communicate so many details of the last things as to that of the Thessalonians. For in one of his Epistles to them we find the most circumstantial prediction of the first ascension of the saints ; while in the other there are many particulars respecting the subsequent career of Antichrist.

The planting of their Church is described in the seventeenth chapter of the "Acts." And from the account there given, as well as from the Epistles, we may infer that Paul spoke much to the converts of the coming and Kingdom of Christ. It may be that the Spirit, foreseeing the persecutions and tribulations which

[1] Luke xxi. 36.

awaited them, had, on that account, directed the apostle to dwell on the glory that should be. For even of the Lord Himself we are told that, for the joy that was set before Him, He endured the cross, despising the shame.

The prominence given in the teachings of Paul to the future reign of Christ may be discovered in the accusation by which the Jews sought to prejudice the rulers against him. "These," they said, "that have turned the world upside down are come hither also; whom Jason hath received: and these all do contrary to the decrees of Cæsar, saying that there is another king, one Jesus." [1]

But, however Jews or Greeks may have distorted the apostle's meaning, the revelation of that blessed hope and glorious appearing of the great God and our Saviour, Jesus Christ, had lifted up the Thessalonian Church to enthusiasm. And so, indeed, it has ever affected those whose hearts have been opened for its reception. It was that hope which stimulated the early Church to the extraordinary exertions of the first two and a half centuries: it is that which oftentimes since has supported believers throngh days of trial; for whenever persecution has arisen on account of the word, the Apocalypse and the prophetic Psalms have almost invariably formed the great stay and comfort of the persecuted. And, at this present time, the same hope is again exercising a powerful influence in arousing the Church to renewed efforts, and in separating off a people for the presence of the Lord.

Yet, although the Thessalonians received the spirit-stirring message with joy, even they did not rightly

[1] Acts xvii. 6, 7

understand it in all its bearings, and the consequence of their imperfect knowledge was seen in certain false and mischievous inferences.

Excited by expectation, and assuming that the Lord must come immediately, they could no longer settle down to the ordinary routine of life, and Paul found it necessary to exhort them to be quiet, and do their own business, and labour with their own hands, that their conduct might be seemly to those that were without, and that they might not, by neglecting their duty, be compelled to depend upon the help of others.

And then again, while they had heard of the coming of the Lord and their gathering together unto Him, they had not yet been instructed in regard to the first resurrection. Consequently, knowing only of the final resurrection and last judgment, being well aware that these events would not take place until after the Millennium, and distinguishing clearly between the Millennium and the Eternal State, they naturally concluded that all who had the misfortune to die before the Lord's return would lose the glories of the Kingdom.

What wonder, then, that they mourned immoderately when the spirit of a beloved one passed away from their midst; since they thought to see his face no more until after the long lapse of the thousand years; unless, indeed, they too should be called to follow him before the Lord came, and so be themselves deprived of the coveted glory.

To lift this gloom from their eyes, and reveal to them the glad truth, is Paul's object in the latter part of the fourth chapter. "We would not have you ignorant, brethren," he says, " concerning them which have been laid to sleep; that ye sorrow not, even as the rest, which have no hope."

And then he reveals the wondrous truth, that each of the great events in our Lord's life has its correspondence in the lives of His members; that if, in our measure, we are called to suffer as He did, to be men of sorrows and acquainted with grief, to endure the contradiction of sinners and the hatred of the world, ay, and presently, should He tarry, to gaze for the last time upon the light of the natural sun; we may, nevertheless, look up to the eminence on the other side of the dark valley, where He sits in glory, and know that, by His grace, we too cannot fail to emerge from the night of death into the resurrection-morning.

Mourn not so hopelessly for your dead, he says to the sorrowing Thessalonians: you know that Christ died and rose again, and His Church must share in all things with her great Head. When He appears as the Risen One, then all those who have been laid to sleep through Him must God bring with Him.

The expression "laid to sleep through Jesus," is very beautiful. In the idea of sleep we have, of course, a hint that there is no intermission of life, and that there will soon be an awakening. The phraseology is that of the Lord Himself. "Our friend Lazarus sleepeth," He said, "and I go that I may awaken him out of sleep."

But of these saints, we are told that they have been laid to sleep by means of the Lord Jesus, that is, by His death and mediation. Yes: for, without His interposition, they had now been not asleep, but dead.

The wicked, when they relinquish natural life, do not sleep: they are dead, and have parted for ever with

THE FIRST RAPTURE.

all hope of life: they are shut out from God. They must, indeed, stand before the Great White Throne, but that will be in the miserable existence which is called death: for death, in the Scriptural sense, is no cessation of being, but eternal separation from Him in Whom alone we may find light and love and rest. And all who pass from this world in wilful rejection of Christ must be thus shut out. For "this is the record, that God gave unto us eternal life, and this life is in His Son. He that hath the Son, hath the life: he that hath not the Son of God, hath not the life."

But all those departed ones who have obtained the life from the Lord Jesus will God bring with Him. Like their Saviour, they have disappeared from the world; and, when He returns to sight, they also must be seen in His company. Now that He is invisible, He and His Church are mystically united: He is the Vine, and they are the branches. But that which is mystical is nothing, unless it has a reality behind it which shall presently be revealed. Therefore, as soon as the Lord is seen again, the connection between Himself and His Church must also become visible. "When Christ Who is our Life shall appear, then shall ye also appear with Him in glory."[1]

And so Paul proceeds to tell us how this consummation will be brought about: and he does so "by the word of the Lord," that is, by a direct revelation to himself.

The words, "we which are alive," are of great doctrinal importance: for they give clear evidence that Paul contemplated the occurrence of the advent in his own lifetime as a possibility. He was, however,

[1] Col. iii. 4.

well aware that none might know the day and the hour, and, therefore, expressed no definite expectation.

But he had a very definite desire, and gave utterance to it in unmistakable terms in another place. "For we that are in this tabernacle do groan being burdened; not for that we would be unclothed, but that we would be clothed upon, that what is mortal may be swallowed up of life."[1]

Yet Paul and many others have passed away, and still the Lord tarries. There is, however, no reason to believe that their expectant attitude is in any way changed: the spirits of those who sleep are also waiting for the Lord from the high heavens, and longing for the time when the sons of God shall be manifested and their bodies redeemed. In this respect the hope of the whole Church, on both sides of the river of death, is the same. And when the hour comes, whether they be upon earth or in the Paradise of God, they shall be glorified together, and neither quick nor dead have the precedence.

The words, "the Lord shall descend," utterly preclude the "spiritual" interpretation to which some Christians even now cling. For His spiritual presence is already with us, and so will remain even unto the end. It is, therefore, to His glorified body, which can be only in one place at a time, that allusion is here made. And the descent is the first stage in the fulfilment of the angels' words, that He should so come in like manner as He was seen to go up into heaven.

And as He passes through His illimitable realms,

[1] 2 Cor. v. 4.

THE FIRST RAPTURE.

upon wings of lightning, followed by His glittering hosts, and causing the countless stars which stud His heavens to pale with His glory, He will utter the word of command, and the dead shall hear the voice of the Son of God ; and they that hear, for all will not do so, shall live.

Forth from Paradise and the grave they will come, from the poor thief, whose mortal agony was prolonged until Heaven and Hades had thrilled with the mighty words, "It is finished," to the last who shall have been laid to sleep, just as the trump of God is proclaiming the arrival of the King.

And scarcely less wonderful will be the change in the case of the living.

It was a glad sight to see the warm flush returning to the leper's face, and his decayed limbs filling out and brightening into ruddy health.

It must have made the hearts of the bystanders rejoice to look on when blind Bartimæus received the reward of his faith, and opened his wondering eyes for the first time on God's fair world and on the tender and loving face of God's own Son.

And hard of heart must he have been who could restrain tears of sympathy when he beheld the poor demoniac ceasing from his mad ravings, his wanderings among the tombs, and his cruel self-mutilations, and sitting clothed, and in his right mind, at the feet of Him Who had saved him from his fiendish tormentors.

But even these miracles of love will seem as nothing to the deliverances of that glorious night, when the Lord shall call His people, and, in response, the bedridden invalid of years, the blind, the halt, the maimed, the consumptive, the fever-stricken, the poor oppressed lunatic or demoniac, the bowed down with age, and pain, and care, and bereavement, and persecution, and hard toil—all shall come forth from the places of durance in which they have been graciously enabled to possess their souls in patience, and shout for joy that the year of the Lord's redeemed has come.

And dropping every fetter of mortality, losing every scar and disfigurement as they rise, and joined by the company of those who had slept, they shall ascend in one glorious body to the presence of the King.

How precious will Christ then seem to them! How unspeakable the breadth and length and height and depth of His love, as separated from every evil thing, and caught up in clouds to the place where He is awaiting them, they utter their rapturous cry;—"Unto Him that loveth us, and loosed us from our sins by His blood; and He made us to be a Kingdom, priests unto His God and Father; to Him be the glory and the dominion for ever and ever. Amen."

Those who shall be summoned to this exultant gathering will find themselves suddenly rapt away, doubtless by the forceful power of that Spirit by Whom they were sealed unto the Day of Redemption. Woe, then, to all who shall have grieved the Spirit of God on that unknown and fateful night!

The Greek words εἰς ἀπάντησιν imply that they who go to meet the Lord in the air will subsequently return to earth with Him,[1] not without Him. For there shall be no more parting from the beloved

[1] That is, when He descends upon the Mount of Olives to deliver Jerusalem. "And the Lord my God shall come, and all the saints with Thee." See Zech. xiv. 3-5, and compare Jude 14, 15.

Saviour, or from the friends which He has restored to us. Thenceforth we shall be ever with the Lord : we shall follow the Lamb whithersoever He goeth.

And with thoughts of this glorious future we are to comfort one another in our bereavements. Not by intercourse with demons, who feign to be the spirits of our dead that they may allure us into paths of destruction ; but by looking on to the time when Christ shall come, and, with every other blessing, restore to us for ever those whom we have loved and lost for a while.

XXII.

The Mystery Finished.

IN writing to the Corinthians, the Apostle Paul bids them regard himself and his colleagues as " stewards of the mysteries of God "—an expression often twisted by sacerdotalists into accord with their own views, and interpreted to mean " dispensers of the sacraments."

But neither Baptism, nor the Lord's Supper, is ever called a mystery in the New Testament : the term is invariably applied to revelations given by the Spirit for communication to the Church. And the nature of the mysteries of which Paul was steward may be readily understood from the following complete list of those which are mentioned in his Epistles.

The mystery of Israel's present condition and
    future deliverance . . . . . Rom. xi. 25, 26.
The mystery of the wisdom of God . . 1 Cor. ii. 7.
The mystery that we shall not all sleep, but
    shall all be changed . . . . 1 Cor. xv. 51, 52.
The mystery of God's will , , . . Eph. i. 9.

The mystery of marriage as a type of Christ and His Church	Eph. v. 32.
The mystery of the Gospel	Eph. vi. 19.
The mystery of Christ	Col. iv. 3.
The mystery of lawlessness	2 Thess. ii. 7.
The mystery of the faith	1 Tim. iii. 9.
The mystery of Godliness	1 Tim. iii. 16.
The mystery[1] of the Church	Rom. xvi. 25. Eph. iii. 3-12. Col. i. 26, 27. Col. ii. 2.

The last on the list is the great mystery of the present dispensation, and the most frequently mentioned of all. It is said to have been hidden from the ages, and its secret was that God would invite Jews and Gentiles, without distinction, to be one in Christ, to become members of His body, of His flesh and of His bones, and to be partakers of a heavenly destiny. As we have already seen, the Lord began to reveal some of its details in the Seven Parables, and in so doing is said to have fulfilled the prophecy;—"I will utter things which have been kept secret from the foundation of the world."[2]

Of its termination we are told that, "in the days of

---

[1] There are two other instances of the use of this word by Paul. In 1 Cor. xiii. 2, he says;—"Though I understand all mysteries": and in 1 Cor. xiv. 2, he describes the speaker with tongues as uttering mysteries in spirit. In the synoptic Gospels it is applied to the parables by which the Lord disclosed the future of the Church. See Matt. xiii. 11, Mark. iv. 11, and Luke viii. 10. In the Apocalypse, it is used of the stars which are the angels of the churches (i. 20); of the Church itself (x. 7); and of the Woman seated on the Beast (xvii. 5, 7). Mysteries are, therefore, secrets revealed by God, with which every one who is made a disciple for the Kingdom of the Heavens must become acquainted, that he may be like a householder which bringeth forth out of his treasure things new and old (Matt. xiii. 52).

[2] Matt. xiii. 35.

THE MYSTERY FINISHED

the voice of the seventh angel, when he is about to sound, then is finished the mystery of God."[1] For, at that time, the last member of the Church of the Firstborn will have been made ready, and, at the blast of the seventh trumpet, its general assembly will take place.

But now the question arises—Is this event the same as that which is described by Paul in the First Epistle to the Thessalonians?

Several reasons induce us to think that it is not.

And, first, Paul does not preface his description with any notice of the violent persecutions, or supernatural judgments, which are to take place just before the mystery is finished.

Again; in the first five verses of the next chapter he manifestly treats the rapture as the introduction to the Day of the Lord, just as Christ Himself gives it as the sign of His Presence in the air. So, too, in the Second Epistle, when he adjured the Thessalonians, by the coming of Christ and our gathering together unto Him, not to be persuaded that the Day of the Lord was then in progress,[2] he clearly implied that the coming and the gathering must take place before that Day.

On the other hand, the blast which signals the conclusion of the mystery sounds just at the close of the time of judgment. For the seventh angel's period includes the final outpouring of wrath from the vials, the plagues of which are of such a nature that their duration must be very limited, or no flesh would be saved. Moreover, their horrors appear to be cumulative; since, under the fifth vial, men are represented as

[1] Rev. x. 7. [2] 2 Thess. ii. 1, 2. See p. 418 and note.

blaspheming God for what they are still suffering from the first.[1]

It would seem, then, that the rapture of which Paul speaks and the fulfilment of the mystery of God are distinct events, and there is no lack of proof that the Church will be gathered to the Lord in two translations, one taking place before, and the other after, the Great Tribulation and the persecutions of Antichrist. But we will not adduce the evidence for this truth until we have considered a difficulty which has troubled many.

If, it is asked, Paul does not include the whole Church in the translation which he describes, why does he say, " Then we which are alive, and remain, shall be caught up,' without a hint of possible exceptions to the rule ?

The difficulty may be removed by two considerations.

First ; Paul merely says "we shall be caught up," and not "we shall *all* be caught up." The significance of the omission will appear presently.

In the second place, the testimony of other Scriptures shows that there will be a second rapture at the appointed time for the assembly of the Church,[2] and,

[1] Rev. xvi. 2, 11.
[2] The reader will find proofs of this further on. Some complain that, unless all believers be taken away at the same time, the Church will be divided into two parts ; but this is a fallacy. It will be no more divided then than it is now by the circumstance that its members are found among the quick as well as among the dead, and that some of them may not yet have been born. But in the days of the voice of the seventh angel, and before the manifestation, all will be safely gathered in : not one will then be missing.

Others do not deny the second rapture, but suppose that all believers will be taken away at the time of the first, and that the

THE MYSTERY FINISHED. 437

therefore, that the Apostle's words are to be regarded as a general statement, expressing what should be, and potentially may be, the case with every Christian. We may compare the passage in which he says, "It is appointed unto men once to die"; and then, in the very next verse, reveals the secret that some will escape death,[1] or, as he puts it in his Epistle to the Corinthians, that " we shall not all sleep."[2]

In the same general way the Lord gave the promise to His disciples;—" Verily, I say unto you, That ye which have followed Me . . . ye also shall sit upon twelve thrones, judging the twelve tribes of Israel."[3] Now Judas had followed Him, and was at the time one of the Twelve. But it is not possible that the Betrayer should occupy a throne in the regeneration, since the Lord shortly afterwards speaks of him as a lost "son of perdition."[4]

How much may be signified by the omission of the word "all" is seen in the discourse contained in the fifth chapter of John. There the Lord reveals the three acts of power by which He will show that, " as the Father raiseth up the dead, and quickeneth them, even so the Son quickeneth whom He will."[5]

The first of these is the resurrection of the spirit, or conversion.[6]

The second is the bodily resurrection of His own at His coming. And although He will at that time raise only some from among the dead, yet He says

members of the second will be entirely made up of sinners subsequently converted. Such an explanation does indeed cut the Church in twain: for if all its members were removed from earth, it could only resume its work after an absolute replanting.

[1] Heb. ix. 27, 28.   [3] Matt. xix. 28   [5] John v. 21.
[2] Cor. xv. 51.   [4] John xvii. 12.   [6] John v. 24.

simply ;—" The dead shall hear the voice of the Son of Man."[1]

But when He speaks of the third act, or resurrection of the whole number of the dead, He describes them as "*all* that are in the graves."[2]

There is, then, little difficulty in regard to the passage in the Epistle to the Thessalonians. But in the First Epistle to the Corinthians we have to deal with a far more precise statement. "We shall not all sleep," says the Apostle, "but we shall *all* be changed, in a moment, in the twinkling of an eye, at the last trump."[3] There is no possibility of misunderstanding this assertion: it can only mean that *all* true Christians who are alive at the time to which reference is made will be changed and translated. But the time is that of the last trumpet: and the word "last" evidently implies that others have previously sounded. Hence it is probable that Paul means the seventh trumpet of the Book of Revelation, the blast of which will announce that the mystery is finished.

We may now be prepared to understand the repeated allusions in the Apocalypse to two raptures;[4] the first of

[1] John v. 25.
[2] John v. 28.
[3] 1 Cor. xv. 51, 52.
[4] In Rev. xvi. 15, we find the words ;—"Behold, I come as a thief. Blessed is he that watcheth and keepeth his garments, lest he walk naked and they see his shame." This verse is often explained of the Church; and would, in that case, indicate a third rapture. But—without pressing the fact that the mystery of God has been already finished—there is nothing in its terms at all suggestive of removal from earth. It is rather a last warning to Jews, that the Lord is on the point of descending, and all His saints with Him (Zech. xiv. 5).

The figure in the latter part of the verse seems to be appropriately taken from a Jewish custom, which—since it is preserved in the sixth section of the *Mishnah*, under the heading *Middoth*,

THE MYSTERY FINISHED.

which, as we have already remarked, will break up the Church as an institution upon earth, and so clear the way for the resumption of God's work with the Jews. For He never yet has had, and is never likely to have, two elect peoples upon earth at the same time under different covenants and different laws. The second, on the other hand, will complete the numbers of the Church in heaven.

To mention some of the traces of these two ascensions—we have already pointed out the distinction between the rapture which Paul describes and the completion of the mystery of God.

We have also shown that the first three chapters of the Apocalypse deal only with matters that concern the Christian dispensation; whereas from the fourth chapter, in the beginning of which John is typically summoned to heaven, the Church altogether disappears, the Tribes of Israel come to the front, and the dispensation is changed, the Old Testament cries for vengeance being again heard among the people of God.[1] And yet this period, during which the Church is not recognised upon earth, is the time of Antichrist's persecution, the victims of which are afterwards found among the heavenly elect?[2] They must, therefore, have been removed to heaven by a second translation.

Again; the Man-child is caught away before Antichrist receives his power.[3]

---

that is, "Measurements of the Temple"—may not improbably be revived when the Jews return to Palestine. It was as follows; —"The priest that walked the round of the Temple-guards by night had torches borne before him: and if he found any asleep upon the guard, he burnt his clothes with the torches" (*Middoth*, cap. I. hal. 2). See Lightfoot's Works, vol. iii, p. 357.

[1] See pp. 332-5. [2] Rev. xx. 4. [3] See pp. 111-2.

But, in the seventh chapter, there stands before the Throne a vast multitude of those who have come out of " the Tribulation the Great one "—for such is a literal rendering of the Greek—and who complete the numbers of the First Resurrection.

Similarly the fourteenth chapter begins with the description of a hundred forty and four thousand standing with the Lamb on Mount Zion,[1] having been redeemed from the earth, and from among men, as a Firstfruits to God and the Lamb.

Then follow three angelic messages, one of which has special reference to the persecution of Antichrist.

Immediately afterwards our attention is directed to the Harvest, which is gathered in by the Lord Himself with " a sharp sickle." And doubtless the adjective alludes to the terrible discipline to which those Christians will be subjected who remain on earth during the reign of the Beast.

Following the Harvest we have, still in the order of nature, the Vintage, or destruction of the wicked; so that the chapter seems to present us with the contrasted end of all those who shall be alive when Christ descends into the air.

Another indication of the two raptures may be found in the sea of glass which John saw before the Throne, and was probably well able to understand.[2] For the appearance of the two altars with the seven torches of fire to represent the lampstand, and the Throne with the Cherubim in the place of the Ark, must immediately

---

[1] That is, of course, the heavenly Mount Zion. For the sound of the harps comes out of heaven (v. 2); the hundred forty and four thousand sing before the Throne; and they have been redeemed from the earth (v. 3).

[2] Rev. iv. 6.

have suggested to him that the sea of glass was the heavenly pattern of the laver and the molten sea.

Now the laver, standing in the court of the Tabernacle, represented sanctification, even as the brazen altar did justification. It was for the priests to wash in before they proceeded into the Holy Place for service. And so the sea which John saw appears to be the purifying element through which those must pass who would go on without fear to do service before the Throne. And what this element is Paul discloses when he speaks of Christ loving the Church, and giving Himself for it, "that he might sanctify and cleanse it with the washing of water by the word."[1]

Hence those who pass through this sea of glass are men so gifted with faith in the revelations of God that His Spirit can apply the word with power to their hearts, and cleanse their way by making them take heed thereto according to it. Clear as crystal, and without any admixture,[2] was the heavenly laver when John saw it prepared for the sanctification of those whose ascension was represented by his own. But a little later, in the fifteenth chapter, he beheld it in a very changed condition.

It was then "a sea of glass mingled with fire." Another purifying element had been added to the water, one which, throughout the New Testament, is used as a figure of the agonizing chastisement of God, whereby

[1] Eph. v. 26.
[2] This does not, of course, imply that those who have part in the first rapture will suffer no affliction. But the word of God, made effectual by His Spirit, will be the chief means of their sanctification: they will need no more than ordinary trouble, and will, therefore, be accounted worthy to escape the appalling woes and persecutions of the Great Tribulation.

the flesh is consumed and destroyed, while the spirit is cleansed and made white.

What it specially means in this case we are at no loss to discover : for upon the shore of the sea nearest to the Throne stands a joyous multitude who have passed through and emerged triumphantly from its painful waters, and they are those "that have gotten the victory over the Beast, and over his image, and over his mark, and over the number of his name."[1] Left behind upon the earth, they have endured to the end through the time of fiery trial, through the hour of temptation : they are the Harvest which the Lord reaped with a sharp sickle, but which is now safely gathered into the heavenly garner, whither the First-fruits had been already conveyed.

With so much testimony in regard to the two raptures, we are not surprised to find that, when, at last, heaven opens, and the Lord and His Church are revealed in glory, He is said to be followed by the "armies[2] in the heaven," the different divisions which make up the one body.

Finally, in the twentieth chapter, the full assembly of the Church of the First-born is described in these terms ;—"And I saw thrones, and they sat upon them, and judgment was given to them : and I saw the souls of them which had been beheaded for the testimony of Jesus, and for the word of God, and such

[1] Rev. xv. 2.
[2] τὰ στρατεύματα. Rev. xix. 14. "Heaven," in the singular, usually means the heaven of this earth, or the Kingdom of the air, where the Church has been tabernacling with Christ. The plural, on the other hand, generally signifies the whole system of the heavens, or, the heaven of heavens, as in the phrases, "the Kingdom of the heavens"; "Our Father Which art in the heavens," and others.

THE MYSTERY FINISHED. 443

as worshipped not the Beast, neither his image, and received not the mark upon their forehead and upon their hand; and they lived and reigned with Christ a thousand years. The rest of the dead lived not until the thousand years should be finished. This is the first resurrection."[1]

Now in this passage we can discern three different classes of glorified believers. There are, first, those who are seen sitting upon thrones, and who are probably the company which will be caught up to the Lord at the beginning of the Presence. Then there are those who, being left behind, will be martyred for the testimony of Jesus during the Seventieth Week; and, lastly, those who will be faithful witnesses for Christ in the times of trial, neither worshipping the Beast nor his image, but will, nevertheless, escape death, or, at least, death by persecution. The first class appears to occupy a higher position than the others: but all live and reign with Christ for a thousand years; while the rest of the dead are not recalled to life until the end of that period.

Thus the glorified saints which John saw are those who, in the Lord's words, shall be accounted worthy to obtain that age—$\tau o\hat{v}$ $ai\hat{\omega}vo\varsigma$ $\dot{\epsilon}\kappa\epsilon ivov$—and the resurrection out of the dead.[2] For they will live and reign during the Millennial age, while others are still confined to the abode of disembodied spirits: they will not wait for the general awakening, but be raised up from the great multitudes of the dead, and have part in the First Resurrection.

We should not omit to notice that their reign is limited to a fixed time: therefore, this Kingdom is not

[1] Rev. xx. 4, 5. [2] Luke xx. 35.

identical with eternal life, nor yet with the inheritance which, as Peter tells us, "fadeth not away." It is something additional to both of these, and special. And, whenever it is mentioned in the New Testament, it appears to be connected rather with the fruits of faith than with faith in the abstract.

The expression, the *souls* of them that had been beheaded, is peculiar, and its possible meaning not very apparent to the merely English reader. In Greek the same word signifies 'soul' and 'life'—that kind of life which enables us to rejoice in all that God has created. Now this word is used by the Lord in the oft-quoted saying ;—" Whosoever would save his life— or, soul—shall lose it : and whosoever shall lose his life for My sake shall find it." Of the promise in the last clause, all who spend and are spent in His service are inheritors, and especially those whose love urges them forward on the path of obedience, even though Death appear standing in the way.

There is a gracious recognition of this in a previous vision, in which the souls of martyrs were seen lying under the great altar, poured out as the blood of a sacrifice which had been offered to God. Such a sacrifice, with which He is well pleased, was presented by those who had been beheaded for the testimony of Jesus : at His command they had cast their lives upon the ground, and now, in return for the few and evil years of mortal existence, He has given them length of days, even life for evermore.

It is, then, the manifest teaching of Scripture that the Church will ascend to the Lord in two divisions, the first of which will leave the earth at the beginning of the Presence, the other towards its close. But it is

THE MYSTERY FINISHED.

most important to remember that the set time for its full assembly is at the sounding of the seventh trumpet. Then the mystery of God will be finished, and the invitation to Jew and Gentile to become one in Christ, as a heavenly people, be withdrawn.

Hence, so far, at least, as the living are concerned, to have part in the first rapture is a reward and privilege given only to those whom the Lord, when He comes, shall find watching. It involves immunity from the terrific woes of the end: it is that blessing for which the Lord urges us to strive, when He bids us take heed, lest, coming suddenly, He find us sleeping. And those who obtain it will have secured the fulfilment of His promise;—"Because thou hast kept the word of My patience, I also will keep thee from the hour of temptation, which shall come upon all the world, to try them that dwell upon the earth."[1]

Surely such a promise is of vital interest to us, standing, as we seem to be, hard by the end of the age. It cannot be misunderstood: it has nothing to do with Jews, but occurs in one of the Epistles to the Churches: it is not given unconditionally to mere believers, but only to those who walk consistently, and are willing to endure with Christ. To them it brings assurance of escape from a temptation by which all other men must be tried, since it is to come upon the whole world. And, as the next verse intimates, their deliverance will be wrought by the personal advent of the Lord.

And how earnestly He is longing to rescue His own from the frightful ordeal, through which they otherwise must pass, we may see by the memorable but much neglected command in the Gospel of Luke which He

[1] Rev. iii. 10.

uttered just after He had been portraying the terrors of the Last Week;—"Watch ye, therefore, and pray always, that ye may be accounted worthy to escape all these things that shall come to pass, and to stand before the Son of Man."[1]

Of these words also it is impossible to mistake the meaning, unless we do so wilfully. They certainly intimate that a Christian, though sure of eternal life, is not sure of being removed from earth before the troubles of the Last Week. This favour will be granted only to those who have progressed in holiness, only to those who have been so strengthened with might in the inner man that they can watch and pray. Such a growth in grace *may*, indeed, be attained by all believers: the *power* of watching and prayer is given to every man at his conversion; but if he would be able to bring it into action, he must be willing to deny himself, to take up his cross, and to follow his Master. Then there will be no doubt as to the issue: for "faithful is He That calleth you, Who will also do it."[2]

But the Lord has no thought of translating worldly-minded believers from the toils of life into the joy of His Presence, of admitting them to honour and immortality by the gate of glory instead of by the dark valley of Death. Those who vainly expect such a thing are like the Jews, who would have had Christ put Himself at their head as the all-victorious King, when as yet He had not saved them from their sins. But He will not grant to the careless and slothful servant that blessing which Paul craved, yet did not receive, the joy of being clothed upon, without the necessity of shuffling off this mortal coil.

[1] Luke xxi. 36.   [2] 1 Thess. v. 24.

THE MYSTERY FINISHED.

And so He bids us watch and pray always, that we may be accounted worthy to escape the time of greatest trouble, and to stand before Him while it is going on. Who obeys the command? How many even of the readers of this book? But His words may not be slighted with impunity, and we would suggest a solemn thought. Among those who first ascend to meet Him in the air, it is not likely that a single person will be found who has neglected this loving command from His own mouth.

Hence we cannot but see the guile of the Adversary, craftily working to throw Christians off their guard, in the arguments by which many strive to escape the responsibility of the Lord's injunction, and to cast it upon the Jews. Such an evasion is, however, impossible: for—

The Gospel of Luke has no Jewish complexion, like that of Matthew; but is specially addressed to Christians, whether they were previously Jews or Gentiles.

The discourse on the Mount of Olives was delivered after the Lord had, so far as His first advent was concerned, finally rejected the Jew. He had just departed from the Temple with the ominous words;— "Behold, *your* house is left unto you desolate!" Not even the very Holy of holies itself was any longer owned of God: His relations with the Jews had been suspended, because they had rejected the King.

Consequently, the whole discourse is addressed to the disciples as the representatives of that body which should now take the place of Israel as witnesses for God.

To them, and to them alone, could the prediction be applied. The synagogues would be inimical to them [1] : they would suffer persecution *for Christ's sake* before the overthrow of Jerusalem by Titus : [2] the promised signal for their flight is that of which the Christians did actually avail themselves [3] ; but by which, so far as we know, not a single Jew was saved : the interval between the Sixty-Ninth and the Seventieth Week is plainly marked out as " the times of the Gentiles," [4] and not merely understood, as it is in Jewish prophecies : and, lastly, but little is said of the Seventieth Week with which Jews are mainly concerned.

Thus, since both the setting and the whole contents of the prediction show it to be distinctively Christian, we cannot consent to disjoin, and refer to Jews, the command at the close of it, by which a practical application is made of all that has been previously spoken.

The further objection that the title " Son of Man " has nothing to do with our Lord's relations to the Church, and, on that account, is never used by Paul, being a mere conjecture could not, in any case, be allowed to stand against the argument stated above. And those who raise it do not appear to display much critical acumen : for the facts are as follows.

The Lord in describing Himself frequently makes use of the term Son of Man ; but, with a single exception, it is never applied to Him by His followers in any part of the New Testament. Possibly the reason is that the title was felt to be one of humiliation, which, therefore, would not come well from the servants' lips, but must be left for the gracious condescension of the Master.

[1] Luke xxi. 12. [3] Luke xxi. 20. See note to p. 241.
[2] Luke xxi. 12, 17. [4] Luke xxi. 24.

THE MYSTERY FINISHED.

However, the only man who is recorded to have used it, the martyr Stephen, was a member of the Church. Just before his death, he exclaimed;—"Behold, I see the heavens opened, and the Son of Man standing on the right hand of God."[1] This does not lead us to regard the title as void of significance for the heavenly election. Nor does the fact that, when the Lord appeared to John—certainly at the time a representative of the Church—He was "like unto a son of man";[2] and that the Apostle afterwards described Him in the same terms when he saw Him seated on the white cloud, and waiting to reap the Harvest which should be borne away from the field[3] into His own garner above.[4]

But, if thoughtless and inconsistent believers are to be left upon earth during the greater part of the last Week, though they are no longer recognised as a Church, we should, nevertheless, expect to find some slight traces of their presence during the times of trouble. And this we do in the passages which tell us of their oppression by and victory over the Beast, as well as in the following instances.

When the Jewish martyrs cry for vengeance, they are bidden to rest in patience until "their fellow-servants also and their brethren" should be killed.[5] And while the brethren are doubtless the Jewish remnant, the fellow-servants are probably Christians.

Again; we have gathered that the travailing Woman represents the system of God upon earth, whether Christian or Jewish. Now after the rapture of her

[1] Acts vii. 56.
[2] Rev. i. 13.
[3] Matt. xiii. 38.
[4] Rev. xiv. 14.
[5] Rev. vi. 11.

child, and her own escape from the Dragon, the latter returns to make war upon the remnant of her seed, "which keep the commandments of God and have the testimony of Jesus Christ."[1] This description, as we have already remarked, appears to include all the people of God who are within the Dragon's reach at the time ; the first clause referring to pious Jews, the second to Christians.

And, perhaps, when we read of the much incense which is given to an angel that he may add it to the prayers of "all the saints,"[2] we are to understand that, at the solemn crisis of renewed Judgment, supplications are ascending to God from both classes of those who fear Him, and who are then suffering oppression upon the earth.

Before closing this subject, we may notice that in the future of Israel there is an exact analogy to the case of those Christians who will have to endure the Great Tribulation.

In the seventh chapter of the Apocalypse, an angel brings the seal of the living God to impress it upon the foreheads of His servants ; and twelve thousand men are thus distinguished in each of the twelve tribes of Israel. But these tribes are not *the* Twelve : their number is made up in an unwonted manner, by reckoning the usually omitted tribe of Levi and leaving out that of Dan.

Many reasons may be found for the exclusion of the latter. A dark cloud overhangs the whole history of the clan whose founder saw the light through the rebellious impatience of Rachel, and was the first offspring of a bond-woman introduced into the family of Jacob.

[1] Rev. xii. 17. [2] Rev. viii. 3.

THE MYSTERY FINISHED.

When blessing his sons on his death-bed, the patriarch could find but the sinister comparison of a serpent for Dan. Moses did, indeed, speak of the tribe as "a lion's whelp";[1] but the ominous addition of the words, "he shall leap from Bashan," rather connects it with that roaring lion which walketh about seeking whom he may devour than with the Lion of the Tribe of Judah. For the Hill of Bashan sets itself in opposition to the Hill of God:[2] its bulls roar against the Son of God:[3] its kine oppress the poor, and crush the needy:[4] its oaks are high, and lifted up in proud rebellion.[5]

The tribe did not belie the predictions concerning it: cunning skill and strength were its characteristics. In the wilderness it was inferior in numbers only to Judah, and brought up the rear of the march: it furnished one of the two skilled artists who were employed upon the Tabernacle:[6] Solomon's chief workman was connected with it:[7] and from its ranks sprang Samson, the great deliverer, but by no means perfect servant of God.[8]

On the other hand, the Israelitish mother of the man stoned for blasphemy was a Danite:[9] and, soon after the entrance of the people into Canaan, some of the same tribe were the first to establish idolatry;[10] so that, in subsequent times, their town was a fitting locality for the setting up of Jeroboam's calf.[11] And perhaps it is because they had thus proved a stumbling-block to Israel that nothing is said of Dan in the genealogies of the First Book of Chronicles.

[1] Deut. xxxiii. 22.
[2] Psalm lxviii. 15, 16.
[3] Psalm xxii. 12, 13.
[4] Amos iv. i.
[5] Isa. ii. 13.
[6] Exod. xxxi. 6.
[7] 2 Chron. ii. 14.
[8] Judges xiii. 2, 24.
[9] Lev. xxiv. 11
[10] Judges xviii.
[11] 1 Kings xii. 29, 30.

These particulars may point to reasons why the tribe is excluded from the sealing: but what is the import of the exclusion? Is it that the Danites will be finally destroyed, and disappear for ever from among the sons of Israel?

Not so: for the sealing takes place before the trumpets and vials, and we have in the last chapter of Ezekiel two other lists of the tribes, connected with later and Millennial times, in both of which the name of Dan again appears. He will have his portion in the recovered land of Canaan; but it will be in the extreme north, at the furthest distance from the Temple which Messiah will build.[1] And one of the twelve gates in the Millennial Jerusalem will be the gate of Dan.[2]

Not, then, for extinction is this tribe excluded from the sealing, but for discipline. The angel with the seal appears just as four other ministers of God are about to let loose His judgments upon the earth, and with a loud voice bids them refrain until he has sealed the servants of God for preservation.[3] And, accordingly, when the infernal locusts are released from the Abyss, their commission is to hurt the men which have not the seal of God in their foreheads.[4]

Hence the tribe of Dan will have no exemption from the torments of this and other plagues; and we may thus see the parallelism between their case and that of the unready Christians.

It was not, then, without meaning that Jacob, when speaking of the future of Dan, uttered the abrupt exclamation;—"I have waited for Thy salvation, O Lord!"[5]

[1] Ezek. xlviii. 1. [2] Ezek. xlviii. 32.
[3] Rev. vii. 1-3. [4] Rev. ix. 4. [5] Gen. xlix. 18.

For he seems, with prophetic eye, to have discerned that there were difficulties in the way of saving this tribe, which could be overcome only by peculiar discipline and longer delay.

XXIII.

CONCLUSION.

WE trust that enough has been said in the preceding chapters to set forth the great secret which the Lord has revealed to them that fear Him. At any moment, of any day or hour, He may descend into the air, and require our instant attendance.[1] And for us the whole duty of life is to maintain a state of continual readiness to leave our earthly habitations, and stand before Him face to face.

This we can do only by keeping closely to Him in spiritual communion, by ever waiting and watching for Him, and by occupying the remaining time of His absence in those works to which He has called us. Like Paul, we must labour that we may be accepted of Him.[2]

And if it be asked, Who is sufficient for these things?—we reply, No man in his own strength; but power shall be given to every one who earnestly and sincerely desires it. The revelation of God declares that all grace is freely offered to us; and that the

[1] To realise this, and act upon it, is the highest perfection of the Christian life. "So that ye come behind in no gift, waiting, as ye are, for the revelation of our Lord Jesus Christ, Who shall also confirm you unto the end, that ye may be blameless in the Day of our Lord Jesus Christ" (1 Cor. i. 7, 8).

[2] 2 Cor. v. 9.

only hindrance arises from hesitation on our part to receive His gifts, because we shrink from the responsibilities which they involve, and love this present world.

Sometimes the phraseology of Scripture is very instructive in regard to this point.

"Be not drunken with wine, wherein is riot," says Paul; "but be filled with the Spirit."[1] Is not the second clause of this verse as direct a command as the first? And, in another place, the same Apostle, after quoting the words, "Yet once more I shake not the earth only, but also the heaven," adds;—"Wherefore, since we are receiving a Kingdom which cannot be shaken, *let us have grace* whereby we may serve God acceptably with reverence and awe."[2]

But many Christians are unable to obtain this necessary grace, because they refuse to confront the future which God's word sets before them. They either reject the doctrine of the Lord's personal coming in plain terms, or, at least, practically ignore it.

But if they love not His appearing, how shall they obtain a crown of Righteousness?[3] If they have not this hope in them, how shall they purify themselves even as He is pure?[4]

It is, again, no uncommon thing to hear those who have some idea of the truth, but dare not put forth their trembling hands to grasp it, excusing themselves

---

[1] Eph. v. 18. If we render, "Be filled in spirit," the sense is still the same. Our spirit must be filled either with the Holy Spirit or with the spirits of evil, and Paul certainly does not refer to the latter.
[2] Heb. xii. 28.
[3] 2 Tim. iv. 8.
[4] 1 John iii. 3.

CONCLUSION. 155

with the remark, that, although they may not care to think of the Lord's return, they, nevertheless, prepare for death; and if they are ready for that, so will they be for His coming, should it happen in their lifetime.

Is this certain? Upon what principle, then, are we to explain the fact that, throughout the New Testament, we are never once commanded to prepare for death; but are repeatedly and urgently warned that the Lord is at hand, and exhorted to watch and pray, lest, coming suddenly, He should find us sleeping? Are we not forced to an inference directly opposed to the opinion that it suffices to keep death in view?

And a very little reflection will enable even our feeble minds to justify the course which God has taken in the matter.

When a disembodied spirit passes into the unseen world, it goes, indeed, to its own place, to its own side of the impassable gulf. But, if it be a saved spirit, is it likely that its condition remains unchanged until the resurrection? All analogy with God's known works forbids such a supposition.

He that is freed from the body of sin, and from the distractions of sense, is able to concentrate his attention upon the glorious Being Who is, and will be, all to Him. And could he do this, and enjoy the near spiritual presence[1] of His Saviour, without progressing,

[1] We must not forget that the spirits of the departed can have nothing more than spiritual intercourse with the Lord, and are unable to behold Him as He is. That they can do only when their bodies are, like His, redeemed and glorified by resurrection. And so John says;—"We know that when He shall appear, we shall be like Him; for we shall see Him as He is"—words which plainly imply that disembodied spirits cannot so see Him. But they have the advantage of an intermediate stage in their knowledge, and by attaining, during the period of uninterrupted

without becoming more and more fit to appear with Christ in glory? Impossible!

In the case, then, of redeemed spirits, it would seem that some preparation for the glory is going on during the intermediate state.

On the other hand, those who are alive when the Lord comes will have no such advantage; but will be required to pass immediately from the scenes of earth to the full light of His majesty. This will be a far more abrupt and serious change, so that we need not wonder at the direction taken by Scriptural admonition. And certainly he who is thus prepared to meet his Judge and King has little need to trouble himself in regard to death. But the converse of the proposition can be by no means maintained.

Perhaps, however, the error of some of us leads in an opposite direction to that which we have been discussing. It may be that we acknowledge the certainty of the Lord's return, and even love to converse on the solemn subject; but do we mean what we say? Are the desires which we express real, and our words unfeigned?

At the time of the first advent, the Pharisees had for many years been talking of the coming Messiah: they had made their boast in Him, and magnified themselves above others on His account. And yet, when they heard the inquiry, "Where is He That is born King of the Jews?" they were troubled, and all Jerusalem with them. Their professions had been suddenly brought to the test, and lo! they cared neither for God nor for His Christ.

spiritual intercourse, to a closer acquaintance with Him than is possible upon earth, they may become more prepared for the beatific vision of His unveiled presence.

They had been using the sacred names merely to add authority to their own teachings, to support a system which they had evolved, and which set them in positions of honour and influence. And feeling instinctively that the Lord of glory could never be persuaded to promote aims so selfish as theirs, they were troubled at His birth, and when He afterwards presented Himself as their Prophet and King, they hated rejected and crucified Him.

Is this sad story of hypocrisy to be repeated? There is too much reason to fear that it will be in the case of many—will be, that is, so far as it may.

For when He comes again, glorious in His apparel, and travelling in the greatness of His strength, we shall be powerless to deny Him: but He may reject us.

"And now, little children, abide in Him, that when He shall appear we may have confidence, and not shrink with shame from Him at His coming."[1]

Our task is completed: for we do not propose to speak, in the present volume, of the Last Week, the Millennial Age, and the Final Judgment. We have considered the great Gentile and Jewish prophecies in order that we might better understand the times of the Church, and we have traced the career of the latter, until we left her in heaven with her Lord.

Her glorified members have exhausted the sufferings appointed for her sanctification, and now they live and reign with Him. Not one of them could avoid the pains, the anxieties, the cares, and the pettiness, of life; but they were lifted up above them all by the power of

[1] 1 John ii. 28.

His resurrection, and lo! the former things have passed away, and the days of their mourning are ended.

O weary and care-worn souls, look up and behold the glorious vision! It is no mere dream of delight to be presently swept away by the never failing stream of woe: nay, it is the joy which our Lord of love, Who cannot lie, has set before us. And, if we but cleave to Him with purpose of heart, He, by His almighty power, will bring us safely to it, though, perhaps, through much tribulation.

Does not the very thought of His promises lighten the burden of the cross? Sorrows, conflicts, and perplexities, may be thickening around us: let them only cause us to cry with greater earnestness;—"Thy Kingdom come!" In the sick chamber, or the place of heart-breaking toil; in the lonely garret, or the full house in which we must sojourn as strangers among ungenial spirits; by the newly opened grave, or in the forsaken home; wherever the load of human anguish presses most heavily, let us, even in sorrow, rejoice that the time of suffering will soon be over. For He has said, "Behold I come quickly"; and then God shall wipe away all tears from our eyes, and death shall be no more, neither shall there any more be mourning, nor crying, nor pain.

BIBLIOLIFE

Old Books Deserve a New Life
www.bibliolife.com

Did you know that you can get most of our titles in our trademark **EasyScript**™ print format? **EasyScript**™ provides readers with a larger than average typeface, for a reading experience that's easier on the eyes.

Did you know that we have an ever-growing collection of books in many languages?

Order online:
www.bibliolife.com/store

Or to exclusively browse our **EasyScript**™ collection:
www.bibliogrande.com

At BiblioLife, we aim to make knowledge more accessible by making thousands of titles available to you – quickly and affordably.

Contact us:
BiblioLife
PO Box 21206
Charleston, SC 29413

Lightning Source UK Ltd.
Milton Keynes UK
UKOW06f0653131217
314385UK00010B/371/P

9 781117 086255